Forms
of the
Essay

The American Experience

Forms of the Essay

Essay

The American Experience

Deanne K. Milan

Naomi Cooks Rattner

City College of San Francisco

HARCOURT BRACE JOVANOVICH, INC.

New York   San Diego   Chicago   San Francisco   Atlanta

Preface

Learning to write well—perhaps the greatest challenge facing the first-year student—is certainly not easy, but neither is it impossible. This book does not pretend to solve all the problems that confront the beginning writer. Rather, its aim is to provide, through instruction and example, materials that will help student writers to extend and refine the skills they already have. To this end, *Forms of the Essay* is a collection of readings, chiefly expository, chosen to involve students in the kind of active, careful, and analytic reading that provides the best foundation for their own writing.

Most of the forty-eight essays are brief—1,000 to 3,000 words. Among them are many familiar authors and classic essays, along with a large sampling of fresh and interesting pieces, all emphasizing excellence in both thought and style. We have tried to offer a selection of readings that will serve as models for writing while at the same time stimulating the student's own intellect and imagination.

The collection represents the diverse forms of the modern essay, arranged along familiar lines. The essays are classified according to the traditional rhetorical modes, with the major emphasis on exposition. As examples of contemporary prose forms frequently encountered by the general reader or required of the everyday writer, we also include two new categories: the profile, and observing and reporting. In addition, all the essays are linked by a common focus on contemporary American life and culture.

We have also included apparatus that builds on the reading of the essays themselves, again emphasizing those skills common to both good reading and good expository writing. Each section begins with a brief discussion of a particular rhetorical mode or technique, showing how it is exemplified in the individual readings that follow. Each essay is introduced by a biographical note, and most are followed by exercises designed to measure comprehension and to develop vocabulary and usage, as well as by suggestions for discussion and writing.

Finally, we want to express our appreciation to those friends who gave us suggestions and encouragement as we prepared the manuscript: Ann Morehead and Georgia Cornell of City College of San Francisco, and Andrew Griffin at the

University of California at Berkeley. Several people at Harcourt Brace Jovanovich also deserve thanks for their contributions: Robert Wanetick; Jeff Samuels; Judy Gelman; Dee Angell; Sylvia Newman, manuscript editor; and Drake Bush, our editor, who guided us from start to finish.

Deanne K. Milan
Naomi Cooks Rattner
San Francisco, California

Contents

Thematic Table of Contents

*The essays marked with an asterisk indicate selections for extra reading.

BEHAVIOR AND INSTITUTIONS

PROBLEMS

VALUES AND BELIEFS

The Essay

Although the works of some earlier writers are today also called "essays," the essay was more or less invented in the sixteenth century by Michel de Montaigne, a writer and philosopher who produced several volumes of brief, personal prose writings. Following no particular pattern, he set down his primarily subjective views, opinions, feelings, and called the results "essais," or "trials," from the French verb "essayer" ("to try"). Today, the term essay still means any brief, personal prose work that demands no particular form in expressing a subjective attitude or opinion rather than a totally objective or scientific view of its subject. But the word has also come to signify a large, loosely defined literary genre that includes almost all short nonfiction prose: the freshman student's weekly composition, a New York *Times* editorial, the President's latest speech, any magazine article.

Any subject or issue may provoke an essay—Montaigne's own topics ranged from "The Affection of Fathers for Their Children" to "On Cannibals." Those collected in this book, the products of many different minds, represent an even wider scope of taste and interest. Essays also vary greatly in form, including pieces as informally arranged as Terkel's profile-interviews, as individualized and unique in shape as the memoirs of Kingston and Anderson, or as formal as Campa's carefully arranged study. They come in almost every length, too, as the selections here demonstrate, exhibiting every shade of tone and style, from the light, amusing touch of White to the solemn or impassioned words of Davis or Baruch.

In fact, the essay in its various forms represents virtually every aspect of *rhetoric*—the term that in modern usage describes the whole art of prose writing. This is why the study of the essay is usually the basis of the first-year composition course. It is also why the selections in this text are arranged according to the four traditional rhetorical patterns or forms of discourse: Narration, Description, Exposition, and Argument and Persuasion. (In addition, we have included two nontraditional categories: Observing and Reporting, and Profiles. While these are not basic forms of discourse, they are forms of the essay commonly encountered by students in both reading and writing.) The essays chosen for each category emphasize a basic rhetorical pattern, but of course most of them employ other forms of development or arrangement as well.

1

Because you may not be reading the essays in the order in which they appear in the text, it is a good idea to begin this book by reading the explanatory headnotes for each of the major rhetorical forms. (Pay special attention to the discussion of *thesis*. Unlike the other divisions in the book, it represents neither a mode of discourse nor a rhetorical device. Rather, it is the central idea that every reader and writer must find or develop in every essay.) This preliminary study will help you to a general understanding of the basic forms of the essay and its fundamental patterns of organization before you attempt a thorough study of any single rhetorical pattern or device.

Narration

The mode of discourse called narration follows a pattern we are all familiar with from earliest childhood—the pattern of storytelling, in which events are often arranged in chronological sequence, in their order in time. As you will see in this section, narration may deal not only with the imaginative events of story ("Once upon a time . . ."), but with the subjective impressions of personal experience ("When I was in my teens") and the factual events of history as well ("It all began with Christopher Columbus").

The storytelling impulse itself, however, is the major force behind all narrative: readers want to know how things happened and what happened next; the writer's task is to make the series of events both clear and interesting. All four essays in this section are primarily narrative—that is, their main function is to tell a story. Elsewhere, however, you will see narration employed as a secondary technique, to support other types of discourse, primarily exposition or persuasion.

There is, of course, usually a point, a special meaning that gives coherence to every narrative. If there were not, the sequence of events would be simply a list (9:00, arrive at castle; 10:00, meet Princess; 10:01, fall in love with Princess; 11:00, slay dragon). In narration this point or main idea is usually shown—implied through dialogue or action—rather than expressed directly in a thesis statement. (One exception is the fable. For example, in Aesop's "The Hare and the Tortoise," the moral, "slow but steady wins the race," is not simply a neat way to end a suspenseful tale, but a direct statement of the theme, the *meaning* of the narrative.)

In general the meaning behind the events determines the emphasis and pace of a narrative; thus, the writer need not treat every portion in the same way. Anderson, for example, summarizes a number of incidents in a sentence or two, but devotes several paragraphs to the central episode; White telescopes the main event into a single paragraph, which is nevertheless effective because it has been so skillfully anticipated. Brown, whose narrative does not focus on any single event, reveals a more regular, chronologically balanced pattern of narration, though he, too, treats some incidents expansively and summarizes others. Unlike the others, Kingston's narrative does not follow chronological sequence, but moves impressionistically backward and forward in time according to what she *feels* is most important.

Without this meaningful variation, a narrative would be dull, like the novel Mark Twain once scornfully criticized as merely "one damn thing after another."

Afternoon of an American Boy

E. B. WHITE

E. B. White is one of America's best-known writers. An essayist, poet, and storyteller, he has written for *The New Yorker*, *Harper's Magazine*, and *The Atlantic Monthly*. He is also the author of the well-known children's books *Stuart Little*, *Charlotte's Web*, and *The Trumpet of the Swan*. Now a full-time resident of Maine, he tends his garden, raises animals, and continues writing. This essay is a narrative describing his first date, which, though painful at the time, came to assume a new meaning.

The House Committee on Un-American Activities (HUAC), which plays an important role in this selection, was the congressional committee charged with investigating communist infiltration in both government and the arts—especially in the movie industry—and membership in supposedly subversive organizations. Often its investigations were conducted without sufficient evidence. J. Parnell Thomas's committee, described here in an imaginary "guilt sequence," was the forerunner of the infamous and more powerful McCarthy Senate Committee of the early 1950s.

1   When I was in my teens, I lived in Mount Vernon, in the same block with J. Parnell Thomas, who grew up to become chairman of the House Committee on Un-American Activities. I lived on the corner of Summit and East Sidney, at No. 101 Summit Avenue, and Parnell lived four or five doors north of us on the same side of the avenue, in the house the Diefendorfs used to live in.

2   Parnell was not a playmate of mine, as he was a few years older, but I used to greet him as he walked by our house on his way to and from the depot. He was a good-looking young man, rather quiet and shy. Seeing him, I would call "Hello, Parnell!" and he would smile and say "Hello, Elwyn!" and walk on. Once I remember dashing out of our yard on roller skates and executing a rink turn in front of Parnell, to show off, and he said, "Well! Quite an artist, aren't you?" I remember the words. I was delighted at praise from an older man and sped away along the flagstone sidewalk, dodging the cracks I knew so well.

3   The thing that made Parnell a special man in my eyes in those days was not his handsome appearance and friendly manner but his sister. Her name was Eileen. She was my age and she was a quiet, nice-looking girl. She never came over to my yard to play, and I never went over there, and, considering that we lived so near each other, we were remarkably uncommunicative; nevertheless, she was the girl I singled out, at one point, to be of special interest to me. Being of special interest to me involved practically nothing on

AFTERNOON OF AN AMERICAN BOY   From *Essays of E. B. White* by E. B. White. Originally appeared in *The New Yorker*. Copyright 1947 by E. B. White. Reprinted by permission of Harper & Row, Publishers, Inc.

a girl's part—it simply meant that she was under constant surveillance. On my own part, it meant that I suffered an astonishing disintegration when I walked by her house, from embarrassment, fright, and the knowledge that I was in enchanted territory.

4   In the matter of girls, I was different from most boys of my age. I admired girls a lot, but they terrified me. I did not feel that I possessed the peculiar gifts or accomplishments that girls liked in their male companions—the ability to dance, to play football, to cut up a bit in public, to smoke, and to make small talk. I couldn't do any of these things successfully, and seldom tried. Instead, I stuck with the accomplishments I was sure of: I rode my bicycle sitting backward on the handle bars, I made up poems, I played selections from *Aïda* on the piano. In winter, I tended goal in the hockey games on the frozen pond in the dell. None of these tricks counted much with girls. In the four years I was in the Mount Vernon High School, I never went to a school dance and I never took a girl to a drugstore for a soda or to the Westchester Playhouse or to Proctor's. I wanted to do these things but did not have the nerve. What I finally did manage to do, however, and what is the subject of this memoir, was far brassier, far gaudier. As an exhibit of teen-age courage and ineptitude, it never fails to amaze me in retrospect. I am not even sure it wasn't un-American.

5   My bashfulness and backwardness annoyed my older sister very much, and at about the period of which I am writing she began making strong efforts to stir me up. She was convinced that I was in a rut, socially, and she found me a drag in her own social life, which was brisk. She kept trying to throw me with girls, but I always bounced. And whenever she saw a chance she would start the phonograph and grab me, and we would go charging around the parlor in the toils of the one-step, she gripping me as in a death struggle, and I hurling her finally away from me through greater strength. I was a skinny kid but my muscles were hard, and it would have taken an unusually powerful woman to have held me long in the attitude of the dance.

6   One day, through a set of circumstances I have forgotten, my sister managed to work me into an afternoon engagement she had with some others in New York. To me, at that time, New York was a wonderland largely unexplored. I had been to the Hippodrome a couple of times with my father, and to the Hudson-Fulton Celebration, and to a few matinées; but New York, except as a setting for extravaganzas, was unknown. My sister had heard tales of tea-dancing at the Plaza Hotel. She and a girl friend of hers and another fellow and myself went there to give it a try. The expedition struck me as a slick piece of arrangement on her part. I was the junior member of the group and had been roped in, I imagine, to give symmetry to the occasion. Or perhaps Mother had forbidden my sister to go at all unless another member of the family was along. Whether I was there for symmetry or for decency I can't really remember, but I was there.

7   The spectacle was a revelation to me. However repulsive the idea of dancing was, I was filled with amazement at the setup. Here were tables where a fellow could sit so close to the dance floor that he was practically on

it. And you could order cinnamon toast and from the safety of your chair observe girls and men in close embrace, swinging along, the music playing while you ate the toast, and the dancers so near to you that they almost brushed the things off your table as they jogged by. I was impressed. Dancing or no dancing, this was certainly high life, and I knew I was witnessing a scene miles and miles ahead of anything that took place in Mount Vernon. I had never seen anything like it, and a ferment must have begun working in me that afternoon.

8   Incredible as it seems to me now, I formed the idea of asking Parnell's sister Eileen to accompany me to a tea dance at the Plaza. The plan shaped up in my mind as an expedition of unparalleled worldliness, calculated to stun even the most blasé girl. The fact that I didn't know how to dance must have been a powerful deterrent, but not powerful enough to stop me. As I look back on the affair, it's hard to credit my own memory, and I sometimes wonder if, in fact, the whole business isn't some dream that has gradually gained the status of actuality. A boy with any sense, wishing to become better acquainted with a girl who was "of special interest," would have cut out for himself a more modest assignment to start with—a soda date or a movie date—something within reasonable limits. Not me. I apparently became obsessed with the notion of taking Eileen to the Plaza and not to any darned old drugstore. I had learned the location of the Plaza, and just knowing how to get to it gave me a feeling of confidence. I had learned about cinnamon toast, so I felt able to cope with the waiter when he came along. And I banked heavily on the general splendor of the surroundings and the extreme sophistication of the function to carry the day, I guess.

9   I was three days getting up nerve to make the phone call. Meantime, I worked out everything in the greatest detail. I heeled myself with a safe amount of money. I looked up trains. I overhauled my clothes and assembled an outfit I believed would meet the test. Then, one night at six o'clock, when Mother and Father went downstairs to dinner, I lingered upstairs and entered the big closet off my bedroom where the wall phone was. There I stood for several minutes, trembling, my hand on the receiver, which hung upside down on the hook. (In our family, the receiver always hung upside down, with the big end up.)

10   I had rehearsed my first line and my second line. I planned to say, "Hello, can I please speak to Eileen?" Then, when she came to the phone, I planned to say, "Hello, Eileen, this is Elwyn White." From there on, I figured I could ad-lib it.

11   At last, I picked up the receiver and gave the number. As I had suspected, Eileen's mother answered.

12   "Can I please speak to Eileen?" I asked, in a low, troubled voice.

13   "Just a minute," said her mother. Then, on second thought, she asked, "Who is it, please?"

14   "It's Elwyn," I said.

15   She left the phone, and after quite a while Eileen's voice said, "Hello, Elwyn." This threw my second line out of whack, but I stuck to it doggedly.

16   "Hello, Eileen, this is Elwyn White," I said.

17   In no time at all I laid the proposition before her. She seemed dazed and asked me to wait a minute. I assume she went into a huddle with her mother. Finally, she said yes, she would like to go tea-dancing with me at the Plaza, and I said fine, I would call for her at quarter past three on Thursday afternoon, or whatever afternoon it was—I've forgotten.

18   I do not know now, and of course did not know then, just how great was the mental and physical torture Eileen went through that day, but the incident stacks up as a sort of unintentional un-American activity, for which I was solely responsible. It all went off as scheduled: the stately walk to the depot; the solemn train ride, during which we sat staring shyly into the seat in front of us; the difficult walk from Grand Central across Forty-second to Fifth, with pedestrians clipping us and cutting in between us; the bus ride to Fifty-ninth Street; then the Plaza itself, and the cinnamon toast, and the music, and the excitement. The thundering quality of the occasion must have delivered a mental shock to me, deadening my recollection, for I have only the dimmest memory of leading Eileen onto the dance floor to execute two or three unspeakable rounds, in which I vainly tried to adapt my violent sister-and-brother wrestling act into something graceful and appropriate. It must have been awful. And at six o'clock, emerging, I gave no thought to any further entertainment, such as dinner in town. I simply herded Eileen back all the long, dreary way to Mount Vernon and deposited her, a few minutes after seven, on an empty stomach, at her home. Even if I had attempted to dine her, I don't believe it would have been possible; the emotional strain of the afternoon had caused me to perspire uninterruptedly, and any restaurant would have been justified in rejecting me solely on the ground that I was too moist.

19   Over the intervening years, I've often felt guilty about my afternoon at the Plaza, and many years ago, during Parnell's investigation of writers, my feeling sometimes took the form of a guilt sequence in which I imagined myself on the stand, in the committee room, being questioned. It went something like this:

20   PARNELL: Have you ever written for the screen, Mr. White?

21   ME: No, sir.

22   PARNELL: Have you ever been, or are you now, a member of the Screen Writers' Guild?

23   ME: No, sir.

24   PARNELL: Have you ever been, or are you now, a member of the Communist Party?

25   ME: No, sir.

26   Then, in this imaginary guilt sequence of mine, Parnell digs deep and comes up with the big question, calculated to throw me.

27   PARNELL: Do you recall an afternoon, along about the middle of the second decade of this century, when you took my sister to the Plaza Hotel for tea under the grossly misleading and false pretext that you knew how to dance?

28   And as my reply comes weakly, "Yes, sir," I hear the murmur run through the committee room and see reporters bending over their notebooks, scrib-

bling hard. In my dream, I am again seated with Eileen at the edge of the dance floor, frightened, stunned, and happy—in my ears the intoxicating drumbeat of the dance, in my throat the dry, bittersweet taste of cinnamon.

29   I don't know about the guilt, really. I guess a good many girls might say that an excursion such as the one I conducted Eileen on belongs in the un-American category. But there must be millions of aging males, now slipping into their anecdotage, who recall their Willie Baxter period with affection, and who remember some similar journey into ineptitude, in that precious, brief moment in life before love's pages, through constant reference, had become dog-eared, and before its narrative, through sheer competence, had lost the first, wild sense of derring-do.

Exercises

COMPREHENSION

Organization and Development

Narrative essays are usually difficult to outline, but White's essay does exhibit a definite structure. After finding the thesis statement and writing it in the space provided, state the main divisions of his essay in the remaining spaces and indicate the paragraphs for each.

Thesis statement: _____

_____

I.   _____   [   ]
II.   _____   [   ]
III. _____   [   ]
IV.   _____   [   ]

Content

Choose the answer that correctly completes each statement.

1. The incident White describes occurred about (a) 1915 (b) 1925 (c) 1945.
2. J. Parnell Thomas, Eileen's brother, grew up to become the chairman of (a) NATO (b) the Senate Committee on Patriotic American Activities (c) the House Committee on Un-American Activities.
3. Whenever White walked by Eileen's house, he felt as if he were in (a) enemy territory (b) an interrogation room (c) enchanted territory.
4. With respect to girls, White felt that he lacked (a) good looks to attract them (b) special accomplishments to impress them (c) a reputation as an athlete to dazzle them.
5. White's description of his sister's teaching him to dance is intended to show how (a) enthusiastic he was about learning to dance (b) inept and graceless his dancing with Eileen must have been (c) fond his sister was of him.

6. White intends the reader to view his imaginary interrogation by J. Parnell Thomas as (a) humorous (b) frightening (c) insulting.
7. White compares love metaphorically to a(n) (a) intoxicating drink (b) journey into ineptitude (c) book.
8. In retrospect, White thinks his experience at the Plaza with Eileen was actually an example of (a) incredible embarrassment and ineptitude (b) an un-American activity comparable to treason (c) a daring, yet precious excursion into life and romance.

Paragraph Structure

Reorder the following sentences to form a unified, coherent paragraph. Identify one sentence as the topic sentence. Then check your version with the original.

1. I was a skinny kid but my muscles were hard, and it would have taken an unusually powerful woman to have held me long in the attitude of the dance.
2. She was convinced that I was in a rut, socially, and she found me a drag in her own social life, which was brisk.
3. And whenever she saw a chance she would start the phonograph and grab me, and we would go charging around the parlor in the toils of the one-step, she gripping me as in a death struggle, and I hurling her finally away from me through greater strength.
4. My bashfulness and backwardness annoyed my older sister very much, and at about the period of which I am writing she began making strong efforts to stir me up.
5. She kept trying to throw me with girls, but I always bounced.

VOCABULARY AND USAGE

Word Formation Table

Complete the following table by changing word endings or root forms to make new grammatical forms. Use your dictionary if necessary.

	NOUN	VERB	ADJECTIVE	ADVERB
1.	revelation	_____	_____	_____
2.	_____	xxx	_____	vainly
3.	_____	justify	_____	_____
4.	_____	_____	_____	annoyingly
5.	ineptitude	xxx	_____	_____

Fill-Ins

Complete each of the sentences below using the words on the following list. You may need to use some words more than once. You may also find that some blanks can be completed correctly with more than one word. Add plural endings to nouns and change verb forms where necessary.

special	peculiar	balance
seldom	solely	apparently
sophisticated	nevertheless	show
alone	impress	vainly
awkward	exhibit	stun

| symmetry | inept | worldly |
| however | deterrent | unique |

1. White feels that he did not possess the _____ accomplishments, nor did he _____ the courage that would _____ girls.
2. White had _____ been to New York; _____, he knew that tea dancing at the Plaza was considered a _____ activity for a boy from Mount Vernon.
3. _____, White's parents did not allow their daughter to go _____ to New York; White had to go along to give the group _____.
4. The fact that White did not know how to dance was not a _____; he hoped the Plaza would _____ even the most _____ girl.
5. White tried _____ to adapt his dancing experience with his sister into something graceful; _____, the harder he tried, the more _____ his dancing was.
6. _____ embarrassed he was at the time, his description _____ that such embarrassing, _____ experiences are not _____.

DISCUSSION

1. What was HUAC? What is the irony in White's asking Eileen Parnell to accompany him to the Plaza?
2. In what ways was White different from most boys his age? What were the two sides of White's personality? Find phrases or sentences that reveal them.
3. What is the topic sentence in paragraph 4?
4. What rhetorical method does White use in paragraph 9?
5. Despite what White says about his careful planning, what did he fail to foresee?
6. Of the actual incident with Eileen at the Plaza, White says very little. Is this a flaw in the narrative, or not? Why? What does the reader know about the tea-dancing episode that is not said? How does White accomplish this?
7. Why does White say that his excursion with Eileen was "un-American"? Is he serious or not? What does the tea-dancing incident really represent to him?
8. What would be the effect on the narrative if White had invited Jane Doe—in other words, someone without a brother who went on to be the chairman of HUAC? Would the narrative have the same impact? How does the HUAC connection serve to unify or perhaps revise the essay's theme?

SUGGESTIONS FOR WRITING

1. Write a narrative sketch—a memoir—in which you describe some particularly embarrassing or awkward incident from your own adolescence. Use concrete details to reinforce your dominant impression.
2. Describe your first date or any first experience from your present point of view, that is, as an adult looking back at a past experience.

From Christopher Columbus to Wounded Knee

DEE BROWN

Dee Brown, a librarian, educator, and author, was born in Louisiana in 1908, and holds degrees from George Washington University and the University of Illinois. He has written fifteen books on the American West, the most famous of which is *Bury My Heart at Wounded Knee.*

The selection printed here is an excerpt from the opening chapter of this documented history of the destruction of the American Indian. Of his unique and disturbing account, Brown says, "I have tried to fashion a narrative of the conquest of the American West as the victims experienced it, using their own words whenever possible. Americans who have always looked westward when reading about this period should read this book facing eastward." Brown's history focuses on the events—the broken treaties, the battles, the massacres—of the last half of the nineteenth century, what he calls "this doom period of their civilization." But this doom had its real beginnings long before, in the explorations of Christopher Columbus, ending finally in 1890 with the massacre at Wounded Knee, South Dakota—the symbolic end of Indian freedom.

Where today are the Pequot? Where are the Narragansett, the Mohican, the Pokanoket, and many other once powerful tribes of our people? They have vanished before the avarice and the oppression of the White Man, as snow before a summer sun.

Will we let ourselves be destroyed in our turn without a struggle, give up our homes, our country bequeathed to us by the Great Spirit, the graves of our dead and everything that is dear and sacred to us? I know you will cry with me, "Never! Never!"

—TECUMSEH OF THE SHAWNEES

1   It began with Christopher Columbus, who gave the people the name *Indios.* Those Europeans, the white men, spoke in different dialects, and some pronounced the word *Indien,* or *Indianer,* or Indian. *Peaux-rouges,* or redskins, came later. As was the custom of the people when receiving strangers, the Tainos on the island of San Salvador generously presented Columbus and his men with gifts and treated them with honor.

2   "So tractable, so peaceable, are these people," Columbus wrote to the King and Queen of Spain, "that I swear to your Majesties there is not in the world a

FROM CHRISTOPHER COLUMBUS TO WOUNDED KNEE   From *Bury My Heart at Wounded Knee* by Dee Brown. Copyright © 1970 by Dee Brown. Reprinted by permission of Holt, Rinehart and Winston, Publishers.

better nation. They love their neighbors as themselves, and their discourse is ever sweet and gentle, and accompanied with a smile; and though it is true that they are naked, yet their manners are decorous and praiseworthy."

3   All this, of course, was taken as a sign of weakness, if not heathenism, and Columbus being a righteous European was convinced the people should be "made to work, sow and do all that is necessary and to *adopt our ways*." Over the next four centuries (1492–1890) several million Europeans and their descendants undertook to enforce their ways upon the people of the New World.

4   Columbus kidnapped ten of his friendly Taino hosts and carried them off to Spain, where they could be introduced to the white man's ways. One of them died soon after arriving there, but not before he was baptized a Christian. The Spaniards were so pleased that they had made it possible for the first Indian to enter heaven that they hastened to spread the good news throughout the West Indies.

5   The Tainos and other Arawak people did not resist conversion to the Europeans' religion, but they did resist strongly when hordes of these bearded strangers began scouring their islands in search of gold and precious stones. The Spaniards looted and burned villages; they kidnapped hundreds of men, women, and children and shipped them to Europe to be sold as slaves. Arawak resistance brought on the use of guns and sabers, and whole tribes were destroyed, hundreds of thousands of people in less than a decade after Columbus set foot on the beach of San Salvador, October 12, 1492.

6   Communications between the tribes of the New World were slow, and news of the Europeans' barbarities rarely overtook the rapid spread of new conquests and settlements. Long before the English-speaking white men arrived in Virginia in 1607, however, the Powhatans had heard rumors about the civilizing techniques of the Spaniards. The Englishmen used subtler methods. To ensure peace long enough to establish a settlement at Jamestown, they put a golden crown upon the head of Wahunsonacook, dubbed him King Powhatan, and convinced him that he should put his people to work supplying the white settlers with food. Wahunsonacook vacillated between loyalty to his rebellious subjects and to the English, but after John Rolfe married his daughter, Pocahontas, he apparently decided that he was more English than Indian. After Wahunsonacook died, the Powhatans rose up in revenge to drive the Englishmen back into the sea from which they had come, but the Indians underestimated the power of English weapons. In a short time the eight thousand Powhatans were reduced to less than a thousand.

7   In Massachusetts the story began somewhat differently but ended virtually the same as in Virginia. After the Englishmen landed at Plymouth in 1620, most of them probably would have starved to death but for aid received from friendly natives of the New World. A Pemaquid named Samoset and three Wompanoags named Massasoit, Squanto, and Hobomah became self-appointed missionaries to the Pilgrims. All spoke some English, learned from explorers who had touched ashore in previous years. Squanto had been

kidnapped by an English seaman who sold him into slavery in Spain, but he escaped through the aid of another Englishman and finally managed to return home. He and the other Indians regarded the Plymouth colonists as helpless children; they shared corn with them from the tribal stores, showed them where and how to catch fish, and got them through the first winter. When spring came they gave the white men some seed corn and showed them how to plant and cultivate it.

8   For several years these Englishmen and their Indian neighbors lived in peace, but many more shiploads of white people continued coming ashore. The ring of axes and the crash of falling trees echoed up and down the coasts of the land which the white men now called New England. Settlements began crowding in upon each other. In 1625 some of the colonists asked Samoset to give them 12,000 additional acres of Pemaquid land. Samoset knew that land came from the Great Spirit, was as endless as the sky, and belonged to no man. To humor these strangers in their strange ways, however, he went through a ceremony of transferring the land and made his mark on a paper for them. It was the first deed of Indian land to English colonists.

9   Most of the other settlers, coming in by thousands now, did not bother to go through such a ceremony. By the time Massasoit, great chief of the Wampanoags, died in 1662 his people were being pushed back into the wilderness. His son Metacom foresaw doom for all Indians unless they united to resist the invaders. Although the New Englanders flattered Metacom by crowning him King Philip of Pokanoket, he devoted most of his time to forming alliances with the Narragansetts and other tribes in the region.

10   In 1675, after a series of arrogant actions by the colonists, King Philip led his Indian confederacy into a war meant to save the tribes from extinction. The Indians attacked fifty-two settlements, completely destroying twelve of them, but after months of fighting, the firepower of the colonists virtually exterminated the Wampanoags and Narragansetts. King Philip was killed and his head publicly exhibited at Plymouth for twenty years. Along with other captured Indian women and children, his wife and young son were sold into slavery in the West Indies.

11   When the Dutch came to Manhattan Island, Peter Minuit purchased it for sixty guilders in fishhooks and glass beads, but encouraged the Indians to remain and continue exchanging their valuable peltries for such trinkets. In 1641, Willem Kieft levied tribute upon the Mahicans and sent soldiers to Staten Island to punish the Raritans for offenses which had been committed not by them but by white settlers. The Raritans resisted arrest, and the soldiers killed four of them. When the Indians retaliated by killing four Dutchmen, Kieft ordered the massacre of two entire villages while the inhabitants slept. The Dutch soldiers ran their bayonets through men, women, and children, hacked their bodies to pieces, and then leveled the villages with fire.

12   For two more centuries these events were repeated again and again as the European colonists moved inland through the passes of the Alleghenies and

down the westward-flowing rivers to the Great Waters (the Mississippi) and then up the Great Muddy (the Missouri).

13   The Five Nations of the Iroquois, mightiest and most advanced of all the eastern tribes, strove in vain for peace. After years of bloodshed to save their political independence, they finally went down to defeat. Some escaped to Canada, some fled westward, some lived out their lives in reservation confinement.

14   During the 1760's Pontiac of the Ottawas united tribes in the Great Lakes country in hopes of driving the British back across the Alleghenies, but he failed. His major error was an alliance with French-speaking white men who withdrew aid from the *peaux-rouges* during the crucial siege of Detroit.

15   A generation later, Tecumseh of the Shawnees formed a great confederacy of midwestern and southern tribes to protect their lands from invasion. The dream ended with Tecumseh's death in battle during the War of 1812.

16   Between 1795 and 1840 the Miamis fought battle after battle, and signed treaty after treaty, ceding their rich Ohio Valley lands until there was none left to cede.

17   When white settlers began streaming into the Illinois country after the War of 1812, the Sauks and Foxes fled across the Mississippi. A subordinate chief, Black Hawk, refused to retreat. He created an alliance with the Winnebagos, Pottawotamies, and Kickapoos, and declared war against the new settlements. A band of Winnebagos, who accepted a white soldier chief's bribe of twenty horses and a hundred dollars, betrayed Black Hawk, and he was captured in 1832. He was taken East for imprisonment and display to the curious. After he died in 1838, the governor of the recently created Iowa Territory obtained Black Hawk's skeleton and kept it on view in his office.

18   In 1829, Andrew Jackson, who was called Sharp Knife by the Indians, took office as President of the United States. During his frontier career, Sharp Knife and his soldiers had slain thousands of Cherokees, Chickasaws, Choctaws, Creeks, and Seminoles, but these southern Indians were still numerous and clung stubbornly to their tribal lands, which had been assigned them forever by white men's treaties. In Sharp Knife's first message to his Congress, he recommended that all these Indians be removed westward beyond the Mississippi. "I suggest the propriety of setting apart an ample district west of the Mississippi . . . to be guaranteed to the Indian tribes, as long as they shall occupy it."

19   Although enactment of such a law would only add to the long list of broken promises made to the eastern Indians, Sharp Knife was convinced that Indians and whites could not live together in peace and that his plan would make possible a final promise which never would be broken again. On May 28, 1830, Sharp Knife's recommendations became law.

20   Two years later he appointed a commissioner of Indian affairs to serve in the War Department and see that the new laws affecting Indians were properly carried out. And then on June 30, 1834, Congress passed *An Act to Regulate Trade and Intercourse with the Indian Tribes and to Preserve Peace* *on the Frontiers.* All that part of the United States west of the Mississippi "and not within the States of Missouri and Louisiana or the Territory of Arkansas" would be Indian country. No white persons would be permitted to trade in the Indian country without a license. No white traders of bad character would be permitted to reside in Indian country. No white persons would be permitted to settle in the Indian country. The military force of the United States would be employed in the apprehension of any white person who was found in violation of provisions of the act.

21   Before these laws could be put into effect, a new wave of white settlers swept westward and formed the territories of Wisconsin and Iowa. This made it necessary for the policy makers in Washington to shift the "permanent Indian frontier" from the Mississippi River to the 95th meridian. (This line ran from Lake of the Woods on what is now the Minnesota-Canada border, slicing southward through what are now the states of Minnesota and Iowa, and then along the western borders of Missouri, Arkansas, and Louisiana, to Galveston Bay, Texas.) To keep the Indians beyond the 95th meridian and to prevent unauthorized white men from crossing it, soldiers were garrisoned in a series of military posts that ran southward from Fort Snelling on the Mississippi River to forts Atkinson and Leavenworth on the Missouri, forts Gibson and Smith on the Arkansas, Fort Towson on the Red, and Fort Jesup in Louisiana.

22   More than three centuries had now passed since Christopher Columbus landed on San Salvador, more than two centuries since the English colonists came to Virginia and New England. In that time the friendly Tainos who welcomed Columbus ashore had been utterly obliterated. Long before the last of the Tainos died, their simple agricultural and handicraft culture was destroyed and replaced by cotton plantations worked by slaves. The white colonists chopped down the tropical forests to enlarge their fields; the cotton plants exhausted the soil; winds unbroken by a forest shield covered the fields with sand. When Columbus first saw the island he described it as "very big and very level and the trees very green . . . the whole of it so green that it is a pleasure to gaze upon." The Europeans who followed him there destroyed its vegetation and its inhabitants—human, animal, bird, and fish—and after turning it into a wasteland, they abandoned it.

23   On the mainland of America, the Wampanoags of Massasoit and King Philip had vanished, along with the Chesapeakes, the Chickahominys, and the Potomacs of the great Powhatan confederacy. (Only Pocahontas was remembered.) Scattered or reduced to remnants were the Pequots, Montauks, Nanticokes, Machapungas, Catawbas, Cheraws, Miamis, Hurons, Eries, Mohawks, Senecas, and Mohegans. (Only Uncas was remembered.) Their musical names remained forever fixed on the American land, but their bones were forgotten in a thousand burned villages or lost in forests fast disappearing before the axes of twenty million invaders. Already the once sweet-watered streams, most of which bore Indian names, were clouded with silt and the wastes of man; the very earth was being ravaged and squandered. To

the Indians it seemed that these Europeans hated everything in nature—the living forests and their birds and beasts, the grassy glades, the water, the soil, and the air itself.

Exercises

COMPREHENSION

Organization and Development

Complete the following outline. Find the thesis statement and write it in the space provided. Then find the main divisions in the essay and fill in the remaining spaces. Note the paragraphs for each section.

Thesis statement: _____

_____

_____	[ ]
I. _____	[ ]
II. _____	[ ]
III. _____	[ ]
IV. _____	[ ]
V. _____	[ ]

Content

Choose the answer that correctly completes each statement.

1. The Europeans saw what Columbus described as the "decorous and praiseworthy" manners of the Indians as a(n) (a) model to emulate (b) unconvincing act (c) sign of weakness, if not of heathenism itself.
2. The natives of the New World were called Indians because (a) that was what they called themselves (b) Christopher Columbus gave them the name *Indios* (c) they were first encountered by white men in a place called *Indianer*.
3. Brown includes the details of the Tainos greeting Columbus with gifts and the Massachusetts Indians sharing their corn with the Pilgrims, whom they saw as helpless children, in order to strengthen his picture of the Indians as (a) always ready to use trickery and deception, rather than violence, to keep the white intruders at bay (b) originally friendly and predisposed to peaceful coexistence with the white man (c) conscious from the beginning of the white man's superiority and anxious to placate him with material offerings.
4. Brown's selection of incidents for this history implies that the white man's oppression of the Indian was motivated mainly by a desire to (a) appropriate the Indians' land (b) convert the Indians to Christianity and thus save their souls (c) civilize the Indians and teach them European methods of agriculture and husbandry.
5. Indian attempts at confederation and retaliation against the white man's oppression failed (a) because the Indians had no sense of unity and could never form a lasting alliance among tribes (b) largely because of the white man's consistently superior

firepower (c) because the Indians lost heart when they saw that the white man had unshakable faith in the divine justice of his cause.

6. The fact that the Indians deeded land to the white settlers merely to humor them demonstrates the (a) vast disparity between the two peoples in their sense of man's right relationship to nature (b) utter simplicity and ignorance of the Indians with regard to property rights (c) white man's clever and intelligent handling of the necessary transfer of great tracts of land.

7. Brown's conclusion leaves us with the sense that the (a) white man's destruction of the New World Indian is another impressive example of the law of survival of the fittest (b) white man was sadly conscious of his obligation to destroy in order to tame and civilize the wilderness (c) white man was a savage destroyer of everything in nature.

8. Most of the factual information in Brown's history is already familiar to us; its important distinction from other narratives of early America lies in its (a) stress on the ecological impact of the European colonists (b) reversal of the usual perspective in that it narrates the familiar history from the unfamiliar point of view of the Indians (c) emphasis on the Europeans' efforts to colonize rather than on their heroic impulse to discover and explore the new continent.

Paragraph Structure

Reorder the following sentences to form a unified, coherent paragraph. Write a topic sentence for the paragraph. Then check your version with the original.

1. He created an alliance with the Winnebagos, Pottawotamies, and Kickapoos, and declared war against the new settlements.
2. After he died in 1838, the governor of the recently created Iowa Territory obtained Black Hawk's skeleton and kept it on view in his office.
3. When white settlers began streaming into the Illinois country after the War of 1812, the Sauks and Foxes fled across the Mississippi.
4. A band of Winnebagos, who accepted a white soldier chief's bribe of twenty horses and a hundred dollars, betrayed Black Hawk, and he was captured in 1832.
5. A subordinate chief, Black Hawk, refused to retreat.
6. He was taken East for imprisonment and display to the curious.

VOCABULARY AND USAGE

Word Formation Table

Complete the following table by changing word endings or root forms to make new grammatical forms. Use your dictionary if necessary.

	NOUN	VERB	ADJECTIVE	ADVERB
1.	_____	xxx	decorous	_____
2	_____	convince	_____	_____
3.	_____	hasten	_____	_____
4.	_____	_____	valuable	_____
5.	extinction	_____	_____	_____

Fill-Ins

Complete each of the sentences below using the words on the following list. You may need to use some words more than once. You may also find that some blanks can be completed correctly with more than one word. Add plural endings to nouns and change verb forms where necessary.

ravaged	discourse	because	barbarities
squandered	manner	resistance	cultivate
utterly	tractable	law	share
alliance	unite	defeat	corn
colony	destruction	join	settlement

1. The story of the white man's relations with the Indian is one of countless _____, broken _____, and ultimate _____ for the Indian.
2. Although the Indians' _____ were decorous and their _____ gentle, these qualities did not save them from being _____ destroyed.
3. The fact that the Indians were gentle and _____ is important _____ these qualities seemed to have aided the white man as he _____ the Indians' lands.
4. Even the white man's _____ helped to accelerate the _____ and to ensure the ultimate _____ of the Indians.
5. The Indians were at first willing and eager to _____ their knowledge and supplies; they even gave the white men _____ and showed them how to _____ it.
6. After three centuries of the white man's _____ and _____, the very land of North America was _____ _____ and _____.

DISCUSSION

1. Brown's tone is often ironic, especially in the opening paragraphs. Point to specific words and phrases in paragraphs 1–9 that contribute to his ironic posture.
2. The basic method of development in this piece is narrative. Find and underline the main transitional words and phrases in paragraphs 1–10 or 11–20. What is Brown's most characteristic method of moving the narrative forward? Try substituting other words, phrases, or methods of transition. What is the effect on the narrative movement?
3. This selection presents a familiar history, but from an unaccustomed perspective—that of the Indian. What important differences can you note between Brown's version and the usual textbook or popular accounts of such familiar historical events as the purchase of Manhattan Island, the Pilgrims' first winter in Massachusetts, the activities of the Bureau of Indian Affairs, etc.?
4. Brown's essay begins with the statement, "It began with Christopher Columbus. . . ." To what does the pronoun "it" actually refer?
5. What difference between the Spanish and the English treatment of the Indians is indicated in paragraph 6? Were the end results of these "civilizing techniques" different? (You might wish to compare Arthur Campa's discussion in "Anglo vs. Chicano: Why?")

6. Tecumseh's statement characterizes the relationship of the white man to the Indian as one of "avarice and oppression." How does Brown's narrative illustrate and support this statement? Does his narrative move beyond these qualities in characterizing that relationship?
7. What essential difference does Brown reveal between the Indian's and the European's relationship to nature? What contemporary problems might be attributed to this essential difference and to the fact that it is the white man's way that has prevailed?

SUGGESTIONS FOR WRITING

1. Write an essay in which you narrate or describe a familiar event or scene but, like Brown, alter the point of view from which we are accustomed to hearing the story or viewing the scene. (For example, what would some fairy tales sound like if the dragon told the story?)
2. Compare the treatment of American Indians to Hitler's treatment of the Jews of Europe during World War II. What similarities and/or differences can you find in the attitudes toward the victims and the motivation for these two separate instances of genocide?
3. Write an essay in which you define an "advanced" civilization and a "primitive" civilization.
4. Write an essay in which you argue for or against the colonization of underdeveloped areas by more technologically advanced societies. (You may want to consider here the possibility of extraterrestrial exploration and colonization.)

Chinese-Feminine, American-Feminine

MAXINE HONG KINGSTON

Maxine Ting Ting Hong Kingston was born in Stockton, California, the daughter of immigrant parents who came to America in the 1930s from a small Chinese peasant village. A graduate of the University of California at Berkeley, she now lives with her husband and small son in Honolulu, where she teaches English and creative writing.

The following selection is from *The Woman Warrior: Memoirs of a Girlhood Among Ghosts,* a unique autobiographical narrative that mingles fact, impression, and legend as Kingston chronicles her struggle to accommodate her bicultural heritage to her female identity and her creative powers. The opening chapter explains the purpose of the book and the ghosts so prominently featured: "Those of us in the first American generations have had to figure out how the invisible world the emigrants built around our childhoods fit in solid America."

This "invisible world" includes spirits as Westerners know them—the ghosts of the dead (and their curses), demons and phantoms, and the powerful figure of Fa Mu Lan, the Woman Warrior of Chinese legend. But by "ghosts" the Chinese also mean white people—Sales Ghosts, Druggist Ghosts, Teacher Ghosts—all caucasians, who are ghostly not only in color, but unreal, less than human, yet nonetheless threatening to the emigrants.

Finally, the invisible world of superstition expands to include the alien customs and beliefs of emigrant parents that embarrass and constrain a child growing up in America: "That is the way the Chinese do it." For Maxine, this means especially the incident of the tongue cutting—which was, in fact, a custom of Chinese peasants who thought their children were tongue-tied. But whether Maxine's mother actually committed "such a powerful act" is not clear—to her or to the reader.

1 In fact, it wasn't me my brother told about going to Los Angeles; one of my sisters told me what he'd told her. His version of the story may be better than mine because of its bareness, not twisted into designs. The hearer can carry it tucked away without it taking up much room. Long ago in China, knot-makers tied string into buttons and frogs, and rope into bell pulls. There was one knot so complicated that it blinded the knot-maker. Finally an emperor outlawed this cruel knot, and the nobles could not order it anymore. If I had lived in China, I would have been an outlaw knot-maker.

2 Maybe that's why my mother cut my tongue. She pushed my tongue up and sliced the frenum. Or maybe she snipped it with a pair of nail scissors. I don't remember her doing it, only her telling me about it, but all during

childhood I felt sorry for the baby whose mother waited with scissors or knife in hand for it to cry—and then, when its mouth was wide open like a baby bird's, cut. The Chinese say "a ready tongue is an evil."

3   I used to curl up my tongue in front of the mirror and tauten my frenum into a white line, itself as thin as a razor blade. I saw no scars in my mouth. I thought perhaps I had had two frena, and she had cut one. I made other children open their mouths so I could compare theirs to mine. I saw perfect pink membranes stretching into precise edges that looked easy enough to cut. Sometimes I felt very proud that my mother committed such a powerful act upon me. At other times I was terrified—the first thing my mother did when she saw me was to cut my tongue.

4   "Why did you do that to me, Mother?"

5   "I told you."

6   "Tell me again."

7   "I cut it so that you would not be tongue-tied. Your tongue would be able to move in any language. You'll be able to speak languages that are completely different from one another. You'll be able to pronounce anything. Your frenum looked too tight to do those things, so I cut it."

8   "But isn't 'a ready tongue an evil'?"

9   "Things are different in this ghost country."

10   "Did it hurt me? Did I cry and bleed?"

11   "I don't remember. Probably."

12   She didn't cut the other children's. When I asked cousins and other Chinese children whether their mothers had cut their tongues loose, they said, "What?"

13   "Why didn't you cut my brothers' and sisters' tongues?"

14   "They didn't need it."

15   "Why not? Were theirs longer than mine?"

16   "Why don't you quit blabbering and get to work?"

17   If my mother was not lying she should have cut more, scraped away the rest of the frenum skin, because I have a terrible time talking. Or she should not have cut at all, tampering with my speech. When I went to kindergarten and had to speak English for the first time, I became silent. A dumbness—a shame—still cracks my voice in two, even when I want to say "hello" casually, or ask an easy question in front of the check-out counter, or ask directions of a bus driver. I stand frozen, or I hold up the line with the complete, grammatical sentence that comes squeaking out at impossible length. "What did you say?" says the cab driver, or "Speak up," so I have to perform again, only weaker the second time. A telephone call makes my throat bleed and takes up that day's courage. It spoils my day with self-disgust when I hear my broken voice come skittering out into the open. It makes people wince to hear it. I'm getting better, though. Recently I asked the postman for special-issue stamps; I've waited since childhood for postmen to give me some of their own accord. I am making progress, a little every day.

18   My silence was thickest—total—during the three years that I covered my

school paintings with black paint. I painted layers of black over houses and flowers and suns, and when I drew on the blackboard, I put a layer of chalk on top. I was making a stage curtain, and it was the moment before the curtain parted or rose. The teachers called my parents to school, and I saw they had been saving my pictures, curling and cracking, all alike and black. The teachers pointed to the pictures and looked serious, talked seriously too, but my parents did not understand English. ("The parents and teachers of criminals were executed," said my father.) My parents took the pictures home. I spread them out (so black and full of possibilities) and pretended the curtains were swinging open, flying up, one after another, sunlight underneath, mighty operas.

19   During the first silent year I spoke to no one at school, did not ask before going to the lavatory, and flunked kindergarten. My sister also said nothing for three years, silent in the playground and silent at lunch. There were other quiet Chinese girls not of our family, but most of them got over it sooner than we did. I enjoyed the silence. At first it did not occur to me I was supposed to talk or to pass kindergarten. I talked at home and to one or two of the Chinese kids in class. I made motions and even made some jokes. I drank out of a toy saucer when the water spilled out of the cup, and everybody laughed, pointing at me, so I did it some more. I didn't know that Americans don't drink out of saucers.

20   I liked the Negro students (Black Ghosts) best because they laughed the loudest and talked to me as if I were a daring talker too. One of the Negro girls had her mother coil braids over her ears Shanghai-style like mine; we were Shanghai twins except that she was covered with black like my paintings. Two Negro kids enrolled in Chinese school, and the teachers gave them Chinese names. Some Negro kids walked me to school and home, protecting me from the Japanese kids, who hit me and chased me and stuck gum in my ears. The Japanese kids were noisy and tough. They appeared one day in kindergarten, released from concentration camp, which was a tic-tac-toe mark, like barbed wire, on the map.

21   It was when I found out I had to talk that school became a misery, that the silence became a misery. I did not speak and felt bad each time that I did not speak. I read aloud in first grade, though, and heard the barest whisper with little squeaks come out of my throat. "Louder," said the teacher, who scared the voice away again. The other Chinese girls did not talk either, so I knew the silence had to do with being a Chinese girl.

22   Reading out loud was easier than speaking because we did not have to make up what to say, but I stopped often, and the teacher would think I'd gone quiet again. I could not understand "I." The Chinese "I" has seven strokes, intricacies. How could the American "I," assuredly wearing a hat like the Chinese, have only three strokes, the middle so straight? Was it out of politeness that this writer left off strokes the way a Chinese has to write her own name small and crooked? No, it was not politeness; "I" is a capital and "you" is lower-case. I stared at that middle line and waited so long for its black center to resolve into tight strokes and dots that I forgot to pronounce

it. The other troublesome word was "here," no strong consonant to hang on to, and so flat, when "here" is two mountainous ideographs. The teacher, who had already told me every day how to read "I" and "here," put me in the low corner under the stairs again, where the noisy boys usually sat.

23   When my second grade class did a play, the whole class went to the auditorium except the Chinese girls. The teacher, lovely and Hawaiian, should have understood about us, but instead left us behind in the classroom. Our voices were too soft or nonexistent, and our parents never signed the permission slips anyway. They never signed anything unnecessary. We opened the door a crack and peeked out, but closed it again quickly. One of us (not me) won every spelling bee, though.

24   I remember telling the Hawaiian teacher, "We Chinese can't sing 'land where our fathers died.'" She argued with me about politics, while I meant because of curses. But how can I have that memory when I couldn't talk? My mother says that we, like the ghosts, have no memories.

25   After American school, we picked up our cigar boxes, in which we had arranged books, brushes, and an inkbox neatly, and went to Chinese school, from 5:00 to 7:30 P.M. There we chanted together, voices rising and falling, loud and soft, some boys shouting, everybody reading together, reciting together and not alone with one voice. When we had a memorization test, the teacher let each of us come to his desk and say the lesson to him privately, while the rest of the class practiced copying or tracing. Most of the teachers were men. The boys who were so well behaved in the American school played tricks on them and talked back to them. The girls were not mute. They screamed and yelled during recess, when there were no rules; they had fist-fights. Nobody was afraid of children hurting themselves or of children hurting school property. The glass doors to the red and green balconies with the gold joy symbols were left wide open so that we could run out and climb the fire escapes. We played capture-the-flag in the auditorium, where Sun Yat-sen and Chiang Kai-shek's pictures hung at the back of the stage, the Chinese flag on their left and the American flag on their right. We climbed the teak ceremonial chairs and made flying leaps off the stage. One flag headquarters was behind the glass door and the other on stage right. Our feet drummed on the hollow stage. During recess the teachers locked themselves up in their office with the shelves of books, copybooks, inks from China. They drank tea and warmed their hands at a stove. There was no play supervision. At recess we had the school to ourselves, and also we could roam as far as we could go—downtown, Chinatown stores, home—as long as we returned before the bell rang.

26   At exactly 7:30 the teacher again picked up the brass bell that sat on his desk and swung it over our heads, while we charged down the stairs, our cheering magnified in the stairwell. Nobody had to line up.

27   Not all of the children who were silent at American school found voice at Chinese school. One new teacher said each of us had to get up and recite in front of the class, who was to listen. My sister and I had memorized the lesson perfectly. We said it to each other at home, one chanting, one

listening. The teacher called on my sister to recite first. It was the first time a teacher had called on the second-born to go first. My sister was scared. She glanced at me and looked away; I looked down at my desk. I hoped that she could do it because if she could, then I would have to. She opened her mouth and a voice came out that wasn't a whisper, but it wasn't a proper voice either. I hoped that she would not cry, fear breaking up her voice like twigs underfoot. She sounded as if she were trying to sing though weeping and strangling. She did not pause or stop to end the embarrassment. She kept going until she said the last word, and then she sat down. When it was my turn, the same voice came out, a crippled animal running on broken legs. You could hear splinters in my voice, bones rubbing jagged against one another. I was loud, though. I was glad I didn't whisper. There was one little girl who whispered.

28   You can't entrust your voice to the Chinese, either; they want to capture your voice for their own use. They want to fix up your tongue to speak for them. "How much less can you sell it for?" we have to say. Talk the Sales Ghosts down. Make them take a loss.

29   We were working at the laundry when a delivery boy came from the Rexall drugstore around the corner. He had a pale blue box of pills, but nobody was sick. Reading the label we saw that it belonged to another Chinese family, Crazy Mary's family. "Not ours," said my father. He pointed out the name to the Delivery Ghost, who took the pills back. My mother muttered for an hour, and then her anger boiled over. "That ghost! That dead ghost! How dare he come to the wrong house?" She could not concentrate on her marking and pressing. "A mistake! Huh!" I was getting angry myself. She fumed. She made her press crash and hiss. "Revenge. We've got to avenge this wrong on our future, on our health, and on our lives. Nobody's going to sicken my children and get away with it." We brothers and sisters did not look at one another. She would do something awful, something embarrassing. She'd already been hinting that during the next eclipse we slam pot lids together to scare the frog from swallowing the moon. (The word for "eclipse" is *frog-swallowing-the-moon.*) When we had not banged lids at the last eclipse and the shadow kept receding anyway, she'd said, "The villagers must be banging and clanging very loudly back home in China."

30   ("On the other side of the world, they aren't having an eclipse, Mama. That's just a shadow the earth makes when it comes between the moon and the sun."

31   "You're always believing what those Ghost Teachers tell you. Look at the size of the jaws!")

32   "Aha!" she yelled. "You! The biggest." She was pointing at me. "You go to the drugstore."

33   "What do you want me to buy, Mother?" I said.

34   "Buy nothing. Don't bring one cent. Go and make them stop the curse."

35   "I don't want to go. I don't know how to do that. There are no such things as curses. They'll think I'm crazy."

36   "If you don't go, I'm holding you responsible for bringing a plague on this family."

37   "What am I supposed to do when I get there?" I said, sullen, trapped. "Do I say, 'Your delivery boy made a wrong delivery'?"

38   "They know he made a wrong delivery. I want you to make them rectify their crime."

39   I felt sick already. She'd make me swing stinky censers around the counter, at the druggist, at the customers. Throw dog blood on the druggist. I couldn't stand her plans.

40   "You get reparation candy," she said. "You say, 'You have tainted my house with sick medicine and must remove the curse with sweetness.' He'll understand."

41   "He didn't do it on purpose. And no, he won't, Mother. They don't understand stuff like that. I won't be able to say it right. He'll call us beggars."

42   "You just translate." She searched me to make sure I wasn't hiding any money. I was sneaky and bad enough to buy the candy and come back pretending it was a free gift.

43   "Mymotherseztagimmesomecandy," I said to the druggist. Be cute and small. No one hurts the cute and small.

44   "What? Speak up. Speak English," he said, big in his white druggist coat.

45   "Tatatagimme somecandy."

46   The druggist leaned way over the counter and frowned. "Some free candy," I said. "Sample candy."

47   "We don't give sample candy, young lady," he said.

48   "My mother said you have to give us candy. She said that is the way the Chinese do it."

49   "What?"

50   "That is the way the Chinese do it."

51   "Do what?"

52   "Do things." I felt the weight and immensity of things impossible to explain to the druggist.

53   "Can I give you some money?" he asked.

54   "No, we want candy."

55   He reached into a jar and gave me a handful of lollipops. He gave us candy all year round, year after year, every time we went into the drugstore. When different druggists or clerks waited on us, they also gave us candy. They had talked us over. They gave us Halloween candy in December, Christmas candy around Valentine's day, candy hearts at Easter, and Easter eggs at Halloween. "See?" said our mother. "They understand. You kids just aren't very brave." But I knew they did not understand. They thought we were beggars without a home who lived in back of the laundry. They felt sorry for us. I did not eat their candy. I did not go inside the drugstore or walk past it unless my parents forced me to. Whenever we had a prescription filled, the druggist put candy in the medicine bag. This is what Chinese druggists normally do, except they give raisins. My mother thought she taught the Druggist Ghosts a lesson in good manners (which is the same word as "traditions").

56   My mouth went permanently crooked with effort, turned down on the left side and straight on the right. How strange that the emigrant villagers are shouters, hollering face to face. My father asks, "Why is it I can hear Chinese from blocks away? Is it that I understand the language? Or is it they talk loud?" They turn the radio up full blast to hear the operas, which do not seem to hurt their ears. And they yell over the singers that wail over the drums, everybody talking at once, big arm gestures, spit flying. You can see the disgust on American faces looking at women like that. It isn't just the loudness. It is the way Chinese sounds, chingchong ugly, to American ears, not beautiful like Japanese sayonara words with the consonants and vowels as regular as Italian. We make guttural peasant noise and have Ton Duc Thang names you can't remember. And the Chinese can't hear Americans at all; the language is too soft and western music unhearable. I've watched a Chinese audience laugh, visit, talk-story, and holler during a piano recital, as if the musician could not hear them. A Chinese-American, somebody's son, was playing Chopin, which has no punctuation, no cymbals, no gongs. Chinese piano music is five black keys. Normal Chinese women's voices are strong and bossy. We American-Chinese girls had to whisper to make ourselves American-feminine. Apparently we whispered even more softly than the Americans. Once a year the teachers referred my sister and me to speech therapy, but our voices would straighten out, unpredictably normal, for the therapists. Some of us gave up, shook our heads, and said nothing, not one word. Some of us could not even shake our heads. At times shaking my head no is more self-assertion than I can manage. Most of us eventually found some voice, however faltering. We invented an American-feminine speaking personality, except for that one girl who could not speak up even in Chinese school.

Exercises

COMPREHENSION

Organization and Development

Complete the following outline. Find the main sequences or episodes in the narrative and label them in the spaces provided. Note the paragraphs for each section. Then, in your own words, write the main idea or ideas that these actions express. If you can, indicate specific paragraphs in which the author comes closest to making a direct statement of her implied theme or thesis.

I. _____   [   ]
II. _____   [   ]
III. _____   [   ]
IV. _____   [   ]
Main idea(s): _____
_____   [   ]

Content

Choose the answer that correctly completes each statement.

1. When Kingston says, "If I had lived in China, I would have been an outlaw knot-maker," she is referring to (a) her inability to follow rules, laws, or conventions (b) the intricacy and complexity of her writing style (c) her desire to establish a truly unique Chinese identity.
2. According to Kingston, her mother cut her tongue when she was an infant (a) in order to punish her (b) because all Chinese mothers perform this operation on their children (c) so she wouldn't be tongue-tied.
3. The Chinese proverb "a ready tongue is an evil," so closely associated in Kingston's mind with the tongue-cutting incident, emphasizes the (a) traditional values that most emigrant parents try to maintain in America (b) author's own hostility toward and desire to escape from her Chinese heritage (c) basic ambiguity and uncertainty the author feels about whether the tongue-cutting incident actually occurred and its significance if it did.
4. The statement "I did not speak and felt bad each time I did not speak" describes Kingston's silence in grade school and also expresses (a) her feelings of ambivalence about the two cultures to which she had to adjust (b) the terrible shyness that plagued her all her life and that she could overcome only by writing (c) her anger at the teachers who did not help her to learn English.
5. Kingston mentions an eclipse in her narrative of the Druggist Ghost episode because both incidents emphasize the (a) fact that Kingston's mother, with her Chinese superstitions, was always doing something embarrassing in her children's eyes (b) folk wisdom of the Chinese peasants, who were able to predict eclipses with great accuracy and to cure many illnesses with natural medicines (c) terror that the superstitious peasants felt in the face of any mystery.
6. Maxine's black-covered paintings worried her teachers; to her the blackness represented (a) the isolation of her total silence during those three years (b) a hostile refusal to reveal herself to the white ghosts (c) a stage curtain ready to rise, making the black paintings seem full of possibilities.
7. The Chinese designation of caucasians as "ghosts" indicates that Chinese people saw white people as (a) emotionally cold and dead (b) insubstantial yet dangerous (c) colorless and unimportant.
8. Kingston's sisters and friends "invented an American-feminine speaking personality" to (a) mask their timidity and attract American boyfriends (b) overcome their shyness and fear at having to speak English (c) disguise their foreignness, since normal Chinese women's voices are strong and bossy.

Paragraph Structure

Reorder the following sentences to form a unified, coherent paragraph. Identify one sentence as the topic sentence. Then check your version with the original.

1. Make them take a loss.
2. They want to fix up your tongue to speak for them.
3. "How much less can you sell it for?" we have to say.
4. Talk the Sales Ghosts down.
5. You can't entrust your voice to the Chinese either; they want to capture your voice for their own use.

VOCABULARY AND USAGE

Word Formation Table

Complete the following table by changing word endings or root forms to make new grammatical forms. Use your dictionary if necessary.

	NOUN	VERB	ADJECTIVE	ADVERB
1.	_____	_____	_____	unpredictably
2.	therapists	xxx	_____	_____
3.	_____	sound	_____	_____
4.	_____	xxx	_____	responsible
5.	medicine	_____	_____	_____

Fill-Ins

Complete each of the sentences below using the words on the following list. You may need to use some words more than once. You may also find that some blanks can be completed correctly with more than one word. Add plural endings to nouns and change verb forms where necessary.

value	imposed	ghost	superstition
peasant	ambivalence	caucasian	tradition
Chinese	voice	belief	school
painting	speak	embarrassing	silence
whisper	noise	speech	conflict

1. Kingston's parents were _____ who came to America and brought with them many _____ _____ on their children, who found this very _____.

2. The author's _____ about which _____ she should follow is symbolized by the _____ between _____ and _____ that actually kept her in a self _____ _____ for three years.

3. This narrative _____ of a _____ faced by the children of _____ emigrants, a _____ between the world of their parents' _____ and the world of the _____ _____.

4. Another way in which the essay reveals the author's dilemma, her _____ about _____, is its comparison of the _____ she attended, one _____ and one _____.

5. Kingston says that while Japanese _____ is pleasing to Western ears, the _____ language sounds awful to _____, partly because the _____ make so much _____.

6. Although as a child at _____ the author admired the Black _____ and Japanese _____, mostly because they made so much _____, she herself seemed condemned to _____, barely able to _____, and unable to raise her _____ above a _____.

DISCUSSION

1. Examine the narrative carefully and determine what method or methods Kingston uses to maintain its progression. What are the main incidents and how are they connected? In what ways does this essay follow, or deviate from, standard chronological sequence?
2. A fundamental opposition between silence and speech marks this narrative. With this in mind, examine the essay carefully, and then list the figures who speak freely, those who are mostly silent, and those who can be either one or the other. Which situations or figures seem to promote silence, which seem to foster speech, and what is the author's relationship to them?
3. The strongest figure in this narrative is Kingston's mother; Chinese women are described as having loud, bossy voices; the author says that her quiet, "American-feminine" personality is "invented"; and the book itself is dominated by the figure of the powerful Woman Warrior. At the same time, it is suggested that silence and passivity have something to do with being a Chinese girl. According to what you have read here, which of the two cultures do you think is more conducive to promoting strength and independence in women? Which image would you prefer: Chinese-feminine or American-feminine? What evidence, apart from this essay, can you produce to support your conclusions?
4. Find two or three incidents in the narrative that reveal misunderstanding, embarrassment, or total lack of communication as a result of cultural differences. What are the essential conflicts in the values of the Chinese emigrants and those of the American "ghosts," and how are these conflicts imposed on the children of the emigrants?
5. What attitude toward speech and language (at once the author's particular problem *and* gift) is suggested by the introductory anecdote about a complicated knot that blinded the knot-makers of ancient China until it was finally outlawed?
6. Analyze the author's relationship to her mother. In what respects does it seem to be formed mainly by the stress of the conflicts between Chinese and American values, and in what respects is it peculiar to these two individuals?

SUGGESTIONS FOR WRITING

1. Write an essay in which you describe the ways in which your family, especially by its customs, habits, or beliefs, embarrassed you as a child.
2. Establish a cause-effect relationship between some incident in your childhood and a whole behavior pattern that you see as its result (somewhat like Kingston's severed frenum and her subsequent difficulty in speaking).
3. Write a narrative of a typical day in your grade school, high school, summer camp, or any other regularly scheduled activity of your childhood. Refer to Kingston's description of her Chinese school and, if you wish, consult Joyce Maynard's essay, "The Lion Tamers."

4. Write an essay in which you analyze the ways in which your family expressed its expectations for you according to your sex. If you have a sibling of the opposite sex, describe the differences between your family's upbringing of, attitude toward, and expectations for males and females.

5. Write a short narrative history of your family and its origins: where they came from, what forces motivated their immigration to the United States (and/or to the particular area where you now live), and the process by which they became "Americans." Be sure to include some reference to any values, beliefs, and customs of the ancestral country that have been preserved. (You may wish to consult Irving Howe's essay, "At Ellis Island.")

Discovery of a Father

SHERWOOD ANDERSON

Sherwood Anderson (1876–1941) grew up in Clyde, Ohio, the fourth of seven children of an unsuccessful harnessmaker, a man apparently much like the father in this selection. Although he never attended school regularly because of his mother's need for help in supporting the family, Anderson read widely and became a serious thinker. He had a varied career, including periods as a successful businessman and newspaper editor in addition to his career as a writer of fiction. He is most recognized for his powerful collection of short stories, *Winesburg, Ohio,* his letters, and three "autobiographies." All the versions of his life story are highly impressionistic, even fictionalized.

The selection that appears below is from the last of those three volumes, *Sherwood Anderson's Memoirs*. This brief narrative reveals, as do most of his writings, Anderson's interest in human behavior as a reaction to the realities of the subconscious or to experiences hidden or forgotten in the individual's past.

1   You hear it said that fathers want their sons to be what they feel they cannot themselves be, but I tell you it also works the other way. A boy wants something very special from his father. I know that as a small boy I wanted my father to be a certain thing he was not. I wanted him to be a proud, silent, dignified father. When I was with other boys and he passed along the street, I wanted to feel a flow of pride. "There he is. That is my father."

2   But he wasn't such a one. He couldn't be. It seemed to me then that he was always showing off. Let's say someone in our town had got up a show. They were always doing it. The druggist would be in it, the shoe-store clerk, the horse doctor, and a lot of women and girls. My father would manage to get the chief comedy part. It was, let's say, a Civil War play and he was a comic Irish soldier. He had to do the most absurd things. They thought he was funny, but I didn't.

3   I thought he was terrible. I didn't see how mother could stand it. She even laughed with the others. Maybe I would have laughed if it hadn't been my father.

4   Or there was a parade, the Fourth of July or Decoration Day. He'd be in that, too, right at the front of it, as Grand Marshal or something, on a white horse hired from a livery stable.

5   He couldn't ride for shucks. He fell off the horse and everyone hooted with

DISCOVERY OF A FATHER   Adapted from *Sherwood Anderson's Memoirs: A Critical Edition,* edited by Ray Lewis White. © 1969 The University of North Carolina Press. By permission of the publisher.

laughter, but he didn't care. He even seemed to like it. I remember once when he had done something ridiculous, and right out on Main Street, too. I was with some other boys and they were laughing and shouting at him and he was shouting back and having as good a time as they were. I ran down an alley back of some stores and there in the Presbyterian Church sheds I had a good long cry.

6   Or I would be in bed at night and father would come home a little lit up and bring some men with him. He was a man who was never alone. Before he went broke, running a harness shop, there were always a lot of men loafing in the shop. He went broke, of course, because he gave too much credit. He couldn't refuse it and I thought he was a fool. I had got to hating him.

7   There'd be men I didn't think would want to be fooling around with him. There might even be the superintendent of our schools and a quiet man who ran the hardware store. Once I remember there was a white-haired man who was a cashier of the bank. It was a wonder to me they'd want to be seen with such a windbag. That's what I thought he was. I know now what it was that attracted them. It was because life in our town, as in all small towns, was at times pretty dull and he livened it up. He made them laugh. He could tell stories. He'd even get them to singing.

8   If they didn't come to our house they'd go off, say at night, to where there was a grassy place by a creek. They'd cook food there and drink beer and sit about listening to his stories.

9   He was always telling stories about himself. He'd say this or that wonderful thing had happened to him. It might be something that made him look like a fool. He didn't care.

10   If an Irishman came to our house, right away father would say he was Irish. He'd tell what county in Ireland he was born in. He'd tell things that happened there when he was a boy. He'd make it seem so real that, if I hadn't known he was born in southern Ohio, I'd have believed him myself.

11   If it was a Scotchman the same thing happened. He'd get a burr into his speech. Or he was a German or a Swede. He'd be anything the other man was. I think they all knew he was lying, but they seemed to like him just the same. As a boy that was what I couldn't understand.

12   And there was mother. How could she stand it? I wanted to ask but never did. She was not the kind you asked such questions.

13   I'd be upstairs in my bed, in my room above the porch, and father would be telling some of his tales. A lot of father's stories were about the Civil War. To hear him tell it he'd been in about every battle. He'd known Grant, Sherman, Sheridan and I don't know how many others. He'd been particularly intimate with General Grant so that when Grant went East to take charge of all the armies, he took father along.

14   "I was an orderly at headquarters and Sim Grant said to me, 'Irve,' he said, 'I'm going to take you along with me.' "

15   It seems he and Grant used to slip off sometimes and have a quiet drink together. That's what my father said. He'd tell about the day Lee surrendered and how, when the great moment came, they couldn't find Grant.

16   "You know," my father said, "about General Grant's book, his memoirs. You've read of how he said he had a headache and how, when he got word that Lee was ready to call it quits, he was suddenly and miraculously cured.

17   "Huh," said father. "He was in the woods with me.

18   "I was in there with my back against a tree. I was pretty well corned. I had got hold of a bottle of pretty good stuff.

19   "They were looking for Grant. He had got off his horse and come into the woods. He found me. He was covered with mud.

20   "I had the bottle in my hand. What'd I care? The war was over. I knew we had them licked."

21   My father said that he was the one who told Grant about Lee. An orderly riding by had told him, because the orderly knew how thick he was with Grant. Grant was embarrassed.

22   "But, Irve, look at me. I'm all covered with mud," he said to father.

23   And then, my father said, he and Grant decided to have a drink together. They took a couple of shots and then, because he didn't want Grant to show up potted before the immaculate Lee, he smashed the bottle against the tree.

24   "Sim Grant's dead now and I wouldn't want it to get out on him," my father said.

25   That's just one of the kind of things he'd tell. Of course the men knew he was lying, but they seemed to like it just the same.

26   When we got broke, down and out, do you think he ever brought anything home? Not he. If there wasn't anything to eat in the house, he'd go off visiting around at farmhouses. They all wanted him. Sometimes he'd stay away for weeks, mother working to keep us fed, and then home he'd come bringing, let's say, a ham. He'd got it from some farmer friend. He'd slap it on the table in the kitchen. "You bet I'm going to see that my kids have something to eat," he'd say, and mother would just stand smiling at him. She'd never say a word about all the weeks and months he'd been away, not leaving us a cent for food. Once I heard her speaking to a woman in our street. Maybe the woman had dared to sympathize with her. "Oh," she said, "it's all right. He isn't ever dull like most of the men in this street. Life is never dull when my man is about."

27   But often I was filled with bitterness, and sometimes I wished he wasn't my father. I'd even invent another man as my father. To protect my mother I'd make up stories of a secret marriage that for some strange reason never got known. As though some man, say the president of a railroad company or maybe a Congressman, had married my mother, thinking his wife was dead and then it turned out she wasn't.

28   So they had to hush it up but I got born just the same. I wasn't really the son of my father. Somewhere in the world there was a very dignified, quite wonderful man who was really my father. I even made myself half believe these fancies.

29   And then there came a certain night. He'd been off somewhere for two or three weeks. He found me alone in the house, reading by the kitchen table.

30 It had been raining and he was very wet. He sat and looked at me for a long time, not saying a word. I was startled, for there was on his face the saddest look I had ever seen. He sat for a time, his clothes dripping. Then he got up.

31 "Come on with me," he said.

32 I got up and went with him out of the house. I was filled with wonder but I wasn't afraid. We went along a dirt road that led down into a valley, about a mile out of town, where there was a pond. We walked in silence. The man who was always talking had stopped his talking.

33 I didn't know what was up and had the queer feeling that I was with a stranger. I don't know whether my father intended it so. I don't think he did.

34 The pond was quite large. It was still raining hard and there were flashes of lightning followed by thunder. We were on a grassy bank at the pond's edge when my father spoke, and in the darkness and rain his voice sounded strange.

35 "Take off your clothes," he said. Still filled with wonder, I began to undress. There was a flash of lightning and I saw that he was already naked.

36 Naked, we went into the pond. Taking my hand he pulled me in. It may be that I was too frightened, too full of a feeling of strangeness, to speak. Before that night my father had never seemed to pay any attention to me.

37 "And what is he up to now?" I kept asking myself. I did not swim very well, but he put my hand on his shoulder and struck out into the darkness.

38 He was a man with big shoulders, a powerful swimmer. In the darkness I could feel the movement of his muscles. We swam to the far edge of the pond and then back to where we had left our clothes. The rain continued and the wind blew. Sometimes my father swam on his back and when he did he took my hand in his large powerful one and moved it over so that it rested always on his shoulder. Sometimes there would be a flash of lightning and I could see his face quite clearly.

39 It was as it was earlier, in the kitchen, a face filled with sadness. There would be the momentary glimpse of his face and then again the darkness, the wind and the rain. In me there was a feeling I had never known before.

40 It was a feeling of closeness. It was something strange. It was as though there were only we two in the world. It was as though I had been jerked suddenly out of myself, out of my world of the schoolboy, out of a world in which I was ashamed of my father.

41 He had become blood of my blood; he the strong swimmer and I the boy clinging to him in the darkness. We swam in silence and in silence we dressed in our wet clothes, and went home.

42 There was a lamp lighted in the kitchen and when we came in, the water dripping from us, there was my mother. She smiled at us. I remember that she called us "boys."

43 "What have you boys been up to," she asked, but my father did not answer. As he had begun the evening's experience with me in silence, so he ended it. He turned and looked at me. Then he went, I thought, with a new and strange dignity out of the room.

44   I climbed the stairs to my own room, undressed in the darkness and got into bed. I couldn't sleep and did not want to sleep. For the first time I knew that I was the son of my father. He was a story teller as I was to be. It may be that I even laughed a little softly there in the darkness. If I did, I laughed knowing that I would never again be wanting another father.

Description

Unlike the other major modes of discourse, description is almost never used solely for its own sake, appearing generally in the service of one of the other modes. Each of the selections here, too, uses description to some extent as a springboard to other ends. For example, Trillin's display of the treasures of the Bubble Gum Store leads to a more general exploration of life in New York City; Hoffman's description of a gay bar provides a basis for the objective analysis of gay social life that follows.

The word *description* comes from the Latin *describere*, which means "to copy off" and it is this root meaning that governs most description, whose aim is to present an accurate *verbal* copy of the thing described, a picture in words. While one picture may be worth a thousand words, the picture itself is not always at hand, and so our need for word pictures, descriptions. The subjects of description are usually concrete objects—persons, places, or things, like Reverend Dick Evers, the Yazoo High School, a gumball machine. But the writer may also present a verbal portrait of a feeling, like boredom ("One middle-aged woman . . . bows her head as the reverend asks the Lord for guidance, and doesn't raise it again until the end of the service"), or of an abstraction, like evil ("the night Martin Luther King was killed in Memphis").

Some description is objective, or realistic; that is, it is totally, or nearly totally, factual. Encyclopedia descriptions and scientific writing represent one extreme of this category. At the other extreme is the subjective or impressionistic description, in which the feelings of the observer color or even constitute the information ("It's a good ole town").

But all good description depends on concrete and specific detail. A *concrete* word refers to something tangible—perceivable by the senses of touch, taste, sight, sound, smell—and is the opposite of *abstract*, something intangible—not directly connected to a material object. When Willie Morris says his wife believed that Mississippi was "elementally evil," "a symbol of all that was wrong with all of us," his description is largely abstract (can you touch "evil" or see "wrong"?). When he later mentions "the night Martin Luther King was killed" and his wife's bitter indictment of "you Southern boys," he supplies concrete images of those abstractions.

And Morris's example is also *specific* (that is, precise, definite, limited), specifying racism and murder as Mississippi's particular evils, distinguishing them from others of their *general* class, other evils or wrongs—like child abuse or grand larceny. The more general a description, the less specific and therefore the less vivid and impressive it is—and also the more that is left up to the imagination of the reader, because so many specific items can be accommodated by a general category. For example, while you may be thinking of pickled bees' wings or rum-tangerine ice cream when Trillin makes a general reference to "a lot of food not found in the ordinary corner store," *he* limits your imaginings (and also the possibility of misunderstanding) by also supplying the specifics—"marinated mushrooms . . . garlic carrots, and stringbeans vinaigrette."

While words that are specific and concrete are important in any description, even more important is the organization, the arrangement that a writer chooses. Notice, for example, how Morris's perspective on Yazoo moves from close-up to distance shots, paralleling his own movement, both physically and emotionally, away from his home town. Trillin begins by describing a tiny crowded room, but focuses on the bubble gum machines, which for him express most vividly the significance of Ken and Eve's enterprise. And Hoffman emphasizes first the physical surroundings, then the postures, and finally the appearance of the patrons as keys to understanding the sociology of the gay bar. Descriptive organization, whether objective or impressionistic, usually aims to stress a single aspect of the thing described, to convey some dominant impression; therefore, its order, when not absolutely dictated by some essential aspect of the object described, is most often determined by the relation of the subject to the writer and the writer's purpose.

The Bubble Gum Store

CALVIN TRILLIN

Calvin Trillin was born in Kansas City, Missouri, the location, according to him, of the world's best restaurant, Arthur Bryant's Barbeque. As a staff writer for *The New Yorker* since 1963, he has traveled around the country writing about restaurants and eating, and about larger issues in American culture as well, under the title "U.S. Journal." Several of his *New Yorker* pieces have been collected in *U.S. Journal* and *American Fried.* "The Bubble Gum Store" is a description of a small New York grocery store reminiscent of those of a century ago.

1   A year or so ago, I became aware that a corner grocery store in our neighborhood was being operated with peculiar warmth. I don't mean that the other storekeepers are unfriendly. The laundry, for instance, is run by a pleasant couple with whom we exchange inquiries about the family in an en-route-to-the-subway sort of way. One of the checkers at the supermarket is a kindly woman who has always been a favorite of my daughters, both of whom are still young enough to consider a bank of gumball machines the store's other attraction, although the relentless line at a supermarket check-out counter is designed to put a quick end to conversation after the money has been collected. (By the time I have reached the register, I have often been made slightly irritable anyway by counting thirteen or fourteen items in the shopping cart of the woman ahead of me in the eight-items-or-under express line—thirteen or fourteen even if she counts, as I'm certain she would if I ever worked up the courage to challenge her, a selection of tonic water and Dr. Pepper and Tab as one item of soft drinks.) We have friends and neighbors who run retail businesses in the neighborhood, so we may find ourselves in an antique shop around the corner or a saloon on the square just saying hello or delivering something for a school fair rather than transacting retail business. Our neighborhood is on the edge of what has remained a strongly Italian section of Greenwich Village, and many of the Italian food shops retain the warmth of businesses run by families who have reason to be proud of what they sell—places like Frank's Pork Store, where a few bottles of liquor and some paper cups are left on a counter around Christmas week, so that the customers aren't put in the position of offering each other holiday greetings empty-handed. I might as well admit that because a spectacular delicacy called "hot cooked salami" is produced by Frank's every morning I

would probably patronize the place if it were run by the kind of people who kept their thumbs on the scale and snarled at my daughters. It stands to reason that a baker of fresh bread or a maker of homemade chocolates could be forgiven a sullenness intolerable in a purveyor of canned goods.

2   We live in a neighborhood, at any rate, where civility and informality and friendliness in shops are sufficiently widespread to be taken for granted; we have our grouches, but they are few enough to permit us to husband most of our pure Manhattanite venom for use against Con Edison or the Telephone Company or one of those faceless voices that speak for the uptown department stores. Still, the atmosphere in the corner grocery store seemed unique. The people who ran it, a couple named Ken and Eve, were young, but the store was old-fashioned—a tiny, crowded room with a worn linoleum floor and a marble counter that had been placed toward the rear, so that the customers tended to collect in the center of the store rather than to pause briefly at a register on their way out. Ken and Eve seemed to call all of the customers by name, and the conversation often drew in anyone who just happened to be standing in front of the counter waiting to pay for a quart of milk or studying the canned goods along the wall trying to find the appropriate soup. The customers chatted among themselves, some of them apparently having been introduced by Ken, who (sometimes as a disembodied voice from behind the meat-slicing machine) had a habit of saying, "Hey, you two might as well know each other—you're neighbors." Somehow, space had been found in the center of the store for a rocking chair—a wooden one, with worn spots on the arms and a worn pad on the seat—and it was often occupied. At first glance, the place seemed to have the predictable inventory—when I try to envision the inside of a New York corner store, my mind fills with walls of cat food—but on the counter were two or three plates of homemade cookies. And what a gumball machine! Inside of it, a cheerful little man with a necktie and a grocer's apron stood waiting with his scoop in hand. For only a penny, he would nod, turn to the cupboard on his left, open it, withdraw a gumball, and, turning in the other direction, drop it down a chute that led to the outside world. My daughters were captivated. From the start, they referred to Ken and Eve's as the Bubble Gum Store, and that is what we have called it ever since.

3   I know that part of my interest in the Bubble Gum Store was based on regret that my daughters had missed growing up near an old-fashioned grocery on our own corner that had closed just before we moved into the neighborhood—a store that a friend of ours who spent part of her childhood on the block can still recall in detail. It was a regret tinged with irritation for a while when the tenants who replaced the grocer seemed to be a succession of the kind of shops that these days have names held together by a contraction of the uncontractable "and"—Rings 'n' Things, 'n' names like that. I was also interested to find Ken and Eve—a bright, open, obviously educated couple—running an old-fashioned store. It even occurred to me that, considering the way a large percentage of New York families arrived in the city, Ken might have had a grandfather who in order to get a toehold in the New

World slaved away for years in such a store (as Greek and Portuguese immigrants are doing in our neighborhood now), giving his son the opportunity to amass enough capital to send Ken comfortably to college—so that he could run a corner grocery store. In the cultural flip-flops of the sixties, of course, New York abounded in such minor generational ironies—middle-aged couples who shuddered at having to return from Long Island to the lower East Side every other Sunday to visit a father who had never left his tenement, only to find that their own son, having had the blessings of the Great Neck school system and superior orthodontics bestowed on him, made directly for a lower-East Side tenement that differed from his grandfather's only in its lack of cleanliness. The likelihood that Ken and Eve were in the Bubble Gum Store more or less by choice, of course, distinguished them from any earlier generation of storekeepers—or, for that matter, from most of the other merchants in our neighborhood. I suppose there are aspects of the grocery business that are satisfying to the Portuguese couple running a place a few blocks from the Bubble Gum Store, but I suspect that their store represents to them mainly a way to pay the rent and educate their children. Ken and Eve really seemed to be having a good time.

4   As it turned out, Ken and Eve had thought they might enjoy running a corner store in our neighborhood partly because they had so enjoyed the neighborhood. In recent years, neighborhoodism has been growing in New York, particularly in neighborhoods dominated by brownstones rather than high-rises—the Village, Chelsea, a half-dozen partly renovated areas in Brooklyn. The new version of neighborhoodism, often led by middle-class house renovators, is geographical rather than ethnic; it is organized around residence on a block rather than membership in, say, an Italian Catholic Church. I have always thought that when one of the new tree-planting, block-party-holding, neighbor-meeting block associations is scratched deeply, what scratches back has some attributes of the old, exclusionary, property-crazed homeowners associations. On the other hand, I like the block parties. Geographical neighborhoodism does reflect some of the reasons that New Yorkers who have some choice about where to live may choose the agonies of renovating a brownstone in Chelsea or Cobble Hill rather than move into an apartment in a West Side high-rise—a manageable number of people on the block, next-door neighbors, buildings constructed on a scale that human beings can grasp, the casual neighborliness that comes with sitting on a stoop for a chat on a spring evening rather than exchanging quick hellos between floors in an elevator. What some people are seeking in the low-rise neighborhoods of New York is not adventure or the bright lights but some qualified urban version of what people in other parts of America would consider a normal life.

5   Ken has not been a consistent block-association activist; although he is not overtly political, Eve always says that at heart he is too much of an anarchist to sit through the meetings. But even before he began running the Bubble Gum Store he took great pleasure in the block it is on—a lively Village

mixture of renovated brownstones and unrenovated brownstones and small apartment buildings occupied by Irish and Italian families who have lived in them for three or four generations. He lived and worked on the block as a building superintendent. My guess about his background had not been far off, although he is the first person in his family to run a store. His grandfather was an immigrant, his father has prospered in a manufacturing business, his brother is an architect. Ken dropped out of college and tried a number of jobs, none of which he liked, until he more or less settled down to being a super. Eve lived on the same block. She was working in an insurance-company office after having spent several years teaching retarded adults. She was introduced to Ken by the president of the block association.

6   Ken did not feel philosophically or psychologically prepared to hold the kind of job that might traditionally be associated with his background; he often says he has "a little trouble with authority." The man who had run the corner grocery store on the block for years, an Armenian immigrant, was about ready to retire. ("He was not an uninteresting man, and he ran a profitable store," Ken says, "but he didn't have a good time.") Both Ken and Eve liked the idea of doing something they could do together. Ken liked the idea of not having a boss. Ken's father was willing to put up some money for the purchase. And the corner store had the final appeal of being right on the corner of their own block. Ken now says, "Down to the corner was about as far as I wanted to go."

7   For an American who finds himself running a small grocery store these days, the normal channels for ambition are expansion or escape. "A whole bunch of things pressure you to become bigger," Ken says. "The nature of business in America is to grow. The customers want more variety. You can buy things cheaper from suppliers in large quantities." Ken and Eve had a different sort of ambition. They did want to make a profit, of course, and Ken says that they have greatly improved on the volume of the previous owner. But they are horrified at anything they believe might detract from the intimacy of the store, and they have no interest in the chain-grocery business. When they talk about how the store is doing, they discuss not just sales volume but whether the atmosphere is quite right or how well the store is filling its role as a place where neighbors can have a relaxed and impromptu chat. In that sense, as Ken and Eve are quick to acknowledge, the store is "artificial"—something they can see themselves doing, something they do because it interests them rather than because the alternative is penury. Ken tends to analyze reasons for, say, having gumball machines the way block-association organizers analyze reasons for having block parties.

8   There are, as it happens, four gum machines now in the Bubble Gum Store. Ken says he bought the first one while he was looking for ways to "warm the place up a little." He says a gumball machine can be seen as an investment, the way, say, printing up advertising circulars would be an investment—although he sees the return in this case as being in "depth rather than breadth" of patronage. Ken and Eve also consider the gumball machines a way to attract the children of the old Irish and Italian families in

the neighborhood—families they are particularly interested in attracting, since they believe the patronage now has an overrepresentation of younger people who live in the Village because they enjoy the informality and an underrepresentation of older people who live in the Village because they were born there. Adults use the machines, too; it is not unusual for a customer to slap a nickel on the counter and say, out of the corner of his mouth, "Gimme five singles" or "Break this five for me." But the kids, by hitting a home run on the baseball gum machine or a hole in one on the golf gum machine, are eligible for stickers that, according to a complicated formula, can be traded in for candy bars or super-hero decals. There is no sign announcing such a system, of course; Ken says it is "not for strangers." Ken and Eve can name three or four other reasons for having gumball machines in a corner store. Among them is that Ken happens to be a sucker for gumball machines.

9   Three years of ownership by Ken and Eve have brought some physical changes to the Bubble Gum Store—although not enough of them to alter my impression that it is dominated by cat food. On the side of the building Ken now has a long flower box about six feet off the ground—high enough, he says, to foil dogs and to force anyone who wants to steal a flower to do so with a conscious effort rather than a casual swipe. The store-front windows on either side of the entrance still have brands of beer spelled out in neon, but one of them also has an attractive gold-leaf window sign that includes the names of Ken and Eve on intertwined hearts. (Ken has just become a notary public—partly, he claims, because the notary symbol will look terrific on the other window.) The Bubble Gum Store has conventional freezers and coolers jammed into it, but one of them is covered with pictures that Ken took of customers with a Polaroid he got once as a gift, and one of them is festooned with decals of the sort that can be won by a quick pair of hands at the golf gumball machine. A few waiters' trays and old-fashioned advertisements and old cracker boxes are around, but not enough to give the impression that the place sells knick-knacks rather than milk and eggs. The air space in the Bubble Gum Store seems just about fully occupied. There is a clown who can be made to cycle across the store on a tightrope, and a couple of hanging ceramic pieces done by Ken's mother, and a rope that is often climbed by a wooden bear, and a mop that I took to be part of some sort of artistic assemblage until Eve informed me that it was a mop display.

10   Ken and Eve do a pretty good take-out-sandwich business at noon with people who work in the neighborhood, and, partly because Ken enjoys preparing salads, they can pull out of the delicatessen case a lot of food not found in the ordinary corner store—marinated mushrooms, for instance, and garlic carrots, and stringbeans vinaigrette. They also keep some steak and hamburger in the deli case, on the theory that someone ought to be able to assemble a full meal in the store if necessary. I have occasionally assembled a full meal there myself, but it consists entirely of homemade cookies—Rosie's Cinnamon Butter Crunchies, Meg's Scottish Short Bread, Karen's Nut

Brownies, Jean's Banana Nut Bread, and, for dessert, Keen Specials, which are to chocolate-chip cookies what Frank's hot cooked salami is to salami. The idea of selling homemade cookies began, Ken told me, when they told a friend who had become seriously interested in baking that they would sell what she baked on consignment. Then Ken saw that carrying cookies on consignment was one way of keeping traffic in the store; it guarantees the presence of the cookiemakers checking on their cookies, if no one else. The cookie system is the most obvious way that the distinctions between buyers and sellers become blurred at the Bubble Gum Store; the Rosie who makes Rosie's Cinnamon Butter Crunchies is a customer and a supplier and a friend and, as it happens, the block-association president who introduced Ken and Eve.

11   A bookcase full of books next to the door also came about more or less accidentally, Eve told me—starting when a new cooler freed some space there and it was decided that whatever went into the space ought to be something that could be stolen without inflicting serious financial damage. That led to the idea of using the space for something free, and that led to the idea of an informal book-trading pool—unidentified as that, of course, because it, too, is not for strangers. Ken says that some people only bring books and some people only take books and a few do both. Some people, he thinks, use the book supply to rationalize spending a few more cents per item in the Bubble Gum Store than they might spend at the supermarket, but so many people seem uncomfortable about taking hardcover books that Ken periodically goes around the corner to a store that seems to specialize in secondhand books and whipping-and-bondage magazines, and trades his hardcovers in for paperbacks.

12   Ken and Eve were pleased with how the bookshelves worked out, and they liked the response to their bean-guessing contest. (The winner got two tickets to a Bette Midler show; second prize was, naturally, the beans.) They think they're getting better and better at the more routine aspects of running the store—knowing how much ice cream to order and maintaining the right kind of variety. They still poke around other grocery stores looking for items they might want to stock. The challenge of improving the store is, of course, part of the enjoyment. Sooner or later, of course, Ken and Eve are likely to decide that they are doing what they set out to do about as well as it can be done. Then, I suspect, my daughters and I will again be without an old-fashioned corner store.

Exercises

COMPREHENSION

Organization and Development

Descriptive essays are quite difficult to outline, and this one is no exception. However, you should be able to look through the essay again and find examples of details that support the author's dominant impression, or thesis. Write the sentence that best expresses that dominant impression. Then in the space that follows list the details that contribute to conveying that impression.

Dominant impression: _____
_____
_____

Specific details: _____
_____
_____
_____
_____

Content

Choose the answer that correctly completes each statement.

1. In general, the section of Greenwich Village where the author lives is known for its (a) intolerance (b) large number of family-run stores (c) friendliness.
2. When Trillin says, "It stands to reason that a baker of fresh bread or a maker of homemade chocolates could be forgiven a sullenness intolerable in a purveyor of canned goods," he means that he (a) refuses to patronize stores whose owners are rude, no matter what they sell (b) will put up with rudeness from a storeowner who sells homemade goods more readily than from an ordinary storeowner (c) can forgive sullenness in most storeowners because their life is hard no matter what they sell.
3. The Bubble Gum Store is unusual because (a) its owners do not run it for profit (b) it has an old-fashioned, informal atmosphere not usually associated with New York City (c) it is run by descendants of immigrants.
4. The new "neighborhoodism" in New York is determined by (a) religion (b) ethnic background (c) geography.
5. Ken wanted to own a store because (a) he didn't want to have a boss (b) his father had owned one (c) he had become bored with his teaching job.
6. In addition to earning a living, Ken and Eve are concerned about (a) improving the volume and quality of goods they sell (b) opening more stores like the original one in other neighborhoods (c) preserving the intimate, relaxed atmosphere for the neighborhood's residents.
7. The best example of how distinctions between customers and sellers are blurred is the (a) noon sandwich business (b) homemade cookie system (c) free lending library.
8. Trillin uses his description of the Bubble Gum Store as a departure point to discuss a related idea, namely, the (a) kinds of changes New York neighborhoods are undergoing (b) difficulties young people face trying to start a new business (c) contrast between this store and large supermarket chains.

Paragraph Structure

Reorder the following sentences to form a unified, coherent paragraph. Identify one sentence as the conclusion. Then check your version with the original.

1. Sooner or later, of course, Ken and Eve are likely to decide that they are doing what they set out to do about as well as it can be done.
2. They still poke around other grocery stores looking for items they might want to stock.
3. Ken and Eve were pleased with how the bookshelves worked out, and they liked the response to their bean-guessing contest.

4. The challenge of improving the store is, of course, part of the enjoyment.
5. (The winner got two tickets to a Bette Midler show; second prize was, naturally, the beans.)
6. Then, I suspect, my daughters and I will again be without an old-fashioned corner store.
7. They think they're getting better and better at the more routine aspects of running the store—knowing how much ice cream to order and maintaining the right kind of variety.

VOCABULARY AND USAGE

Word Formation Table

Complete the following table by changing word endings or root forms to make new grammatical forms. Use your dictionary if necessary.

	NOUN	VERB	ADJECTIVE	ADVERB
1.	_____	_____	predictable	_____
2.	_____	regret	_____	_____
3.	_____	xxx	_____	sullenly
4.	_____	xxx	intolerable	_____
5.	irritation	_____	_____	_____

Fill-Ins

Complete each of the sentences below using the words on the following list. You may need to use some words more than once. You may also find that some blanks can be completed correctly with more than one word. Add plural endings to nouns and change verb forms where necessary.

transact	politeness	distinguish	different
retain	distinction	civility	opportunity
informal	seldom	picture	usually
envision	for	generally	intimate
or	conduct	relaxed	keep

1. The atmosphere in the Bubble Gum Store is _____, which _____ it from most other New York grocery stores.
2. The store's primary _____ is that people go there _____ other reasons than just to _____ business.
3. Ken and Eve are concerned about how to _____ the store's _____ atmosphere, but they have also found new _____ to increase business at the same time.
4. Although the shops in the author's neighborhood are _____ known for their _____, Ken and Eve's store is _____ from the others; for example, one of the freezer compartments is covered with _____ of the customers.
5. When the author _____ a grocery store, he thinks of shelves of cat food, and the Bubble Gum Store is not any _____ in this respect.
6. Most shopkeepers are _____ in business _____ profit _____ because they don't have an _____ to make a living in any other way.

DISCUSSION

1. What is the function of the long first paragraph? How does it relate to Trillin's thesis? And what would be the effect if it were omitted?
2. What does Trillin mean by "generational ironies" in paragraph 3?
3. Underline the transitional expressions in paragraph 4.
4. In paragraph 4, Trillin writes, "when one of the . . . block associations is scratched deeply, what scratches back has some attributes of the old, exclusionary, property-crazed homeowners associations." What does he mean here? And what is the connotation of "scratched"?
5. In paragraph 8, what does Ken mean when he says that gumball machines provide a return in "depth rather than breadth" of patronage?
6. Does paragraph 9 use description, narration, exposition, or persuasion as the dominant method of discourse?
7. In what ways are the owners of the Bubble Gum Store unique in their goals? How does their management of the store reflect a new attitude among young people toward enterprise and business?

SUGGESTIONS FOR WRITING

1. Describe a place that had special significance for you during your childhood. Be sure to use concrete details that appeal to the senses and to explain the features that made the place so important to you.
2. Write an essay describing a small store in your neighborhood. Begin by establishing a dominant impression. Then describe the organization and layout of the store, giving special emphasis to those features that give it its characteristic atmosphere. You might also want to describe a few of the store's regular customers or one or two representative ones.
3. Describe the neighborhood you live in and explain the characteristics that make it unique.
4. Since the 1960s, the young people who have begun businesses of their own have brought a freshness, occasionally even a radical approach, to merchandising. In the same way that Trillin describes Ken and Eve's Bubble Gum Store, describe a store you are familiar with that reflects the values of its owners.

God's Garage: Beeping for the Lord

DENNIS TROUTE

Dennis Troute, an NBC correspondent in Saigon during the last days of the Vietnam war, now lives and writes in Stockton, California.

The best-known drive-in church was started in southern California by the Reverend Robert Schuller, whose slogan was "Come As You Are—In Your Family Car." He has since moved to larger quarters at the Garden Grove Community Church, where the overflow audiences listen to the service on their car radios. Schuller's service is nationally televised as "The Hour of Power," and it is probably this service to which the woman refers at the end of the essay. The church described in "God's Garage" is considerably more modest than Schuller's.

1   Highway 99 below Sacramento isn't a bad stretch of road, as places like this go. The south end of the valley is much worse, cluttered with truck stops, used-car lots, and billboards. But here miles of brown grain fields leave an unbroken view of one another, dotted occasionally with an old clapboard house, as constant and wearisome as summers that start before June and stretch their blanket of heat over September and beyond. Up north a very few businesses signal the beginning of a suburb: a Standard service station, the Western Mobile Home Park, and a drive-in. The drive-in seems misplaced out here, as its director, Dick Evers, admits.

2   "We didn't expect a change in the zoning, so we were sure the town was going to grow this way," he acknowledges, glancing at the rows of steel posts with speakers attached. But with the buoyant confidence that only youth and a managerial position, or a thick strain of Calvinism, can foster, Evers greets every visitor energetically and sincerely. Tall and sinewy, with thick blond hair, he has the big hands and quick movements of a young athlete, constantly working at improvement. "We'd hoped to move everything indoors by now," he says, "so the schedule has been set back some, but we'll make it."

3   How about popcorn machines or a snack bar, to pick things up?

4   "Well, this *is* a church," he intones, half smiling at what he hopes was a joke.

5   Indeed it is. The sign says "Sacramento Community Drive-in Church," and just below announces Sunday school, indoor-outdoor services, and a nursery. Only two beige-and-brown shingle buildings are on the lot. One, at the front, has a podium and a glassed-in section for the choir, or foul-weather services.

The other sits just to the side, dominated by a picture window allowing parishioners to view services from the chapel. A grass-covered embankment on the far side provides some privacy from the road, but those less spiritually inclined still can be seen driving cars and campers into the hills for a Sunday outing. More distracting is the noise, the drone of automobile engines and the blaring of horns.

6   So the service must be on a grand scale, interesting enough visually to focus attention away from the movement on the road, and sufficiently persuasive to give the tinny voice coming through the box in each car some human touch. The Reverend Evers appears in a long white robe with a purple chasuble, wearing dark sunglasses against the reflected glare from the as-phalt and shining cars in front of him. His delivery is breathless and excited, reaching at times for emotional heights, at others softening words to a reverent whisper. He speaks at one point of the conversion of a reluctant Saint Paul, pounding his hands like cymbals as he hits the climax of the story.

7   If success can be defined by involvement rather than economics, the Reverend Evers fares just about as well as more conventional pastors. At the front of the lot, devout churchgoers follow the service with inexhaustible attention, their eyes like headlights, blank and staring. During common prayers they can be seen through their windshields, chanting, in silent unison, invocations from prayer sheets passed out earlier.

8   The unwashed and the unwilling congregate at the back, fulfilling a duty or perhaps hoping that a surplus of saintliness will flow back to them. The excited reference to Saint Paul's fate brings up two heads in a maroon Impala that at first revealed only one, but the interest of the second party is short-lived. In a Volkswagen camper, a man with a Marine haircut plays with his little boy during the sermon but sets the child aside on the seat next to him during prayers. One middle-aged woman driving an Eskimo Pie ice-cream truck bows her head as the reverend asks the Lord for guidance, and doesn't raise it again until the end of the service. Statistically, what loses back-row people most often are exegeses of the Scriptures. Even a staccato treatment that would do justice to a faith healer cannot hold them.

9   "If you are justified by the courts," the pastor begins, "or you are justified by someone else, what are you doing? You are bringing proof that you're all right. Even though there were some doubts, you're okay! That's not the meaning of the Greek word. The meaning of the Greek word—and there's no other way to translate it, with its ending—is that which is reckoned to someone who doesn't have it. So that means the righteousness is given to an unrighteous person."

10   Almost on cue, one of the least deserving, a girl who has spent most of the last half hour fixing her hair in the rearview mirror, slips the speaker quietly off her window and onto its stand. She ponders for a moment the problem of starting a car quietly, and decides finally to slouch in the seat. Those not completely absorbed by the sermon are treated to a miracle of sorts, as a seemingly driverless Chevrolet glides toward the rear exit.

11   The departure only raises greater excitement in the pastor, who speeds up his delivery, bouncing from one side of the podium to the other as the tempo increases. The rest of the automobiles sit quietly before him, just slightly less active than their occupants, as though hypnotized by the motion of the figure in white. They come to life at the end, upon request, in salute to an activist.

12   "Thank you for sending out those newsletters," says the pastor, smiling in the direction of a late-model sedan at the front. "Let's give her a drive-in welcome—a real good toot." The lot echoes with a chorus of greetings, from punchy little Volkswagen bursts to the deeper tones of Oldsmobiles and Buicks.

13   Most of the cars then jockey into lines forming at the exit gate; others remain as their occupants assemble for coffee in the hall leading to the nursery school. The congregation is a cross section of middle America, its men bright and buoyant in Palm Springs casuals, its milk-shake-fed ladies poured into lightweight polyester knits. Those who come to a drive-in because it's easy have left; those who want to be part of things are sipping coffee and chatting, content in the knowledge that they are pursuing the Right Way in another way, ready even for further experiments. A woman with brightly tinted hair recommends a visit to one of the Los Angeles congregations. "You really should see it," she gushes. "It's really much bigger—and it's televised."

Exercises

COMPREHENSION

Organization and Development

Complete the following outline. In your own words write Troute's thesis statement, which is implicit rather than stated directly, in the space provided. Then find the main divisions in the essay and fill in the remaining spaces. Note the paragraphs for each section.

Thesis statement: _____

_____

I. Description of _____   [   ]
II. Description of _____   [   ]
III. Description of _____   [   ]

Content

Choose the answer that correctly completes each statement.

1. The Sacramento Community Drive-in Church is located (a) in the center of the city (b) in the middle of farmlands (c) along a heavily-traveled highway.

2. The church is located on the premises of a drive-in (a) restaurant (b) laundry (c) theater.
3. Troute emphasizes that (a) most of the congregation are just as devout as members of a conventional church (b) many members are less attentive and behave differently from the way they would at a conventional church (c) many members are distracted by the noise from the passing cars and trucks.
4. To salute a particularly hard-working member, the congregation (a) claps and cheers (b) honks their horns (c) gives a donation.
5. One young woman who fixed her hair during the service (a) stayed for coffee afterward (b) sang and prayed during the invocation (c) drove away slouched in her seat.
6. Apparently, the congregation is bored (a) in spite of the minister's excited manner (b) by analyses of the Scriptures (c) by the newsletters.
7. Reverend Evers wears a robe, a chasuble, and (a) a straw hat (b) a perpetual smile (c) sunglasses.
8. The difference between this drive-in church and those in Los Angeles is that the Los Angeles services are (a) less successful (b) more popular (c) televised.
9. The minister thinks that soon the church will (a) sell popcorn and snacks (b) move indoors (c) begin advertising in newspapers.
10. We can infer that the author considers the phenomenon of drive-in churches (a) sacrilegious (b) sensible (c) bizarre.

Paragraph Structure

Reorder the following sentences to form a unified, coherent paragraph. Identify one sentence as the topic sentence and underline the key words. Then check your version with the original.

1. But here miles of brown grain fields leave an unbroken view of one another, dotted occasionally with an old clapboard house, as constant and wearisome as summers that start before June and stretch their blanket of heat over September and beyond.
2. Highway 99 below Sacramento isn't a bad stretch of road, as places like this go.
3. Up north a very few businesses signal the beginning of a suburb: a Standard service station, the Western Mobile Home Park, and a drive-in.
4. The drive-in seems misplaced out here, as its director, Dick Evers, admits.
5. The south end of the valley is much worse, cluttered with truck stops, used-car lots, and billboards.

VOCABULARY AND USAGE

Word Formation Table

Complete the following table by changing word endings or root forms to make new grammatical forms. Use your dictionary if necessary.

	NOUN	VERB	ADJECTIVE	ADVERB
1.	_____	_____	reverent	_____
2.	_____	_____	persuasive	_____
3.	_____	xxx	_____	conventionally
4.	_____	admit	_____	_____
5.	_____	dominate	_____	_____

Fill-Ins

Complete each of the sentences below using the words on the following list. You may need to use some words more than once. You may also find that some blanks can be completed correctly with more than one word. Add plural endings to nouns and change verb forms where necessary.

admit	customary	permanent	even though
content	conventional	constant	common
ordinary	least	satisfied	confident
assemble	distraction	cue	ponder
signal	acknowledge	gather	salute

1. The reverend _____ that the noise from the highway is a _____.
2. Apparently, drive-in churches are fairly _____ in California _____ they are not at all like _____ churches.
3. Reverend Evers is _____ that his congregation will be able to move to _____ quarters.
4. When the minister gives a _____, the congregation _____ one hard-working member.
5. Some of the congregation leave the church _____ that they have _____ their weekly obligation in an unusual way.
6. At _____ the minister _____ that his job is not the same as a(n) _____ minister's job.

DISCUSSION

1. What is the central impression of the Sacramento Valley conveyed by the author's description? Which details suggest it?
2. What is your opinion of a drive-in church? What do you think the author's opinion is? The congregation's? How are these points of view revealed?
3. In paragraph 5, what does "it" refer to?
4. In paragraph 13, what does Troute mean when he says some members are "ready even for further experiments"?
5. What are the special problems involved in holding a religious service in a drive-in theater? How does Evers accommodate to those special requirements?
6. How does the behavior of some churchgoers differ from the way they would behave if they were in a conventional church?
7. Where does Troute state his main characterization of this congregation?

SUGGESTIONS FOR WRITING

1. Following Troute's organizational pattern of describing the location, the people, and their behavior, describe a public place—any place where people gather. So that you can provide a fairly thorough picture, the place you choose should not be too large. Some suggestions are a shoe repair shop, a hardware store, a coffee shop, delicatessen or drug store counter, a boutique, a department store bargain basement, a discothèque, or a farm implement store.

2. We all know that the automobile has fostered traffic jams, freeways, and air pollution. However, it is clear that an institution like the Sacramento Community Drive-in Church can exist only because America is so dependent on the automobile. Write about some other out-of-the-ordinary institutions or practices that are the direct result of Americans' dependence on and fondness for the automobile.

3. Go through Troute's essay carefully and find examples of diction (word choice) that reveal his attitude toward the drive-in church and its members. Then, in an essay, explain his attitude toward his subject, using these examples to support your contention.

Yazoo, Mississippi, 1970

WILLIE MORRIS

Willie Morris, a native of Yazoo, is a writer and a former editor of *Harper's Magazine*. Besides *Yazoo,* he has written *North Toward Home,* the book Henjie Henick, his friend, refers to in this selection as causing complaints from some of Yazoo's residents.

In 1954 the Supreme Court reached a landmark decision, *Brown* v. *the Board of Education,* striking down the concept of "separate but equal" education for blacks and whites as it was practiced in many school districts throughout the nation. In response, many districts, both in the North and in the South, either ignored the decision or dragged their feet in implementing integration. In Mississippi, fifteen years later, the Supreme Court ordered 30 school districts, among them Yazoo's, that had not complied with lower court rulings to desegregate by January 7, 1970. The local chapter of the NAACP organized an effective boycott against white-owned businesses to pressure the district into complying. What is described in this essay occurred on the eve of that day.

1   The town has changed remarkably little in twenty years, and as I drive these streets which are a map on my consciousness, I see the familiar places—the hills and trees and houses—in a strange, dreamlike quality, as if what I am seeing here is not truly real, but faintly blurred images caught in my imagination from a more pristine time. I see people walking on the sidewalks on Main Street or Broadway or Grand Avenue who should have been dead long ago, unexpected wisps from the past, but their names come back right away, and with the names the recognition of encounters, conversations, fragments of experience from a quarter of a century ago.

2   Main Street on this cold and wistfully mournful January day is all but deserted, the result, people tell me, of the Negroes' boycott. Tommy Norman's Drug Store, across from the Taylor & Roberts Feed & Seed Store and Radio Station WAZF, is boarded up and dead; a generation ago, on Saturdays, great crowds of Negroes would have been in front of Tommy's, and inside, along a long wooden counter, whites and blacks, segregated on each side, would have drunk their beer or Nehi strawberry, face-to-face and juxtaposed. On Saturday nights, when we were in high school, we would have taken our girls to the midnight show at either the Palace or the Dixie, finding out in advance which one our friends had chosen so we could all go together. The

Palace is now a burnt-out hull, and the Dixie, at Broadway and Main, has vanished from the face of the earth; most of the boys and girls who ate popcorn and held hands and wished the show would finish so they could go park and rub up together on Brickyard Hill, have long since departed for other places. Only the Yazoo Theater, over on Washington Street, remains; it is showing an Elvis Presley picture, *Change of Habit*. Several cars parked in front, next to the building which quarters the Chamber of Commerce, have bumper stickers which say, "YAZOO'S ALIVE AND DOING WELL."

3   The lumberyard and paint store on Canal, across from the Confederate monument, still displays the big sign, "VISIT OUR COLOR BAR." Behind it, in the colored section, a white postman has put his mailbag on the ground near a house and is playing cards with three Negroes. Further down Main, I see a tall, thin man wearing glasses shuffling along in front of the furniture store. I know the walk, and from fifty yards away, out of the instinct of recognition, I see it is my companion Henjie Henick, who runs the tire store. "People here are complaining about what you wrote," he once said in a letter to me. "I tell them, everything he says happened, and it happened just like he said it did." I haven't seen Henjie in fifteen years, but I do not stop now to say hello. At the Yazoo Motel earlier that day, the lady behind the counter had said, when I checked in, "I haven't seen you since you were this big," extended an arm, waving it downward about ten inches from the floor. "I wouldn't have recognized you. Why, you're a grown man!" with a look of exasperation and despair.

4   I drove by my old high school, where the next morning the white students would be joined and outnumbered by the Negro high school students coming in a group from their school. It was as pleasant and settled at the end of the broad avenue as it was eighteen years before; the inscription on the entrance said, "Education—Knowledge" over the statue of Plato holding a book, and the plaque bearing the Ten Commandments was there, as it had always been. Here, in front of this entrance, we once waited for the bell to ring, sitting in small groups on the grass on warm spring mornings, enjoying the pleasant, driftless Southern life, talking parties and baseball and school spirit, and giving hardly a mind to our colored contemporaries who went to "Yazoo High Number 2" on the other side of town; giving little thought to the "separate-but-equal" *modus vivendi* under which, in the early 1950s, the sovereign state of Mississippi was providing us with our education. We were sheltered, I suppose, from much of the humanity around us, privileged white benefactors of our honored and acknowledged Mississippi way of life, and we grew to love the town and the school as our departing came nearer. The school ground is empty on this day, and I have three companions I am showing the town to—two New Yorkers and an editor from Alabama—and they remark on the loveliness of my old schoolhouse. I would like to show them the good old boys lazing there in the yard, and the soft-skinned, double-named belles who shared those days: Daisye Love and Werdna Dee and Libby Terrell and Nettie Taylor and Barbara Nell and Ina Rae, and all the others who should be sitting here, precisely where I left them in May of 1952.

I have taken my friends all over town, showing them the houses surrounded by magnolias and elms and locusts, and also the lean-tos and shacks with stilts on the dirt roads of the colored section. The Alabama editor complains that I have not shown him the jailhouse, but the dark has set in, and he says, knowing the South as well as I, "It's a good ole town."

5   I had a wife, a Texas girl, who hated this place, hated the town and its people with a terrible and disparaging contempt. She believed it elementally evil. She hated everything about Mississippi, and once she wrote a graduate school treatise calling William Faulkner a second-rater. I believe her contempt sprang largely from the fear which often works on outsiders when they come here, fear among other things of its extraordinary apposition of violence and gentleness. For her, Mississippi was a symbol of all that was wrong with all of us, so that even what it inspired in the way of literary sensibility was, to any sound and secure academic mind, also an aberration. On the night Martin Luther King was killed in Memphis, as forlorn and grief-laden a night as I have ever lived, she slapped me across the face and said, "*You Southern boys have a lot to be guilty about.*"

6   There are those who say New York City is a provincial enclave, and that it is unrepresentative of the rest of the nation. I have lived on Manhatten Island eight years now, and for the first two or three in the Big Cave, in the dreadful hardening of one's senses for survival in the cultural capital, I shared in many of these fears. But gradually I grew to feel that New York, far from being an estuary of our national life, is if anything more *representative* than not, more American than otherwise, precisely because it brings together the whole range and spectrum, manifestation and extreme, of the American temperament, of the American races, of all our ways of living and our ways of speaking. New York has become to me the crux and apogee of our contemporary experience, and yet it drives me back almost against the will toward my past. Growing up in a small isolated town of the Deep South a generation ago, I became aware of the life of that place as a cross section and a microcosm of my time and region, and much that was typical of humanity was there for me to judge and to comprehend. What I missed a generation ago were the great exertions of the national presence, the manifestations of the relentless movement toward homogeneity and nationalization—the farthest nerve endings of Americans as a civilization—toward some kind of accommodation, however fragile and illusory this would seem, among our races and peoples and our separate collective pasts. This generation of children, white and black, in Yazoo will not, I sense, be so isolated as mine, for they will be confronted quite early with the things it took me years to learn, or that I have not learned at all.

Exercises

COMPREHENSION

Organization and Development

Like most descriptive essays, Morris's piece cannot be outlined in the traditional manner, nor does it contain an explicit thesis statement. It can, however, be summarized. In a sentence or two, write a summary of this essay, being sure to include a statement of Morris's conclusion.

Summary: _____

_____

_____

_____

Content

Choose the answer that correctly completes each statement.

1. According to Morris, in 25 years Yazoo's appearance has (a) improved (b) not changed (c) deteriorated.
2. One sign of the Negro boycott's effectiveness is that (a) no blacks are shopping in any white-owned stores (b) blacks and whites are never seen together (c) Main Street is deserted.
3. Apparently, Yazoo's residential areas are (a) segregated (b) integrated (c) haphazardly laid out.
4. When Yazoo's schools are integrated, (a) blacks will outnumber whites (b) whites will outnumber blacks (c) the number of blacks and whites will be equal.
5. Morris mentions his wife and her fear and hatred of Mississippi because (a) he wants to show how foolish her ideas were (b) she represents the feelings of many outsiders who come to the South (c) he eventually accepted her evaluation.
6. After moving from Yazoo, Morris decided that New York was in reality (a) representative of the entire spectrum of American culture (b) as provincial and isolated from American culture as Yazoo (c) the place where he wanted to live for the rest of his life.
7. Morris concludes that by growing up in Yazoo he missed (a) contact with different races and ethnic groups (b) an understanding of what it means to live in a big city (c) a realization of the national push for racial equality.
8. With respect to the impending integration of Yazoo's schools, Morris is apparently (a) indifferent (b) approving (c) disapproving.

Paragraph Structure

Reorder the following sentences to form a unified, coherent paragraph. Then check your version with the original.

1. Further down Main, I see a tall, thin man wearing glasses shuffling along in front of the furniture store.
2. The lumberyard and paint store on Canal, across from the Confederate monument, still displays the big sign, "VISIT OUR COLOR BAR."
3. "People here are complaining about what you wrote," he once said in a letter to me.
4. Behind it, in the colored section, a white postman has put his mailbag on the ground near a house and is playing cards with three Negroes.

5. "I tell them, everything he says happened, and it happened just like he said it did."
6. I know the walk, and from fifty yards away, out of the instinct of recognition, I see it is my companion Henjie Henick.

VOCABULARY AND USAGE

Word Formation Table

Complete the following table by changing word endings or root forms to make new grammatical forms. Use your dictionary if necessary.

	NOUN	VERB	ADJECTIVE	ADVERB
1.	homogeneity	_____	_____	_____
2.	_____	xxx	provincial	_____
3.	aberration	xxx	_____	_____
4.	_____	_____	disparaging	_____
5.	inscription	_____	_____	xxx

Fill-Ins

Complete each of the sentences below using the words on the following list. You may need to use some words more than once. You may also find that some blanks can be completed correctly with more than one word. Add plural endings to nouns and change verb forms where necessary.

segregated	consequently	as a result	representative
wistful	aberration	melancholic	equality
disparaging	now	protected	sheltered
typical	confront	contempt	isolated
oppose	deviation	experience	derogatory

1. Blacks and whites were _____ both in businesses and in schools; _____, the drive for _____ was _____ by many whites.
2. The courts ruled that schools in Yazoo could no longer be _____; _____, the white community's _____ for the court order was _____ by blacks who, in turn, started a boycott.
3. Morris's high school was _____, and he admits that his upbringing was _____ from the kind of _____ that the younger generation in Yazoo, both black and white, _____ must _____.
4. Morris's former wife showed _____ for Mississippi, and she made _____ comments about the southern way of life.
5. Morris's wife evidently felt that his interest in literature was only a(n) _____, and that such sensibility was not _____ of the southern way of life.
6. Morris thinks that Yazoo, a small _____ town, was _____ of the American temperament and _____ a generation ago; it was his _____ in New York that taught him that the rest of the country was engaged in a fight for _____.

DISCUSSION

1. At what place in the essay does Morris end his description? What is the relationship between the descriptive part and the final paragraphs?
2. Description conveys a dominant impression, either stated or implied. What dominant impression does Morris convey about Yazoo, especially in paragraphs 1, 2, and 4? Underline the key words that convey the mood in paragraph 2.
3. What method of organization does Morris use to order his impressions in paragraphs 2 and 4?
4. What order does Morris use to organize the details in paragraph 3? Underline the transitional devices as a way to help you see the order.
5. What is the function of paragraph 5? What is Morris's wife supposed to represent? What did she mean by her notion that "Mississippi was a symbol of what was wrong with all of us"?
6. In what way was Yazoo a microcosm of life in the United States a generation ago?
7. What did New York City teach Morris?
8. Morris's feelings in 1970 toward Yazoo and toward integration are different from his adolescent feelings. How precisely have they changed, and what caused him to reevaluate his ideas?

SUGGESTIONS FOR WRITING

1. Can you go home again? If you've already left home, how do you feel about returning? For example, how do you feel about seeing your old high school friends? Have you been to a high school reunion? Discuss.
2. Write an essay describing a scene using space order (left to right, right to left, near to far) as Morris does in the beginning of paragraph 3. Some suggestions for topics: the street you live on, a street in a nearby business district, your bedroom, your kitchen, your old high school.
3. Write a descriptive essay in which you present a scene from two points of view: the past (as you remember it) and the present (as you see it now). You might choose a house you once lived in, a school you once attended, or a favorite haunt, like a park or a playground.
4 In Morris's final paragraph, he sums up what he has learned since his youth and adolescence in Yazoo. In an essay, discuss some of the "discoveries" you have made since reaching adulthood—in particular, you might consider your ideas about politics, race, morality, education, religion, or your system of values.

The Gay Bar

MARTIN HOFFMAN

Martin Hoffman was born in Chicago in 1935 and educated at the University of Illinois. He is a psychiatrist on the staff of the San Francisco Health Department, an assistant professor of clinical psychiatry at the University of California Medical School in San Francisco, a consultant to the Gender Identity Program at the UCLA School of Medicine, and has taught courses in sexual deviance as a visiting lecturer in Criminology at the University of California at Berkeley. He was the recipient of a grant from the National Institute of Mental Health for a study of male homosexuality in San Francisco and the Bay Area. "The Gay Bar" is an excerpt from *The Gay World*, in which he reports the findings of his research into the San Francisco gay scene.

1   The gay bar has almost become a social institution in America. It is the central public place around which gay life revolves and is to be found in all large and medium-sized cities across the country. We would like to describe here the "typical gay bar," although, of course, there is no such thing, any more than there is a "typical straight bar." Perhaps, narrowing our focus a bit, what we want to describe is what I call the "middle-class" gay bar, by which I mean not that all its members are necessarily middle-class socioeconomically, but rather that middle-class proprieties are observed and that there is nothing unique or specialized about the bar. We will not, for example, be concerned with the leather-jacket motorcycle bars, nor with the hustler bars so beautifully described by Rechy,[1] nor with those bars which provide entertainment such as drag shows and male go-go dancers.

2   Perhaps the most important fact about a gay bar is that it is a sexual marketplace. That is, men go there for the purpose of seeking sexual partners, and if this function were not served by the bar there would be no gay bars, for, although homosexuals also go there to drink and socialize, the search for sexual experience is in some sense the core of the interaction in the bar. It should, however, be obvious that there must be more going on in the bar than simply people meeting and leaving; otherwise the bar could not exist as a commercial enterprise. People have to come there for a time long enough to drink, in order to make it profitable to the management to run these bars. And gay bars are very profitable and have sprung up in large numbers. It is estimated that there are about 60 gay bars in Los Angeles and

THE GAY BAR   From *The Gay World: Male Homosexuality and the Social Creation of Evil,* by Martin Hoffman. © 1968 by Basic Books, Inc., Publishers, New York.
[1]John Rechy, *City of Night* (1963).

about 40 in San Francisco. A number of heterosexuals have converted their own taverns into gay bars simply because they have found it more profitable to run a gay bar, even though they are sometimes not particularly delighted with the clientele. The gay bar plays a central role in the life of very many homosexuals—one which is much more important than the role played by straight bars in the life of all but a few heterosexuals. This is connected intimately with the use of the gay bar as a sexual marketplace and, of course, with the fact that homosexuals, as homosexuals, have really no place else where they can congregate without disclosing to the straight world that they are homosexual.

3   What does a gay bar look like? In the first place, unlike most middle-class straight bars, it is almost exclusively populated by males. Sometimes non-homosexuals accidentally walk into a gay bar and it is usually this lack of women that makes them aware that they may have inadvertently walked into a homosexual setting. There are a few bars in which lesbians congregate along with male homosexuals, especially in cities which are not large enough to support a lesbian bar. But even in the larger cities, lesbian bars are not very common. They are never as large as the large metropolitan male gay bars. This is because female homosexuals are much less promiscuous than male homosexuals and really not able to support a sexual marketplace on the scale that males do.

4   Occasionally, "fruit flies," i.e., women who like to associate with male homosexuals, are found in gay bars, although they are not a very prominent part of any gay bar scene. Why a woman who is not a lesbian would like to associate with male homosexuals is a question which cannot be altogether answered in general, except to say that some of these women obviously find homosexual men a lot less threatening than heterosexual men, since the former are not interested in them sexually. Since these women are not potential sexual partners for the males, they are not potential sources of rejection for them either, and thereby they find themselves the subject of much attention by the male clientele. Consequently, they are the beneficiaries of a great deal of sociability without being objects of seduction. Some women find this a very appealing position.

5   In the gay world there is a tremendous accent on youth and this is reflected in the composition of the bar clientele. Youth is very much at a premium and young men will go to the bars as soon as they have passed the legal age limit. This varies from state to state; it is 18 in New York and 21 in California. Along with the younger men, there are somewhat older men who are trying to look young. They attempt to accomplish this primarily by dress. The typical bar costume is the same style of dress that an average college undergraduate might wear. It would consist of a sport shirt, Levis, and loafers or sneakers. In this "typical" middle-class gay bar which I am attempting to describe, extremely effeminate dress and mannerisms are not well tolerated. Nevertheless, it would not be correct to say that the scene in a gay bar looks like a fraternity stag party. There is a tendency toward effeminacy in the overall impression one gets from observing the bar, although this

may not necessarily be anything striking or flagrant. There is a certain softness or absence of stereotypical masculine aggression present in the conversations and behavior of the bar patrons. Also, in spite of the fact that the model bar costume is very much like what one would see on a college campus, there is a good deal of special attention paid by the bar patrons to their dress, so that they seem almost extraordinarily well groomed. There is thus a feeling of fastidiousness about the appearance of the young men in the bar which, along with their muted demeanor, rather clearly differentiates the overall *Gestalt* of the gay bar from that which would be experienced upon entering a gathering of young male heterosexuals. There are usually a few clearly identifiable homosexuals, although the majority of individuals in the bar are not identifiable and would not be thought homosexual in another setting. It seems to be the general consensus of gay bar observers that fights are less likely to break out in a gay than in a straight bar. This is, I think, probably attributable to the psychological characteristics of the clientele rather than to anything about the structure of the bar itself. Male homosexuals would certainly rather make love than war.

6   One of the clearest differences between the gay and the straight bar is that in the gay bar the attention of the patrons is focused directly on each other. In a gay bar, for example, the patrons who are sitting at the bar itself usually face away from the bar and look toward the other people in the room and toward the door. When a new patron walks in, he receives a good deal of scrutiny, and people engaged in conversation with each other just naturally assume that their interlocutors will turn away from them to watch each new entering patron. All this is, of course, part of the pervasive looking and cruising which goes on in the bar.

7   There is a great deal of milling about in the bar and individuals tend to engage in short, superficial conversations with each other. They try to make the circuit around the bar to see everyone in it, perhaps stopping to chat with their friends but usually not for very long. In a way, the shortness and superficiality of the conversations in the bar mirror that same brevity and shallowness of interpersonal relations which characterize gay life as a whole.

8   Heterosexual observers and even homosexuals who are not habitués of the bar scene often express great perplexity about the bars—they cannot quite understand what's going on there. They seem to be bewildered by the sight of all these young men standing around and communicating so little with one another. The patrons stand along the walls, it seems, for hours, without speaking. They move around the room and talk at length with almost no one. One heterosexual observer said that he felt as if everyone in the room were standing around waiting for some important figure to come in, but of course he never comes. He likened the scene to a reception for a foreign ambassador, where everyone stands around simply marking time until the dignitary arrives. In a sense, this observer was correct, for the young men *are* waiting for some important person to arrive, one who will never arrive—but it is not a foreign ambassador. Each is waiting for a handsome young prince to come and carry him off in his arms. They're waiting for the ideal sexual object, and

if they don't find him they may very well go home alone, in spite of the fact that there are sometimes hundreds of other attractive young men right there in the bar.

9   The gay bar, then, in a sense may be thought of as a stage on which is played out a fantasy in which the hero never arrives. The reason why heterosexuals and even some homosexuals cannot understand what is going on is because they are not a party to this fantasy. They imagine that if you are going to a place to seek a sexual partner, you go in, look around a little bit, walk up to somebody that you like, engage in a conversation, and then go out together. And sometimes this is precisely what does occur in the gay bar. Very often, in fact, but the bewildering problem which confronts the uninitiated observer is why this does not happen more often: why, in fact, all these good-looking and well-dressed young men are standing around uncommunicative.

10   Sherri Cavan[2] has made the suggestion that in the homosexual pickup bar it may happen that encounters are never begun because each party is waiting for the other to offer the first words of greeting. This is presumably due to the fact that when the situation involves two males, it is not clear who is expected to make the initial overture. One cannot deny the saliency of this observation. Nevertheless, I do not think it alone accounts fully for the strange situation in the gay bar, since one would expect the reverse to occur just as well, i.e., since both parties can make the initial overture, one would think that at least one of the members of the hypothetical pair could overcome his shyness. I think the sociological explanation fails to take into account the psychological factors involved. As many observers have noted, homosexuals are very much afraid of rejection, and hence, have an inordinate hesitancy about making an approach. I think this is due to the following reason: the only aspect of their self which male homosexuals are able to adequately present in a bar situation is their physical appearance. If they are rejected in making a conversational opening, this is interpreted (probably correctly) to mean a rejection of that crucial part of themselves, namely, their desirability as a sexual partner. Hence, their self-esteem is very much at stake and they have a great deal to lose by being rejected.

11   It must be remembered that in the gay world the only real criterion of value is physical attractiveness; consequently, a rejection by a desired partner is a rejection of the only valued part of one's identity in that world. When we understand this, I think we understand why the fear of rejection is so prevalent among homosexual men.

12   The gay bar, is, then, a lot less licentious than people who are not aware of what is going on there might be inclined to think. When heterosexual men enter a gay bar for the first time for the purpose of simply visiting it, they often seem afraid that somehow they will be rapidly approached, or perhaps even attacked, by the sexual deviants present inside the bar. This, of course, is about as far from reality as it is possible to imagine. It would not be unusual

[2]Sherri Cavan, *Liquor License: An Ethnography of Bar Behavior* (1966), p. 192.

if none of the patrons would engage them in conversation during the entire course of the evening. If they are not young and handsome, they may well have great difficulty in communicating with anyone after even a great deal of effort on their part.

13   A word should be said, I suppose, about the function of the gay bar as a source of group solidarity and as a place where one can meet one's friends and exchange gossip. I think, however, that this function is obvious and that it need not be elaborated upon. Many homosexuals frequent gay bars for reasons other than seeking sexual partners. If sex eventuates from the bar interaction, this is fine, but it is not the reason they went there in the first place. They went there for sociability. And yet this too must be qualified, for in the back of their minds is usually the thought that perhaps that special person will walk through the door tonight and they will meet him and go home with him.

14   The "cosmetic" quality of the gay bar is a result, in large part, of the need for anonymity which pervades all the public places of the gay world. If one can only present the visible and nonidentifying aspect of one's identity, one's physical appearance will be the central aspect that can be displayed to others. If homosexuals could meet *as homosexuals* in the kinds of social settings in which heterosexuals can (e.g., at school, at work) where the emphasis on finding sexual partners is not the controlling force behind all the social interaction which transpires, a great deal of the anonymous promiscuity which now characterizes homosexual encounters would be replaced by a more "normal" kind of meeting between two persons. Perhaps, then, the sexual relationships which develop would become more stable. Maybe the gay bar itself would not change—this can only be a matter for conjecture—but, at any rate, it would not be so central to gay life.

Observing
and Reporting

One of the most common and important kinds of writing is the report. Its effectiveness is based on the ability of the reporter—whether student researcher or international news correspondent—to observe carefully and then to communicate those observations to others with clarity and accuracy. While modern media reporting and scientific research, carried on by television satellite and computer, may seem remote from ancient times, when messengers were slain for bringing bad news, good reporting still depends on the observer's careful attention to detail, correctness in diction, precision of emphasis and, above all, his accuracy. Inaccurate observation and reporting can have serious consequences: the lab technician who is careless may endanger the patient's life; the businessman who incorrectly reports his sales will lose commissions, or his job; the student who records the chemistry experiment carelessly may undermine his grade—or the lab—the next time he tries it.

It is important for the reader to question the credentials and position of the observer. Is he objective, unbiased, without a special interest in the subject—as, presumably, are news reporters, scientists, and other researchers? Or does he approach his subject, as do three of the observers in this section, from a position of some personal involvement? While newspaper and other media reporting, along with scientific observation, should be the most objective of all reporting, concentrating solely on the communication of observable facts, it is important to note that this is not always so. Newspaper editors have been "bought" by special interests, and even a scientist as great as Galileo had to save his neck by swearing falsely that the sun moved around the earth.

Further, the newspaper piece in this section is *not* a straight news article (for examples of which you should consult your own local paper), but a feature article. Such a piece differs from the news report in that it may reveal, from the start, not just the journalistic essentials of who, where, what, when, and why, but also the observer's personal attitude toward some person, place or thing that has interest beyond the news of the day. (Does Harris, for example, reveal a particular feeling about the "dinosaur man"?) Also, feature articles frequently have a by-line; that is, the reporter's name appears along with the article, while straight news reporting (where, presumably, as in scientific experiment, any trained eye can function as objective recorder) is mostly anonymous. The distinction is very much like that between an impressionistic painting and a news photograph.

Harris remains, however, the only one of the four observers in this section who maintains an objective distance from his subject. Northrup and Smith are observers of activities in which they have an essential role; and their own involvement—Northrup as one of the slaves about to be auctioned and Smith as one of the novice transcendental meditators—colors their reports. Involvement is not necessarily *bad*, however—the participant-observer can provide the kind of eye-witness account, or close-up, that an objective observer cannot. But the reader should be aware of the observer's position and possible bias so that he can evaluate potential distortion of the facts.

Finally, Ephron presents other problems to the careful analyst of reportage: she is not a participant, and her ironic and even wicked tone reveals a definite feeling about her subject. Yet one might ask, what is her motive for adopting this perspective on one of America's homegrown traditions? The ability to answer that question is one mark of a careful reader.

The Dinosaur Man

ROY J. HARRIS, JR.

Roy J. Harris, Jr., a staff writer for the *Wall Street Journal,* reports in the article below on a California man with an unusual mission—to build replicas of dinosaurs in his back yard.

1   Along Interstate 10 northwest of Palm Springs, the wind-scoured desert, ringed with bare and jagged peaks, has an almost lunar beauty. Suddenly, as you drive along, there rises out of the desert a creature from the dimmest past. It grows in your car's windshield—and grows some more.

2   The monster is four stories high and half a football field long, and it weighs hundreds of tons. It is a brontosaurus almost triple the size of the actual dinosaur of the Jurassic period—the largest animal ever to walk the earth.

3   Looking at the bulging shoulder muscles, the curling tail, the rough-textured green hide, it is possible to forget for a moment that it is just steel and sculptured concrete. It is even possible briefly to ignore the fire escape (a grudging concession to safety) and the surroundings—a gas station, the Wheel-Inn Cafe, and other features of the roadside economy of Cabazon, population 750.

4   The dinosaur is much more than just another tourist attraction, however. It is the realized lifelong dream of one man, who built it himself, for its own sake, over 11 years at a personal cost of more than $100,000. Some men aspire to be board chairmen and retire as clerks; others want to be great athletes and wind up weekend bowlers. Claude Bell wanted to build with his own hands something memorable, something permanent, above all something big. He did it.

5   Mr. Bell is a small, wiry man who has been an artist-artisan all his life. At 78 years of age, operator of a portrait studio that has regularly grossed $140,000 a year, he could have retired in comfort long ago. Yet he still spends most of his spare time, in fact half of every week, puttering around his giant reptile. To the residents of Cabazon, the figure in the flower-printed cap is so identified with his creation that he is known simply as "the dinosaur man."

6   Mr. Bell, who lives with his wife in a Spartan cabin near the dinosaur when he's in town, says that maybe he'll get a little of his investment back by charging admission to a museum he's installing in the beast's cavernous belly. But profit clearly has little to do with it. "If all he wanted to do was

make money, he'd have had that lizard up in a year or two," says Alice Richmond, a waitress at the Wheel-Inn, which Mr. Bell also owns. "I think he's building a monument to himself."

7   Says Mr. Bell: "When you're doing something like this, you can forget about eating and sleeping, and just live on that tingle of enthusiasm. I've worked all through the night sometimes. A younger man probably couldn't plan this and do it; you need to build up the money, and the dedication, too. When you're young, you're too dumb, you run crazy after girls."

8   For Claude Bell, the idea of building his very own colossus goes back to his boyhood in Atlantic City, where he used to sculpt sand on the beach. One day he left his coat on the sand while he worked and found that appreciative patrons had thrown coins on it. "So I went home and got a bedsheet. When the coins started dropping, I was in business right then," he recalls. At the same time he saw a wooden house near Atlantic City built in the shape of an elephant. "I was only a kid, but I knew I could do something like that for myself," he says.

9   But the project had to wait a few decades. After leaving Atlantic City as a young man, he worked as an artist, sculpting sand and concrete for various fairs and expositions around the country. Finally, 22 years ago, he got a job in Southern California at Knott's Berry Farm, a big amusement complex, where he made concrete figures and got the portrait studio concession. He still works there.

10   At about the same time he bought 76 acres in windy, desolate Cabazon; his investment paid off years later when Interstate 10 was routed right across his property. In 1958 he opened the Wheel-Inn. He prospered. The childhood idea that had never really left him grew more vivid, more compelling. And now the time was ripe.

11   Mr. Bell had long been fascinated with the great dinosaurs. The one that fit his dream was, of course, the biggest—far bigger, far grander than any mere elephant. Clearly, only a brontosaurus, and an outsize one at that, would do. And, since it would be his brontosaurus, there would have to be a few modifications on the basic Jurassic model. The head, for example, displeased him: too small. He made it a little bigger. The project took shape in his drawings and plans, and in 1964 he broke ground.

12   Working week after week, Mr. Bell scrounged what he could and paid for the rest. He got steel from a washed-out bridge and concrete for the foundation from a road-builder's surplus. The construction, which he originally figured would only take a couple of years, stretched to four, five, a decade. An average of $10,000 a year was swallowed up by the beast.

13   No detail was too small to see to, nothing could be skimped or hurried. Forced to air-condition the monster, Mr. Bell even sculpted a concrete turtle to conceal the compressor unit outside near the tail. His perfectionism and deep personal involvement made him a trying taskmaster at times. "He's old and he's got his own ways," says Steve Spencer, a teenager who works for the artist. "If you don't want to do something his way, you're not going to do it at all."

14   When he sensed a threat to his creation, he fought fiercely. A few years ago, former Cabazon Mayor Thomas De Luca tried to get Mr. Bell to obtain an outside engineering opinion on the structure's safety; Mr. Bell joined others in a successful drive to recall the mayor, with the dinosaur being one of the issues. Mr. De Luca is still a bit bitter, saying he was wrongfully characterized as an enemy of the beast. Mr. Bell says: "Anyone who tries to buck something clean like the dinosaur is in trouble."

15   The artist defends the animal's safety. With its steel frame and concrete skin up to five inches thick, it's built to withstand the howling winds and earthquakes that often strike here, he says. And he vows that everyone in town except Mr. De Luca has favored the reptile all along. Considering Cabazon's reliance on luring people off the highway, by means of everything from a poker casino (now defunct) to a fortune-telling parlor, it isn't surprising that such an attention-getter as a four-story dinosaur would be welcome. Homer Shepard, principal of the Cabazon school, echoes typical sentiments when he calls it "a brilliant idea."

16   To all outward appearances, the creature seems complete. But Mr. Bell always finds something new to improve it, like a large tongue that he plans to add and that will sway in the wind. The thought that someday his dream might actually be finished disturbs him. "Finished?" he says. "I'll never be finished. After the brontosaurus, I'm going to build a tyrannosaurus 65 feet high with a viewing platform in the head. After that, more, a whole dinosaur garden. I'm going on 80 and I've got 25 or 30 years left to live, I figure, and I'm going to work until I can't work anymore."

17   Is he serious? "I'm afraid so," Mrs. Bell says with a sigh.

Exercises

COMPREHENSION

Organization and Development

Complete the following outline. Find the thesis statement and write it in the space provided. Then find the three main divisions in the article and fill in the remaining spaces. Note the paragraphs for each section.

Thesis statement: _____

_____

I.   _____   [   ]

II.   _____   [   ]

III. _____   [   ]

Content

Choose the answer that correctly completes each statement.

1. Mr. Bell built the brontosaurus to (a) make money (b) satisfy a lifelong dream (c) attract tourists to Cabazon.
2. Harris emphasizes Mr. Bell's (a) obsession with money and fame (b) energy and perfectionism (c) stubbornness and irrationality.
3. Mr. Bell began constructing his dinosaur (a) when he was a young man in New Jersey (b) after he retired in 1959 (c) in 1964 when he was still working at Knott's Berry Farm.
4. Mr. Bell's brontosaurus is (a) an exact copy of the original animal (b) unsafe structurally (c) a modified version of the original animal.
5. Since he began the project, Mr. Bell each year has spent on the average about (a) $100 (b) $1000 (c) $10,000.
6. Most of Cabazon's residents like the dinosaur because they think it (a) is a fascinating work of art (b) will help Cabazon's economy by bringing visitors (c) creates jobs for the town's unemployed teenagers.
7. Mr. Bell's next project will be a (a) second brontosaurus with moving head and legs (b) tyrannosaurus with a movable tongue (c) tyrannosaurus with a viewing platform in the head.
8. Mrs. Bell (a) has accepted her husband's hobby (b) helped him build the monster (c) worries about the project's cost.

Paragraph Structure

Reorder the following sentences to form a unified, coherent paragraph. Identify one sentence as the topic sentence. Then check your version with the original.

1. Claude Bell wanted to build with his own hands something memorable, something permanent, above all something big.
2. It is the realized lifelong dream of one man, who built it himself, for its own sake, over 11 years at a personal cost of more than $100,000.
3. The dinosaur is much more than just another tourist attraction, however.
4. He did it.
5. Some men aspire to be board chairmen and retire as clerks; others want to be great athletes and wind up weekend bowlers.

VOCABULARY AND USAGE

Word Formation Table

Complete the following table by changing word endings or root forms to make new grammatical forms. Use your dictionary if necessary.

	NOUN	VERB	ADJECTIVE	ADVERB
1.	_____	_____	creative	_____
2.	_____	appreciate	_____	_____
3.	_____	_____	_____	economically
4.	origin	_____	_____	_____
5.	_____	_____	characteristic	_____

Fill-Ins

Complete each of the sentences below using the words on the following list. You may need to use some words more than once. You may find that some blanks can be completed correctly with more than one word. Add plural endings to nouns and change verb forms where necessary.

also	attract	resident
threat	prosperous	dreary
lure	although	known
desolate	still	because
characterized	in spite	primitive
demand	entice	inhabitant
spartan	rich	challenge

1. Mr. Bell is _____ by the _____ of Cabazon as "the dinosaur man."
2. _____ of the dinosaur, Cabazon's surroundings are fairly _____ and don't offer much to _____ tourists.
3. _____ Mr. Bell is now _____, he _____ holds his regular job and lives in a _____ cabin.
4. The _____ of Cabazon hope that the town will become _____ to travelers _____ of the dinosaur.
5. The former mayor was _____ as an enemy of the dinosaur _____ he _____ an engineering report.
6. _____ of the mayor's _____ to its existence, the dinosaur is _____ standing in Cabazon.

DISCUSSION

1. What is ironic about the dinosaur's location? What is the dominant impression of the area around Cabazon, and what words reveal it?
2. What was Bell's purpose in building the dinosaur? Did he have any ulterior motives? If so, what were they?
3. Underline the transitional devices in paragraphs 8 and 9 and explain how each is appropriate for the supporting idea it governs.
4. What attitude do Bell and his wife display in the last two paragraphs?
5. What is the author's attitude toward Bell and his creation throughout the article? Point to examples that reveal his point of view.
6. After reading this article, someone said that Claude Bell could only be an American. Why?
7. Would you characterize this article as factual and objective or as interpretive and subjective? Explain your answer by citing references from the article.

SUGGESTIONS FOR WRITING

1. Describe a goal or desire of yours that might seem eccentric or useless to the outside world.
2. Write an essay describing a nonconforming or unusual person you know. Be sure to include an explanation of how others view his or her behavior.

3. Describe an unusual or bizarre place or tourist attraction you have observed.

4. Following Harris's method of organization, report on an unusual scene you have observed. Be sure to follow the standard journalistic procedure of including all the essential information (who, what, where, when, and why) in the beginning.

A Slave Witness of a Slave Auction

SOLOMON NORTHRUP

Slave narratives were common before the Civil War, and abolitionists frequently used them in their campaign against slavery. As a result, many were sensational, although this one seems fairly objective. It was published in 1853 in a book entitled *Twelve Years a Slave: Narrative of Solomon Northrup, a Citizen of New York, Kidnapped in Washington City in 1841, and Rescued in 1853, from a Cotton Plantation near the Red River in Louisiana.* Northrup was finally given his freedom when he was able to get a letter sent to friends in New York. The governor arranged for his release, enabling him to return to his family in Glens Falls, New York.

1   The very amiable, pious-hearted Mr. Theophilus Freeman, partner or consignee of James H. Burch, and keeper of the slave pen in New-Orleans, was out among his animals early in the morning. With an occasional kick of the older men and women, and many a sharp crack of the whip about the ears of the younger slaves, it was not long before they were all astir, and wide awake. Mr. Theophilus Freeman bustled about in a very industrious manner, getting his property ready for the sales-room, intending, no doubt, to do that day a rousing business.

2   In the first place we were required to wash thoroughly, and those with beards, to shave. We were then furnished with a new suit each, cheap, but clean. The men had hat, coat, shirt, pants and shoes; the women frocks of calico, and handkerchiefs to bind about their heads. We were now conducted into a large room in the front part of the building to which the yard was attached, in order to be properly trained, before the admission of customers. The men were arranged on one side of the room, the women on the other. The tallest was placed at the head of the row, then the next tallest, and so on in the order of their respective heights. Emily was at the foot of the line of women. Freeman charged us to remember our places; exhorted us to appear smart and lively,—sometimes threatening, and again holding out various inducements. During the day he exercised us in the art of "looking smart," and of moving to our places with exact precision.

3   After being fed, in the afternoon, we were again paraded and made to dance. Bob, a colored boy, who had some time belonged to Freeman, played on the violin. Standing near him, I made bold to inquire if he could play the

A SLAVE WITNESS OF A SLAVE AUCTION   From *A Southern Reader*, edited by Willard Thorp (Alfred A. Knopf, 1955).

"Virginia Reel." He answered he could not, and asked me if I could play. Replying in the affirmative, he handed me the violin. I struck up a tune, and finished it. Freeman ordered me to continue playing, and seemed well pleased, telling Bob that I far excelled him—a remark that seemed to grieve my musical companion very much.

4   Next day many customers called to examine Freeman's "new lot." The latter gentleman was very loquacious, dwelling at much length upon our several good points and qualities. He would make us hold up our heads, walk briskly back and forth, while customers would feel of our hands and arms and bodies, turn us about, ask us what we could do, make us open our mouths and show our teeth, precisely as a jockey examines a horse which he is about to barter for or purchase. Sometimes a man or woman was taken back to the small house in the yard, stripped, and inspected more minutely. Scars upon a slave's back were considered evidence of a rebellious or unruly spirit, and hurt his sale.

5   One old gentleman, who said he wanted a coachman, appeared to take a fancy to me. From his conversation with Freeman, I learned he was a resident of the city. I very much desired that he would buy me, because I conceived it would not be difficult to make my escape from New-Orleans on some northern vessel. Freeman asked him fifteen hundred dollars for me. The old gentleman insisted it was too much, as times were very hard. Freeman, however, declared that I was sound and healthy, of a good constitution, and intelligent. He made it a point to enlarge upon my musical attainments. The old gentleman argued quite adroitly that there was nothing extraordinary about the nigger, and finally, to my regret, went out, saying he would call again. During the day, however, a number of sales were made. David and Caroline were purchased together by a Natchez planter. They left us, grinning broadly, and in the most happy state of mind, caused by the fact of their not being separated. Lethe was sold to a planter of Baton Rouge, her eyes flashing with anger as she was led away.

6   The same man also purchased Randall. The little fellow was made to jump, and run across the floor, and perform many other feats, exhibiting his activity and condition. All the time the trade was going on, Eliza was crying aloud, and wringing her hands. She besought the man not to buy him, unless he also bought herself and Emily. She promised, in that case, to be the most faithful slave that ever lived. The man answered that he could not afford it, and then Eliza burst into a paroxysm of grief, weeping plaintively. Freeman turned round to her, savagely, with his whip in his uplifted hand, ordering her to stop her noise, or he would flog her. He would not have such work—such snivelling; and unless she ceased that minute, he would take her to the yard and give her a hundred lashes. Yes, he would take the nonsense out of her pretty quick—if he didn't, might he be d—d. Eliza shrunk before him, and tried to wipe away her tears, but it was all in vain. She wanted to be with her children, she said, the little time she had to live. All the frowns and threats of Freeman, could not wholly silence the afflicted mother. She kept on begging and beseeching them, most piteously, not to separate the three. Over

and over again she told them how she loved her boy. A great many times she repeated her former promises—how very faithful and obedient she would be; how hard she would labor day and night, to the last moment of her life, if he would only buy them all together. But it was of no avail; the man could not afford it. The bargain was agreed upon, and Randall must go alone. Then Eliza ran to him; embraced him passionately; kissed him again and again; told him to remember her—all the while her tears falling in the boy's face like rain.

7   Freeman damned her, calling her a blubbering, bawling wench, and ordered her to go to her place, and behave herself, and be somebody. He swore he wouldn't stand such stuff but a little longer. He would soon give her something to cry about, if she was not mighty careful, and *that* she might depend upon.

8   The planter from Baton Rouge, with his new purchases, was ready to depart.

9   "Don't cry, mama. I will be a good boy. Don't cry," said Randall, looking back, as they passed out of the door.

10   What has become of the lad, God knows. It was a mournful scene indeed. I would have cried myself if I had dared.

Exercises

COMPREHENSION

Organization and Development

Complete the following outline. Write a sentence stating the *purpose* of Northrup's essay in the space provided. Then find the main divisions in the essay and fill in the remaining spaces. Note the paragraphs for each section.

Statement of purpose: _____

_____

I. _____   [   ]

II. _____   [   ]

Content

Choose the answer that correctly completes each statement.

1. When Northrup describes Mr. Theophilus Freeman, keeper of the slave pen, as "amiable" and "pious-hearted," he is being (a) realistic (b) sarcastic (c) complimentary.

2. Freeman exercised the slaves so they would (a) be in good physical condition for their future labors (b) look sharp to the customers (c) be kept busy before the auction began.

3. Northrup's violin playing is meant to call attention to (a) his superiority to the other slaves (b) his desire to ingratiate himself to the slave keeper (c) the disparity between his position as a slave and his culture and education.

4. Throughout the essay Northrup implies that Freeman treated the slaves like (a) family members (b) objects (c) animals.

5. Uppermost on a slave's mind was (a) not being separated from his family (b) being purchased by a kind owner (c) living in a place from which escape would be easy.

6. When Randall, Eliza's son, was sold to a planter, he behaved (a) bravely (b) childishly (c) stubbornly.

7. Northrup dwells on the scene with Eliza and her son to show (a) the inhumanity of slavery as an institution (b) Northrup's own unselfish attempts to intercede on Eliza's behalf (c) how hard the times were, since the planter could afford to buy only one slave.

8. The scene described in this essay occurred in (a) Baton Rouge (b) New Orleans (c) Natchez.

Paragraph Structure

Reorder the following sentences to form a unified, coherent paragraph. Then check your version with the original. Finally, decide what method of organization the paragraph exhibits.

1. The men had hat, coat, shirt, pants and shoes; the women frocks of calico, and handkerchiefs to bind about their heads.

2. The men were arranged on one side of the room, the women on the other.

3. In the first place we were required to wash thoroughly, and those with beards, to shave.

4. We were now conducted into a large room in the front part of the building to which the yard was attached, in order to be properly trained, before the admission of customers.

5. We were then furnished with a new suit each, cheap but clean.

6. During the day he exercised us in the art of "looking smart," and of moving to our places with exact precision.

7. The tallest was placed at the head of the row, then the next tallest, and so on in the order of their respective heights.

8. Freeman charged us to remember our places; exhorted us to appear smart and lively,—sometimes threatening, and again holding out various inducements.

VOCABULARY AND USAGE

Word Formation Table

Complete the following table by changing word endings or root forms to make new grammatical forms. Use your dictionary if necessary.

	NOUN	VERB	ADJECTIVE	ADVERB
1.	_____	argue	_____	_____
2.	_____	_____	rebellious	_____
3.	grief	_____	_____	_____
4.	_____	_____	_____	passionately
5.	_____	inquire	_____	_____

Fill-Ins

Complete each of the sentences below using the words on the following list. You may need to use some words more than once. You may also find that some blanks can be completed correctly with more than one word. Add plural endings to nouns and change verb forms where necessary.

amiable	then	thoroughly	during
grief	because	loquacious	talkative
attempt	precision	as	plaintive
dare	obedient	quality	asset
mournful	threaten	work	sorrowful

1. _____ the first day, Freeman trained the slaves _____ and made them learn their places with _____.
2. Although Freeman was described as pious-hearted and _____, he _____ the slaves if they _____ to challenge his authority.
3. Freeman was a _____ salesman, _____ he spoke at length about each slave's _____.
4. Although the old man said he could not buy Northrup, _____ times were hard, Freeman emphasized Northrup's intelligence and willingness to _____ hard.
5. The purchaser said he could not buy Eliza's son; _____ she burst into a fit of _____, but her _____ cries went unheard.
6. Northrup writes that this _____ scene filled him with such _____ that he would have cried if he _____.

DISCUSSION

1. What is Northrup's attitude toward Mr. Freeman? Is it consistent throughout the chronicle, or does it shift? Point to references in the essay to support your view.
2. What is the dominant method of development in paragraph 2?
3. What is the real purpose of Freeman's exercising and training the slaves? And what does Northrup's description of the day's exercise reveal about Freeman's attitude toward the slaves?
4. What is the point of including the passage about Northrup's familiarity with the violin? What does this little incident reveal about Northrup's background?
5. What seems to be the slaves' central concern? How would you characterize the behavior of Randall, Eliza's son, after he was purchased?
6. In what way does Northrup's account of Eliza's grief over being separated from her son contrast with his earlier method of reporting?

SUGGESTIONS FOR WRITING

1. Northrup is both an observer and a participant in the slave auction he describes. Following his example, describe an incident that you have at once observed and participated in. Do not state your opinion but, like Northrup, let your illustrations and choice of words reveal your dominant impression.
2. Northrup's account is a masterpiece of understatement. Despite the horror of the

scene he recounts, his report is nonetheless objective. In an essay discuss some of the techniques—diction, point of view, metaphors, narrative techniques—that contribute to the success of this piece.

3. Northrup's chronicle ends with a long, detailed anecdote about Eliza's distress at being separated from her children, and this anecdote constitutes a powerful argument against the institution of slavery. Write an essay that argues for something you strongly believe in. Your essay should either begin or end with an anecdote that convinces the reader of the validity of your opinion.

Baking Off

NORA EPHRON

Nora Ephron is a journalist who writes a column on the media for *Esquire*. She lives in New York and Washington with her husband, Carl Bernstein, a reporter for the *Washington Post*. Several of her pieces on women and the women's movement have been collected in an anthology called *Crazy Salad*. Among them is "Baking Off," a humorous, acerbic look at the 24th annual Pillsbury Bake-Off.

1   Roxanne Frisbie brought her own pan to the twenty-fourth annual Pillsbury Bake-Off. "I feel like a nut," she said. "It's just a plain old dumb pan, but everything I do is in that crazy pan." As it happens, Mrs. Frisbie had no cause whatsoever to feel like a nut: it seemed that at least half the 100 finalists in the Bake-It-Easy Bake-Off had brought something with them—their own sausages, their own pie pans, their own apples. Edna Buckley, who was fresh from representing New York State at the National Chicken Cooking Contest, where her recipe for fried chicken in a batter of beer, cheese, and crushed pretzels had gone down to defeat, brought with her a lucky handkerchief, a lucky horseshoe, a lucky dime for her shoe, a potholder with the Pillsbury Poppin' Fresh Doughboy on it, an Our Blessed Lady pin, and all of her jewelry, including a silver charm also in the shape of the doughboy. Mrs. Frisbie and Mrs. Buckley and the other finalists came to the Bake-Off to bake off for $65,000 in cash prizes; in Mrs. Frisbie's case, this meant making something she created herself and named Butterscotch Crescent Rolls—and which Pillsbury promptly, and to Mrs. Frisbie's dismay, renamed Sweet 'N Creamy Crescent Crisps. Almost all the recipes in the finals were renamed by Pillsbury using a lot of crispy snicky snacky words. An exception to this was Sharon Schubert's Wiki Wiki Coffee Cake, a name which ought to have been snicky snacky enough; but Pillsbury, in a moment of restraint, renamed it One-Step Tropical Fruit Cake. As it turned out, Mrs. Schubert ended up winning $5,000 for her cake, which made everybody pretty mad, even the contestants who had been saying for days that they did not care who won, that winning meant nothing and was quite beside the point; the fact was that Sharon Schubert was a previous Bake-Off winner, having won $10,000 three years before for her Crescent Apple Snacks, and in addition had walked off with a trip to Puerto Vallarta in the course of this year's festivities. Most of the

contestants felt she had won a little more than was really fair. But I'm getting ahead of the story.

2   The Pillsbury Company has been holding Bake-Offs since 1948, when Eleanor Roosevelt, for reasons that are not clear, came to give the first one her blessing. This year's took place from Saturday, February 24, through Tuesday, February 27, at the Beverly Hilton Hotel in Beverly Hills. One hundred contestants—97 of them women, 2 twelve-year-old boys, and 1 male graduate student—were winnowed down from a field of almost 100,000 entrants to compete for prizes in five categories: flour, frosting mix, crescent main dish, crescent dessert, and hot-roll mix. They were all brought, or flown, to Los Angeles for the Bake-Off itself, which took place on Monday, and a round of activities that included a tour of Universal Studios, a mini-version of television's *Let's Make a Deal* with Monty Hall himself, and a trip to Disneyland. The event is also attended by some 100 food editors, who turn it from a mere contest into the incredible publicity stunt Pillsbury intends it to be, and spend much of their time talking to each other about sixty-five new ways to use tuna fish and listening to various speakers lecture on the consumer movement and food and the appliance business. General Electric is co-sponsor of the event and donates a stove to each finalist, as well as the stoves for the Bake-Off; this year, it promoted a little Bake-Off of its own for the microwave oven, an appliance we were repeatedly told was the biggest improvement in cooking since the invention of the Willoughby System. Every one of the food editors seemed to know what the Willoughby System was, just as everyone seemed to know what Bundt pans were. "You will all be happy to hear," we were told at one point, "that only one of the finalists this year used a Bundt pan." The food editors burst into laughter at that point; I am not sure why. One Miss Alex Allard of San Antonio, Texas, had already won the microwave contest and $5,000, and she spent most of the Bake-Off turning out one Honey Drizzle Cake after another in the microwave ovens that ringed the Grand Ballroom of the Beverly Hilton Hotel. I never did taste the Honey Drizzle Cake, largely because I suspected—and this was weeks before the *Consumers Union* article on the subject—that microwave ovens were dangerous and probably caused peculiar diseases. If God had wanted us to make bacon in four minutes, He would have made bacon that cooked in four minutes.

3   "The Bake-Off is America," a General Electric executive announced just minutes before it began. "It's family. It's real people doing real things." Yes. The Pillsbury Bake-Off is an America that exists less and less, but exists nonetheless. It is women who still live on farms, who have six and seven children, who enter county fairs and sponsor 4-H Clubs. It is Grace Ferguson of Palm Springs, Florida, who entered the Bake-Off seventeen years in a row before reaching the finals this year, and who cooks at night and prays at the same time. It is Carol Hamilton, who once won a trip on a Greyhound bus to Hollywood for being the most popular girl in Youngstown, Ohio. There was a lot of talk at the Bake-Off about how the Bake-It-Easy theme had attracted a new breed of contestants this year, younger contestants—housewives, yes,

but housewives who used whole-wheat flour and Granola and sour cream and similar supposedly hip ingredients in their recipes and were therefore somewhat more sophisticated, or urban, or something-of-the-sort than your usual Bake-Off contestant. There were a few of these—two, to be exact: Barbara Goldstein of New York City and Bonnie Brooks of Salisbury, Maryland, who actually visited the Los Angeles County Art Museum during a free afternoon. But there was also Suzie Sisson of Palatine, Illinois, twenty-five years old and the only Bundt-pan person in the finals, and her sentiments about life were the same as those that Bake-Off finalists presumably have had for years. "These are the beautiful people," she said, looking around the ballroom as she waited for her Bundt cake to come out of the oven. "They're not the little tiny rich people. They're nice and happy and religious types and family-oriented. Everyone talks about women's lib, which is ridiculous. If you're nice to your husband, he'll be nice to you. Your family is your job. They come first."

4   I was seven years old when the Pillsbury Bake-Off began, and as I grew up reading the advertisements for it in the women's magazines that were lying around the house, it always seemed to me that going to a Bake-Off would be the closest thing to a childhood fantasy of mine, which was to be locked overnight in a bakery. In reality, going to a Bake-Off *is* like being locked overnight in a bakery—a very bad bakery. I almost became sick right there on Range 95 after my sixth carbohydrate-packed sample—which happened, by coincidence, to be a taste of the aforementioned Mrs. Frisbie's aforementioned Sweet 'N Creamy Crescent Crisps.

5   But what is interesting about the Bake-Off—what is even significant about the event—is that it is, for the American housewife, what the Miss America contest used to represent to teen-agers. The pinnacle of a certain kind of achievement. The best in the field. To win the Pillsbury Bake-Off, even to be merely a finalist in it, is to be a great housewife. And a creative housewife. "Cooking is very creative." I must have heard that line thirty times as I interviewed the finalists. I don't happen to think that cooking is very creative—what interests me about it is, on the contrary, its utter mindlessness and mathematical certainty. "Cooking is very relaxing"—that's my bromide. On the other hand, I have to admit that some of the recipes that were concocted for the Bake-Off, amazing combinations of frosting mix and marshmallows and peanut butter and brown sugar and chocolate, were practically awe-inspiring. And cooking, it is quite clear, is only a small part of the apparently frenzied creativity that flourishes in these women's homes. I spent quite a bit of time at the Bake-Off chatting with Laura Aspis of Shaker Heights, Ohio, a seven-time Bake-Off finalist and duplicate-bridge player, and after we had discussed her high-protein macaroons made with coconut-almond frosting mix and Granola, I noticed that Mrs. Aspis was wearing green nail polish. On the theory that no one who wears green nail polish wants it to go unremarked upon, I remarked upon it.

6   "That's not green nail polish," Mrs. Aspis said. "It's platinum nail polish that I mix with green food coloring."

7   "Oh," I said.

8   "And the thing of it is," she went on, "when it chips, it doesn't matter."

9   "Why is that?" I asked.

10   "Because it stains your nails permanently," Mrs. Aspis said.

11   "You mean your nails are permanently green?"

12   "Well, not exactly," said Mrs. Aspis. "You see, last week they were blue, and the week before I made purple, so now my nails are a combination of all three. It looks like I'm in the last throes of something."

13   On Sunday afternoon, most of the finalists chose to spend their free time sitting around the hotel and socializing. Two of them—Marjorie Johnson of Robbinsdale, Minnesota, and Mary Finnegan of Minneota, Minnesota—were seated at a little round table just off the Hilton ballroom talking about a number of things, including Tupperware. Both of them love Tupperware.

14   "When I built my new house," Mrs. Johnson said, "I had so much Tupperware I had to build a cupboard just for it." Mrs. Johnson is a very tiny, fortyish mother of three, and she and her dentist husband have just moved into a fifteen-room house she cannot seem to stop talking about. "We have this first-floor kitchen, harvest gold and blue, and it's almost finished. Now I have a second kitchen on my walk-out level and that's going to be harvest gold and blue, too. Do you know about the new wax Congoleum? I think that's what I put in—either that or Shinyl Vinyl. I haven't had to wash my floors in three months. The house isn't done yet because of the Bake-Off. My husband says if I'd spent as much time on it as I did on the Bake-Off, we'd be finished. I sent in sixteen recipes—it took me nearly a year to do it."

15   "That's nothing," said Mrs. Finnegan. "It took me twenty years before I cracked it. I'm a contest nut. I'm a thirty-times winner in the *Better Homes & Gardens* contest. I won a thousand dollars from Fleischmann's Yeast. I won Jell-O this year, I'm getting a hundred and twenty-five dollars' worth of Revere cookware for that. The Knox Gelatine contest. I've won seven blenders and a quintisserie. It does four things—fries, bakes, roasts, there's a griddle. I sold the darn thing before I even used it."

16   "Don't tell me," said Mrs. Johnson. "Did you enter the Crystal Sugar Name the Lake Home contest?"

17   "Did I enter?" said Mrs. Finnegan. "Wait till you see this." She took a pen and wrote her submission on a napkin and held it up for Mrs. Johnson. The napkin read "Our Entry Hall." "I should have won that one," said Mrs. Finnegan. "I did win the Crystal Sugar Name the Dessert contest. I called it 'Signtation Squares.' I think I got a blender on that one."

18   "Okay," said Mrs. Johnson. "They've got a contest now, Crystal Sugar Name a Sauce. It has pineapple in it."

19   "I don't think I won that," said Mrs. Finnegan, "but I'll show you what I sent in." She held up the napkin and this time what she had written made sense. "Hawaiian More Chant," it said.

20   "Oh, you're clever," said Mrs. Johnson.

21   "They have three more contests so I haven't given up," said Mrs. Finnegan.

22   On Monday morning at exactly 9 a.m., the one hundred finalists marched four abreast into the Hilton ballroom, led by Philip Pillsbury, former chairman of the board of the company. The band played "Nothin' Says Lovin' Like Somethin' from the Oven," and when it finished, Pillsbury announced: "Now you one hundred winners can go to your ranges."

23   Chaos. Shrieking. Frenzy. Furious activity. Cracking eggs. Chopping onions. Melting butter. Mixing, beating, blending. The band perking along with such carefully selected tunes as "If I Knew You Were Coming I'd Have Baked a Cake." Contestants running to the refrigerators for more supplies. Floor assistants rushing dirty dishes off to unseen dishwashers. All two hundred members of the working press, plus television's Bob Barker, interviewing any finalist they could get to drop a spoon. At 9:34 a.m., Mrs. Lorraine Walmann submitted her Cheesy Crescent Twist-Ups to the judges and became the first finalist to finish. At 10 a.m., all the stoves were on, the television lights were blasting, the temperature in the ballroom was up to the mid-nineties, and Mrs. Marjorie Johnson, in the course of giving an interview about her house to the Minneapolis *Star*, had forgotten whether she had put one cup of sugar or two into her Crispy Apple Bake. "You know, we're building this new house," she was saying. "When I go back, I have to buy living-room furniture." By 11 a.m., Mae Wilkinson had burned her skillet corn bread and was at work on a second. Laura Aspis had lost her potholder. Barbara Bellhorn was distraught because she was not used to California apples. Alex Allard was turning out yet another Honey Drizzle Cake. Dough and flour were all over the floor. Mary Finnegan was fussing because the crumbs on her Lemon Cream Bars were too coarse. Marjorie Johnson was in the midst of yet another interview on her house. "Well, let me tell you," she was saying, "the shelves in the kitchen are built low. . . ." One by one, the contestants, who were each given seven hours and four tries to produce two perfect samples of their recipes, began to finish up and deliver one tray to the judges and one tray to the photographer. There were samples everywhere, try this, try that, but after six tries, climaxed by Mrs. Frisbie's creation, I stopped sampling. The overkill was unbearable: none of the recipes seemed to contain one cup of sugar when two would do, or a delicate cheese when Kraft American would do, or an actual minced onion when instant minced onions would do. It was snack time. It was convenience-food time. It was less-work-for-Mother time. All I could think about was a steak.

24   By 3 p.m., there were only two contestants left—Mrs. Johnson, whose dessert took only five minutes to make but whose interviews took considerably longer, and Bonnie Brooks, whose third sour-cream-and-banana cake was still in the oven. Mrs. Brooks brought her cake in last, at 3:27 p.m., and as she did, the packing began. The skillets went into brown cartons, the measuring spoons into barrels, the stoves were dismantled. The Bake-Off itself was over—and all that remained was the trip to Disneyland, and the breakfast at the Brown Derby . . . and the prizes.

25   And so it is Tuesday morning, and the judges have reached a decision, and any second now, Bob Barker is going to announce the five winners over

national television. All the contestants are wearing their best dresses and smiling, trying to smile anyway, good sports all, and now Bob Barker is announcing the winners. Bonnie Brooks and her cake and Albina Flieller and her Quick Pecan Pie win $25,000 each. Sharon Schubert and two others win $5,000. And suddenly the show is over and it is time to go home, and the ninety-five people who did not win the twenty-fourth annual Pillsbury Bake-Off are plucking the orchids from the centerpieces, signing each other's programs, and grumbling. They are grumbling about Sharon Schubert. And for a moment, as I hear the grumbling everywhere—"It really isn't fair." . . . "After all, she won the trip to Mexico"—I think that perhaps I am wrong about these women: perhaps they are capable of anger after all, or jealousy, or competitiveness, or something I think of as a human trait I can relate to. But the grumbling stops after a few minutes, and I find myself listening to Marjorie Johnson. "I'm so glad I didn't win the grand prize," she is saying, "because if you win that, you don't get to come back to the next Bake-Off. I'm gonna start now on my recipes for next year. I'm gonna think of something really good." She stopped for a moment. "You know," she said, "it's going to be very difficult to get back to normal living."

Exercises

COMPREHENSION

Organization and Development

Complete the following outline. Find the thesis statement and write it in the space provided. Then find the main divisions in the essay and fill in the remaining spaces. Note the paragraphs for each section.

Thesis statement: _____

_____

_____ [   ]

  I.   _____ [   ]

  II. _____ [   ]

 III. _____ [   ]

 IV. _____ [   ]

  V.   _____ [   ]

Content

Choose the answer that correctly completes each statement.

1. The author feels that the annual Pillsbury Bake-Off is a (a) means for housewives to get together and exchange recipes (b) hyped-up publicity stunt to publicize Pillsbury products (c) waste of time, money, and energy for everyone concerned.

2. Throughout the essay, Ephron's tone can be described as (a) hostile and derogatory (b) bitterly scornful (c) mildly sarcastic and cynical.
3. General Electric co-sponsors the Bake-Off because it (a) likes to organize tours and lectures for the food editors who also attend (b) believes in the values the contest represents (c) can promote its microwave ovens there.
4. Pillsbury apparently renames some of the contestants' winning recipes to (a) reflect more accurately the contest's five categories (b) make them sound cuter and flashier (c) make them describe more accurately what the entry really is.
5. For Ephron, that year's "Bake-It-Easy" theme produced a(n) (a) array of overly sweet, carbohydrate-filled convenience snacks (b) childhood dream come true about being locked in a bakery overnight (c) series of easily-prepared convenience dinners for the overworked modern housewife.
6. Ephron's emphasis on Mrs. Johnson, the contestant with the new house, and Mrs. Finnegan, the contest nut, reveals their (a) obsession with competition and winning (b) shallowness and foolish concern with nonessential things (c) resemblance to the other 98 contestants.
7. The dominant impression conveyed by Ephron's description of the actual baking part of the contest is (a) regimentation (b) frivolity (c) confusion.
8. Despite their statements to the contrary, many of the contestants turned out to be (a) poor losers (b) bad cooks (c) discouraged about entering the contest another time.

Paragraph Structure

Reorder the following sentences to form a unified, coherent paragraph. Then check your version with the original.

1. All the contestants are wearing their best dresses and smiling, trying to smile anyway, good sports all, and now Bob Barker is announcing the winners.
2. Sharon Schubert and two others win $5,000.
3. And so it is Tuesday morning, and the judges have reached a decision, and any second now, Bob Barker is going to announce the five winners over national television.
4. They are grumbling about Sharon Schubert.
5. Bonnie Brooks and her cake and Albina Flieller and her Quick Pecan Pie win $25,000 each.
6. And suddenly the show is over and it is time to go home, and the ninety-five people who did not win the twenty-fourth annual Pillsbury Bake-Off are plucking the orchids from the centerpieces, signing each other's programs, and grumbling.

VOCABULARY AND USAGE

Word Formation Table

Complete the following table by changing word endings or root forms to make new grammatical forms. Use your dictionary if necessary.

	NOUN	VERB	ADJECTIVE	ADVERB
1.	_____	_____	_____	presumably
2.	restraint	_____	_____	_____
3.	fantasy	_____	_____	_____
4.	chaos	xxx	_____	_____
5.	coincidence	_____	_____	_____

Fill-Ins

Complete each of the sentences below using the words on the following list. You may need to use some words more than once. You may also find that some blanks can be completed correctly with more than one word. Add plural endings to nouns and change verb forms where necessary.

in addition	trait	frenzy	opinion
compete	chaos	quality	on the contrary
significant	represent	concoction	characteristic
awe-inspiring	largely	amazing	vie
sentiment	presumably	ingredients	mostly

1. One hundred contestants came to Los Angeles to _____ for money _____ to a free stove in the Pillsbury Bake-Off, in an atmosphere of complete _____.

2. What Ephron finds interesting and _____ about the contest is that it _____ the pinnacle of success to a certain group of American housewives, _____ those women who have strong _____ against women's liberation.

3. Apparently, the dominant _____ of the food produced by the contestants was excessive sweetness; _____, she noted that the recipes were _____ for snack or convenience foods.

4. Ephron found the _____ some contestants made _____, because they had managed to combine _____ sweet _____ in unusual ways.

5. One finalist who praised the virtues and good _____ of the other contestants _____ reflected the _____ of most women who enter the annual Bake-Off.

6. Many contestants claimed that winning meant nothing; Ephron notes that, _____, many contestants revealed their true _____ by complaining about one contestant who won again after _____ in a previous year's contest.

DISCUSSION

1. Why does Ephron deliberately "get ahead of the story" in paragraph 1? What are the effect and purpose of the many details she summons up? What is the connotation, for example, of "snicky snacky"?

2. In paragraph 2, Ephron notes that the annual Pillsbury Bake-Off is an "incredible publicity stunt." Why do you think a contest such as this would be good publicity for Pillsbury? What intangible qualities does the contest represent?

3. What is the difference between this spectacle and the traditional county fair, in which housewives compete for prizes in several categories such as jams, pies, and pickles? What do you think Ephron's opinion would be about old-fashioned county fairs?

4. From her characterization of some of the contestants (see in particular paragraphs 3, 6–12, and 13–21), what do you think Ephron's attitude is toward these women? Where does she reveal explicitly her feelings for the majority of contestants?

5. Three of the contestants were male: two twelve-year-old boys and one graduate student. Why didn't she interview them?

6. What order of development does Ephron use in the last portion of the essay, from paragraph 22 to the end?

7. Ephron mentions Mrs. Johnson and her new house in paragraphs 14, 23 (twice), 24, and 25. Why so many times?

8. In the last paragraph, Mrs. Johnson unwittingly reveals two motivations for entering the Bake-Off. What are they? What needs or deficiencies—perhaps unconscious ones—does this contest satisfy? What satisfactions might it provide?

SUGGESTIONS FOR WRITING

1. Describe a place (or event or institution) you are familiar with that you believe is a "hype"—that is, a place that promotes idealistic or virtuous qualities but whose actual function is money-making or self-promotion. Some examples might be leadership classes, rock concerts, beauty contests, baby contests, or Little League.

2. Write an essay in which you offer a rebuttal to Ephron's rather wicked portrayal of the Pillsbury Bake-Off.

8. Cite and discuss illustrations of some of the devices Ephron uses in "Baking Off"—in particular, those that convey its satiric effect.

You Deserve a Break Today

ADAM SMITH

Adam Smith is the pseudonym of George J. W. Goodman. His career has been primarily in finance and investments, first as a vice president of a mutual fund, then as editor of *Institutional Investor* magazine, and currently as vice president of *New York Magazine.* His two best-known books are *The Money Game,* a witty look at the stock market and its devotees, and *Powers of Mind,* an exploration of contemporary "pop" psychology, from which this piece is taken. In it Smith describes with his characteristically wry sense of humor the phenomenon of TM.

1   Transcendental Meditation is the McDonald's of the meditation business. Or maybe the Howard Johnson's. Whatever suggests: a relatively low fixed price, a standard item, and increasing numbers of franchises, or outlets. Like McDonald's, TM suggests, "You deserve a break today," in fact, you deserve two, twenty minutes in the morning and twenty minutes in the evening. TM has processed somewhere between 400,000 and 500,000 Americans, most of them in the last four or five years, and that gives it respectable size among service organizations.

2   In one sense, TM is a pioneer. Indians have been bringing the vedanta, or Hindu scriptures, here for almost a hundred years, but TM made a meditation technique work with an audience that didn't want to hear any Hindi. And for de-Hindizing the technique, TM deserves its success, which has been spectacular. It took the strangeness—and the threat—from the second definition of meditation, and once the threat was gone, even the Rotary Club and the Illinois State Legislature took to it.

3   Transcendental Meditation comes from a gentleman called Maharishi Mahesh Yogi—born Mahesh Prasad Varma in 1918 in the Central Provinces, father forest ranger, degree in physics from Allahabad University in 1942, says the official biography. (Maharishi, or Maharaj Ji, appears as a title before a number of figures from the East, since it means Sage, or Wise One, and if you mix among the followers of several of them it can get confusing. There is Maharishi the TM leader, and Maharaj Ji the sixteen-year-old guru, and Maharishi the late guru of Baba Ram Dass. I once had file folders organized by my favorite technique among all the Maharishis, e.g., Maharishi—Sound, Maharishi—Light, Maharishi—Reads Minds.) Maharishi was on his way to

become, like the members of his caste, a merchant or a clerk, and to have a marriage arranged for him when he met one of the major religious leaders of India: Swami Brahmanada Saraswati, the Jadgadguru Bhagwan Shankaracharya, and he became a disciple and spent thirteen and a half years with him. His assignment, given when it became time for the master to leave his body, was to find a simple form of meditation for everyone to practice. Maharishi spent two years in a cave in the Himalayas and emerged with TM. (Two years in a cave, for a religious Indian, is like two years at the Harvard Business School for a commercial banker.)

4   Maharishi seems to have started his efforts quite innocently, without any great world plan, talking to Indian businessmen. His instincts steered him in the direction of acceleration; things moved faster in the West, so by 1960 he was setting up the International Meditation Society in London. Being pragmatic in nature, he was not afraid to use radio, television and public relations—an approach that, needless to say, did not go down well with the gurus left in India. By the late 1960's he had, as followers, the Beatles and Mia Farrow; John Lennon, a former Beatle, once spent eight hours a day meditating with the Maharishi in the Himalayas. The bearded, giggly presence of the Maharishi became familiar on the talk shows: there was Maharishi on Johnny Carson.

5   And that crested and passed. John Lennon said that the gurus of India were like rock stars in the West, if you couldn't be Mick Jagger you could be a maharishi. The Maharishi went on a nationwide tour with the Beach Boys, another rock group, and nobody came. The tour had to be canceled, and it looked like TM was another one of those Sixties Things, fading with the natural rhythms of time. Within a couple of years, the Maharishi was to say he had failed in his mission, and yet even as he spoke another wave was beginning to curl.

6   Before we complete that story, it might be useful to see what this is all about. When I signed up for TM, I had already been through a year of other trips that involved meditations, and my attitude was more that of an engineer taking apart somebody else's widget—well, let's see how *they* do it. Unlike most of my TM classmates, I did not have a friend who had just done it, and also unlike my TM classmates, I had been through much of the literature of meditation.

7   I happened to do this at a university, so our first lecture was in a university building. On the table in our room were glossy reprints of articles telling us how TM would fix us up, color charts in them of stress relief. Not only was there TM's own literature, but also reprints from *Scientific American* and *The Wall Street Journal*. Our instructor was a clean-cut junior called Buzz, who wore a sport jacket and loafers, and who smiled a lot. The audience was naturally mostly students, but with a sprinkling of older people, for the TM lectures were advertised—mostly in diners and on tree trunks, it seemed to me—over a wide area.

8   "Anybody can do this," Buzz said, "no matter how old or how smart. As we meditate we become clearer, you can do more, students get better grades,

the mind doesn't wander. TM rest is deeper than sleep. It gets rid of really deep stresses. It helps your relationship with other people. You will get along better with your roommates."

9   What we would do, if we wanted to sign up, was to come to two lectures, and then be initiated on the weekend, and then one more lecture and one more weekend—that's all there was.

10   "Previously, we had three states of consciousness," Buzz said. "Waking, sleeping and dreaming. This is the fourth state, cosmic and all-inclusive. The mind is evolutionary, a blessing of the Creator, approaching the Infinite One"—Buzz giggled a bit, and the audience got restless—"but there's nothing to believe in TM. You don't have to believe in anything. And nothing to give up."

11   "Is this the same as yoga?" somebody wanted to know.

12   "No, all you do in TM is sit still," Buzz said. "Yoga will give you a charley horse. Zen monks meditate for twenty-five years to get the same result TM will give you in two weeks. It's different from concentration, and from contemplation."

13   TM, said Buzz, used a sound. Different sounds match different people— you and your roommate might not like the same music. A sound in the Vedic tradition is a mantram. Each of us would get his own mantram. Were all the mantrams really individual? They were, though there were far more people than mantrams, since 20,000 people a month were signing up for TM. How do the instructors match the mantram to the individual? I wanted to know. Buzz said you went to a teacher training course—ten or twelve weeks—and learned how to do this, but it was privileged information how it was done. We would fill out a questionnaire, have an interview, and get our mantram.

14   "Never," Buzz said, "tell anybody your mantram. That will ruin the whole effect." How come? "We have found that through experience. Your mantram is secret. Every once in a while somebody goes through TM, and then a friend gets interested, and they tell the friend the mantram, just to save the initiation fee. It doesn't work. There was a guy in Rhode Island who used somebody else's mantram and he got edgy and irritable and lost energy. It's worth the fee." The fee was $45 for students and $75 for adults. The fee for adults is now up to $125.

15   All kinds of medical tests had showed that TM relieved stress, Buzz said. The body was carrying stress, the imprint of the daily activities, but sleep didn't relieve all the stress. Every mental condition has a corresponding physical one: the release of stress—Buzz drew bubbles rising on the blackboard—is an activity, maybe a chemical change, and that activity creates a mental activity, a thought.

16   If we got so relaxed, how would we ever get around to do anything?

17   The mind is spontaneously capable, said Buzz. When anxiety is down, capabilities develop. It doesn't lead to inertia. Just twenty minutes, twice a day, would leave us refreshed.

18   If meditation was so good, why only twenty minutes?

19   So you can adjust to the change, Buzz said. You have to have a balance of meditation and activity.

20   We filled out questionnaires, rather brief questionnaires, age, occupation, and so on. The only unusual question was: had we used any drugs?

21   We made appointments for Saturday.

22   "Bring six to twelve fresh flowers, two to three sweet fresh whole fruit, and a clean white handkerchief. And the fee for the course," Buzz said. "Don't eat a lot. And we ask that you not use any recreational chemicals while you are learning TM. Give it a chance to work. We find that many people cut down on their recreational chemicals after learning meditation."

23   Hands went up in the audience. What kind of fruit? What kind of flowers? They wanted to be told exactly. *All* recreational chemicals?

24   On Saturday I reported with one apple, one orange, one white handkerchief, and a bouquet from the florist. We were in the basement of a university building. No English 212 today. One at a time, we went into the initiation room (English 212). Candles, incense, bowls of fruit, lots of flowers, very pretty.

25   It was so dark in the room I could barely see the pictures scotch-taped on the wall: Maharishi, I supposed, and Guru Dev, his teacher. The offerings, said Buzz, were symbolic, flower of life, fruit the seed of life, and the handkerchief, the cleansing of the spirit. We were both in our socks. Buzz went through a ten-minute ceremony, all by himself and all in Sanskrit, with rice, salt and sandalwood.

26   "What was that?" I said when he stopped.

27   "That's the ceremony, initiation," Buzz said. "Some of it is the names of the masters who preserved the technique. We're grateful to the Vedic tradition for having preserved it, it's as applicable today as thousands of years ago. Okay, I'm going to give you your mantram. The mantram is meaningless, a sound whose effect is known. Your mantram is *Shiam*."

28   "*Shiam?*" I said. "*Shiam? You sure Shiam* is mine?"

29   Buzz looked stunned. What's the matter with Shiam? And I was thinking: You sure it's Shiam and not Shiom? And I had been looking for some basic Sanskrit sound, Hum or Aum or Hrim or Bam, I didn't exactly remember Shiam. And I was also remembering an unpublished article on the "rise times" of sounds in physiological psychology, how mantra were always soft and mellifluous, never any k's, nothing sharp, lots of soft mmm's and o's, see, Campbell's Soup is secretly conditioning you, they have you going mmm-mmm good.

30   "Shiam," Buzz said. "Let's say it." We said it. "Okay, just keep it going, to yourself, and if thoughts come let them come, and don't try." We closed our eyes. I could see the letters: SHIAM. Then I thought, I bet these guys screwed up my mantram, that one doesn't sound quite right, there's no quality these days, car mechanics fake repairs; plumbers, no craftsmen left; but at the same time I knew just as many mantrams as Buzz, so I thought, well, what the hell, they all work, and I kept it going. It was very quiet. Toward the end

of the twenty-minute period I peeked a couple of times. Buzz had his eyes shut and was breathing evenly. I tried it a couple of different speeds. S h i a m, slow, and Shiam Shiam Shiam, fast. It doesn't have to stay consistent. "Very slowly, open your eyes," Buzz said. "Take a couple of minutes to come out." Was it easy? Yes. Was it pleasant? Yes. Did the mantram change, get faster or slower or disappear? Yes. Did thoughts come? Yes. "Good," said Buzz.

31   Some people have reported dizziness and nausea and all sorts of wild things. I guess all that is possible, magnetism without imagination is nothing, imagination without magnetism can produce convulsions, as they told Louis XVI, but it's not my experience.

32   Buzz said I could have my handkerchief and flowers and fruit back. I took the handkerchief, I ate the apple, and I left the orange and the flowers.

Profiles

The profile is a specialized report that can best be defined as a sort of verbal silhouette—a portrait in words which, like the curious black on white paper designs so popular with our grandparents, offers to the reader a full outline of the subject, but no real depth of information. A profile is not and does not pretend to be a complete biographical study, but is rather a sketch of a particular person at a particular time and in a particular place. Though all three of the authors in this section appear to have studied their subjects with care, and while in the Coles and Willwerth essays we can even see the evidence of rather lengthy observation, these profiles show only highpoints of interest and identity and do not presume to offer full, three-dimensional pictures.

The profile is, in fact, fundamentally a journalistic technique (*The New Yorker* magazine runs a regular feature called "Profiles"), and the examples here reveal this origin. All the subjects have been skillfully questioned, all are permitted to speak for themselves, and all three reports reveal the careful and selective use of quotation and illustrative detail that marks such writing, designed as it is for quick, pleasant, often fairly casual reading.

The techniques of profile writing can be applied not only to persons, but to groups, places, or even institutions. (The essays by Campa, Sevareid, and Michener, for example, are in some senses profiles.) The profile can be useful in fields other than journalism as well. Coles, for instance, is a psychiatrist with a strong interest in social psychology, and his observation of the Allen family, in conjunction with other techniques, serves as the base for broader inferences and generalizations about other similar families and other socioeconomic problems. In this sense, the profile can be viewed as a specialized kind of example or illustration, one which has its own intrinsic interest, but which also illustrates or represents other individuals, other propositions. What, for example, can be inferred about petty criminals, ghetto life, and poverty from the overview of Jones? How are Ward Quaal and the Allens representative of American attitudes about work, family, and home?

The basic "outlining" technique of profile writing can also be put to use in business (consider the profile of the type of employee a particular firm is searching for); community affairs (the town council wants a profile of the community's future recreational needs); or even psychology and criminology (the homicide bureau presents a profile of the typical domestic murder). In fact, the profile is of value in any situation where the broad outlines and features of a subject—or some aspect of it—need to be described simply, clearly, and briefly.

"We Do the Best We Can"—Profile of an Appalachian Family

ROBERT COLES

Robert Coles is a child psychiatrist at Harvard University. During the 1960s he began to do extensive research on the problems of hunger and malnutrition, the plight of migrant workers, and the effects of school integration on children in the South. From these investigations came the five-volume series, *Children of Crisis*. Volume II, *Migrants, Sharecroppers, and Mountaineers*, and Volume III, *The South Goes North*, won Pulitzer prizes. The following profile of the Allens of Swain County, North Carolina, is from Volume II.

1   They live up alongside the hills, in hollow after hollow. They live in eastern Kentucky and eastern Tennessee and in the western part of North Carolina and the western part of Virginia and in just about the whole state of West Virginia. They live close to the land; they farm it and some of them go down into it to extract its coal. Their ancestors, a century or two ago, fought their way westward from the Atlantic seaboard, came up on the mountains, penetrated the valleys, and moved stubbornly up the creeks for room, for privacy, for a view, for a domain of sorts. They are Appalachian people, mountain people, hill people. They are white yeomen, or miners, or hollow folk, or subsistence farmers. They are part of something called "the rural poor"; they are sometimes called "hillbillies." They are people who live in a "depressed area"; and they have been called part of a "subculture." They have also been called "backward," and more inscrutably, "privatistic." They are known as balladeers and they are thought to have a tradition of music and poems and stories that is "pure"—right from old England and old Scotland and early if not old America.

2   As for the minds of those mountaineers, the rest of us outside their region are not supposed to have any way of really getting around certain traits that (so it is claimed) make the inhabitants of the hollows hard to reach psychologically, even as their territory and their cabins can be virtually unapproachable. Up in the hollows, the story goes, one finds sullen, fearful, withdrawn men and women who distrust outsiders, shun much of the twentieth century, cling to old and anomalous customs, take to liquor rather

freely, and in general show themselves to be survivors of a rural, pioneer America for the most part long since gone. Up in the hollows, one is also told, the worst poverty in the nation exists, with hundreds of thousands of people condemned to a life of idleness, meager employment, long, snowbound winters and summers that can be of limited help to a man who has only an acre or two for planting on the side of a steep, rocky hill. Finally, up in the hollows history's cruel lessons are supposed to be unmistakably apparent: an ignored and exploited people have become a tired people, a worn-out people, a frivolous or unresponsive people, the best of whom, the ones with any life at all in them, continue to leave, thereby making an already dismal situation an almost impossible one.

3   No one, least of all the people in or near the hollows themselves, would want to deny all of that. Appalachia is indeed cut off in some respects from the rest of us; and the region's people are indeed quiet and reserved and often enough full of misgivings about "city people" and "outsiders," and the declarations of concern and the offers of help that have lately come from "them," whom one mountaineer I have known since 1964 goes on to describe as follows: "They're full of sugar when they come, and they say they want to do something for you; but I can't stand the sight of them, not one of them, because they're two-faced and wanting to treat you like you are dumb, a fool, and someone that needs to be told everything he should do and can't figure anything out for himself."

4   Yet, that same, man, who lives way up one of those hollows (in Swain County, North Carolina) has other things to say about visitors and tourists, and by implication, other things to say about himself and his own kind of people: "A lot of cars come riding through here, you know. Everyone wants to look at the hills, and the bigger the waterfall you have to show, the better. They'll stop their driving and ask you directions to things, if you're down there on the main road, and I always try to help. You see, we're not against those people. It's beautiful here, right beautiful. You couldn't make it better if you could sit down and try to start all over and do anything you want. If they come here from clear across the country and tell you how they love what they've seen and they want to see more, I'm ready to help them, and I always act as polite as I can, and so do they, for the most part. The ones I don't like one bit are different. They don't want to look and enjoy your land, like you do yourself; no sir, they want to come and sit down and tell you how sorry you are, real sorry, and if something isn't done soon, you're going to 'die out,' that's what one of them said. I wasn't there, but I heard he came from Asheville, or from some big city, maybe not in North Carolina; and he was supposed to get us meeting together, and if we did there'd be some money in it for us, and he kept saying we're in bad shape, they tell me he did, and worst of all are the kids, he said, and didn't we know that.

5   "I didn't hear him or his exact words, of course, but it's not the first time it's happened like that, because a year ago I heard someone talk the very same. He came to the church and we all listened. He said we should have a program here, and the kids should go to it before they start school. He said the

government would pay for it, from Washington. He said they'd be teaching the kids a lot, and checking up on their health, and it would be the best thing in the world. Well, I didn't see anything wrong with the idea. It seemed like a good idea to me. But I didn't like the way he kept repeating how bad off our kids are, and how they need one thing and another thing. Finally I was about ready to tell him to go home, mister, and leave us alone, because our kids are way better than you'll ever know, and we don't need you and your kind around here with nothing good to say, and all the bad names we're getting called. I didn't say a word, though. No, I sat through to the end, and I went home. I was too shy to talk at the meeting, and so were a lot of the others. Our minister was there, and he kept on telling us to give the man a break, because he'd come to help us. Now, I'm the first to admit we could stand some help around here, but I'm not going to have someone just coming around here and looking down on us, that's all, just plain looking down on us—and our kids, that's the worst of it, when they look down on your own kids.

6   "My kids, they're good; each of them is. They're good kids, and they don't make for trouble, and you couldn't ask for them any better. If he had asked me, the man out of the East, Washington or someplace, I would have told him that, too. We all would have. But he didn't want to ask us anything. All he wanted was to tell us he had this idea and this money, and we should go ahead and get our little kids together and they would go to the church during the summer and get their first learning, and they would be needing it, because they're bad off, that's what he must have said a hundred times, how bad off our kids are, and how the President of the United States wants for them to get their teeth fixed and to see a doctor and to learn as much as they can. You know what my wife whispered to me? She said, he doesn't know what our kids have learned, and still he's telling us they haven't learned a thing and they won't. And who does he think he is anyway? I told her it's best to sit him out and we could laugh out loud later when we left the church."

7   Later, when they left the church, they went home to their children, who were rather curious about the reason their parents had seen fit to go out to a meeting after supper in the middle of the week. There are five of those children and they range from four months to nine years. All the children were born in Swain County, North Carolina, as were their parents and grandparents and great-grandparents going back a century and more. Nor does Mrs. Allen want her children to be born anyplace else, or for that matter, under any other circumstances: "This is good country, as anybody will likely admit once he's seen it, and there's no reason to leave that I can see. You ask about the children I've borne; well, they're all good children, I believe they are. I've lost two, one from pneumonia we thought, and one had trouble from the moment he was alive. He was the only child that ever saw a doctor. We brought him down to Bryson City and there was a doctor there, waiting to see him. The Reverend Mason had called over, and he went with us.

8   "The doctor looked over the child real good, and I kept on fearing the news was going to be bad, the longer he looked and the more tests he did. Then he

said he'd need extra tests, even beyond what he did, and we would have to come back. Of course I told him we'd try, but it's real hard on us to get a ride, and there's the other children I have, and my mother's gone, so they have to be left with one another the whole day, and there's a baby that needs me for feeding. The doctor said he could understand, but he needed those tests, and he was going to have to call some other doctor way over in Asheville or someplace and ask him some things. Mr. Mason said he'd drive us again, and we'd better do what the doctor said. Mr. Mason asked the doctor if there was much hope, even if we did everything and kept on coming back, so long as we had to, and the doctor shook his head, but he didn't say anything, one way or the other. But then my husband, Mr. Allen, he decided we'd better ask right there and then what was happening, and he did. He told the doctor that we're not much used to going to see doctors, and we'd like to know where we stand—it's just as plain and simple as that. The doctor asked if he could talk to Mr. Mason alone, and we said yes, that would be fine by us, but please couldn't they decide between themselves and then come and tell us something before we go back. And they did. They didn't talk too long before they came out, and said they would be honest with us, like we wanted, and the problem was with little Edward's muscles, and they weren't good from the start, and chances are they'd never be much good, and if we come back for the tests we might find out the exact disease, but he was pretty sure, even right then the doctor was, that Edward had a lot of bad trouble, and there wasn't much that could be done for him, and we might as well know it, that he'd not live to be grown up, and maybe not more than a year was the best we could hope for.

9   "I was real upset, but I was relieved to be told; I was thankful as can be for that. I guess Jim and I just nodded our heads and since we didn't say a word, and it was getting along, the time, the doctor came over and he asked if we had any questions to ask of him. I looked at Jim and he looked at me, and we didn't think of anything, and then Mr. Mason said it was all right, because if we did think of something later, we could always tell him and he could tell the doctor. The doctor said yes, and he said we were good people, and he liked us for being quiet and he wished he could do more. Jim said thank you, and we were glad he tried to help, and to be truthful we knew that there was something real bad wrong, and to us, if there isn't anything we can do, then chances are there isn't anything that anyone can do, even including a doctor, if he didn't mind us saying so. Mr. Mason said he wasn't sure we were in the right, and I said we could be wrong, and maybe they could have saved little Anne from her fever that burned her up—it was the pneumonia, we were sure. The doctor said there wasn't much use going back to what was over and done with, and I agreed. When we left, Mr. Mason said we could take the child back to the doctor anytime and he would drive us, and the doctor told the reverend he wouldn't charge us, not a penny. But Edward died a few weeks later. He couldn't breathe very good, like the doctor explained to us, because of his muscles, and the strain got to be more than he could take, so he stopped breathing, the little fellow did, right there in my arms. He could

have lived longer, they said, if we'd have let them take him and put him in a hospital, you know, and they have motors and machines, to work on you. But I don't believe the Lord meant for Edward to go like that, in a hospital. I don't."

10   Her words read sadder than they sounded. She is tall, thin, but a forceful and composed woman, not given to self-pity. She has delicate bones, narrow wrists, thin ankles, decidedly pale blue eyes, and a bit surprisingly, a very strong, almost aquiline nose. She was thirty and, I thought, both young and old. Her brown hair was heavily streaked with gray, and her skin was more wrinkled than is the case with many women who are forty or even fifty, let alone thirty. Most noticeable were her teeth; the ones left were in extremely bad repair, and many had long since fallen out—something that she is quite willing to talk about, once her guest has lost *his* embarrassment and asked her a question, like whether she had ever seen a dentist about her teeth. No, she had never done anything like that. What could a dentist do, but take out one's teeth; and eventually they fall out if they are really no good. Well, of course, there *are* things a dentist can do—and she quickly says she knows there must be, though she still isn't quite sure what they are, "those things." For a second her tact dominates the room, which is one of two the cabin possesses. Then she demonstrates her sense of humor, her openness, her surprising and almost awesome mixture of modesty and pride: "If you want to keep your teeth, you shouldn't have children. I know that from my life. I started losing my teeth when I started bringing children into the world. They take your strength, your babies do, while you're carrying them, and that's as it should be, except if I had more strength left for myself after the baby comes, I might be more patient with them. If you're tired you get sharp all the time with your children.

11   "The worst tooth to lose is your first one, after that you get used to having them go, one by one. We don't have a mirror here, except a very small one and it's cracked. My mother gave it to me. When I pick it up to catch a look at myself I always fix it so that I don't see my teeth. I have them in front of the crack instead of the glass. I'd like to have the teeth back, because I know I'd look better, but you can't keep yourself looking good after you start a family, not if you've got to be on the move from the first second you get up until right before you go to sleep. When I lie down on the bed, it's to fall asleep. I never remember thinking about anything. I'm too tired. So is Jim; he's always out there working on something; and so are the kids, they're real full of spirits. No wonder I lost so many teeth. When you have kids that are as rowdy and noisy as mine, they must need everything a mother's got even before they're born. Of course, even now Jim and I will sacrifice on their account, though they'll never know it.

12   "I always serve myself last, you know. I serve Jim first, and he's entitled to take everything we have, if he wants to, because he's the father, and it's his work that has brought us what we have, all of it. But Jim will stop himself, and say he's not so hungry, and nod toward the kids, and that means to give them the seconds before him. We don't always have seconds, of course, but

we do the best we can. I make corn bread every day, and that's filling. There's nothing I hate more than a child crying at you and crying at you for food, and you standing there and knowing you can't give them much of anything, for all their tears. It's unnatural. That's what I say; it's just unnatural for a mother to be standing in her own house, and her children near her, and they're hungry and there isn't the food to feed them. It's just not right. It happens, though—and I'll tell you, now that you asked, my girl Sara, she's a few times told me that if we all somehow could eat more, then she wouldn't be having trouble like me with her teeth, later on. That's what the teacher told them, over there in the school.

13   "Well, I told Sara the only thing I could tell her. I told her that we do the best we can, and that's all anyone put here on this earth can ever do. I told her that her father has worked his entire life, since he was a boy, and so have I, and we're hoping for our kids that they may have it a lot better than us. But this isn't the place to be, not in Swain County here, up in this hollow, if you want to sit back and say I'd like this and I'd like that, and you'd better have this and something else, because the teacher says you should. I told Sara there's that one teacher, and maybe a couple more, and they get their salaries every week, and do you know who the teacher's uncle is—he's the sheriff over there in Needmore. Now, if Sara's daddy made half that teacher's salary in cash every week, he'd be a rich man, and I'd be able to do plenty about more food. But Sara's daddy doesn't get a salary from no one, no one, you hear! That's what I said to her, word for word it was. And she sat up and took notice of me, I'll tell you. I made sure she did. I looked her right in the eyes, and I never stopped looking until I was through with what I had to say. Then she said, 'Yes, ma'am,' and I said that I didn't want any grudges between us, and let's go right back to being friends, like before, but I wanted her to know what the truth was, to the best of my knowledge, and nothing more. She said she knew, and that was all that was said between us."

14   In point of fact Mrs. Allen is usually rather silent with her children. She almost uncannily signals them with a look on her face, a motion of her hand, a gesture or turn of her body. She doesn't seem to have to talk, the way so many mothers elsewhere do, particularly in our suburbs. It is not that she is grim or glum or morose or withdrawn or stern or ungiving or austere; it is that she doesn't need words to give and acknowledge the receipt of messages. The messages are constantly being sent, but the children, rather like their mother, do things in a restrained, hushed manner—with smiles or frowns, or if necessary, laughs and groans doing the service of words. Yet, there are times when that cabin on the side of a mountain will become a place where songs are sung and eloquent words are spoken. Once, after a series of winter storms had worn them all down, Mr. Allen spoke to his wife and children, at first tentatively and apologetically and then firmly: "It's been a tough winter, this one, but they all are until they're over, and then you kind of miss them. You don't get a thing free in this world, that's what was handed down to me by my father. He said if I knew that, I knew all I'd ever have to know. I heard some of you kids the other day wondering if we couldn't go and live some-

place else, where maybe there wouldn't be so much snow and ice, and us shivering even under every blanket your mother made and her mother and my mother, and that's a lot of blankets we're lucky to have. I'm sure there's better land than this, better counties to live in. You could probably find a house way off far from here, where they never get any snow, not once in the winter, and where there's more money around for everyone. Don't ask me where, or how you'll get there. I don't know.

15   "I was out of here, this county, only once, and it was the longest three years of my life. They took me over to Asheville, and then to Atlanta, Georgia, and then to Fort Benning, and then to Korea. Now, that was the worst time I ever had, and when I came back, I'll tell you what I did. I swore on my Bible to my mother and my father, in front of both of them, that never again would I leave this county, and maybe not even this hollow. My daddy said I shouldn't be so positive, because you never can tell what might happen—like another war—and I said they'd have to come up here and drag me off, and I'd have my gun out, and I couldn't truthfully say right now if I'd use it on them or not, but I believe the word would get down to them that they'd better think it over very carefully, if they decide to come another time and take me and others who've given them three years already. Why do they always want us to go and fight those wars? It wasn't only the fighting, though. It was leaving here; and once you're over there, you never see this hollow for months and months and then you sure do know what you're missing. Oh, do you!

16   "When you ask me to say it, what we have here that you can't find anyplace else, I can't find the words. When I'd be in Georgia and over in Korea my buddies would always be asking me why I was more homesick than everyone in the whole Army put together. I couldn't really answer them, but I tried. I told them we have the best people in the world here, and they'd claim everyone says that about his hometown folks. Then I'd tell them we take care of each other, and we've been here from as far back almost as the country, and we know every inch of the hollow, and it's the greatest place in the world, with the hills and the streams and the fish you can get. And anyone who cared to come and visit us would see what I mean, because we'd be friendly and they'd eat until they're full, even if we had to go hungry, and they'd never stop looking around, and especially up to the hills over there, and soon they'd take to wishing they could have been borned here, too."

17   Mr. Allen never stops saying such things. That is, every week or so, sometimes every day or so, he rises to the occasion—when his visitor is still recognized as just that, a visitor. A year or more later Mr. Allen still will talk affectionately of the hollow he loves, the county he loves, the region whose hills must be, so he once told me, "the most beautiful things God ever made"; still, he has his rough times, and if he bears them most of the time in silence and even pretended joy, he can slip and come out with urgent and plaintive exclamations, once he knows a visitor reasonably well: "Why can't we have a little more money come into these hills? I don't mean a lot of tourists coming around and prying, like you hear some people say we need. I mean some work we could get, to tide us over the winter. That's the worst time. You start

running out of the food you've stored, and there's nothing you can do but hope you make it until the warm weather. We all help each other out, of course; but there'll come times when we none of us has much of anything left, and then it's up to the church, and the next hollow. Once they had to fly in food, it was so bad, because of the snow and the floods we had. I can't find the littlest bit of work, and it makes you wonder sometimes. They move factories into every other part of the country, but not here. I guess it's hard, because of the hills. We'd be good workers, though. I was taught to work from sunrise to sunset by my folks. You might think this little farm we've got is all that we need, but it isn't. We'd have nothing to eat without the land we plant, but it's money we lack, that's for sure, and you can't grow that. You can pick up a little money here and there—for instance they'll come and recruit you to do work for the county on the roads or cleaning things up. But it's not very much money you ever make, and if we didn't really love it here, we might have left a long time ago. I've been all set to—but then I can't do it. When my kids will ask me if I ever thought of leaving, I'll say no, and why should they ask, I say to them. I guess they know I don't want much to talk about some things, so they never push me too much. I wouldn't let them. They'll find out soon enough—about the misery in this world. The way I see it, life's never easy, and you just have to choose whether you'll stay here and live where it's best to live—or go someplace else, where you're feeling sad and homesick all the time, but they've got a lot of jobs, and you can make good money. I hope my kids think it over real hard before they decide—when they get older."

18   His children love the hollow, and maybe they too will never really be able to leave. They are unmistakably poor children, and they need all sorts of things, from medical and dental care to better and more food; but they love the land near their cabin, and they know that land almost inch by inch. Indeed, from the first days of life many of the Appalachian children I have observed are almost symbolically or ritualistically given over to the land. One morning I watched Mrs. Allen come out from the cabin in order, presumably, to enjoy the sun and the warm, clear air of a May day. Her boy had just been breast-fed and was in her arms. Suddenly the mother put the child down on the ground, and gently fondled him and moved him a bit with her feet, which are not usually covered with shoes or socks. The child did not cry. The mother seemed to have almost exquisite control over her toes. It all seemed very nice, but I had no idea what Mrs. Allen really had in mind until she leaned over and spoke very gravely to her child: "This is your land, and it's about time you started getting to know it."

Exercises

COMPREHENSION

Organization and Development

Coles's essay does not contain an explicit thesis; however, his purpose is readily apparent. In your own words, state Coles's purpose in writing about the Allens. Then find the three main divisions of the essay and fill in the remaining spaces. Note the paragraphs for each section.

Statement of purpose: _____

_____

_____

I.   _____   [   ]
II. _____   [   ]
III. _____   [   ]

Content

Choose the answer that correctly completes each statement.

1. Contrary to what most people think, Coles found the people of the hollows to be (a) sullen and fearful of outsiders (b) proud of their heritage and fiercely independent (c) backward and ignorant of modern ways.
2. The mountaineers especially dislike outsiders who say (a) the mountain children are so badly off (b) only educated people or government officials know what's best for children (c) the mountain people are unable to help themselves.
3. Evidently, Mr. Allen, a mountaineer from Swain County, North Carolina, regards the land he lives in as (a) so poor that it's hardly worth farming (b) beautiful as any place in the world (c) rich in natural resources such as coal and other minerals.
4. To support his family, Mr. Allen depends mainly on (a) food stamps and welfare (b) a small salary from working on the roads (c) the food he raises on his small farm.
5. According to Mrs. Allen, she has lost many teeth because (a) babies took her strength away (b) she doesn't eat the proper foods (c) the dentist was unable to save them.
6. Coles's essay emphasizes that the Allens (a) would leave the hollows if they could save the money (b) despite their hardships have no intention of ever leaving the land they are so wedded to (c) need more training from government programs so they can work in nearby factories.
7. Evidently Mrs. Allen is most upset by her children's (a) poor schooling (b) lack of sufficient food (c) lack of proper medical care.
8. In sum, the author portrays this mountain family as (a) enviable (b) admirable and deserving of respect rather than scorn (c) pitiably ignorant and stubborn.

Paragraph Structure

Reorder the following sentences to form a unified, coherent paragraph. Identify one sentence as the topic sentence. Then check your version with the original.

1. The child did not cry.
2. The boy had just been breast-fed and was in her arms.

3. Indeed, from the first days of life many of the Appalachian children I have observed are almost symbolically or ritualistically given over to the land.
4. "This is your land, and it's about time you started getting to know it."
5. One morning I watched Mrs. Allen come out from the cabin in order, presumably, to enjoy the sun and the warm, clear air of a May day.
6. Suddenly the mother put the child down on the ground, and gently fondled him and moved him a bit with her feet, which are not usually covered with shoes or socks.
7. The mother seemed to have almost exquisite control over her toes.
8. It all seemed very nice, but I had no idea what Mrs. Allen really had in mind until she leaned over and spoke very gravely to her child.

VOCABULARY AND USAGE

Word Formation Table

Complete the following table by changing word endings or root forms to make new grammatical forms. Use your dictionary if necessary.

NOUN	VERB	ADJECTIVE	ADVERB
1. _____	_____	noticeable	_____
2. _____	penetrate	_____	_____
3. _____	_____	symbolical	_____
4. _____	xxx	austere	_____
5. _____	_____	apparent	_____

Fill-Ins

Complete each of the sentences below using the words on the following list. You may need to use some words more than once. You may also find that some blanks can be completed correctly with more than one word. Add plural endings to nouns and change verb forms where necessary.

bear	prevent	shun
austere	eventually	serious
apparent	for instance	glum
grave	endure	clear
tradition	distrust	stern
noticeable	custom	tolerate
avoid	rather	prefer

1. The stereotype of the mountaineers is that they _____ contact with outsiders and that they cling to their old _____.
2. Mr. Allen particularly _____ government officials from Washington who say they want to help, because he says mountaineers would _____ do without than have people feel sorry for them.
3. It is quickly _____ that the Allens must _____ many hardships; _____, they often don't have enough food during the winter.
4. Most _____ were Mrs. Allen's missing teeth, and though she admits a visit to the dentist might have _____ their loss, she has never been to one.
5. Mrs. Allen is neither _____ nor _____ in disciplining her children; _____, she disciplines them by gesture or facial expression.

6. Survival for mountaineers like the Allens is a ＿＿＿＿＿＿ matter, and the author suggests they may ＿＿＿＿＿＿ have to give up their ＿＿＿＿＿＿ of independence.

DISCUSSION

1. What are some reasons Appalachians might distrust outsiders?
2. In spite of all the hardships they must endure, why do the Allens not want to leave Swain County? Does Coles find their tenacity admirable or not? Explain.
3. Explain the structure of the central portion of Coles's essay which begins with paragraph 4. Is his commentary necessary? What function does it serve? Would the essay be more or less convincing (or unified) if he had omitted the commentary and simply let the Allens speak for themselves?
4. What do we learn about Mrs. Allen from her description of her two children's deaths? [See paragraphs 7–9.]
5. What are the Allenses' feelings about the land they live on? How do they demonstrate those feelings?
6. What is Coles's attitude toward the Allens? Point to specific examples of word choice that reveal how he feels about this family.
7. Explain some differences in the level of language used by Coles in his commentary and by the Allens in their dialog. Again, cite specific examples to support your explanation.
8. What peculiarly American traits do the Allens exhibit?

SUGGESTIONS FOR WRITING

1. One of Coles's purposes is to correct the stereotype most of us have about Appalachian people by presenting a profile of one family. Following Coles's method of showing and convincing by an extended example, write an essay in which you correct a false picture or a common stereotype of a particular group.
2. Certainly the people who live in the hollows of Appalachia must bear many hardships—poverty, lack of jobs, and poor farm land. Yet they are not a defeated people. Write an essay explaining the characteristics of the mountain people, as represented by the Allens, that you consider admirable (or perhaps that you find foolishly stubborn), being sure to cite specific examples from the essay.
3. It is clear that the Allens resent and distrust the government's attempts to intervene in their lives. Discuss some of the advantages and disadvantages of government intervention or attempts to make "substandard" institutions conform. You might consider, for example, the real price the Appalachians might pay if they submit to outsiders' recommendations. What would they gain? What would they give up?

Jones: Portrait of a Mugger

JAMES WILLWERTH

James Willwerth was born in Detroit, Michigan, in 1943. He received a B.A. and M.A. in journalism from the University of California at Berkeley where, while still a student, he wrote a prize-winning article on Berkeley's "street people." During the 1960s he was a correspondent for *Time* in San Francisco, New York, and Saigon. His experiences in Vietnam are recorded in *Eye in the Last Storm: A Reporter's Journal of One Year in Southeast Asia*. His other full-length works are *Clive: Inside the Music Business,* and *Jones: Portrait of a Mugger,* from which the following essay is an excerpt.

1   "I hit the streets each day about twelve and I walk around."
        . . . Jones was telling me about a typical day's work during this period.
2   "This day I was wearing jeans and cut-off sneakers and a dark knit. It was early in November and starting to get cool. The dude I worked with then was the best crime partner I ever had. He's doin' five-to-ten for robbery now."
3   Jones was living at home. From that sanctuary, he moved into the larger city as a hunter might.
4   "We walked up First Avenue and stood in front of a supermarket. This dude came out. He had given the woman a check, and she had given him a lot of bills. You can watch people through the glass and see this.
5   "He lived about a block away, and we followed him into his building. It was quick; he had the bags in his arms, and I put the knife right above his heart. He said he was a working man and all that bullshit and then we took the roll; it was big, but it was only ones, like maybe thirty-five dollars. We went back to the projects to let things cool off in case he called the cops."
6   If the police were called, the victim would be put in a patrol car and driven around the neighborhood. The police would take a description of Jones and his accomplice. But most likely, the man would walk to his apartment and open the door with his passkey before he called the police. By the time they arrived, Jones would be blocks away.
7   "Then we saw this dude coming out of the building across from us. It was later in the afternoon by now, and he was between the doors. He had let the first door lock behind him, and we came in through the other way—he couldn't go in or out. I had the knife out, but I didn't even touch him. He kept on saying, 'Just take it—don't hurt me . . .'"

8   The man, middle-aged and wise, survived. He had the sense not to frighten or anger his assailant; so he endured fear and humiliation and theft—but not violence or death.

9   "He might have been around forty. Sometimes you don't remember the faces, just the things they say. He had about fifty dollars and change. We left the change. We went into another part of the projects and let things cool off again.

10   "We caught the next dude, who was thirty-nine or forty, the same way. He was the kind you had to show you wasn't playing. I pulled the knife and I said, 'Look, we just want your money.' He said, 'What? what?' So I hit him with the handle of the knife. That didn't faze him. I put the knife up against here"—Jones pokes his finger into my stomach—"and wow, he almost had a heart attack! He goes, 'Ah! Ahhhhhhhhhh!' and wow, I was feelin' bad. Then he says something about how you can't leave your house any more, you get robbed, you know? My man says to check his belt. So far we had about thirty-five dollars. I pulled the belt out and it had two hundred-dollar bills behind a zipper."

11   As the man says, you can't leave your house any more.

12   "Then we saw this white dude. If you see a white dude down here, something's strange; this one had come to get dope. We said, 'Hey, man, why don't you come over here? We'd like to talk to you.' He had about seventy dollars. He said he would come back for us, and there's a lot of racketeers around that area, so we decided to cool it for a few days. We split up the cash and I laid up with my share. We had wanted to put together some money and cop a lot of dope. This wasn't enough, but I figured we should stay off the streets for a while anyway."

13   Not bad. Half of $337 for a day's work. Yet *not* enough. It would not sustain Jones very long, for as always the Law of Easy Money was at work. Anything above the price of a day's habit would be spent blindingly fast.

14   "This was in the daytime. We were downtown, and the guy I was with had a lot of heart. We saw a dude coming out of a store with a bag in his arms; he was dressed nice. We followed him to his building and got in the elevator with him; he pressed nine, so we pressed seven. Then we ran up the two flights of stairs, and got there as he got out. The elevator door had closed behind him.

15   "The dude was strong, and he knew what was happening. He dropped the bag and started to fight. We both went for him. I grabbed his shirt collar—you can lead a dude around that way—but my nails broke and I lost my grip. My man got scared now; he stabbed him with his K-55."

16   The K-55 is a smaller version of the .007. Both knives are favorite muggers' tools. The K-55 has a long metal handle, and a locking blade that is at most three or four inches long. The .007, which Jones has, is more expensive, with a hefty wooden handle and a longer blade. Neither is spring-action; a practiced thumb and forefinger action forces the blade out of the handle. A powerful wrist snap and a click! complete the movement. With practice the knife opens as fast as any switch-blade.

17   "It was a quick thing, and that did it."

18   Jones's accomplice has "heart." It means that he is capable of sudden, reckless violence. Jones does not approve of this; one part of him does not. He grinds his teeth at the memory.

19   "He was against the wall holding himself. He was stabbed now, and he was screaming and we took his money—one hundred and fifty dollars—and split. I was scared! We ran down nine flights of stairs. I knew if I got busted, the courts would hang me."

20   Jones's face is tight, tense. He looks at me, and the tension reaches across the space between us. Several seconds pass before he says anything.

21   "I dreamed about this for three days. It was the horror of the thing; I was part of it. My man had trouble pulling the blade out of the dude. He had to pull hard, and the blood ran all down him."

22   Jones sits forward. "I don't know if I want to talk about it." Silence. He puts his hand under his chin, and says nothing for seconds. Then he starts again.

23   "The dream went almost the way it happened. It would start to happen, and I would wake up; I would go back to sleep and see him being stabbed. Moms and Pops thought I was crazy—I was punching the wall in my sleep. They asked what I was doing—I told them it was nothing. I had been down with stabbings as a kid; but then I knew the dude. He had done something to abuse me."

24   Jones is lost in his grim memory.

25   "When you don't know the person you are doing the harm to, taking his money is enough. This dude hadn't done shit to me and now he was being stabbed and I was part of it. There are dudes out there I wouldn't mind killing, but it's a bitch to stab someone you don't know.

26   "We ran to a park. When we stopped, I asked my man why he did it. He said he didn't know why. I didn't want to show I was afraid, so I dropped it."

27   "It isn't so safe in the streets. The cops are out; everybody is uptight. Buildings are better."

28   The man in the hallway might have been thirty-five years old. He was Chinese; but his face was hardly inscrutable; it showed pain and fright and humiliation. He had managed to shut the street door in time to keep one of his assailants out of the hallway. But the other was upon him. He flailed and pushed and moved as fast as he could.

29   "I hit him in the face a couple of times. Then I hit him again. I felt the blow crush something, something went squish. I looked at my hand and it was okay—so it had to be him."

30   In the darkness the man moaned and became silent. Jones let him fall. He turned to let his partner into the building. No one had heard the fight.

31   "It was kinda funny. He had been up against the wall and he was goin' uhhhhh, uhhhhhhh . . . and he didn't have any place to go. When I let go, he just dropped. I let my man in. We was in a hurry—we took the dude's money and ran, it was about twenty dollars. There was cops all over that night."

32   "Did the man die?" I ask, sick at the thought.

33   "I don't know. I never read the newspapers afterward—I don't want to feel

sorry about what happened. Some dudes are different. They want everybody to know about it. Not me."

34   A neon-colored night. Jones and I walk down Houston Street, past the mute wilderness of an empty park. "I've got to get some fresh air," he'd said. "Sometimes when I've been sleeping and smoking, I get to thinking and my nerves start bothering me. I've got a lot of things on my mind."

35   We are talking now about women and old people—as victims. Jones is opposed to the idea.

36   "An old man can have a weak heart and die from the shock of the beating—that can be Murder One. It's premeditated because they say you planned the mugging. Mugging by itself is a robbery and assault charge, which is easier to beat."

37   This is a recurring bit of ambivalence. Jones will not mug women or old men he considers helpless. It is not just a matter of ethics; pragmatism is involved. A murder charge means a lot of prison time. And women tend to scream; you have to silence them, fast. More prison time.

38   A middle-aged woman hurries by, clutching her purse tightly. Jones pauses to watch her.

39   "Now that's a *shame*. She's alone, and she's afraid of being mugged. I see women like that, and I think of Moms. If a dude hurt her, that would bring me out in the streets like a wild man! I would *really* hurt someone. If someone hits Pops, he can take it. A woman is a different thing."

40   It's nice to have ideals, I am thinking. Then I ask: "Who *does* hit women?"

41   "Dudes afraid to face men."

42   He drifts for a moment as the middle-aged woman disappears.

43   "If a woman starts screaming, somebody, even a punk, will want to help her. Then you got two people to deal with. A woman like this can make you want to hurt her, which is a drag. I think about my mother. If someone took her off, it would hurt me; she can't really get down with a dude and win."

44   "If you saw a woman being mugged, would you help her?"

45   Jones says nothing. We pass a patrol car idling outside an all-night coffee shop. Then he nods.

46   "Yeah. If the woman was getting hurt, I would help her. Dudes who get down with women have no heart. I would definitely get into it."

47   Jones spreads clear polish on his thumbnail with a tiny brush to toughen the sharpened surface. We are talking about mugging techniques.

48   "I'm into drops now. You lay outside a bank, or a check-cashing place; you know the dudes have cash. You can be even more selective if you want. Today, like, I watched faces going in and out of this bank. Tomorrow I'll go back again. If I see those faces again, I'll know they aren't going to the bank for themselves. So I'll pick a face and follow it to its store. As a rule, stores make one drop a day. They usually make those drops between two and three o'clock. I'll time this dude for a few days. Say he's pretty close to between two and two-thirty. I make it my business to be there."

49   He turns to his other thumb, dipping the brush into the small jar again.

50   "You have to remember the faces you've taken off. You see a dude twice, you give him a rest; because if your face becomes familiar, it's trouble. I don't walk much in the areas where I work."

51   "You'll mug a man twice?"

52   "Oh yeah. He'll be slick for a while after the first time. But he'll drop his guard again. It ain't *his* money. He isn't going to risk his life for it."

53   Jones is into the talk now. His hands loop and dive in the space in front of him.

54   "It's not worth it to fuck with people on the street. The regular dude, he's like you and me. He's working, he's got a wife and kids. He don't carry much money—and he might fight. The dude with the drop, he's got more money, and he's got insurance."

55   "Do you still hit people randomly?"

56   "Yeah, sometimes. I prefer drops, but you have to plan for them. If you need money right away, you resort to the old street thing."

57   "How do you spot the right person to mug?"

58   "You walk behind a dude. If he keeps looking around, if he's leery, you know something is up. If he's got no money, he's got nothing to worry about, right? You walk beside him, and if he's looking over his shoulder—if he's got eyes in the back of his head—you've got your man."

59   "What's the most you've gotten?"

60   "One time me and my man saw this fat dude, and I just had this feeling, you know? We followed him into this building and *wow*, he had cash everywhere! In his pockets, in his belt, in his shoes, in a case he was carrying . . . we got a thousand dollars. Sometimes a good drop is worth that much, too."

61   I am thinking. When Jones works regularly, he says he makes more than a hundred dollars a day. Perhaps several thousand dollars a month, perhaps $20,000 a year. It is tax free. A $1,200 paycheck has about $900 left after the government gets its bite. So he has the equivalent of a $25,000 job.

62   Let's assume Jones is bragging—that he makes only half that amount. Thus he is making ten thousand tax-free dollars a year. He may be short on social security and medical plans, but at ten thousand after taxes he is doing better than most of New York City's office workers, delivery men, factory people, cops, and firemen. Not to mention free-lance writers. And he pays no rent.

63   Twenty thousand—if he was not exaggerating—means he does as well as the middle-level executives of Madison Avenue and Wall Street. He could drink in Sardi's after the theater, shop on Fifth Avenue, attend Lincoln Center concerts, and consult *The New York Times* restaurant guide for three-star French restaurants.

64   Yet Jones is constantly broke. He takes money from his women, borrows from his parents, and hits me up practically every time we get together (and always pays me back). He dresses well and uses expensive drugs—but they can't possibly account for all the money he spends. Yet beyond the drugs and clothes, he lives like a welfare recipient. *Why?* There never seems to be a satisfactory answer.

65   One reason may be the blackly ironic economics of the ghetto. Goods and services cost more. Groceries in a bodega cost as much as gourmet foods on the fashionable Upper East Side; small stores must have a high margin to survive. Even supermarkets, as congressional studies have shown, are higher. Public transportation is usually poorer, and gypsy cabs cost plenty. Rent is cheap, but the tenants often must put money into the apartments to make them livable. Cheap furniture and household items are sold at exorbitant prices through deceptive time payment plans. The furniture wears out before the payments are finished.

66   But economics is not the answer, even the largest part of it. The problem is lifestyle.

67   "A thousand-dollar rip-off means you can relax for a while, right?"

68   "Oh no! I go through it in three or four days. I buy clothes, I go out, I get high. I get shoes, or a knit, or slacks—I get a lot of things I don't need. You just live while the money's there; that's the rule of the street. That's one thing dope did—it made me live for the day. When I've got money, I don't sleep for three or four days—you're just *buying* something all the time. If you've got the money that easy and that fast, it doesn't have any value."

69   Jones and money are like a lion and its latest kill. The meat is eaten now—day-old flesh is for jackals. Let the future take care of itself.

70   Jones doesn't entirely believe this, of course. He feels trapped by street life—somehow heroin disrupted his life in more than chemical ways. He sees cars and nice apartments and legitimate money around him, and he tells himself he should save his resources and buy things that last. But at night, when he is alone and thinking about his life, he sees two images. One reaches out, gently saying work and save, become stable.

71   The other shrieks that nothing matters: get it *now*. And he knows that this vision—and he hates himself for knowing it—has more strength than its cautious, thoughtful twin.

72   "You have a car and cash in the bank," he says to me in gloomy moments. "You *have* things. And I have a yellow sheet and a hole in my arm. Wow, what *happened?*"

Exercises

COMPREHENSION

Organization and Development

Complete the following outline. Determine the main idea or dominant impression of the subject that this profile conveys and write it in the space provided. Then find the main divisions in the essay and fill in the remaining spaces. Note the paragraphs for each section.

Main idea: _____
_____
_____

I.   _____ [   ]
   A. _____ [   ]
   B. _____ [   ]
   C. _____ [   ]
II.   _____ [   ]
III. _____ [   ]
   A. _____ [   ]
   B. _____ [   ]
IV. _____ [   ]

Content

Choose the answer that correctly completes each statement.

1. The image of Jones moving into the city "as a hunter might" emphasizes what aspect of his criminal career? (a) its essentially predatory nature (b) its bestiality (c) its immorality.
2. When Jones says his accomplice has "heart," he means he is (a) warm and affectionate with his friends (b) powerful, courageous, and unafraid (c) capable of sudden, reckless violence.
3. Jones steals mainly to (a) support his expensive sports car and impress women (b) support his heroin habit (c) pay his enormous gambling debts.
4. The fact that Jones does not approve of mugging women or helpless old men is evidence of his (a) ethical values (b) pragmatism: a Murder One charge means more prison time than robbery and assault (c) sentimentality: he thinks of all women as if they were his mother.
5. That Jones's job requires some skill and knowledge is best demonstrated by his (a) choice of weapons (b) comments on the manner in which he selects his victims (c) ability to avoid paying rent.
6. The interviewer mentions Sardi's, Lincoln Center, Fifth Avenue, and three-star restaurants to (a) emphasize the total absence of culture and refinement in Jones's life (b) show the kinds of establishments Jones might consider robbing if he could see beyond the limited world of the mugger (c) emphasize the disparity between what a middle-class man and Jones do with similar incomes.
7. If Jones seems to spend his money as fast as he makes it, it is because he (a) is uneducated and has no understanding of economics (b) feels that money has no value when you get it as easily and quickly as he does—the Law of Easy Money (c) is fearful of being picked up by the police with his pockets full of money.
8. The interviewer implies that the mugger's inability to do what middle-class people with comparable incomes can afford to do is a result of (a) his limited vision of the possibilities of organized crime (b) the oppression of the poor by the rich—heroin pushing and ghetto economics (c) a total difference in lifestyles and values.

Paragraph Structure

Reorder the following sentences to form a unified, coherent paragraph. Identify one sentence as the topic sentence. Then check your version with the original.

1. The K-55 has a long metal handle, and a locking blade that is at most three or four inches long.
2. With practice the knife opens as fast as any switch-blade.
3. The K-55 is a smaller version of the .007.
4. Neither is spring-action; a practiced thumb and forefinger action forces the blade out of the handle.
5. Both knives are favorite muggers' tools.
6. The .007, which Jones has, is more expensive, with a hefty wooden handle and a longer blade.
7. A powerful wrist snap and a click! complete the movement.

VOCABULARY AND USAGE

Word Formation Table

Complete the following table by changing word endings or root forms to make new grammatical forms. Use your dictionary if necessary.

	NOUN	VERB	ADJECTIVE	ADVERB
1.	ethics	xxx	_____	_____
2.	_____	assail	_____	xxx
3.	_____	frighten	_____	_____
4.	memory	_____	_____	_____
5.	_____	prefer	_____	_____

Fill-Ins

Complete each of the sentences below using the words on the following list. You may need to use some words more than once. You may also find that some blanks can be completed correctly with more than one word. Add plural endings to nouns and change verb forms where necessary.

sanctuary	disrupt	accomplice	legitimate
sustain	heroin	criminal	lifestyle
inscrutable	cautious	work	mugger
ethics	assailant	occupation	because
pragmatic	victim	addiction	narcotics

1. Jones's home is like a _____ from which he moves out into the city to pursue his _____ as a _____.
2. Jones is diligent in his _____, always seeking a new _____ in order to _____ his _____.
3. Yet, Jones has a code of _____, as well as _____ reasons for refraining from making women and helpless old men his _____.
4. If Jones used as much intelligence and energy in some _____ kind of _____, instead of pursuing the _____ _____ of _____, he might be very successful.
5. Jones _____ with an _____, but he is more _____, less violent, than his partner.
6. The interviewer says Jones is always broke in spite of his high-income _____; he is a _____ addict, and the _____ has _____ his entire life.

DISCUSSION

1. What is the purpose of alternating the author's comments with those of the mugger? What effect is produced by this alternation?
2. What purpose is served by this supposedly intimate portrait of someone who lives outside the law?
3. What specific details are emphasized in order to give the reader a really close-up, intimate view of Jones?
4. This essay emphasizes *fear*; it does so principally by making it part of everyone's experience, including that of the mugger himself. Would we see him differently if Jones himself were fearless? How *do* we see him? Is this vision the same as or different from the author's? What details convey the author's dominant impression of Jones? If your attitude toward Jones is different from the impression you think this profile is intended to give, why is it different?
5. Although the essay doesn't focus on this fact, Jones is a heroin addict, and most of the profits of his criminal activity are devoted to the support of his $100-a-day habit. In view of the danger to society represented by Jones and other addicts who must resort to crime to maintain their habits, do you think we might be better off to institute the system of government support of addicts that England established some years ago? Be precise and specific in your supporting arguments.
6. Willwerth suggests that with his income, Jones could be living like a middle-level executive—dinners at little French restaurants, concerts at Lincoln Center, etc. The reason he doesn't is partly economic (the economics of the ghetto), but mostly what Willwerth calls a problem of "lifestyle." What does Willwerth mean by "lifestyle"? Do the specifics he suggests in paragraphs 65–71 *really* constitute a lifestyle, or is he talking about something for which the term lifestyle is a euphemism? Explain.
7. When Willwerth compares Jones to a lion with a fresh kill (paragraph 68), what is he suggesting? What basic qualities are associated with the lion? What values are involved in the notion of "let the future take care of itself"? Is there a basic contradiction or ambivalence here? What is it?
8. Do you feel that you have anything in common with Jones? Does the mugger have anything in common with the young executives whose lifestyle is contrasted with his? What do you think is the real purpose and effect of that contrast (paragraphs 61–64)?
9. How much do you know about criminals or the poverty of urban ghettos or about drug addiction? Has this close-up view altered or reinforced your preconceived ideas?

SUGGESTIONS FOR WRITING

1. Following Willwerth's formula of alternating the subject's comments and his own observations, first interview and then write a profile of someone you know who has an unusual or interesting occupation.
2. Compare and contrast the differences in lifestyles—including social and moral values—between a mugger who can earn $20,000 a year and a middle-level executive with a comparable income. Draw some conclusions.
3. Write an essay which, using factual details, establishes a cause-effect relationship between drug addiction and our nation's high crime rate.
4. Write an essay which argues for (or against) the decriminalization of heroin and other addictive drugs, using Jones's profile as supporting evidence.

In Charge: A Profile of Ward Quaal

STUDS TERKEL

Studs Terkel received a bachelor's and a law degree from the University of Chicago. His career has been varied: he has been a radio soap opera actor, a disc jockey, a sports commentator, and a TV host. Currently, he has a daily radio program in Chicago. He has published three books of taped interviews: *Division Street: America, Hard Times: An Oral History of the Great Depression in America,* and *Working: People Talk About What They Do All Day and How They Feel About What They Do.* The following interview from *Working* is with Ward Quaal, a Chicago TV executive.

(Note: This anthology also contains Terkel's "Here Am I, a Worker.")

1   *We're at Tribune Square, Chicago. We're in the well-appointed office of the president of WGN-Continental Broadcasting Corporation—"the most powerful broadcast medium in the Midwest." He has been battling a slight sinus condition, but his presence is, nonetheless, felt.*

2   *"I'm responsible for all its broadcasting properties. We have radio and television here. We have a travel company here. We have a sales company here. We have the Continental Productions Company here. We have radio and television in Minnesota and translator systems in northern Michigan, Wisconsin, as well as Minnesota. We have cable television in Michigan and California. We have television in Denver. We have sales companies in New York and Tokyo. I operate sixteen different organizations in the United States and Japan."*

3   My day starts between four thirty and five in the morning, at home in Winnetka. I dictate in my library until about seven thirty. Then I have breakfast. The driver gets there about eight o'clock and oftentimes I continue dictating in the car on the way to the office. I go to the Broadcast Center in the morning and then to Tribune Square around noon. Of course, I do a lot of reading in the car.

4   I talk into a dictaphone. I will probably have as many as 150 letters dictated by seven-thirty in the morning. I have five full-time secretaries, who do nothing but work for Ward Quaal. I have seven swing girls, who work for me part-time. This does not include my secretaries in New York, Los Angeles,

Washington, and San Francisco. They get dicta-belts from me every day. They also take telephone messages. My personal secretary doesn't do any of that. She handles appointments and my trips. She tries to work out my schedule to fit these other secretaries.

5   I get home around six-thirty, seven at night. After dinner with the family I spend a minimum of two and a half hours each night going over the mail and dictating. I should have a secretary at home just to handle the mail that comes there. I'm not talking about bills and personal notes, I'm talking about business mail only. Although I don't go to the office on Saturday or Sunday, I do have mail brought out to my home for the weekend. I dictate on Saturday and Sunday. When I do this on holidays, like Christmas, New Year's, and Thanksgiving, I have to sneak a little bit, so the family doesn't know what I'm doing.

6   Ours is a twenty-four-hour-a-day business. We're not turning out three thousand gross of shoes, beans, or neckties. We're turning out a new product every day, with new problems. It's not unusual for me to get a phone call on a weekend: "What are your thoughts on it, Mr. Quaal? Would you speak out on it?" I'm not going to hide my posture on it. I'm going to answer that. This may mean going into the studio to make a recording. Or I may do a tape recording at home. Or maybe I'll just make a statement. I am in a seven-day-a-week job and I love it!

7   *"I grew up in a very poor family. Not only did no one come to us for advice, we went to other people for advice. We wondered what we were going to do for the next dollar. We did manage during the Depression. But I know others who didn't extricate themselves from these difficulties. I won't forget them. A letter from one of those individuals asking for help is just as important to me as a suggestion from the chairman of the board of the Chase Manhattan Bank. They get the same weight. They get a personal letter from me. He didn't write to my assistant, he didn't write to my secretary. He wants to hear from Ward Quaal."*

8   When I come to the Broadcast Center, I'll probably have about five or six different stacks of mail. One stack is urgent and should be acted upon before I make any phone calls. Once I handle that, which usually takes about fifteen, twenty minutes, I start the important phone calls. In-between these phone calls and others of lesser importance, I get into the other mail. On a typical day we'll get thirteen hundred pieces of first-class mail addressed to me personally. Every letter is answered within forty-eight hours—and not a form letter. There are no form letters. If they write to the president of the company, they don't want to hear from the third vice president. They hear from the president. Mail and the telephone, that's the name of the game in this business.

9   *I imagine your phone calls are not long in nature?*

10   No, they're not long in nature. I have this ability—I learned this when I was an announcer years ago, and we were feeding six networks out of here. I could listen to all these channels with earphones and I knew when to say the right cue at the right time. I can still do that.

11   *"In high school I wanted to be a good football player, a good basketball player, a good baseball player. I managed to be captain of every team on which I ever played. At the end of my freshman year my coach said, 'There's a shortage of people to do oratory and declamatory work.' He said, 'We've just simply got to have somebody with your voice. If you would do this, I would excuse you from football practice a couple of nights a week.' I won the oratorical and declamatory championship for the state of Michigan. On the night of the finals in Ishpeming, which were broadcast, the chief engineer of a radio station, a Polish gentleman, called my mother and told her I'd be a network announcer someday.*

12   *"I started working during my freshman year in high school as an announcer at WBEO in Marquette. I worked from 10:00 A.M. to 10:00 P.M. and got $17.50 a week. At the same time, I drove a commercial milk truck from four in the morning to eight, and I got $22.50 a week for that. The two jobs gave me money to go to the University of Michigan. I have great pride in my university. I was chairman of the Alumni Fund and its Development Council.*

13   *"I won the job as a Detroit radio announcer at thirty-five dollars a week, while still a student. I hitchhiked or took a bus every day from Ann Arbor to Detroit. On the campus I was promotion manager of the yearbook. I was sports and feature writer for the* Michigan Daily. *I was on the freshman football team, baseball team, and basketball team. And I was president of the fraternity. All at one time. Shows you can do it if you work hard enough.*

14   *"When I applied for admission at the university, I was asked what my goal was after graduation. I said, 'The announcing staff of WGN.' I finished my last exam June 8, 1941, and I started at WGN the next day."*

15   I had no desire to be an announcer forever. I wanted to become general manager. I think this is something anybody can do. The number one thing in any business is to go get a background, so you can show your people you can do anything they can do. My people today know I can announce any show they could, I can write a script, I can produce a show, I can handle a camera. If I still had the voice, I would enjoy being back on the air again.

16   I've had to develop a team effort with all people. I prefer being called Ward rather than Mr. Quaal. Ninety percent of the people do call me by my first name. The young women of the organization do not, although I certainly would not disapprove of them calling me Ward. The last thing I want to be is a stuffed shirt. I'm trying to run this organization on a family basis. I prefer it to be on the informal side.

17   I've always felt throughout my lifetime that if you have any ability at all, go for first place. That's all I'm interested in. That doesn't mean I'm trying to be

an autocrat. Lord knows I'm not a dictator. I try to give all my colleagues total autonomy. But they know there's one guy in charge.

18   Of course, you have to be number two before you become number one—unless you're born into something. I was born into a poor family. I had to create my own paths. Sure, I've been second vice president, first vice president, and executive vice president. But I had only one goal in life and that was to be president.

19   A fellow like Ward Quaal, he's one of the old hands now. That doesn't mean I'm going to vegetate. I intend to devote more time to our subsidiaries and to develop young people who come forth with new ideas. I don't look forward to retirement. I feel I have many useful years ahead of me. When the time comes to step aside, I won't regret it at all. I have a lot of writing to do. I'll have so much to do.

20   *You're more of a philosopher-king than a boss. . .*

21   I think that is true. When I came here sixteen years ago, August first, I never had any desire to be a czar. I don't like to say I ruled with an iron hand, but I had to take charge and clean up the place. I am the captain calling the signals and every once in a while I call the right play and we're pretty lucky.

22   I don't feel any pressure, though my family says I sometimes show it. I'm not under tension. I go to bed at night and I sleep well. The company is doing well. My people are functioning as a team. The success story is not Ward Quaal. It's a great team of people.

23   POSTSCRIPT: *"On a typical day we get about seven hundred phone calls. We average eighty a day long distance."* I estimated that during the time of this conversation, there were about forty phone calls for Ward Quaal.

Exposition

Exposition—or expository prose—is the main business of this book. It is the ordinary, everyday kind of writing found in letters and reports, term papers and essay examinations, newspapers and magazines, as well as in the essay. It forms the bulk of our nonfiction reading, and it is also the kind of writing that most people use in their daily lives.

The purpose of exposition (implied by its Latin root, *exponere*, "to put forth" or "to expound") is to explain, to make clear; its subject matter is ideas. Thus, exposition develops mainly through direct statement of purpose and logical arrangement of ideas, rather than through sensory impressions, as in description, or through actions that express a theme, as in narration.

Exposition employs a number of rhetorical methods, each of which describes a particular form of development or arrangement of ideas. The organization of this book emphasizes the major methods of expository development by selecting in turn essays in which one method dominates. But only rarely is any one of these methods employed alone, as these mainly artificial divisions might imply. Instead, they are almost always used in combinations suited to the subject matter—often along with one or another of the primary modes of discourse as well.

But while it may employ the techniques of narration or description, or while it may be used in the service of an argument, exposition itself never seeks solely to persuade nor does it merely tell a story or present a description: its aim is always the clear presentation or explanation of ideas.

Thesis

Unlike the other subdivisions of Exposition, this first section is not concerned with a rhetorical technique or device designed to promote the development of an idea. The thesis *is* the main idea—what is called the theme in a work of fiction or drama, where an underlying idea or "moral" may be expressed through the speech and actions of the characters. Because the whole purpose of exposition is to explain ideas, to make them clear, the thesis of an expository essay is *what it's all about*, and it is almost always presented directly, or at least implied through the arrangement of other, supporting ideas, rather than through dialog or dramatic action.

The simplest and most direct method of organization puts the thesis statement at or near the beginning of the essay, followed by supporting evidence and ending with a fuller statement of the thesis, a conclusion, or an inference to be drawn from the evidence. In fact, depending on subject and purpose, any one or a combination of these three possibilities will work. This classic arrangement, which might be described as a pyramid of ideas, is the one employed in "Last of the New England Hill Farms." Brown's essay begins with a thesis statement in the opening paragraph, follows with increasingly fuller supporting evidence, and ends in a concluding statement that consolidates thesis and documentation, and also urges the reader to form the same conclusion. But while this is the most straightforward and clearest of arrangements (and also the simplest—a fact that you may want to keep in mind for your own writing), other plans of order are often used with equal effectiveness.

Toffler, for example, does not state his thesis until he has first presented an illustration that embodies it—the phenomenon of the trade-in "Barbie." Then he initially offers the thesis in the sparest of statements, restates it several times and in several ways to ensure coherence, but reserves his fullest expression of the thesis for the last paragraph, where it also functions as a conclusion.

"The American Way of Death" presents two major supporting ideas about the funeral industry that may at first seem to be Mitford's main ideas (and that might also be seen correctly as partial expressions of her thesis, rather than as supporting statements). But her complete thesis is not made fully apparent until the very end of the essay, where thesis, conclusion, and inferences to be drawn from her evidence are posed as a rhetorical question for the reader.

McPhee's article is the only one in this section that is not completely direct in its statement of thesis. Instead, it opens with a lengthy introduction that offers a mosaic of information about Alaska in which are embedded the essential facts that illuminate the central narrative sequence, the experiences of the downed flier, Leon Crane. From all of this the reader must infer the thesis, which is, by essay's end, fairly obvious.

The thesis, then, may appear at any point in the essay. It may be expressed fully in only one place, or it may be restated in several places and in various ways. Or it may not be stated directly, but left to the reader to infer from the information the essay presents. But whatever the position of the thesis statement, it is crucial to both reader and writer—it is the main idea in any piece of exposition.

Last of the New England Hill Farms

RICHARD W. BROWN

Richard W. Brown is a writer and photographer who lives on a 200-acre farm near Barnet, Vermont. First published in *National Wildlife,* this essay examines the forces threatening the survival of small family farms in New England and describes a way of life that is gradually becoming extinct.

1   Hidden away in backcountry pockets of upper New England lie the last remnants of a type of agriculture that once covered the greater portion of the Northeast. These are the few remaining small family hill farms of Vermont, New Hampshire and Maine. Their existence is an anachronism; too remote to be easily reached from Boston or New York, lacking the proper terrain for a ski resort or the necessary shorefront for a second-home development, these farming enclaves have retained much of their original character. And they still exhibit a sense of harmony between man and his natural surroundings.

2   Particularly in northern Vermont, the towns and farms are woven into the earth's contours, their boundaries naturally formed by a streambed or a change in soil or terrain. Fruit trees have been planted in sheltered hollows and massive, thick-barked maples shade the dirt roads that link each farm. The arrangement of the buildings, even the rooflines of the houses and barns, speak of the severe and cantankerous New England weather. Often, the house and much larger barn are connected by a series of shedlike structures, so that winter chores may be done without struggling through heavy drifts or the breath-shortening cold of a January morning.

3   This is not an easy land to farm. Those who first settled here found a rich, well-drained humus formed by the vast deciduous forest that stretched uninterrupted to the horizon. But the ground was stony, uneven and frozen half the year. The glaciers that once covered these hills left thin-skinned bony ledges, and immovable boulders like granite icebergs, their gray shoulders poking obstinately above the earth's surface.

4   Gradually, this obdurate ground was cleared and worked. The Vermont hill farmer learned to plow thin where the soil was shallow and to leave the wet places and bogs to soak up the spring runoff. Nature dictated that what was taken be balanced by what was left alone. After generations of bent-backed labor, the soil was persuaded to trade birch and maple for oats and

LAST OF THE NEW ENGLAND HILL FARMS   From *National Wildlife* magazine, August-September 1976. Copyright 1976 by the National Wildlife Federation. Reprinted by permission of the publisher.

corn, nutgrass and milkweed for beans and squash. The brown corduroy of plowed land lay in patches on green hillsides, and white farmhouses and red barns brightened the landscape.

5   Still, a feeling of wildness remained and remains to this day, for this land could never be completely tamed. Such an attempt would have been foolhardy. Only careful and judicious agriculture, with constant attention to nature's prerogatives, allowed these farms to survive. Those places that were carelessly farmed or cleared unwisely have long since failed or reverted to their natural state. Rectangular stands of softwood now mark hillsides once overgrazed and poplars sprout from countless abandoned cellar holes.

6   The people who have worked this ground have in turn become formed by it. Growing up in these weather-worn hills has made them different from their down-country counterparts. The rural Yankee character is legendary: the wry humor, the thrift, the ability to "make do"—even the inflection and laconic manner of speech.

7   The work of these farmers is wedded to the land and its seasonal variations. In early spring, buckets are hung out in maple orchards to catch the watery sap. The thawing of the earth reawakens the sense of smell and the faint scent of damp tree buds and fiddleheads mingles with the rich smell of manure as the winter's accumulation is spread on the re-emerging fields. Large bands of robins that have arrived prematurely will often follow a spreader, searching for insect larvae in its wake.

8   One late and very cold spring, I watched in amazement, as a flock of 15 scarlet tanagers followed a farmer plowing. I had only seen six of these shy, brilliantly colored birds in my entire lifetime. Their usual diet of insects had not yet hatched and they were desperately snatching at grubs and worms as the plowshare turned back each furrow.

9   Summer is a season of frantic growth, for both wild and cultivated plants must flower, become pollinated and produce their seed in the urgently short span of just three or four months. Miraculously, a countryside that was sterile and white in January is now brilliantly green and alive with the rustle of field corn and the rampant, tropical growth of ostrich fern. The cut hay lies in fragrant windrows under the flat heat of a July noon. During the hours of early morning, and again in the evening, white-tailed deer appear, as many as a dozen silhouetted on a ridge, the white of their tails flickering in the half light, their heads poking up periodically to test the air.

10   In fall, human activity mirrors that of the animals—it is a time spent in preparation for the coming winter. Fields are plowed so that winter's snow and frost will mellow them. Cords of firewood are cut from the woodlot and split (not for this winter's heat, but for the next, as it must season for a year). The old stone foundations are banked against drafts with spruce boughs, maple leaves, or musty hay bales. In the barn, the bats have wedged themselves into protected cracks to hibernate and the barn swallows have long since departed.

11   With the heavy, muffling snowfall and numbing cold of winter, there is a general sense of drawing inward. Deer yard up in cedar swamps and rac-

coons sleep in tree hollows. The farmer occupies himself in the barn as the landscape lies outside, unstirring and quiescent under a brilliant but heatless sun. Great flocks of evening grosbeaks gather around feeders, squabbling and chattering over the sunflower seeds that have been put out for them: large, chunky yellow birds that my neighbor calls his "chickens." In the middle of the night, when temperatures often reach $-30°$, the old houses boom and crack like ice on a pond.

12   Many of the farms that still remain in this region continue to be farmed in a traditional manner. Lying outside the mainstream of American agribusiness, with its vast one-crop acreages, they are all small family holdings. Many are known in this area as "century farms"—farms that have been worked by the generations of one family for over a hundred years—and a few have even passed 200 years. While dairying, lumbering and maple sugaring are the primary sources of income, most farmers continue to keep a small herd of sheep or a few goats, pigs and chickens. A tractor is a necessity on an economically viable farm today, but some of these farmers also keep a team of thick-flanked Belgian horses to do their lighter work, and for hauling the sap sleds through the woods in April.

13   After 200 years of continuous use, northern New England's surviving hill farms are fertile and productive. Yet even these farms face the possibility of extinction in the near future. Tractor fuel and baling twine prices have doubled in the past few years. Property taxes are skyrocketing; fertilizer and machinery prices have jumped alarmingly, too. In the face of this savage inflation, the price the dairyman receives for his milk has not kept pace.

14   These problems affect all farmers, of course, large and small alike. But they often have an especially brutal impact on the small-acreage operator in the hills with a slim profit margin. Unfortunately, these farmers cannot hold out much longer if present trends continue, no matter how skillful their management of land, time and money. Each year, they have increasing difficulty competing with larger valley farms more adaptable to modern machinery and concentrated cropping.

15   These farms are a valuable part of our heritage. They lend beauty and diversity to the countryside and they provide food and habitat for an enormous variety of wildlife. Certain measures, such as tax easements for agricultural land use, would help keep this kind of agriculture alive. Surely, such efforts must be made to see that the old-fashioned New England hill farm does not vanish altogether from the landscape.

Exercises

COMPREHENSION

Organization and Development

Complete the following outline. Find the thesis statement and write it in the space provided. Then find the main divisions in the essay and fill in the remaining spaces. Note the paragraphs for each section.

Thesis statement: _____

_____

_____

I.   _____   [   ]
II. _____   [   ]
III. _____   [   ]
IV. _____   [   ]

Content

Choose the answer that correctly completes each statement.

1. In comparison to earlier farms in the Northeast, the Vermont hill farms are (a) practically unchanged (b) more modern and scientific (c) larger and more numerous.
2. Farming this land successfully requires (a) knowledge of how to tame nature's wilderness (b) careful and constant attention (c) modern fertilizers and pesticides.
3. Two characteristics of these Yankee farmers are thrift and the ability to (a) make up (b) make money (c) make do.
4. One can infer that many small farms close to northeastern cities have been developed for (a) industry (b) suburbs (c) resorts.
5. The farmer's work is dictated by (a) his family's needs (b) the seasons (c) the price he can get for his crops.
6. Brown emphasizes the animals who inhabit this area to show that (a) the farmers are shortsighted in trying to eliminate them (b) these farms provide the animals' food and habitat (c) the animals destroy crops each year worth millions of dollars.
7. The greatest threat to the survival of the hill farms is (a) agribusiness (b) low crop prices (c) inflation.
8. The main idea of this article is that the Vermont hill farms exhibit (a) a wasteful, inefficient, and obsolete agricultural system (b) harmony and interdependence between man and his surroundings (c) an example of how small, family farms can survive and succeed.

Paragraph Structure

Reorder the following sentences to form a unified, coherent paragraph. Then check your version with the original.

1. Each year, they have increasing difficulty competing with larger valley farms more adaptable to modern machinery and concentrated cropping.
2. These problems affect all farmers, of course, large and small alike.
3. Unfortunately, these farmers cannot hold out much longer if present trends continue, no matter how skillful their management of land, time and money.

4. But they often have an especially brutal impact on the small-acreage operator in the hills with a slim profit margin.

VOCABULARY AND USAGE

Word Formation Table

Complete the following table by changing word endings or root forms to make new grammatical forms. Use your dictionary if necessary.

	NOUN	VERB	ADJECTIVE	ADVERB
1.	activity	_____	_____	_____
2.	_____	_____	adaptable	xxx
3.	_____	_____	_____	desperate
4.	_____	continue	_____	_____
5.	_____	dictate	_____	_____

Fill-Ins

Complete each of the sentences below using the words on the following list. You may need to use some words more than once. You may also find that some blanks can be completed correctly with more than one word. Add plural endings to nouns and change verb forms where necessary.

rival	environment	foolhardy	habitat
severe	unfortunately	sterile	reflect
mirror	compete	however	anachronism
once	fertile	harsh	dormant
threat	exhibit	possibility	continuously

1. During the fall, human activity _____ that of the animals; that is, everyone prepares for the _____ winter months.
2. The hill farms provide a(n) _____ for many species of animals and birds who would face the _____ of extinction if the farms were developed.
3. _____, inflation has become a _____ to the hill farmers, who can no longer _____ against agribusiness.
4. In winter the land is _____; _____, in the summer, it is green and vibrant with new life.
5. The existence of the hill farms is a(n) _____; they _____ a way of life that _____ was much more widespread.
6. The hill farms _____ a harmonious relationship between man and his _____; some farms, _____, failed because of _____ attempts to tame the land.

DISCUSSION

1. What are some of the hardships that the hill farmers have to endure to make a living?
2. What is the relationship between the land, the climate, and the people who farm the land?

3. What is the author's tone toward his subject? Where does he reveal his attitude implicitly, and where does he reveal it explicitly?
4. Explain the author's pattern of development in paragraphs 3, 7, 12, and 15.
5. If you are a farm person, is this account sentimentalized? Explain by citing references to the essay. In the same way, if you are a city person, has Brown made this life sound appealing or not? Explain.

SUGGESTIONS FOR WRITING

1. Using the cause and effect method of organization, write an essay in which you explain the reasons for the threat to the survival of the hill farms.
2. Describe a tradition or institution in your part of the country that is in danger of becoming extinct. Include an explanation of the forces that are threatening it.
3. In the library, gather statistics on the decline of the small farm in America and, in particular, on the economic effects of inflation, high taxes, and high prices for farm machinery. Then in an essay discuss the economic factors contributing to the decline of small farms, using the statistical evidence you have gathered as support.

Things: The Throw-away Society

ALVIN TOFFLER

Alvin Toffler is a writer and teacher who lives in Connecticut. He wrote *Future Shock,* from which this excerpt is taken, to explore "the dizzying disorientation brought on by the premature arrival of the future." But *Future Shock* is also social criticism, and this selection examines how Americans' attachment to objects is increasingly temporary, a lesson taught even to little girls who are encouraged to trade in their old Barbie dolls for a new model.

1   "Barbie," a twelve-inch plastic teen-ager, is the best-known and best-selling doll in history. Since its introduction in 1959, the Barbie doll population of the world has grown to 12,000,000—more than the human population of Los Angeles or London or Paris. Little girls adore Barbie because she is highly realistic and eminently dress-upable. Mattel, Inc., maker of Barbie, also sells a complete wardrobe for her, including clothes for ordinary daytime wear, clothes for formal party wear, clothes for swimming and skiing.

2   Recently Mattel announced a new improved Barbie doll. The new version has a slimmer figure, "real" eyelashes, and a twist-and-turn waist that makes her more humanoid than ever. Moreover, Mattel announced that, for the first time, any young lady wishing to purchase a new Barbie would receive a trade-in allowance for her old one.

3   What Mattel did not announce was that by trading in her old doll for a technologically improved model, the little girl of today, citizen of tomorrow's super-industrial world, would learn a fundamental lesson about the new society: that man's relationships with *things* are increasingly temporary.

4   The ocean of man-made physical objects that surrounds us is set within a larger ocean of natural objects. But increasingly, it is the technologically produced environment that matters for the individual. The texture of plastic or concrete, the iridescent glisten of an automobile under a streetlight, the staggering vision of a cityscape seen from the window of a jet—these are the intimate realities of his existence. Man-made things enter into and color his consciousness. Their number is expanding with explosive force, both absolutely and relative to the natural environment. This will be even more true in super-industrial society than it is today.

5   Anti-materialists tend to deride the importance of "things." Yet things are highly significant, not merely because of their functional utility, but also

because of their psychological impact. We develop relationships with things. Things affect our sense of continuity or discontinuity. They play a role in the structure of situations and the foreshortening of our relationships with things accelerates the pace of life.

6   Moreover, our attitudes toward things reflect basic value judgments. Nothing could be more dramatic than the difference between the new breed of little girls who cheerfully turn in their Barbies for the new improved model and those who, like their mothers and grandmothers before them, clutch lingeringly and lovingly to the same doll until it disintegrates from sheer age. In this difference lies the contrast between past and future, between societies based on permanence, and the new, fast-forming society based on transience.

The Paper Wedding Gown

7   That man-thing relationships are growing more and more temporary may be illustrated by examining the culture surrounding the little girl who trades in her doll. This child soon learns that Barbie dolls are by no means the only physical objects that pass into and out of her young life at a rapid clip. Diapers, bibs, paper napkins, Kleenex, towels, non-returnable soda bottles—all are used up quickly in her home and ruthlessly eliminated. Corn muffins come in baking tins that are thrown away after one use. Spinach is encased in plastic sacks that can be dropped into a pan of boiling water for heating, and then thrown away. TV dinners are cooked and often served on throw-away trays. Her home is a large processing machine through which objects flow, entering and leaving, at a faster and faster rate of speed. From birth on, she is inextricably embedded in a throw-away culture.

8   The idea of using a product once or for a brief period and then replacing it, runs counter to the grain of societies or individuals steeped in a heritage of poverty. Not long ago Uriel Rone, a market researcher for the French advertising agency Publicis, told me: "The French housewife is not used to disposable products. She likes to keep things, even old things, rather than throw them away. We represented one company that wanted to introduce a kind of plastic throw-away curtain. We did a marketing study for them and found the resistance too strong." This resistance, however, is dying all over the developed world.

9   Thus a writer, Edward Maze, has pointed out that many Americans visiting Sweden in the early 1950's were astounded by its cleanliness. "We were almost awed by the fact that there were no beer and soft drink bottles by the roadsides, as, much to our shame, there were in America. But by the 1960's, lo and behold, bottles were suddenly blooming along Swedish highways . . . . What happened? Sweden had become a buy, use and throw-away society, following the American pattern." In Japan today throw-away tissues are so universal that cloth handkerchiefs are regarded as old fashioned, not to say unsanitary. In England for sixpence one may buy a "Dentamatic throwaway toothbrush" which comes already coated with toothpaste for its one-time use. And even in France, disposable cigarette lighters are commonplace.

From cardboard milk containers to the rockets that power space vehicles, products created for short-term or one-time use are becoming more numerous and crucial to our way of life.

10   The recent introduction of paper and quasi-paper clothing carried the trend toward disposability a step further. Fashionable boutiques and working-class clothing stores have sprouted whole departments devoted to gaily colored and imaginatively designed paper apparel. Fashion magazines display breathtakingly sumptuous gowns, coats, pajamas, even wedding dresses made of paper. The bride pictured in one of these wears a long white train of lace-like paper that, the caption writer notes, will make "great kitchen curtains" after the ceremony.

11.   Paper clothes are particularly suitable for children. Writes one fashion expert: "Little girls will soon be able to spill ice cream, draw pictures and make cutouts on their clothes while their mothers smile benignly at their creativity." And for adults who want to express their own creativity, there is even a "paint-yourself-dress" complete with brushes. Price: $2.00.

12   Price, of course, is a critical factor behind the paper explosion. Thus a department store features simple A-line dresses made of what it calls "devil-may-care cellulose fiber and nylon." At $1.29 each, it is almost cheaper for the consumer to buy and discard a new one than to send an ordinary dress to the cleaners. Soon it will be. But more than economics is involved, for the extension of the throw-away culture has important psychological consequences.

13   We develop a throw-away mentality to match our throw-away products. This mentality produces, among other things, a set of radically altered values with respect to property. But the spread of disposability through the society also implies decreased durations in man-thing relationships. Instead of being linked with a single object over a relatively long span of time, we are linked for brief periods with the succession of objects that supplant it.

Exercises

COMPREHENSION

Organization and Development

Complete the following outline. Find the thesis statement and write it in the space provided. Then find the main divisions in the essay and fill in the remaining spaces. Note the paragraphs for each section.

Thesis statement: _____

_____

    I.   _____   [   ]
    II. _____   [   ]
    III. _____   [   ]
    IV. _____   [   ]

Content

Choose the answer that correctly completes each statement.

1. Toffler's purpose in this essay is to (a) explain the cultural forces that give rise to materialism (b) convince us not to buy disposable items (c) examine the relationship between human beings and objects in a technological society.
2. Toffler uses the illustration of Mattel's trade-in policy for Barbie dolls to show that (a) Mattel needed a gimmick to increase its profits (b) children learn early in this culture that objects are easily disposed of (c) American companies deliberately foster the impulse to buy new models by making the old models seem either old-fashioned or obsolete.
3. When Toffler writes, "The ocean of man-made physical objects that surrounds us is set within a larger ocean of natural objects," the word "ocean" refers to (a) the ocean in a literal sense (b) a splendid array (c) a vast quantity.
4. In his discussion of material objects, Toffler emphasizes (a) their psychological impact (b) new technological advances (c) their contribution to economic growth.
5. Toffler compares the modern home to a (a) marvelous store with an incredible assortment of things to buy (b) large processing machine in which objects enter and leave at a rapid pace (c) huge garbage pail where one throws disposable objects.
6. People in countries such as Sweden, England, and Japan apparently (a) believe in saving objects and using them over and over again (b) have also adopted our throw-away mentality (c) have successfully resisted the idea of disposable products.
7. To support his contentions, Toffler relies extensively on (a) illustration and example (b) classification (c) comparison and contrast.
8. Toffler concludes that the primary negative effect of throw-away products is (a) they waste the earth's natural resources (b) we are unable to develop strong attachments to our possessions (c) we develop a throw-away mentality that produces a set of radically altered values with respect to property.

Paragraph Structure

Reorder the following sentences to form a unified, coherent paragraph. Identify one sentence as the topic sentence. Then check your version with the original.

1. From birth on, she is inextricably embedded in a throw-away culture.
2. This child soon learns that Barbie dolls are by no means the only physical objects that pass into and out of her young life at a rapid clip.
3. Her home is a large processing machine through which objects flow, entering and leaving, at a faster and faster rate of speed.
4. Diapers, bibs, paper napkins, Kleenex, towels, nonreturnable soda bottles—all are used up quickly in her home and ruthlessly eliminated.
5. That man-thing relationships are growing more and more temporary may be illustrated by examining the culture surrounding the little girl who trades in her doll.

VOCABULARY AND USAGE

Word Formation Table

Complete the following table by changing word endings or root forms to make new grammatical forms. Use your dictionary if necessary.

	NOUN	VERB	ADJECTIVE	ADVERB
1.	_____	_____	disposable	XXX
2.	_____	illustrate	_____	_____
3.	society	_____	_____	_____
4.	materialist ,	_____	_____	_____
5.	_____	XXX	_____	ruthlessly

Fill-Ins

Complete each of the sentences below using the words on the following list. You may need to use some words more than once. You may also find that some blanks can be completed correctly with more than one word. Add plural endings to nouns and change verb forms where necessary.

moreover	critical	illustrate	furthermore
instead of	relationship	trade	importance
disposable	crucial	display	version
society	thing	transient	object
significance	temporary	throw-away	yet

1. Toffler's thesis is that in our new _____, man's _____ with _____ are increasingly _____.
2. Mattel announced a new _____ of a Barbie doll; _____, it announced that any little girl could _____ her old model for a new one.
3. Toffler implies that _____ teaching children to conserve, the Barbie doll policy _____ that _____, even cherished ones, are _____.
4. Anti-materialists deride the _____ of _____; _____ Toffler _____ strongly to this idea.
5. Toffler feels that our _____ with _____ and the attitudes we _____ toward them have psychological _____.
6. The _____ point in Toffler's argument is that we develop a _____ mentality to match our _____ products; _____, life itself becomes more _____.

DISCUSSION

1. What is the function of the Barbie doll illustration at the beginning of the essay? Is this an isolated example?
2. After Toffler states his thesis, he refers to it again in the body. Where does he restate his thesis? Are these restatements necessary to establish coherence?
3. What are the two main methods of development in the section comprising paragraphs 7, 8, and 9?
4. Look up "ruthless" (see paragraph 7) in the dictionary. Has Toffler used this word accurately? What other word could you substitute?
5. What is the topic sentence in paragraph 8? Does the evidence that follows adequately support his assertion about those "steeped in a heritage of poverty"?
6. Toffler states in paragraph 13 that the throw-away mentality produces "a set of radically altered values with respect to property." What exactly do you think he means? What evidence does he provide in the essay to warrant this conclusion?
7. Would you characterize Toffler's essay as subjective and interpretive or objective and factual? Cite examples from the essay to support your answer.

SUGGESTIONS FOR WRITING

1. Discuss the strengths and weaknesses of Toffler's argument and come to a conclusion of your own about the psychological effects of the throw-away culture.
2. Toffler is chiefly concerned with the psychological impact of things and our increasingly temporary relationship with them. Argue against the idea of disposable products from another point of view—for example, from economic or environmental concerns. Use illustrations other than Toffler's as much as possible.
3. If you are familiar with the habits and customs of another culture (or subculture), write an essay contrasting that culture's attitude toward things with the attitude Toffler describes. Use extensive illustrations for your supporting evidence.

Freedom and Survival in the Alaskan Wilderness

JOHN MCPHEE

John McPhee lives in Princeton, New Jersey, and writes for *The New Yorker,* as well as for other magazines, primarily on science and the environment. Some of his books are *A Sense of Where You Are* (about Bill Bradley), *The Pine Barrens,* and *The Survival of the Bark Canoe.* This essay comes from *Coming into the Country,* a book about Alaska. The title refers to Alaskans' penchant for describing Alaska as "the country" and the act of moving there as "coming into the country." Brad Snow, mentioned at the beginning, is the builder of an illegal cabin on the Nation River, and Lilly Allen is his girlfriend. The Gelvins, mentioned in the second paragraph, are an Alaskan family engaged in gold prospecting.

1   Snow was shortly given written notice that the cabin was on federal ground, that its presence conflicted with "the necessary and appropriate use of said land," and that if he left his personal property there it would be removed and stored at his expense. Lilly Allen was mentioned only as "any and all other persons." Alaska had attracted them. The United States had rebuffed them. Sarge Waller got a notice, too, about his cabin at the Kandik. Other notices went down the river. In the hundred and sixty miles between Eagle and Circle, the exact small number of people living on or near the Yukon had always been indeterminate, and as the scrutiny of the Bureau of Land Management drew closer the number became even less determinate than before. Under blue wisps of smoke separated by pieces of land the size of Eastern counties, people did what they could to remain invisible, knowing they were in trespass on federal land.

2   From time immemorial until the nineteen-seventies, anyone who had the drive and spirit to build a cabin in this northern wilderness was not restrained from doing so. For a long time, gold was the almost exclusive draw, and, as Lieutenant Frederick Schwatka had observed when he was sent to scout the region in 1883, "the discovery of gold in paying quantities is probably the only incentive for men to enter the country, and were it not that indications are seen all along the river, white men would probably never venture in." In more recent times, though, as the pressure of population in the Lower Forty-eight increased toward critical levels, a quite different

incentive presented itself as well. Some of the hardiest people in the society were drawn to bush Alaska in search of a sense of release—of a life that remembered the past. The Alaskan wild was, as advertised, the last frontier—where people willing to combat its cold and run its risks could live an existence free from supererogatory rules as long as they did no harm to one another. The government did not interfere, and through the Homestead Act and other legislative provisions it even assisted this dream; but, with the discovery of oil at Prudhoe Bay on the edge of the Arctic Ocean, events began to occur that would change, apparently forever, the use and demarcation of Alaskan land. Meanwhile, certain long-established forms of freedom would disappear—the sort of freedom that drew a family like the Gelvins a generation earlier into the country, the sort of freedom envisioned by young people who set off to live in the wild of the upper Yukon. If the oil had never been discovered, there would not have been an eviction notice prepared for Brad Snow.

3   The discovery of the oil was in 1968, and after it became clear that there would be no pipeline until the land claims of the natives were satisfactorily extinguished, the United States Congress (attempting to satisfy not only the natives but at the same time the conflicting ambitions of conservationists and developers; attempting to promote the economy, protect the ecology, and respond multifariously to the sudden demand for this long-ignored but now prime segment of American national real estate) got together in a single bill the mighty ziggurat of legislation within which the catalytic pipeline would seem, while important, almost minor. Long after the publicity had receded and the pipeline had become as little discussed as the Big Inch, the social and political effects of its progenitive congressional bill would still be poignantly felt. Everyone of any race in all Alaska would be affected by the Alaska Native Claims Settlement Act. In elemental respects, the character of Alaska would change.

4   The natives would be afforded some variety in the choosing of their forty million acres of land, but much of it would be close to established villages. Included, meanwhile, among the epic consolations given the conservationists—the big pieces of land that were to be set aside for consideration as national parks, forests, rivers, wildlife refuges—were more than two million acres along the Yukon between Eagle and Circle. Many millions of additional acres—including the valley where the Gelvins legally staked gold claims—were to be closed to all but those in pursuit of "metalliferous minerals." Meanwhile, the State of Alaska was still choosing the hundred and three million acres awarded to it in the Statehood Act. It had until 1984 to complete the selection, and for the time being the land under scrutiny would remain—to the individual—beyond reach. When one adds in the existing parks, government forests, and wildlife refuges and a vast federal petroleum reserve in the north, not much remains, so it is one of the ironies of Alaska that in the midst of this tremendous wilderness people consider themselves fortunate to have (anywhere at all) a fifty-by-a-hundred-foot lot they can call their own.

5   Meanwhile, down below, outside, people who sit on sidewalks wearing Italian hiking boots and machine-faded jeans imply an extremity somewhere else. Surely, some of them will stand up and leave town, and when they leave they will go toward the wild—probably to the nearest mountain. Some will keep going to an even wilder place. Some will go farther than that. The logical inevitability for this chain of beings is that the ultimates will appear in Eagle (or Circle or Central or somewhere else in Alaska)—where civilization stops. And a very few will then jump free, going deep into the roadless world. By the time they reach Eagle, their momentum is too great to be interrupted by an act of Congress, even if they know of it and understand what it says. What the law now calls for is the removal of the last place in the United States where the pioneer impulse can leap from confinement. It is in the character of the impulse that the impulse will leap anyway—so the Bureau of Land Management, custodian of all the huge acreages under shift and selection, is charged with driving the trespassers away. Whites feel sold out and shoved under by the settlement of the native claims. Reticence has never been a characteristic of people attracted to this kind of terrain. They howl their upset, its focus the B.L.M.

6   "You can't go out and build a cabin and live in the goddamned woods, which people have been doing since the country was founded. Nobody argues with a few parks, but such a big percentage of the land is too much."

7   "It's not as if we're building fifty-thousand-dollar houses with asphalt driveways and stinking cesspools."

8   "Our cabins are more like tents than like most people's homes. They are made with native materials—white spruce, earth, moss. They are biodegradable. When they are abandoned, trees thirty feet high grow up out of the sod on their roofs. Eventually, the cabin collapses and disappears into the ground."

9   "Most people felt if we became a state we'd get rid of some of this federal control, and actually it's got worse."

10   "Alaska's ruined by this native-land deal that's went through. You could build a cabin anywhere, and mine anywhere, when I came. Now Alaska is going to be just like every other state."

11   "What bugs me is that when decisions are made about Alaska, people from Texas and Ohio, California and New York carry more weight than people from Alaska."

12   "Why should people be hassled for building cabins out here? What harm are they doing? Why should they be bothered? Why destroy a life simply because it exists? Slap a mosquito, yes. But if a life is not harming, why destroy it? Every species of animal has a wide genetic base, or they don't exist. Our living out here is a widening of the genetic base. I think the government people are fools to wipe us out."

13   "It's public land. We're the public."

14   "Down at the North Fork are twelve cabins. Mostly, the sites have been in use since the turn of the century, maintained and repaired by trappers and

prospectors. Now the B.L.M. wants to kick these people out. It tells them they can never go to those cabins."

15   "Why should they drive us away? They ought to pay us to be out here—just to keep these places in good shape and well supplied."

16   "There are emergencies in this country, and when they happen sometimes cabins are needed."

17   "More than one life has been saved when someone in trouble has come upon a cabin."

18   The country is full of stories of unusual deaths—old Nimrod Robertson lying down on a creek in overflow and letting it build around him a sarcophagus of ice; the trapper on the Kandik who apparently knocked himself out when he tripped and fell on his own firewood and froze to death before he came to—and of stories also of deaths postponed. There are fewer of the second. I would like to add one back—an account that in essence remains in the country but in detail has largely disappeared.

19   On a high promontory in the montane ruggedness around the upper Charley River lies the wreckage of an aircraft that is readily identifiable as a B-24. This was the so-called Liberator, a medium-range bomber built for the Second World War. The wreckage is in the dead center of the country, and I happened over it in a Cessna early in the fall of 1975, during a long and extremely digressive flight that began in Eagle and ended many hours later in Circle. The pilot of the Cessna said he understood that the crew of the Liberator had bailed out, in winter, and that only one man had survived. I asked around to learn who might know more than that—querying, among others, the Air Force in Fairbanks, the Gelvins, various old-timers in Circle and Central, some of the river people, and Margaret Nelson, in Eagle, who had packed parachutes at Ladd Field, in Fairbanks, during the war. There had been one survivor—everyone agreed. No one knew his name. He had become a symbol in the country, though, and was not about to be forgotten. It was said that he alone had come out—long after all had been assumed dead—because he alone, of the widely scattered crew, was experienced in wilderness, knew how to live off the land, and was prepared to deal with the hostile cold. Above all, he had found a cabin, during his exodus, without which he would have died for sure.

20   "And the government bastards try to stop us from building them now."

21   "Guy jumped out of an airplane, and he would have died but he found a cabin."

22   If the survivor had gone on surviving for what was now approaching thirty-five years, he would in all likelihood be somewhere in the Lower Forty-eight. When I was home, I made a try to find him. Phone calls ricocheted around Washington for some days, yielding only additional phone numbers. The story was just too sketchy. Did I know how many bombers had been lost in that war? At length, I was given the name of Gerard Hasselwander, a historian at the Albert F. Simpson Historical Research Center, Maxwell

Air Force Base, Alabama. I called him, and he said that if I did not even know the year of the crash he doubted he could help me. Scarcely two hours later, though, he called back to say that he had had a free moment or two at the end of his lunch hour and had browsed through some microfilm. To his own considerable surprise, he had found the survivor's name, which was Leon Crane. Crane's home when he entered the Army Air Forces had been in Philadelphia, but Hasselwander had looked in a Philadelphia directory and there was no Leon Crane in it now. However, he said, Leon Crane had had two brothers who were also in service—in the Army Medical Corps—during the Second World War. One of them was named Morris. In the Philadelphia directory, there was a Dr. Morris Crane.

23   When I called the number, someone answered and said Dr. Crane was not there.

24   I asked when he would return.

25   "I don't know" was the reply. "He went to Leon's."

26   The Liberator, making cold-weather propeller tests above twenty thousand feet, went into a spin, dived toward the earth, and, pulling out, snapped its elevator controls. It then went into another spin, and the pilot gave the order to abandon ship. There were five aboard. Leon Crane was the co-pilot. He was twenty-four and he had been in Alaska less than two months. Since the plane was falling like a swirling leaf, he had to drag himself against heavy centrifugal force toward the open bomb bay. He had never used a parachute. The outside air temperature was at least thirty degrees below zero. When he jumped, he forgot his mittens. The day was December 21st.

27   The plane fiercely burned, not far away from where he landed, and he stood watching it, up to his thighs in snow. He was wearing a hooded down jacket, a sweater, winter underwear, two pairs of trousers, two pairs of socks, and felt-lined military mukluks. He scanned the mountainsides but could see nothing of the others. He thought he had been the second one to go out of the plane, and as he fell he thought he saw a parachute open in the air above him. He shouted into the winter silence. Silence answered. Months later, he would learn that there had been two corpses in the aircraft. Of the two other fliers no track or trace was ever found. "Sergeant Pompeo, the crew chief, had a hell of a thick set of glasses. He must have lost them as soon as he hit the airstream. Without them, he really couldn't see. What was he going to do when he got down there?"

28   For that matter, what was Crane going to do? He had no food, no gun, no sleeping bag, no mittens. The plane had been meandering in search of suitable skies for the tests. Within two or three hundred miles, he had no idea where he was.

29   Two thousand feet below him, and a couple of miles east, was a river. He made his way down to it. Waiting for rescue, he stayed beside it. He had two books of matches, a Boy Scout knife. He started a fire with a letter from his father, and for the first eight days he did not sleep more than two hours at a time in his vigilance to keep the fire burning. The cold awakened him anyway. Water fountained from a gap in the river ice, and that is what he lived on. His

hands, which he to some extent protected with parachute cloth or in the pockets of his jacket, became cut and abraded from tearing at spruce boughs. When he spread his fingers, the skin between them would split. Temperatures were probably ranging between a high of thirty below zero and a low around fifty. The parachute, as much as anything, kept him alive. It was twenty-eight feet in diameter, and he wound it around him so that he was at the center of a great cocoon. Still, he said, his back would grow cold while his face roasted, and sparks kept igniting the chute.

30   He was telling me some of this on a sidewalk in Philadelphia when I asked him how he had dealt with fear.

31   He stopped in surprise, and looked contemplatively up the street toward Independence Hall, his graying hair wisping out to the sides. He wore a business suit and a topcoat, and he had bright, penetrating eyes. He leaned forward when he walked. "Fear," he repeated. "I wouldn't have used that word. Think about it: there was not a hell of a lot I could do if I were to panic. Besides, I was sure that someone was going to come and get me."

32   All that the search-and-rescue missions had to go on was that the Liberator had last been heard from above Big Delta, so the search area could not be reduced much below forty thousand square miles. Needless to say, they would not come near finding him. He thought once that he heard the sound of an airplane, but eventually he realized that it was a chorus of wolves. In his hunger, he tried to kill squirrels. He made a spear, and threw it awkwardly as they jumped and chattered in the spruce boughs. He made a bow and arrow, using a shroud line from his parachute, but when he released the arrow it shot off at angles ridiculously oblique to the screeching, maddening squirrels. There was some rubber involved in the parachute assembly, and he used that to make a slingshot, which was worse than the bow and arrow. When he fell asleep by the fire, he dreamed of milkshakes, dripping beefsteaks, mashed potatoes, and lamb chops, with lamb fat running down his hands. Awake, he kicked aside the snow and found green moss. He put it in his mouth and chewed, and chewed some more, but scarcely swallowed any. Incidentally, he was camped almost exactly where, some twenty-five years later, Ed and Virginia Gelvin would build a cabin from which to trap and hunt.

33   Crane is a thoroughly urban man. He grew up in the neighborhood of Independence Hall, where he lives now, with an unlisted number. That part of the city has undergone extensive refurbishment in recent years, and Crane's sons, who are residential builders and construction engineers, have had a part in the process. Crane, more or less retired, works for them, and when I visited him I followed him from building to building as he checked on the needs and efforts of carpenters, bricklayers, plumbers. He professed to have no appetite for wild country, least of all for the expanses of the north. As a boy, he had joined a city Scout troop, and had become a First Class Scout, but that was not to suggest a particular knowledge of wilderness. When he flew out of Fairbanks that morning in 1943, his lifetime camping experience consisted of one night on the ground—with his troop, in Valley Forge.

34   He decided on the ninth day that no help was coming. Gathering up his parachute, he began to slog his way downriver, in snow sometimes up to his waist. It crossed his mind that the situation might be hopeless, but he put down the thought as he moved from bend to bend by telling himself to keep going because "right around that curve is what you're looking for." In fact, he was about sixty miles from the nearest human being, almost a hundred from the nearest group of buildings large enough to be called a settlement. Around the next bend, he saw more mountains, more bare jagged rock, more snow-covered sweeps of alpine tundra, contoured toward another river bend. "Right around that curve is what you're looking for," he told himself again. Suddenly, something was there. First, he saw a cache, high on legs in the air, and then a small cabin, with a door only three feet high. It was like the lamb chops, with the grease on his fingers, but when he pushed at the door it was wood and real. The room inside was nine by ten: earth floor, low ceiling, a bunk made of spruce. It was Alaskan custom always to leave a cabin open and stocked for anyone in need. Split firewood was there, and matches, and a pile of prepared shavings. On a table were sacks of dried raisins, sugar, cocoa, and powdered milk. There was a barrel stove, frying pans on the wall. He made some cocoa, and, after so long a time without food, seemed full after a couple of sips. Then he climbed a ladder and looked in the cache, lifting a tarp to discover hammers, saws, picks, drills, coiled rope, and two tents. No one, he reasoned, would leave such equipment far off in the wilderness. "I figured civilization was right around the corner. I was home free."

35   So he stayed just a night and went on down the river, anxious to get back to Ladd Field. The moon came up after the brief light of day, and he kept going. He grew weak in the deep cold of the night, and when the moon went below the mountains he began to wander off the stream course, hitting boulders. He had been around many corners, but no civilization was there. Now he was sinking into a dream-hazy sleepwalking numbed-out oblivion; but fear, fortunately, struck through and turned him, upriver. He had not retraced his way very far when he stopped and tried to build a fire. He scraped together some twigs, but his cut and bare hands were shaking so—at roughly fifty below zero—that he failed repeatedly to ignite a match. He abandoned the effort, and moved on through the snow. He kept hitting boulders. He had difficulty following his own tracks. He knew now that he would die if he did not get back to the cabin, and the detached observer within him decided he was finished. Left foot, right foot—there was no point in quitting, even so. About noon, he reached the cabin. With his entire body shaking, he worked at a fire until he had one going. Then he rolled up in his parachute and slept almost continuously for three full days.

36   In his excitement at being "right around the corner from civilization," he had scarcely looked in the cache, and now he found rice, flour, beans, powdered eggs, dried vegetables, and beef—enough for many weeks, possibly months. He found mittens. He found snowshoes. He found long

johns, socks, mukluks. He found candles, tea, tobacco, and a corncob pipe. He found ammunition, a .22. In the cabin, he mixed flour, peas, beans, sugar, and snow, and set it on the stove. That would be his basic gruel—and he became enduringly fond of it. Sometimes he threw in eggs and vegetables. He covered his hands with melted candle wax, and the bandage was amazingly effective. He developed a routine, with meals twice a day, a time for hunting, a fresh well chopped daily through the four-foot river ice. He slept eighteen hours a day, like a wintering bear—not truly hibernating, just lying there in his den. He felt a need to hear a voice, so he talked to himself. The day's high moment was a pipeful of tobacco puffed while he looked through ten-year-old copies of *The Saturday Evening Post.* He ransacked the magazines for insights into the woods lore he did not know. He learned a thing or two. In a wind, it said somewhere in the *Post,* build your fire in a hole. He shot and ate a ptarmigan, and had the presence of mind to look in its stomach. He found some overwintering berries there, went to the sort of bushes they had come from, and shot more ptarmigan. Cardboard boxes, the magazines, and other items in the cabin were addressed to "Phil Berail, Woodchopper, Alaska." Contemplating these labels, Crane decided that Alaska was a fantastic place—where someone's name and occupation were a sufficient address. One day, an old calendar fell off the wall and flipped over on its way to the floor. On the back was a map of Alaska. He stared at it all day. He found Woodchopper, on the Yukon, and smiled at his foolishness. From the terrain around him, the northward flow of the stream, the relative positions of Fairbanks and Big Delta, he decided—just right—that he was far up the Charley River. The smile went back where it came from.

37   He decided to wait for breakup, build a raft, and in late May float on down to the Yukon. After five or six weeks, though, he realized that his food was going to give out in March. There was little ammunition with which to get meat, and he had no confidence anyway in his chances with the rifle. If he stayed, he would starve. He felt panic now, but not enough to spill the care with which he was making his plans. He had set off willy-nilly once before and did not want to repeat the mistake. He patched his clothes with parachute cloth, sewing them with shroud lines. He made a sled from some boards and a galvanized tub. He figured closely what the maximum might be that he could drag and carry. On February 12th, he left. The sled would scarcely budge at first, and snow bunched up before it. Wearing a harness he had made, he dragged the sled slowly downriver. Berail's snowshoes had Indian ties. Try as he would, he could not understand how to secure them to his feet. The snowshoes were useless. Up to his knees, and sometimes to his hips, he walked from dawn until an hour before dark each day. He slept beside bonfires that burned all night. Blizzards came up the river some days, and driving williwaws—winds of a force that could literally stop him in his tracks. He leaned against the wind. When he could, he stepped forward. Once, at the end of a day's hard walking, he looked behind him—on the twisting mountain river—and saw where he had started at dawn. The

Charley in summer—clear-flowing within its canyon walls, with grizzlies fishing its riffles, Dall sheep on the bluffs, and peregrines above it in the air—is an extremely beautiful Alaskan river (it has been called the loveliest of all), but for Leon Crane it was little more than brutal. He came to a lead one day, a patch of open water, and, trying to use some boulders as stepping stones, he fell in up to his armpits. Coming out, barging through snowdrifts, he was the center of a fast-forming block of ice. His matches were dry. Shaking as before, he managed this time to build a fire. All day, he sat steaming beside it, removing this or that item of clothing, drying it a piece at a time.

38   After a couple of weeks on the river, he found another cabin, with a modest but welcome food cache—cornmeal, canned vegetables, Vienna sausage. He sewed himself a backpack and abandoned his cumbersome sled. Some seven or eight days on down the river, he came around a bend at dusk and found cut spruce tops in parallel rows stuck in the river snow. His aloneness, he sensed, was all but over. It was the second week of March, and he was eighty days out of the sky. The arrangement of treetops, obviously, marked a place where a plane on skis might land supplies. He looked around in near darkness and found a toboggan trail. He camped, and next day followed the trail to a cabin—under smoke. He shouted toward it. Al Ames, a trapper, and his wife, Neena, and their children appeared in the doorway. "I am Lieutenant Leon Crane, of the United States Army Air Forces," he called out. "I've been in a little trouble." Ames took a picture, which hangs on a wall in Philadelphia.

39   Crane remembers thinking, Somebody must be saving me for something, but I don't know what it is. His six children, who owe themselves to that trip and to Phil Berail's fully stocked Charley River cabin, are—in addition to his three sons in the construction business—Mimi, who is studying engineering at Barnard; Rebecca, who is in the master's program in architecture at Columbia; and Ruth, a recent graduate of the Harvard Medical School. Crane himself went on to earn an advanced degree in aeronautical engineering at the Massachusetts Institute of Technology, and spent his career developing helicopters for Boeing Vertol.

40   "It's a little surprising to me that people exist who are interested in living on that ground up there," he told me.

41   "Why would anyone want to take someone who wanted to *be* there and throw them out? Who the hell could *care?*"

42   Al Ames, who had built his cabin only two years before, harnessed his dogs and mushed Crane down the Yukon to Woodchopper, where a plane soon came along and flew him out.

43   Crane met Phil Berail at Woodchopper, and struggled shyly to express to him his inexpressible gratitude. Berail, sixty-five, was a temporary postmaster and worked for the gold miners there. He had trapped from his Charley River cabin. He was pleased that it had been useful, he said. For his part, he had no intention of ever going there again. He had abandoned the cabin four years before.

Exercises

COMPREHENSION

Organization and Development

Complete the following outline. Write a sentence stating McPhee's thesis, which is implied rather than stated directly, in the space provided. Then find the main divisions in the essay and fill in the remaining spaces. Note the paragraphs for each section.

Thesis statement: _____

_____

_____

    I. _____ [   ]

    II. _____ [   ]

    III. _____ [   ]

Content

Choose the answer that correctly completes each statement.

1. The Bureau of Land Management sent written notices to people stating that their cabins (a) did not meet federal regulations for construction and safety (b) were on federal land and thus the inhabitants were trespassing (c) would have to be moved to make room for the pipeline and a new national park.

2. In the nineteenth century, Alaska attracted gold prospectors; in the twentieth, McPhee says that Alaska has attracted people in search of (a) a sense of release and freedom from rules (b) high wages working on the pipeline (c) the security of owning several acres of wilderness.

3. According to the essay, the catalyst for all the changes that have occurred in Alaska was the (a) quarrel between developers and conservationists over Alaska's future (b) Alaska Native Claims Settlement Act (c) discovery of oil at Prudhoe Bay.

4. The congressional bill dealing with Alaska was especially complicated because (a) the Native Claims Settlement Act had not yet gone into effect (b) most Alaskans were opposed to the pipeline and the public lobby was strong (c) there were conflicting demands from developers, conservationists, and natives.

5. One would expect that land in Alaska would be easy to buy, but in fact (a) land is so expensive that few can afford to buy more than a small lot (b) most land around established villages is reserved for natives under the terms of the Settlement Act (c) so much land is owned by the state or federal government or set aside for gold and oil claims that little is available for private purchase.

6. The lone survivor of the Liberator crash was Leon Crane, who, though nameless, was widely regarded among Alaskans as (a) inexperienced in survival techniques in the wilderness (b) foolish to be flying over uncharted territory with so little equipment and so few supplies (c) a symbol of one who survived an ordeal in the wilderness because he came across a cabin.

7. It is Alaskan custom (a) to leave a cabin unlocked and fully stocked (b) to bury caches of food in the snow and mark the spot with a stick (c) to signal for help by sending smoke signals that might be seen by a plane.

8. "Woodchopper" turned out to be (a) Phil Berail's occupation (b) a town on the Yukon River (c) a prospector's nickname.

9. Crane's ordeal reveals (a) courage and a will to survive (b) fear and the folly of panicking (c) arrogance and overconfidence.
10. The main idea of this essay is that (a) cabins on federal land violate the law and all trespassers should be evicted (b) cabins built on federal land should be allowed to remain, because they have saved lives in emergencies (c) although it is undoubtedly a bad precedent, cabins should be allowed to remain on federal land because Alaska is America's last frontier.

Paragraph Structure

Reorder the following sentences to form a unified, coherent paragraph. Identify one sentence as the topic sentence and underline the key words. Then check your version with the original.

1. In more recent times, though, as the pressure of population in the Lower Forty-eight increased toward critical levels, a quite different incentive presented itself as well.
2. The Alaskan wild was, as advertised, the last frontier—where people willing to combat its cold and run its risks could live an existence free from supererogatory rules as long as they did no harm to one another.
3. From time immemorial until the nineteen-seventies, anyone who had the drive and spirit to build a cabin in this northern wilderness was not restrained from doing so.
4. For a long time, gold was the almost exclusive draw, and, as Lieutenant Frederick Schwatka had observed when he was sent to scout the region in 1883, "the discovery of gold in paying quantities is probably the only incentive for men to enter the country, and were it not that indications are seen all along the river, white men would probably never venture in."
5. Some of the hardiest people in the society were drawn to bush Alaska in search of a sense of release—of a life that remembered the past.

VOCABULARY AND USAGE

Word Formation Table

Complete the following table by changing word endings or root forms to make new grammatical forms. Use your dictionary if necessary.

	NOUN	VERB	ADJECTIVE	ADVERB
1.	_____	_____	_____	ridiculously
2.	_____	xxx	_____	fiercely
3.	_____	_____	_____	comtemplatively
4.	_____	_____	digressive	_____
5.	vigilance	xxx	_____	_____

Fill-Ins

Complete each of the sentences below using the words on the following list. You may need to use some words more than once. You may also find that some blanks can be completed correctly with more than one word. Add plural endings to nouns and change verb forms where necessary.

restrain	complicated	cumbersome	hardly
hardy	rebuff	draw	evacuate
wander	meander	incentive	complex
supply	cache	rugged	attract
abandon	irony	scarcely	burdensome
			refuse

1. The eviction notice stated that the federal government _____ to allow the illegal cabin dwellers to remain and that they must _____ the premises.
2. The _____ for people in earlier times was gold; now, people were _____ by a new _____, a sense of release from the _____ problems and rules of the Lower 48.
3. Developers promoting the Alaska pipeline were _____ from construction until a _____ congressional bill was passed.
4. One of the _____ of Alaska is that _____ any land is left for private ownership.
5. The plane had been _____ in search of a place for its tests, and when Crane _____ ship, he had few _____ to help him survive in such _____ country.
6. When Crane's _____ of food was nearly gone, he_____ to give up; instead, he _____ the cabin and began to search for help.

DISCUSSION

1. What were the Bureau of Land Management's reasons for wanting to get rid of the cabins built on or near the Yukon River? What do you think the government meant by their notice that the cabins were in conflict with "the necessary and appropriate use of said land"? What do you think is the government's idea of how the wilderness should be used? What is McPhee's idea?
2. What was the catalyst for the government's order to the cabin dwellers? What was the real motive behind its decision?
3. What method of development does McPhee use in paragraph 2?
4. Write a topic sentence to govern the facts presented in paragraph 4.
5. How does McPhee reveal the Alaskans' hostility to the government's plan? (See paragraphs 6–17.) Why doesn't he quote the names of the people whose opinions he cites? What effect is he trying to create by stringing together quotations without attributions or transitions?
6. Why doesn't McPhee provide a transition between paragraphs 17 and 18—the end of the residents' quotations and the beginning of Crane's story? Why is the last quotation particularly apt?
7. What did Leon Crane symbolize for Alaskans who knew the sketchy details of his survival? What is ironic about his reputation?
8. McPhee presents insurmountable evidence to support the idea, stated explicitly later in his book, that anyone who wants to build a cabin in the Alaskan wilderness should be allowed to do so. What are the unique circumstances and conditions of Alaska that lead him to this conclusion? Are these circumstances sufficiently unique and special to permit the government to grant an exception, or would this constitute a precedent that the government might regret in the future?

SUGGESTIONS FOR WRITING

1. The first portion of McPhee's essay establishes the background of the government's decision to evict the owners of the illegal cabins. Using a cause and effect pattern of development, explain the causes leading to a particular situation—perhaps the passage of a law, the outbreak of a prison riot, or a change in the policy of an institution that you are familiar with.

2. McPhee's anecdote about Leon Crane can easily stand alone in support of his implied thesis. Write a narrative of your own that suggests a thesis and that argues implicitly for something you strongly believe in.

3. Write an essay analyzing the significance of the frontier for American culture. You might want to refer to Dee Brown's essay, "From Christopher Columbus to Wounded Knee," as well as to McPhee's selection.

4. McPhee's point of view toward the cabin dwellers is clearly sympathetic, and his suspenseful recounting of Crane's ordeal makes a subtly forceful argument. Write an essay in which you take the opposite stand. Defend the government's policy of evicting the illegal residents from federal land in Alaska. In your rebuttal, you should respond to some of the arguments McPhee raises.

The American Way of Death

JESSICA MITFORD

Jessica Mitford was born in England, one of the famous Mitford sisters (described in *Daughters and Rebels*). She now lives in Oakland, California, and is married to a lawyer, Robert Treuhaft. She undertook an investigation of the heretofore shadowy practices of the American funeral industry because of her husband's concern that excessive funeral costs were depleting his clients' small estates. She has also published *Kind and Unusual Punishment*, a critical look at the American prison system. This essay is the first chapter of *The American Way of Death*.

1   *How long, I would ask, are we to be subjected to the tyranny of custom and undertakers? Truly, it is all vanity and vexation of spirit—a mere mockery of woe, costly to all, far, far beyond its value; and ruinous to many; hateful, and an abomination to all; yet submitted to by all, because none have the moral courage to speak against it and act in defiance of it.*

—Lord Essex

O death, where is thy sting? O grave, where is thy victory? Where, indeed. Many a badly stung survivor, faced with the aftermath of some relative's funeral, has ruefully concluded that the victory has been won hands down by a funeral establishment—in disastrously unequal battle.

2   Much has been written of late about the affluent society in which we live, and much fun poked at some of the irrational "status symbols" set out like golden snares to trap the unwary consumer at every turn. Until recently, little has been said about the most irrational and weirdest of the lot, lying in ambush for all of us at the end of the road—the modern American funeral.

3   If the Dismal Traders (as an eighteenth-century English writer calls them) have traditionally been cast in a comic role in literature, a universally recognized symbol of humor from Shakespeare to Dickens to Evelyn Waugh, they have successfully turned the tables in recent years to perpetrate a huge, macabre and expensive practical joke on the American public. It is not consciously conceived of as a joke, of course; on the contrary, it is hedged with admirably contrived rationalizations.

4   Gradually, almost imperceptibly, over the years the funeral men have constructed their own grotesque cloud-cuckooland where the trappings of Gracious Living are transformed, as in a nightmare, into the trappings of Gracious Dying. The same familiar Madison Avenue language, with its peculiar adjectival range designed to anesthetize sales resistance to all sorts of products, has seeped into the funeral industry in a new and bizarre guise. The emphasis is on the same desirable qualities that we have all been schooled to look for in our daily search for excellence: comfort, durability, beauty, craftsmanship. The attuned ear will recognize too the convincing quasi-scientific language, so reassuring even if unintelligible.

5   So that this too, too solid flesh might not melt, we are offered "solid copper—a quality casket which offers superb value to the client seeking long-lasting protection," or "the Colonial Classic Beauty—18 gauge lead coated steel, seamless top, lap-jointed welded body construction." Some are equipped with foam rubber, some with innerspring mattresses. Elgin offers "the revolutionary 'Perfect-Posture' bed." Not every casket need have a silver lining, for one may choose between "more than 60 color matched shades, magnificent and unique masterpieces" by the Cheney casket-lining people. Shrouds no longer exist. Instead, you may patronize a grave-wear couturière who promises "handmade original fashions—styles from the best in life for the last memory—dresses, men's suits, negligees, accessories." For the final, perfect grooming: "Nature-Glo—the ultimate in cosmetic embalming." And, where have we heard that phrase "peace of mind protection" before? No matter. In funeral advertising, it is applied to the Wilbert Burial Vault, with its ⅜-inch precast asphalt inner liner plus extra-thick, reinforced concrete—all this "guaranteed by Good Housekeeping." Here again the Cadillac, status symbol par excellence, appears in all its gleaming glory, this time transformed into a pastel-colored funeral hearse.

6   You, the potential customer for all this luxury, are unlikely to read the lyrical descriptions quoted above, for they are culled from *Mortuary Management* and *Casket and Sunnyside*, two of the industry's eleven trade magazines. For you there are ads in your daily newspaper, generally found on the obituary page, stressing dignity, refinement, high-caliber professional service and that intangible quality, *sincerity*. The trade advertisements are, however, instructive, because they furnish an important clue to the frame of mind into which the funeral industry has hypnotized itself.

7   A new mythology, essential to the twentieth-century American funeral rite, has grown up—or rather has been built up step by step—to justify the peculiar customs surrounding the disposal of our dead. And, just as the witch doctor must be convinced of his own infallibility in order to maintain a hold over his clientele, so the funeral industry has had to "sell itself" on its articles of faith in the course of passing them along to the public.

8   The first of these is the tenet that today's funeral procedures are founded in "American tradition." The story comes to mind of a sign on the freshly sown lawn of a brand-new Midwest college: "There is a tradition on this campus that students never walk on this strip of grass. This tradition goes into effect

next Tuesday." The most cursory look at American funerals of past times will establish the parallel. Simplicity to the point of starkness, the plain pine box, the laying out of the dead by friends and family who also bore the coffin to the grave—these were the hallmarks of the traditional funeral until the end of the nineteenth century.

9   Secondly, there is the myth that the American public is only being given what it wants—an opportunity to keep up with the Joneses to the end. "In keeping with our high standard of living, there should be an equally high standard of dying," says the past president of the Funeral Directors of San Francisco. "The cost of a funeral varies according to individual taste and the niceties of living the family has been accustomed to." Actually, choice doesn't enter the picture for the average individual, faced, generally for the first time, with the necessity of buying a product of which he is totally ignorant, at a moment when he is least in a position to quibble. In point of fact the cost of a funeral almost always varies, not "according to individual taste" but according to what the traffic will bear.

10   Thirdly, there is an assortment of myths based on half-digested psychiatric theories. The importance of the "memory picture" is stressed—meaning the last glimpse of the deceased in open casket, done up with the latest in embalming techniques and finished off with a dusting of makeup. A newer one, impressively authentic-sounding, is the need for "grief therapy," which is beginning to go over big in mortuary circles. A historian of American funeral directing hints at the grief-therapist idea when speaking of the new role of the undertaker—"the dramaturgic role, in which the undertaker becomes a stage manager to create an appropriate atmosphere and to move the funeral party through a drama in which social relationships are stressed and an emotional catharsis or release is provided through ceremony."

11   Lastly, a whole new terminology, as ornately shoddy as the satin rayon casket liner, has been invented by the funeral industry to replace the direct and serviceable vocabulary of former times. Undertaker has been supplanted by "funeral director" or "mortician." (Even the classified section of the telephone directory gives recognition to this; in its pages you will find "Undertakers—see Funeral Directors.") Coffins are "caskets"; hearses are "coaches," or "professional cars"; flowers are "floral tributes"; corpses generally are "loved ones," but mortuary etiquette dictates that a specific corpse be referred to by name only—as, "Mr. Jones"; cremated ashes are "cremains." Euphemisms such as "slumber room," "reposing room," and "calcination— the *kindlier* heat" abound in the funeral business.

12   If the undertaker is the stage manager of the fabulous production that is the modern American funeral, the stellar role is reserved for the occupant of the open casket. The decor, the stagehands, the supporting cast are all arranged for the most advantageous display of the deceased, without which the rest of the paraphernalia would lose its point—*Hamlet* without the Prince of Denmark. It is to this end that a fantastic array of costly merchandise and services is pyramided to dazzle the mourners and facilitate the plunder of the next of kin.

13   Grief therapy, anyone? But it's going to come high. According to the funeral industry's own figures, the *average* undertaker's bill in 1961 was $708 for casket and "services," to which must be added the cost of a burial vault, flowers, clothing, clergy and musician's honorarium, and cemetery charges. When these costs are added to the undertaker's bill, the total average cost for an adult's funeral is, as we shall see, closer to $1,450.

14   The question naturally arises, *is* this what most people want for themselves and their families? For several reasons, this has been a hard one to answer until recently. It is a subject seldom discussed. Those who have never had to arrange for a funeral frequently shy away from its implications, preferring to take comfort in the thought that sufficient unto the day is the evil thereof. Those who have acquired personal and painful knowledge of the subject would often rather forget about it. Pioneering "Funeral Societies" or "Memorial Associations," dedicated to the principle of dignified funerals at reasonable cost, have existed in a number of communities through the country, but their membership has been limited for the most part to the more sophisticated element in the population—university people, liberal intellectuals— and those who, like doctors and lawyers, come up against problems in arranging funerals for their clients.

15   Some indication of the pent-up resentment felt by vast numbers of people against the funeral interests was furnished by the astonishing response to an article by Roul Tunley, titled "Can You Afford to Die?" in *The Saturday Evening Post* of June 17, 1961. As though a dike had burst, letters poured in from every part of the country to the *Post*, to the funeral societies, to local newspapers. They came from clergymen, professional people, old-age pensioners, trade unionists. Three months after the article appeared, an estimated six thousand had taken pen in hand to comment on some phase of the high cost of dying. Many recounted their own bitter experiences at the hands of funeral directors; hundreds asked for advice on how to establish a consumer organization in communities where none exists; others sought information about pre-need plans. The membership of the funeral societies skyrocketed. The funeral industry, finding itself in the glare of public spotlight, has begun to engage in serious debate about its own future course—as well it might.

16   Is the funeral inflation bubble ripe for bursting? A few years ago, the United States public suddenly rebelled against the trend in the auto industry towards ever more showy cars, with their ostentatious and nonfunctional fins, and a demand was created for compact cars patterned after European models. The all-powerful auto industry, accustomed to *telling* the customer what sort of car he wanted, was suddenly forced to *listen* for a change. Overnight, the little cars became for millions a new kind of status symbol. Could it be that the same cycle is working itself out in the attitude towards the final return of dust to dust, that the American public is becoming sickened by ever more ornate and costly funerals, and that a status symbol of the future may indeed be the simplest kind of "funeral without fins"?

Example and Illustration

Developing an idea by means of example or illustration is one of the most effective and one of the most natural ways to translate a general or abstract statement into a meaningful and concrete message. Because examples and illustrations perform the essential function of making prose more concrete and therefore more precise and clear, they are fundamental to all good writing.

We all find it fairly easy to move from a proposition like "I'm all thumbs" to an illustration: "Yesterday while trying to paint the kitchen I dropped my wet brush on the dog, spilled a bucket of paint, and broke a window when I knocked over the ladder." The illustration fixes and limits the scope of the generalization (while I'm terribly clumsy at household chores, I may still be an agile athlete or a clever seamstress). Moreover, it prevents the vagueness or even total misunderstanding that a generalized or abstract proposition alone may leave with the reader. In "Here Am I, a Worker," Terkel asserts that "lately there has been a questioning of this 'work ethic,' especially by the young." If this statement were not supported by examples of the specific dissatisfactions of a series of young workers, the reader would be free to associate mass strikes, hippie drop-outs, or corporate mutiny and white collar crime with the idea of challenge to the work ethic—though Terkel has none of these in mind.

But while they perform the crucial function of making the abstract concrete and the general specific, examples are never in themselves enough. They must also fulfill four requirements. First, they must accurately illustrate the generalities they are intended to illuminate. Compare the examples of "Here Am I, a Worker," with Terkel's profile of Ward Quaal (p. 115), and consider why Quaal, though also a "worker," would be an inappropriate example of Terkel's main idea in the first essay. Second, examples must offer a fair representation of the general idea: if Kuralt had limited his examples of "the good outdoor cooking going on in this country" to the Mississippi fish fry and the hog barbecue in Lexington, N.C., the reader might be left with the impression that the only good outdoor cooking is Southern cooking.

Third, examples must be interesting enough to attract the reader's attention, to fix an otherwise forgettable generalization with a vivid picture—like Kuralt's example of the transplanted Southerner with his hibachi, "touching up a little pork tenderloin with a watercolor brush twenty-three floors above Lexington Avenue," or Terkel's reference to the steel worker who expressed his need for recognition in the complaint, "I feel like the guys who built the pyramids." Fourth, examples must be in harmony with the general intention and the level of difficulty of the essay. Because Kuralt is giving examples, not recipes, his description of hush puppies ("cornmeal, flour, salt, baking powder . . .") is adequate, but it would not be sufficiently detailed for a cookbook. Similarly, a scientific paper on the psychological effects of worker dissatisfaction would probably present case studies and figures on industrial accidents rather than the anecdotal examples Terkel uses.

Finally, a word about the often-neglected distinction between examples and illustrations. In general, examples don't appear singly, but in groups—as do the examples of unhappy workers and memorable outdoor meals in the essays in this section. And they are generally (but not always) factual and verifiable (Kuralt describes presumably real meals in specific detail; Terkel actually names the individuals he interviewed). On the other hand, an illustration may be a single, obvious example, developed as fully as possible, as in Kuralt's illustration of the unfortunate mechanization of outdoor cookery with his portrait of the "four-wheel, gas-fired, smoke-controlled Adjustable Grid Patio Grill," a description intended to encompass the attributes of thousands of such individual outfits. Or it may be an anecdote, fictitious yet "true" (like the story of the man who is looking for a camel to barbecue in Scarsdale), an analogy, or even a parable, designed to give concrete form to an abstract theme or moral.

The Great American Barbe-Queue

CHARLES KURALT

Charles Kuralt has been a correspondent for CBS since 1959. Recently, as a correspondent for "On the Road," broadcast on the CBS Evening News, he has traveled around the country observing an America that few of us ever see in our travels: a man with a whole museum of Cadillacs on a dusty Texas highway or the annual return of the buzzards to a small Ohio town. In this essay, he gives his impression of outdoor cooking from Maine to West Texas during America's bicentennial.

1   An old refrigerator shelf was all you really needed.

2   That was your grill. You laid it on a circle of stones surrounding a bare spot on the lawn in the North Carolina backyard of my youth, started a charcoal fire under it, unwrapped a sirloin from the A & P, iced down a few bottles of beer in the wheelbarrow, and invited the neighbors over. After supper you sat talking quietly in the dusk until the mosquitoes got too bad. Contentment was within the grasp of anybody with an old refrigerator shelf.

3   I should have known something was going wrong when I came home from college to find that my own father had built a brick fireplace in the backyard, with a chimney. The neighbors admired it and set out to exceed it. That was twenty years ago.

4   You, too, have noticed, I assume, how it all turned out. In this summer of our celebration, the electrical hum of the three-speed spit is heard in the land. It is revolving majestically over a four-wheel, gas-fired, smoke-controlled Adjustable Grid Patio Grill with a copper hood and a warming oven. The chef is wearing an apron with a funny saying on it. He is frowning over his *caneton rôti aux pêches flambées*, trying to decide whether the sauce needs more Madeira. Contentment is not his.

5   For many years I have been traveling around America mooching meals from friends where possible and observing the decline of suburban serenity. I think the outdoor cooking machine has a lot to do with it. If we are ever going to win back our innocence, we have to rediscover the refrigerator shelf.

6   The pleasure of outdoor cooking used to be the simplicity of it. This is the ancestral secret of generations of American males that is in danger of being lost: *nothing you can do to a steak cooked outdoors can ruin it.*

7   A man (outdoor cooks are invariably men, for atavistic reasons having to do, I imagine, with knives and fire and ego) can thoughtfully marinate his steak for hours in a mixture of his own invention—wine vinegar, soy sauce, secret herbs, and tequila; then patiently wait for the coals to reach just the right color and temperature; then quickly sear the steak on both sides to contain its juices; then cook it by feel and by experience; he can do all these things—*or not*—and be certain of triumphant approval. "Good steak, George." "You cooked it just right, Daddy." They will say the same if he unwraps it half frozen, drops it on the grill, and remembers to pause in his drinking to turn it once.

8   But let this same man begin to believe himself a chef, acquire, in his pride, an outdoor cooking machine, and attempt dishes having to do with delicate sauces or, worse, flaming swords, and we would all be better off staying indoors. Indoors, Daddy disdains to help with the cooking. It is not cooking he loves; it is his machine.

9   There is still some good outdoor cooking going on in this country, but none of it needs machinery, and none of it comes from Escoffier.

10   The first meal that comes to mind as I ruminate happily through my own recent memories of outdoor eating is a clambake last summer in Maine. Here is the authentic recipe for a clambake: dig a big hole in a beach. If you have a Maine beach to dig your hole in, so much the better, but any beach will do. Line the hole with rocks. Build a big fire on the rocks and take a swim. When the fire is all gone, cover the hot rocks with seaweed. Add some potatoes just as they came from the ground; some corn just as it came from the stalk; then lobsters, then clams, then another layer of seaweed. Cover the whole thing with a tarp and go for another swim. Dinner will be ready in an hour. It will make you very happy. No machine can make a clambake.

11   If there is a next-best thing to a Maine clambake, it is a Mississippi fish fry. I have a friend in Mississippi who is trying to keep Yankees from finding out that beneath the slimy hide of the catfish is concealed the flakiest, most delicate of all gifts from sea, stream, or farm pond. He is trying to keep it secret because there are not enough catfish to go around. I know he is my friend because he took me to a fish fry. You dip your catfish in seasoned flour, then in eggs, then in cornmeal, then into a bubbling pot of fat—that's all. Catfish fry happiest when accompanied in the pot by hush puppies. Hush puppies are cornmeal, flour, salt, baking powder, chopped onion, and ham fat, with enough beer worked in to hold them together. A few Baptists use water instead of beer. A fish fry is wonderful, with either wet or dry hush puppies.

12   Clambakes and fish fries are for fun. I went on a cattle roundup in West Texas this spring and found another brand of outdoor cooking that survives by necessity. Camp cooks are still much honored. They live by the principle that anything that can't be cooked in a heavy black iron skillet over live coals isn't worth eating. Any of the good ones, given a campsite and one hour, can supply from one of those skillets beans, chili, stew, coffee, and even bread

baked over the hot coals with additional coals heaped on the skillet lid. It is simple fare, always delicious, and more welcome to a hungry cowhand than anything Paul Bocuse ever created for jaded palates of the Continent.

13   I know some trout fishermen on the Upper Peninsula of Michigan who meet frequently at streamside to tell lies, play cribbage, and occasionally persuade some young brook trout that a fanciful floating speck of fur and feathers is actually a mayfly. They succeed often enough to eat well. Their specialty is mushrooms, grilled until their caps fill up with juices, served with a little salt, and washed down with bourbon out of an old tin cup. This is a meal I remember with reverence—mushrooms and bourbon—noble in its simplicity.

14   From *barbe to queue*, the French said, to describe the roasting of a whole hog, from whiskers to tail. And thereby started an argument. Barbecue is one of those things Americans can't agree on, like nuclear power or Ronald Reagan. Midwesterners, to whom barbecue is any roasted meat with ketchup on it, think Midwestern barbecue is best. The best barbecue comes from a genius I know in Lexington, N.C., who merely anoints his hog with salt, pepper, garlic, sage, and a mysterious sauce, wraps it in burlap, buries it in coals, covers it with earth, and serves it in precious shreds hours later with hot corn bread and Brunswick stew. It's simple, he says.

15   There are Southerners transplanted to New York who achieve almost the same result working with a hibachi on an apartment balcony. They know enough not to get too fancy with their barbecue sauce, whether swabbing it on a whole hog with a new broom in Lexington, N.C., or touching up a little pork tenderloin with a watercolor brush twenty-three floors above Lexington Avenue.

16   North, South, East, or West, cooking outdoors is a healing and a renewal for those smart enough to keep it simple. Hot dogs and hamburgers, than which nothing is more boring when cooked in the kitchen, become magical delights when grilled outdoors and eaten with your back against an oak tree. Spareribs, sausages, lamb chops, or chicken wings smoked indolently over a section of old stovepipe become greater than they are. Just being outdoors, it is truly said, enhances the flavor of just about everything, but it's not just that. *Is* there a better way of cooking fish than sautéing it, freshly caught, in butter, over a campfire? I have never discovered it. All you need is a fire, a fork, and a frying pan.

17   What you don't need is a machine.

18   But I know I am too late. You probably already have one. This is how far the al fresco escalation has gone: a man of my acquaintance, grown rueful and contemplative over the bigger and better outdoor cooking machines of his neighbors, watching their parties grow in size and sophistication, recently came upon a description of an Arab barbecue. A chicken, it seems, is stuffed into the stomach of a lamb, the lamb into the stomach of a cow, and the cow into the stomach of a camel. Roasting takes three days.

19   He's thinking about it. He says there's a machine at the hardware store that would do the job, but he can't find a camel in Scarsdale.

Exercises

COMPREHENSION

Organization and Development

Complete the following outline. Find the thesis statement, which in this essay is stated twice: once near the beginning and again near the end. Write them in the spaces provided. Then find the main divisions in the essay and fill in the remaining spaces. Note the paragraphs for each section.

Thesis statement: _____

_____

_____

Restatement of thesis: _____

_____

I. _____ [   ]
II. _____ [   ]
III. _____ [   ]

Content

Choose the answer that correctly completes each statement.

1. The main idea and conclusion of this selection is probably best described by the sentence (a) "there is still some good outdoor cooking going on in this country, but none of it needs machinery, and none of it comes from Escoffier" (b) "it is not cooking Daddy loves; it is his machine" (c) "North, South, East, or West, cooking outdoors is a healing and a renewal for those smart enough to keep it simple."

2. According to the author, the outdoor barbeque no longer provides contentment because the (a) simple methods have been replaced by fancy machines (b) barbeque is no longer an occasion for relaxation and socializing (c) American male now considers himself a chef who must produce complicated French dishes.

3. When the author says that outdoor cooks are invariably men, he says it probably has to do with knives and fire and ego, referring to men as (a) great chefs and authors of cookbooks (b) hunters, providing food to assure their family's survival (c) warriors and protectors of the family home.

4. Besides poking fun at Americans' fascination with fancy machines for outdoor cooking, Kuralt also finds amusing the emphasis on (a) roasting a whole animal (b) men becoming the family cooks (c) fancy French cooking.

5. The body of Kuralt's essay consists of (a) contrasting descriptions of old and new barbeque methods (b) examples of simple but memorable meals cooked outdoors (c) a series of reasons to support his contention that outdoor cooking should be simple.

6. The secret of a good steak cooked outdoors is that (a) it should be marinated in oil, wine, and herbs before it is cooked (b) nothing can ruin it (c) it should be covered in burlap and buried in hot coals.

7. The French expression, from *barbe* to *queue*, used to describe the roasting of a whole hog, literally means from (a) nose to tail (b) whiskers to tail (c) ears to feet.

8. The real pleasure of outdoor cooking for the author is that (a) it allows men to take over the cooking and to indulge their creative urges (b) it provides a relaxed atmosphere for entertaining friends (c) food not only tastes better when it is cooked outdoors, but it is also the best and simplest method.

Paragraph Structure

Reorder the following sentences to form a unified, coherent paragraph. Then check your version with the original.

1. After supper you sat talking quietly in the dusk until the mosquitoes got too bad.
2. An old refrigerator shelf was all you really needed.
3. Contentment was within the grasp of anybody with an old refrigerator shelf.
4. That was your grill.
5. You laid it on a circle of stones surrounding a bare spot on the lawn in the North Carolina backyard of my youth, started a charcoal fire under it, unwrapped a sirloin from the A&P, iced down a few bottles of beer in the wheelbarrow, and invited the neighbors over.

VOCABULARY AND USAGE

Word Formation Table

Complete the following table by changing word endings or root forms to make new grammatical forms. Use your dictionary if necessary.

	NOUN	VERB	ADJECTIVE	ADVERB
1.	serenity	xxx	_____	_____
2.	_____	exceed	_____	_____
3.	_____	_____	boring	_____
4.	simplicity	_____	_____	_____
5.	_____	disdain	_____	_____

Fill-Ins

Complete each of the sentences below using the words on the following list. You may need to use some words more than once. You may also find that some blanks can be completed correctly with more than one word. Add plural endings to nouns and change verb forms where necessary.

invariably	enhance	observe	scorn
authentic	simple	primitive	improve
disdain	revere	fancy	honor
accompany	contentment	principle	decline
pleasure	simplicity	atavistic	genuine

1. The author regards with _____ those who ruin the _____ of outdoor cooking by using a _____ machine.
2. The author has been traveling around the country _____ Americans' outdoor cooking styles and noting the _____ in _____ fare.
3. Outdoor cooks are _____ men, an example, according to the author, of _____ behavior, by which American males try to imitate their _____ ancestors.
4. The author provides a(n) _____ recipe for a clambake, which illustrates the _____ that no machine can _____ upon a clambake.
5. Texas camp cooks are still _____ for their ability to serve beans and chili _____ by bread, all cooked in an iron skillet.

6. The ＿＿＿＿＿ of outdoor cooking should be the ＿＿＿＿＿ of it, but it is also true that the flavor of good food is ＿＿＿＿＿ by being cooked over an open fire.

DISCUSSION

1. In paragraphs 1, 2, 4, 17, and 18, Kuralt uses the second person pronoun "you," a practice that many writers and teachers find objectionable in formal prose. How does the use of "you" contribute to the tone, purpose, and style of the essay? Could he have used "you" throughout? What pronoun could he have substituted for "you" in these paragraphs?
2. In paragraph 10, Kuralt offers his first example of a memorable meal. What other method of paragraph development does this paragraph employ?
3. Look up "barbeque" in an unabridged dictionary and note its etymology. What is Kuralt's purpose in using the French term? Why doesn't he provide the original etymology of this term? You might check the *Oxford English Dictionary* for a full explanation.
4. Why does Kuralt provide so many illustrations of good food from various regions of the country? How do these illustrations reinforce his thesis?
5. What is Kuralt implicitly criticizing about other aspects of our lives?

SUGGESTIONS FOR WRITING

1. Write a paragraph summarizing Kuralt's objections to complicated outdoor barbeque machines.
2. Kuralt describes several good meals that he has eaten in his travels around America. Describe a meal you enjoy cooking outdoors and provide instructions for its preparation. Or describe some dishes that are favorites or specialties in your region of the country or among your ethnic group.
3. Kuralt's essay describes the changes—for the worse—that modern equipment has brought to the old-fashioned cookout. Choose another invention or modern convenience that has brought about undesirable changes or that has ruined the pleasures of the old-fashioned way. Include an analysis of the contrasts between the original and the new methods.
4. Several of the essays in this anthology reflect a longing for the simplicity of the past and attempts to regain it, ironically, by substituting technology. Write an essay analyzing this phenomenon in American culture, using two or three of the following essays as the basis for your ideas: Kuralt, Brown, Ephron, Toffler, "The Fine Art of Moonshining," and Ciardi.

Here Am I, a Worker

STUDS TERKEL

Studs Terkel received a bachelor's and a law degree from the University of Chicago. His career has been varied: he has been a radio soap opera actor, a disc jockey, a sports commentator, and a TV host. Currently, he has a daily radio program in Chicago. He has published three books of taped interviews: *Division Street: America; Hard Times: An Oral History of the Great Depression in America;* and *Working: People Talk About What They Do All Day and How They Feel About What They Do.* In the following selection Terkel examines young people's dissatisfaction with their jobs and redefines the traditional work ethic. Many of the workers interviewed in this piece appear in *Working.*
(Note: This anthology also contains Terkel's "In Charge: A Profile of Ward Quaal.")

1   In our society (it's the only one I've experienced, so I cannot speak for any other) the razor of necessity cuts close. You must make a buck to survive the day. You must work to make a buck. The job is often a chore, rarely a delight. No matter how demeaning the task, no matter how it dulls the senses or breaks the spirit, one *must* work or else. Lately there has been a questioning of this "work ethic," especially by the young. Strangely enough, it has touched off profound grievances in others, hitherto silent and anonymous.

2   Unexpected precincts are being heard from in a show of discontent by blue collar and white. Communiqués are alarming concerning absenteeism in auto plants. On the evening bus the tense, pinched faces of young file clerks and elderly secretaries tell us more than we care to know. On the expressways middle-management men pose without grace behind their wheels, as they flee city and job.

3   In all, there is more than a slight ache. And there dangles the impertinent question: Ought there not be another increment, earned though not yet received, to one's daily work—an acknowledgement of a man's *being*?

4   Steve Hamilton is a professional baseball player. At 37 he has come to the end of his career as a major-league pitcher. "I've never been a big star. I've done about as good as I can with the equipment I have. I played with Mickey Mantle and with Willie Mays. People always recognize them. But for someone to recognize me, it really made me feel good. I think everybody gets a kick out of feeling special."

5   Mike Fitzgerald was born the same year as Hamilton. He is a laborer in a

HERE AM I, A WORKER   From *Capitalism: The Moving Target,* edited by Leonard Silk. Copyright © 1974 by Leonard Silk. Reprinted by permission of Quadrangle/The New York Times Book Co.

steel mill. "I feel like the guys who built the pyramids. Somebody built 'em. Somebody built the Empire State Building, too. There's hard work behind it. I would like to see a building, say The Empire State, with a foot-wide strip from top to bottom and the name of every bricklayer on it, the name of every electrician. So when a guy walked by, he could take his son and say, 'See, that's me over there on the 45th floor. I put that steel beam in.' Picasso can point to a painting. I think I've done harder work than Picasso, and what can I point to? Everybody should have something to point to."

6   Sharon Atkins is 24 years old. She's been to college and acridly observes: "The first myth that blew up in my face is that a college education will get you a worthwhile job." For the last two years she's been a receptionist at an advertising agency. "I didn't look at myself as 'just a dumb broad' at the front desk, who took phone calls and messages. I thought I was something else. The office taught me differently."

7   Among her contemporaries there is no such rejection; job and status have no meaning. Blue collar or white, teacher or cabbie, her friends judge her and themselves by their beingness. Nora Watson, a young journalist, recounts a party game, Who Are You? Older people respond with their job titles: "I'm a copy writer," "I'm an accountant." The young say, "I'm me, my name is so-and-so."

8   Harry Stallings, 27, is a spot welder on the assembly line at an auto plant. "They'll give better care to that machine than they will to you. If it breaks down, there's somebody out there to fix it right away. If I break down, I'm just pushed over to the other side till another man takes my place. The only thing the company has in mind is to keep that line running. A man would be more eager to do a better job if he were given proper respect and the time to do it."

9   You would think that Ralph Grayson, a 25-year-old black, has it made. He supervises twenty people in the audit department of a large bank. Yet he is singularly discontented. "You're like a foreman on an assembly line. Or like a technician sitting in a computer room watching the machinery. It's good for a person who enjoys that kind of job, who can dominate somebody else's life. I'm not too wrapped up in seeing a woman, 50 years old—white, incidentally—get thrown off her job because she can't cut it like the younger ones.

10   "I told management she was a kind and gentle person. They said 'We're not interested in your personal feelings. Document it up.' They look over my appraisal and say: 'We'll give her about five months to shape up or ship out.' "

11   The hunger persists, obstinately, for pride in a man's work. Conditions may be horrendous, tensions high, and humiliations frequent, yet Paul Dietch finds his small triumphs. He drives his own truck, interstate, as a steel hauler. "Every load is a challenge. I have problems in the morning with heartburn. I can't eat. Once I off-load, the pressure is gone. Then I can eat anything. I accomplished something."

12   Yolanda Leif graphically describes the trials of a waitress in a quality restaurant. They are compounded by her refusal to be demeaned. Yet pride in

her skills helps her through the night. "When I put the plate down, you don't hear a sound. When I pick up a glass, I want it to be just right. When someone says, 'How come you're just a waitress?' I say, 'Don't you think you deserve being served by me?' "

13   Peggy Terry has her own sense of pride and beauty. Her jobs have varied with geography, climate, and the ever-felt pinch of circumstance. "What I hated worst was being a waitress, the way you're treated. One guy said, 'You don't have to smile, I'm gonna give you a tip anyway.' I said, 'Keep it, I wasn't smiling for a tip.' Tipping should be done away with. It's like throwing a dog a bone. It makes you feel small."

14   Ballplayer. Laborer. Receptionist. Assembly-line worker. Truck driver. Bank official. Waitress. What with the computer and all manner of automation, add scores of hundreds of new occupations and, thus, new heroes and antiheroes to Walt Whitman's old anthem. The sound, though, is no longer melodious. The desperation is unquiet.

15   Perhaps Nora Watson has put her finger on it. She reflects on her father's work. He was a fundamentalist preacher, with whom she had been profoundly at odds.

16   "Whatever, he was, he was. It was his calling, his vocation. He saw himself as a core resource of the community. He liked his work, even though his family barely survived, because that was what he was supposed to be doing. His work was his life. He himself was not separate and apart from his calling. I think this is what all of us are looking for, a calling, not just a job. Most of us, like the assembly-line worker, have jobs that are too small for our spirit. Jobs are not big enough for people."

17   Does it take another, less competitive, less buck-oriented society to make one match the other?

Exercises

COMPREHENSION

Organization and Development

Complete the following outline. Find the thesis statement and write it in the space provided. Then find the main divisions in the essay and fill in the remaining spaces. Note the paragraphs for each section.   •

Thesis statement: _____

_____

_____

    I. _____ [   ]

    II. _____ [   ]

    III. _____ [   ]

Content

Choose the answer that correctly completes each statement.

1. Terkel defines the work ethic as the idea that (a) work not only makes life more worthwhile, but it also builds one's character (b) one must work no matter how boring or demeaning the job may be (c) only those who work hard and endure discontent will be assured of spiritual salvation.

2. One piece of evidence he offers to support his observation that the young are discontented is (a) the high number of young people receiving welfare and unemployment compensation (b) the high number of young people who change jobs frequently (c) absenteeism in auto plants.

3. Terkel suggests that workers should earn another increment, namely, (a) an acknowledgement of one's being (b) profit sharing and bonuses for those who do a particularly good job (c) higher status and more prestige according to one's occupation and salary.

4. Sharon Atkins, the ad agency receptionist, learned a hard lesson, that (a) no one in the office respected her skills or knowledge (b) most jobs are boring or senseless (c) a college education doesn't guarantee a person a worthwhile job.

5. All of the workers whom Terkel quotes feel that their jobs fail to give them (a) respect and a feeling of self-worth (b) a decent wage and generous fringe benefits (c) job security, status, and a promise of advancement.

6. What Ralph Grayson, the bank supervisor, especially dislikes about his job is (a) his employer's indifference to illness or personal problems (b) having to evaluate an older woman who isn't as productive as younger workers (c) the laziness and inefficiency he must tolerate from workers he supervises.

7. One can infer that many workers' feelings of uselessness are aggravated by (a) labor unions and strikes (b) computers and automation (c) inability to find employment in occupations for which they were trained.

8. Terkel concludes by suggesting that (a) modern society should get rid of obsolete notions of working for status or material rewards (b) discontented workers should accept their fate and develop outside interests to improve their leisure hours (c) jobs should match the spirit and pride of the people who do them.

Paragraph Structure

Reorder the following sentences to form a unified, coherent paragraph. Identify one sentence as the topic sentence and underline the key words. Then check your version with the original.

1. You must make a buck to survive the day.
2. The job is often a chore, rarely a delight.
3. Strangely enough, it has touched off profound grievances in others, hitherto silent and anonymous.
4. In our society the razor of necessity cuts close.
5. Lately there has been a questioning of this "work ethic," especially by the young.
6. You must work to make a buck.
7. No matter how demeaning the task, no matter how it dulls the senses or breaks the spirit, one *must* work or else.

VOCABULARY AND USAGE

Word Formation Table

Complete the following table by changing word endings or root forms to make new grammatical forms. Use your dictionary if necessary.

	NOUN	VERB	ADJECTIVE	ADVERB
1.	_____	vary	_____	_____
2.	_____	xxx	profound	_____
3.	humiliation	_____	_____	_____
4.	_____	respect	_____	_____
5.	_____	xxx	anonymous	_____

Fill-Ins

Complete each of the sentences below using the words on the following list. You may need to use some words more than once. You may also find that some blanks can be completed correctly with more than one word. Add plural endings to nouns and change verb forms where necessary.

rarely	profound	demeaning	modern
status	grievance	barely	pride
anonymous	peer	respect	deep
myth	if	dissatisfaction	degrading
contemporary	discontent	complaint	whether

1. The most common _____ of workers in _____ American society is that their jobs are senseless or _____.
2. Terkel says that most jobs are a chore, that they are _____ a delight, and that most workers show a _____ feeling of _____ with how they earn a living.
3. _____ from workers in the past were both silent and _____, probably because even outspoken people felt they had to keep their _____ to themselves.
4. Sharon Atkins used to believe that _____ she went to college, she could get a worthwhile job and take _____ in her work.
5. Although the young workers interviewed feel as most of their _____ do—that employers don't treat them with _____—they also believe that jobs and _____ have no meaning.
6. Nora Watson's father, the minister, was _____ able to support his family, yet _____ or not they had the necessities of life, he never lost his _____.

DISCUSSION

1. What is Terkel's thesis, and what is his purpose? Is there any evidence in the essay to suggest that he is writing from a preconceived idea that is not adequately borne out by the statements of those workers he interviewed?

2. What is the difference between an example and an illustration? Which does Terkel use as the basic means of support?
3. What attitude is common to each of the workers interviewed? Do their statements adequately support his ideas about questioning the work ethic? How have these people redefined the traditional work ethic?
4. How do you think the three workers cited in paragraphs 4–6 view Terkel's notion that "jobs and status have no meaning"?
5. What does Mike Fitzgerald, the steelworker, mean in paragraph 5 when he says that "somebody built the pyramids"?
6. Why doesn't Terkel use transitional phrases to introduce each new example?
7. Terkel ends his essay with a rhetorical question (a question that the author asks only for effect). How do you think Terkel might answer this question? How would you answer it?

SUGGESTIONS FOR WRITING

1. Write an essay in which you discuss the differences between a career and a job. Be sure to include some discussion of the differences in social attitudes toward each.
2. Write an essay summarizing the ideas about work revealed by Terkel's interviews. Your essay should present Terkel's conclusion about the significance of work as well as your own ideas.
3. Describe in detail your ideal job.
4. Terkel says that young people are questioning the work ethic and that jobs and status no longer have meaning for them. Write an essay discussing some reasons that might account for this shift in attitude away from the traditional work ethic among young Americans.
5. Read Terkel's other essay in this anthology, "In Charge: A Profile of Ward Quaal." Then write an essay in which you contrast Quaal's ideas with those of the young workers interviewed in this essay.
6. Terkel's essay uses a series of illustrations and examples to reveal the way a variety of people feel about working and the reasons for their discontent. Using the same technique, interview several people about a subject that interests you. Then state your central impression and organize the comments you collect, using them as supporting examples for your thesis.

Process

Process writing is the method of exposition in which the writer analyzes the steps or stages by which something is accomplished: for example, the owner's manual for an electrical appliance, the directions on a can of condensed soup, or a cookbook. Process writing demands the kind of chronological or time sequence essential to narration, but it is most closely associated with analysis—the expository method in which the parts or components of a thing are isolated from the whole (see p. 193). It is, in fact, often considered a subdivision of analysis and called process analysis.

The distinctions between process and analysis are perhaps best seen by examining the most common kind of process writing—the "how-to" or instructional format—as exemplified in an ordinary household recipe. The recipe for chocolate cake, for instance, presents a classic formula for process writing. It is composed of a list of ingredients (flour, sugar, salt, butter, eggs, chocolate, etc.), followed by a detailed list of instructions for combining these materials, step by step, to produce the desired end product: a chocolate cake. The list of ingredients represents an *analysis* of chocolate cake—that is, the parts of which it is composed, while the steps in the preparation constitute the *process* that leads to a specific result: the cake.

The key factors in successful process writing are easily seen in a recipe. First, the basic ingredients must be clearly indicated. (Or, if the subject is how to do rather than how to make something, the basic equipment—ski poles, skis, gloves—must be noted; if it is how to achieve or be something, the basic qualities—coordination, endurance, motivation—are required.) Then, the stages by which ingredients, equipment or qualities are used or combined to achieve a particular end (a chocolate cake, a perfectly hidden moonshine still, a successful attitude to death) must be written clearly and, with few exceptions, in their exact order of execution. The importance of order cannot be overemphasized: try reversing two steps in a chocolate cake recipe or almost any other how-to-do-it process and see what happens. This, of course, is where narrative order, or something like it, comes in: once you go beyond the listing of steps ("Insert tab A into slot B"; " . . . find a cave"), narrative devices such as transitional phrases and repeated key words (" . . . then a sharp turn to the right; . . . again into lines") are necessary to ensure the coherence of the stages in the process.

Because instructional process writing requires both analysis and chronological order, and because it *won't work* unless it is absolutely precise and clear (have you ever puzzled over the instructions in a carelessly written owner's manual?), it is an excellent method for student writing practice. Unfortunately, not all process writing is as pared down as a recipe or instructions for hiding a still. Process writing is also used to inform the reader of how something happened or was or might be done. The description of a process for informational purposes (how Malcolm X educated himself; how immigrants were examined at Ellis Island; how the dying person faces up to death) is not generally intended to help the reader repeat the process. It may concern a historical event, obviously impossible to duplicate. And it cannot always be as clearly ordered as instructional process. Other kinds of writing—description, narration, or analysis—interrupt the stages of the informational process. (Howe, for example, intervenes in his own process several times with revealing descriptions, quotations, footnotes; Kubler-Ross interpolates anecdotes and a lengthy illustrative letter.) In some cases, like "A Homemade Education," the order in which things happened is not only interrupted or prefaced by other material, it is actually altered as it could never be in a coherently arranged instructional process analysis.

By and large, though, with these particular exceptions—as well as the exception of the process so complicated that it must be analyzed in segments or stages, rather than sequentially (imagine how many things are happening at once as a manned rocket is fired)—the key to clear process writing is precision of detail and absolute accuracy in sequential order.

A Homemade Education

MALCOLM X

Malcolm X was born Malcolm Little in Omaha, Nebraska, in 1925, and spent his early childhood in various Midwestern towns. His family was often the target of hostility and even violence at the hands of whites and blacks alike because of the beliefs of Malcolm's father, a preacher whose mission was to spread the teachings of the black separatist, Marcus Garvey. After the mysterious and violent death of his father, followed by his mother's breakdown and commitment to a state mental hospital, the Little family broke up, and Malcolm began his descent into the shadowy world of hoodlums, thieves, pimps, and addicts—where he was known as "Detroit Red." This spiral was reversed when Malcolm, while in prison for burglary, began to correspond with Elijah Muhammad, leader of the Black Muslims. This correspondence ultimately confirmed Malcolm Little as Muhammad's most talented disciple and propelled him onto the national scene as Malcolm X, one of the most dynamic leaders of the Black Revolution. His controversial career was cut short by an assassin's bullet in Harlem in 1965.

Before his murder, Malcolm X had reversed his militant stand on black separatism and was, at the time of his death, preaching the brotherhood of all men. The following excerpt from his autobiography describes how, through sheer will power, he began the process of his own intellectual salvation.

1   It was because of my letters that I happened to stumble upon starting to acquire some kind of a homemade education.

2   I became increasingly frustrated at not being able to express what I wanted to convey in letters that I wrote, especially those to Mr. Elijah Muhammad. In the street, I had been the most articulate hustler out there—I had commanded attention when I said something. But now, trying to write simple English, I not only wasn't articulate, I wasn't even functional. How would I sound writing in slang, the way I would *say* it, something such as, "Look, daddy, let me pull your coat about a cat, Elijah Muhammad—"

3   Many who today hear me somewhere in person, or on television, or those who read something I've said, will think I went to school far beyond the eighth grade. This impression is due entirely to my prison studies.

4   It had really begun back in the Charlestown Prison, when Bimbi first made me feel envy of his stock of knowledge. Bimbi had always taken charge of any conversation he was in, and I had tried to emulate him. But every book I

picked up had few sentences which didn't contain anywhere from one to nearly all of the words that might as well have been in Chinese. When I just skipped those words, of course, I really ended up with little idea of what the book said. So I had come to the Norfolk Prison Colony still going through only book-reading motions. Pretty soon, I would have quit even these motions, unless I had received the motivation that I did.

5   I saw that the best thing I could do was get hold of a dictionary—to study, to learn some words. I was lucky enough to reason also that I should try to improve my penmanship. It was sad. I couldn't even write in a straight line. It was both ideas together that moved me to request a dictionary along with some tablets and pencils from the Norfolk Prison Colony school.

6   I spent two days just riffling uncertainly through the dictionary's pages. I'd never realized so many words existed! I didn't know *which* words I needed to learn. Finally, just to start some kind of action, I began copying.

7   In my slow, painstaking, ragged handwriting, I copied into my tablet everything printed on that first page, down to the punctuation marks.

8   I believe it took me a day. Then, aloud, I read back, to myself, everything I'd written on the tablet. Over and over, aloud, to myself, I read my own handwriting.

9   I woke up the next morning, thinking about those words—immensely proud to realize that not only had I written so much at one time, but I'd written words that I never knew were in the world. Moreover, with a little effort, I also could remember what many of these words meant. I reviewed the words whose meanings I didn't remember. Funny thing, from the dictionary first page right now, that "aardvark" springs to my mind. The dictionary had a picture of it, a long-tailed, long-eared, burrowing African mammal, which lives off termites caught by sticking out its tongue as an anteater does for ants.

10   I was so fascinated that I went on—I copied the dictionary's next page. And the same experience came when I studied that. With every succeeding page, I also learned of people and places and events from history. Actually the dictionary is like a miniature encyclopedia. Finally the dictionary's A section had filled a whole tablet—and I went on into the B's. That was the way I started copying what eventually became the entire dictionary. It went a lot faster after so much practice helped me to pick up handwriting speed. Between what I wrote in my tablet, and writing letters, during the rest of my time in prison I would guess I wrote a million words.

11   I suppose it was inevitable that as my word-base broadened, I could for the first time pick up a book and read and now begin to understand what the book was saying. Anyone who has read a great deal can imagine the new world that opened. Let me tell you something: from then until I left that prison, in every free moment I had, if I was not reading in the library, I was reading on my bunk. You couldn't have gotten me out of books with a wedge. Between Mr. Muhammad's teachings, my correspondence, my visitors— usually Ella and Reginald—and my reading of books, months passed without my even thinking about being imprisoned. In fact, up to then, I never had been so truly free in my life.

Exercises

COMPREHENSION

Organization and Development

Complete the following outline. Find the thesis statement and write it in the space provided. Then find the main steps in the process that the essay describes and the result or effect of that process, and fill in the remaining spaces. Note the paragraphs for each section.

Thesis statement: _____
_____
_____

I.   _____ [   ]

II. _____ [   ]

III. _____ [   ]

IV. _____ [   ]

V.   Result: _____ [   ]

Content

Choose the answer that correctly completes each statement.

1. Malcolm was motivated to acquire an education because he (a) found he had so much time on his hands while in prison (b) became increasingly frustrated at his inability to express himself in letters to important people (c) felt that his lack of education would prevent him from earning enough money to support himself when he left prison.
2. Malcolm's reference to his "book-reading motions" calls our attention to the fact that before he began his own studies he was (a) really functionally illiterate (b) not really interested in the reading material provided for him by the prison officials (c) checking out books from the prison library only to impress the officials with his "rehabilitation."
3. The author's description of his education as "homemade" is apt because (a) he did most of his studying at home (b) the method he used was "custom-tailored" for him by prison teachers (c) he taught himself by a method that he himself had improvised.
4. The first tangible step in Malcolm X's homemade education was (a) a high school correspondence course (b) his acquisition of a dictionary and some pencils and paper (c) his discovery of the Norfolk Prison Colony library.
5. One of the "morals" of Malcolm X's story is that his real education couldn't begin until he realized that he (a) was doomed to a life of failure and even crime if he remained uneducated (b) found a teacher who cared enough to motivate him to study (c) had a real need for the skills of speech, reading, and writing that he lacked.
6. Malcolm's homemade process of education began with his copying some pages from the dictionary and ended with his (a) copying a million words (b) entry into a whole new world (c) acquiring a college degree.
7. Malcolm's new experiences with books made him feel (a) important and knowledgeable (b) capable of handling any problem (c) truly free for the first time in his life.
8. Malcolm X's narrative implies that (a) even before he began to acquire some education, he was strong, articulate, and a leader (b) before he taught himself to read and write effectively, he was a hopeless failure, and without a future (c) his homemade education was only a beginning that had to be followed by more formal education.

Paragraph Structure

Reorder the following sentences to form a unified, coherent paragraph. Identify one sentence as the topic sentence. Then check your version with the original.

1. But every book I picked up had few sentences which didn't contain anywhere from one to nearly all of the words that might as well have been in Chinese.
2. So I had come to the Norfolk Prison Colony still going through only book-reading motions.
3. When I just skipped those words, of course, I really ended up with little idea of what the book said.
4. It had really begun back in the Charlestown Prison, when Bimbi first made me feel envy of his stock of knowledge.
5. Pretty soon, I would have quit even these motions, unless I had received the motivation that I did.
6. Bimbi had always taken charge of any conversation he was in, and I had tried to emulate him.

VOCABULARY AND USAGE

Word Formation Table

Complete the following table by changing word endings or root forms to make new grammatical forms. Use your dictionary if necessary.

	NOUN	VERB	ADJECTIVE	ADVERB
1.	conversion	_____	_____	_____
2.	_____	_____	_____	increasingly
3.	_____	copy	_____	xxx
4.	_____	_____	articulate	_____
5.	impression	_____	_____	_____

Fill-Ins

Complete each of the sentences below using the words on the following list. You may need to use some words more than once. You may also find that some blanks can be completed correctly with more than one word. Add plural endings to nouns and change verb forms where necessary.

frustrated	acquire	knowledge	articulate
education	book	intelligent	fashion
inability	free	manner	moreover
motivation	illiteracy	copy	study
comprehend	word	obviously	understand

1. When Malcolm X went to prison, he was a street hustler with little or no real _____ to _____ a(n) _____.
2. Probably because he was _____ and _____ possessed a forceful personality, he became _____ by his _____ to _____ the _____ he tried to _____.
3. He had to become conscious of his own _____ and _____ by its effects before he could begin to _____ a(n) _____.
4. Malcolm's _____ for _____ _____ was also _____

based on his _____ to write his thoughts in a _____ that others could easily _____.
5. The most important _____ in Malcolm X's homemade _____ was the dictionary, which he _____ _____ for _____.
6. Malcolm said that his _____ _____ him from the prison of _____; _____, once he could _____ any _____, he could enter into a whole new world.

DISCUSSION

1. Analyze the process that Malcolm X followed in order to educate himself. How many steps were there in the process? Does he write of them in the actual order in which they occurred? Which stage do you consider most crucial, and why?
2. In paragraph 2, Malcolm contrasts his stature on the street ("I had been the most articulate hustler out there") with his inability to communicate in simple English when he wrote ("I not only wasn't articulate, I wasn't even functional"). What basic distinctions between his street life and the life he wanted to participate in can you infer from this contrast? What skills and what qualities did each life require? (You may wish to compare Malcolm X with Jones in "Jones: Portrait of a Mugger.")
3. In paragraph 4, Malcolm refers to an acquaintance in the Charlestown Prison. What role did Bimbi play in Malcolm's education, and what particular quality in Malcolm is revealed by this reference?
4. What basic essential of learning is revealed by the experiences of Malcolm X? If you were a teacher in an urban ghetto, what steps might you take to arrange a program of study for students who, like Malcolm X, were really functionally illiterate after years of "schooling"?
5. Malcolm says, "anyone who has read a great deal can imagine the new world that opened" after he began to understand what his books were saying. He further describes his new relationship with books as one which made him forget he was in prison, one which made him feel "truly free." What is he talking about?
6. Malcolm X was a remarkable man who rose from common hoodlum to become one of the most dynamic leaders of the Black Revolution. How does this narrative of his homemade education reveal his extraordinary qualities of character, and what, in fact, were they? Could anyone do what he did? Why or why not?

SUGGESTIONS FOR WRITING

1. Write an essay in which you explain the steps in a process that you know how to do very well.
2. Describe your own relationship to and experience with books.
3. Compare and contrast Malcolm X and the subject of Willwerth's "Jones: Portrait of a Mugger."
4. Analyze the purposes for which you are acquiring an education.
5. In recent years, there has been much controversy about bilingualism and, particularly, about "soul talk" or Black English. At one extreme are educators of both races who believe the public schools should emphasize standard English to the exclusion of Black English. At the other extreme are those who believe just the opposite—or at least that Black English should be taught as a second language. Explore the arguments for both sides and draw a conclusion of your own, using as much as you can of the "evidence" in Malcolm X's narrative.

At Ellis Island

IRVING HOWE

Irving Howe was born in New York City in 1920. He is a graduate of the City College of New York and has taught at Brandeis University, Stanford University, and the Hunter College division of the City University of New York, where he is currently professor of English. His distinguished career as author, historian, and critic has included numerous fellowships, and he has written extensively on history, politics, and literature, including important critical biographies of Sherwood Anderson and William Faulkner. *World of Our Fathers,* from which this piece is excerpted, is a history of the great wave of immigration that brought thousands upon thousands of Jews from Eastern Europe to the United States at the turn of the century.

1   "The day of the emigrants' arrival in New York was the nearest earthly likeness to the final Day of Judgment, when we have to prove our fitness to enter Heaven." So remarked one of those admirable journalists who in the early 1900's exposed themselves to the experience of the immigrants and came to share many of their feelings. No previous difficulties roused such overflowing anxiety, sometimes self-destructive panic, as the anticipated test of Ellis Island.[1] Nervous chatter, foolish rumors spread through each cluster of immigrants:

> "There is Ellis Island!" shouted an immigrant who had already been in the United States and knew of its alien laws. The name acted like magic. Faces

AT ELLIS ISLAND   From *World of Our Fathers* copyright © 1976 by Irving Howe. Reprinted by permission of Harcourt Brace Jovanovich, Inc.

[1]Ellis Island was opened as an immigration center in 1892, shortly after the federal government took over the supervision of incoming aliens. Until 1890 the matter had been in the hands of the states, and in New York, starting in 1855, immigrants were received at Castle Garden, a massive structure built in 1807 as a fort on a small island close to the west side of the Battery (later attached to it through landfill). During the early 1850's Castle Garden had been used as a concert hall; Jenny Lind and Lola Montez performed there.

By the 1880's it became clear that Castle Garden could not possibly take care of the thousands of immigrants arriving each week. In the late 1880's several government investigations were held into conditions at Castle Garden, at which missionaries testified that immigrants were forced to sleep on hard floors, some were made to pay twice for shipment of their baggage, and others were cheated by moneychangers who hung about the Battery like leeches. One of the New York state commissioners testified that the Castle Garden operation was "a perfect farce."

These scandals were compounded in regard to immigrants detained for medical examination, who were sent to Ward's Island in the East River. Here, writes Edward Corsi, a commissioner of immigration for the New York district at a later time, "riots occurred frequently. Many immigrants escaped by swimming to the Manhattan shore [an exaggeration—I.H.], asking to be arrested and confined in the New York jails, rather than remain there with the insane and, as some charged, in a state of starvation. An investigation on one occasion revealed the startling fact that the bodies of dead immigrants were being used for purposes of dissection."

grew taut, eyes narrowed. There, in those red buildings, fate awaited them. Were they ready to enter? Or were they to be sent back?

"Only God knows," shouted an elderly man, his withered hand gripping the railing.

2   Numbered and lettered before debarking, in groups corresponding to entries on the ship's manifest, the immigrants are herded onto the Customs Wharf. "Quick! Run! Hurry!" shout officials in half a dozen languages.

3   On Ellis Island they pile into the massive hall that occupies the entire width of the building. They break into dozens of lines, divided by metal railings, where they file past the first doctor. Men whose breathing is heavy, women trying to hide a limp or deformity behind a large bundle—these are marked with chalk, for later inspection. Children over the age of two must walk by themselves, since it turns out that not all can. (A veteran inspector recalls: "Whenever a case aroused suspicion, the alien was set aside in a cage apart from the rest . . . and his coat lapel or shirt marked with colored chalk, the color indicating why he had been isolated.") One out of five or six needs further medical checking—H chalked for heart, K for hernia, Sc for scalp, X for mental defects.

4   An interpreter asks each immigrant a question or two: can he respond with reasonable alertness? Is he dull-witted? A question also to each child: make sure he's not deaf or dumb. A check for TB, regarded as "the Jewish disease."

5   Then a sharp turn to the right, where the second doctor waits, a specialist in "contagious and loathsome diseases." Leprosy? Venereal disease? Fauvus, "a contagious disease of the skin, especially of the scalp, due to a parasitic fungus, marked by the formation of yellow flattened scabs and baldness"?

6   Then to the third doctor, often feared the most. He

stands directly in the path of the immigrant, holding a little stick in his hand. By a quick movement and the force of his own compelling gaze, he catches the eyes of his subject and holds them. You will see the immigrant stop short, lift his head with a quick jerk, and open his eyes very wide. The inspector reaches with a swift movement, catches the eyelash with his thumb and finger, turns it back, and peers under it. If all is well, the immigrant is passed on. . . . Most of those detained by the physician are Jews.

7   The eye examination hurts a little. It terrifies the children. Nurses wait with towels and basins filled with disinfectant. They watch for tracoma, cause of more than half the medical detentions. It is a torment hard to understand, this first taste of America, with its poking of flesh and prying into private parts and mysterious chalking of clothes.

8   Again into lines, this time according to nationality. They are led to stalls at which multilingual inspectors ask about character, anarchism, polygamy, insanity, crime, money, relatives, work. You have a job waiting? Who paid your passage? Anyone meeting you? Can you read and write? Ever in prison? Where's your money?

9   For Jewish immigrants, especially during the years before agencies like the Hebrew Immigrant Aid Society (HIAS) could give them advice, these ques-

tions pose a dilemma: to be honest or to lie? Is it good to have money or not? Can you bribe these fellows, as back home, or is it a mistake to try? Some are so accustomed to bend and evade and slip a ruble into a waiting hand that they get themselves into trouble with needless lies. "Our Jews," writes a Yiddish paper,

> love to get tangled up with dishonest answers, so that the officials have no choice but to send them to the detention area. A Jew who had money in his pocket decided to lie and said he didn't have a penny. . . . A woman with four children and pregnant with a fifth, said her husband had been in America fourteen years. . . . The HIAS man learned that her husband had recently arrived, but she thought fourteen years would make a better impression. The officials are sympathetic. They know the Jewish immigrants get "confused" and tell them to sit down and "remember." Then they let them in.

Especially bewildering is the idea that if you say you have a job waiting for you in the United States, you are liable to deportation—because an 1885 law prohibits the importation of contract labor. But doesn't it "look better" to say a job is waiting for you? No, the HIAS man patiently explains, it doesn't. Still, how can you be sure *he* knows what he's talking about? Just because he wears a little cap with those four letters embroidered on it?

10   Except when the flow of immigrants was simply beyond the staff's capacity to handle it, the average person passed through Ellis Island in about a day. Ferries ran twenty-four hours a day between the island and both the Battery and points in New Jersey. As for the unfortunates detained for medical or other reasons, they usually had to stay at Ellis Island for one or two weeks. Boards of special inquiry, as many as four at a time, would sit in permanent session, taking up cases where questions had been raised as to the admissibility of an immigrant, and it was here, in the legal infighting and appeals to sentiment, that HIAS proved especially valuable.

11   The number of those detained at the island or sent back to Europe during a given period of time varied according to the immigration laws then in effect and, more important, according to the strictness with which they were enforced. It is a sad irony, though familiar to students of democratic politics, that under relatively lax administrations at Ellis Island, which sometimes allowed rough handling of immigrants and even closed an eye to corruption, immigrants had a better chance of getting past the inspectors than when the commissioner was a public-spirited Yankee intent upon literal adherence to the law.

12   Two strands of opinion concerning Ellis Island have come down to us, among both historians and the immigrant masses themselves: first, that the newcomers were needlessly subjected to bad treatment, and second, that most of the men who worked there were scrupulous and fair, though often overwhelmed by the magnitude of their task.

13   The standard defense of Ellis Island is offered by an influential historian of immigration, Henry Pratt Fairchild:

> During the year 1907 five thousand was fixed as the maximum number of immigrants who could be examined at Ellis Island in one day; yet during the

spring of that year more than fifteen thousand immigrants arrived at the port of New York in a single day.

As to the physical handling of the immigrants, this is [caused] by the need for haste. . . . The conditions of the voyage are not calculated to land the immigrant in an alert and clear-headed state. The bustle, confusion, rush and size of Ellis Island complete the work, and leave the average alien in a state of stupor. . . . He is in no condition to understand a carefully-worded explanation of what he must do, or why he must do it, even if the inspector had the time to give it. The one suggestion which is immediately comprehensible to him is a pull or a push; if this is not administered with actual violence, there is no unkindness in it.

14   Reasonable as it may seem, this analysis meshed Yankee elitism with a defense of the bureaucratic mind. Immigrants *were* disoriented by the time they reached Ellis Island, but they remained human beings with all the sensibilities of human beings; the problem of numbers *was* a real one, yet it was always better when interpreters offered a word of explanation than when they resorted to "a pull or a push." Against the view expressed by Fairchild, we must weigh the massive testimony of the immigrants themselves, the equally large body of material gathered by congressional investigations, and such admissions, all the more telling because casual in intent, as that of Commissioner Corsi: "Our immigration officials have not always been as humane as they might have been." The Ellis Island staff was often badly overworked, and day after day it had to put up with an atmosphere of fearful anxiety which required a certain deadening of response, if only by way of self-defense. But it is also true that many of the people who worked there were rather simple fellows who lacked the imagination to respect cultural styles radically different from their own.

15   One interpreter who possessed that imagination richly was a young Italo-American named Fiorello La Guardia, later to become an insurgent mayor of New York. "I never managed during the years I worked there to become callous to the mental anguish, the disappointment and the despair I witnessed almost daily. . . . At best the work was an ordeal." For those who cared to see, and those able to feel, there could finally be no other verdict.

Exercises

COMPREHENSION

Organization and Development

Complete the following outline. In your own words write a sentence stating the purpose of the essay. Then find the main divisions in the essay and fill in the remaining spaces. Note the paragraphs for each section.

Statement of purpose: _____

_____

_____

I.   Introduction: _____ [   ]
II. _____ [   ]
     A. _____ [   ]
     B. _____ [   ]
     C. _____ [   ]
     D. _____ [   ]
     E. _____ [   ]
     F. _____ [   ]
     G. _____ [   ]
     H. _____ [   ]
III. _____ [   ]
     A. _____ [   ]
     B. _____ [   ]
     C. _____ [   ]
     D. _____ [   ]

Content

Choose the answer that correctly completes each statement.

1. In the first paragraph, Howe compares the emigrants' arrival at Ellis Island to the (a) torments of hell (b) Day of Judgment (c) entry into Heaven.
2. The metaphor of paragraph 1 is designed to call the reader's attention to the fact that the main function of the procedures at Ellis Island was to (a) turn away as many prospective citizens as possible (b) quarantine new emigrants for contagious diseases before allowing them to enter the United States (c) examine new emigrants to ensure their fitness, mentally, morally, and physically, for entrance into the United States.
3. The period of mass immigration from Europe to the United States about which this essay is concerned was in the (a) early 1900s (b) middle 1800s (c) late 1700s.
4. In paragraphs 2 and 3, the phrases "herded into," "pile into," "set aside in a cage," and "marked with colored chalk" contribute to the impression that at Ellis Island the immigrants were (a) treated like animals (b) processed mechanically (c) considered to be ignorant hoodlums.
5. The two strands of opinion about Ellis Island that come to us from both historians and the emigrants themselves are that the (a) emigrants were needlessly subjected to bad treatment and most of the officials were scrupulous and fair (b) newcomers were never subjected to bad treatment even though the officials often found the task overwhelming (c) emigrants often precipitated unpleasant treatment because they could not make themselves understood and the overworked officials could not be blamed for this.
6. The two opinions about Ellis Island seem contradictory, suggesting that (a) the official view or opinion was designed to justify the bureaucracy (b) Howe is careless in his analysis (c) the emigrants were too bewildered to be accurate in their descriptions.
7. Howe says that the "standard defense" of Ellis Island procedures "meshed Yankee elitism with a defense of the bureaucratic mind," suggesting that (a) any harsh treatment of the emigrants was justified by the belief that they were inferior or that rules took precedence over people (b) the procedures at Ellis Island were designed to give the newcomers their first view of the sophisticated Yankee culture into which they had to assimilate (c) the manner of handling the emigrants at Ellis Island was designed to initiate them into the kinds of bureaucratic procedures they had to master in order to become citizens.

8. Howe's description of Ellis Island during the days of mass emigration from Europe leaves one with the dominant impression that it was a (a) carefully organized, humane, and basically calm operation (b) place of confusion, rush, panic, anguish, and sometimes disappointment and despair (c) place that, despite its enslavement to bureaucratic procedures, was predominantly enthusiastic and joyful in its atmosphere as the first place to welcome the new Americans.

Paragraph Structure

Reorder the following sentences to form a unified, coherent paragraph. Write a sentence of your own that can serve as a topic sentence for the reorganized paragraph. Then check your version with the original.

1. Boards of special inquiry, as many as four at a time, would sit in permanent session, taking up cases where questions had been raised as to the admissibility of an immigrant, and it was here, in the legal infighting and appeals to sentiment, that HIAS proved especially valuable.
2. Except when the flow of immigrants was simply beyond the staff's capacity to handle it, the average person passed through Ellis Island in about a day.
3. As for the unfortunates detained for medical or other reasons, they usually had to stay at Ellis Island for one or two weeks.
4. Ferries ran twenty-four hours a day between the island and both the Battery and points in New Jersey.

VOCABULARY AND USAGE

Word Formation Table

Complete the following table by changing word endings or root forms to make new grammatical forms. Use your dictionary if necessary.

NOUN	VERB	ADJECTIVE	ADVERB
1. _____	judge	_____	_____
2. _____	mistake	_____	_____
3. _____	_____	imagined	_____
4. _____	testify	_____	_____
5. style	_____	_____	_____

Fill-Ins

Complete each of the sentences below using the words on the following list. You may need to use some words more than once. You may also find that some blanks can be completed correctly with more than one word. Add plural endings to nouns and change verb forms where necessary.

emigrant	anticipate	suitability	judgment
arrive	fear	character	imagine
panic	examination	officials	if
test	fitness	treatment	disease
intelligence	health	elitism	disembark

1. It is hard to _____ what the _____ about to _____ at Ellis Island must have felt as he _____ his first landing in America.
2. Some say he _____ with _____ the coming _____ of his _____ to enter the new country.
3. At Ellis Island, the _____ from many lands were _____ for their _____ in _____, _____, and _____.
4. The _____ themselves were not necessarily difficult or unpleasant, but the newcomers could not count on gentle _____ from the _____ in charge of their processing.
5. Many of the newly _____ foreigners were found, in the course of the _____, to have contagious _____.
6. In the _____ of the examiners and doctors, others were found to lack normal _____ or to be of poor _____, and _____ this was the case, they were probably not permitted to remain in the United States.

DISCUSSION

1. Study carefully paragraphs 2–8, and then determine the specific techniques the author uses to show the actual movement of the procedure he is describing.
2. Underline all the verbs in paragraphs 2–8. Can you note any particular patterns of use? If so, what are they, and what effect do they produce?
3. Only in paragraph 13 does Howe refer directly to the magnitude of the number of immigrants who passed through Ellis Island at the peak of the great wave of immigration—on one day in 1907, 15,000! In what way does the author emphasize indirectly the enormity of the job that was carried out by the immigration authorities?
4. Howe quotes one investigator's view of the procedures at Ellis Island: "Our immigration officials have not always been as humane as they might have been." Which specific aspects of the entry and examination procedures do you think were inhumane, and in what ways might they have been improved easily? Which aspects of the Ellis Island process were unavoidably harsh?
5. Does the essay suggest, either directly or indirectly, any reasons for the lack of humaneness other than the vastness of the job and the inadequacy of the facilities? If so, what are they?
6. What does the reference to congressional investigations (paragraph 14) suggest to you about the actual conditions at Ellis Island? What does it suggest to you about the nature of Howe's actual description?
7. It is often noted that with the exception of the native American Indian, every "American" is really an immigrant. Find out as much as you can about the immigrant experience of your ancestors, and note the similarities and differences between what you find and what Howe both describes and suggests in his essay.

SUGGESTIONS FOR WRITING

1. Write a description of a process that, like the entry of the European immigrants, arouses strong emotions in both the participants and observers (for example, gaining admission to an especially important rock concert, registering for the first time in college, preparing for a long-anticipated trip).
2. Compare and contrast the arrival of the Mayflower in Massachusetts in 1620 with the

arrival of the typical immigrant ship about 1900, drawing whatever conclusions you can about the changes in America itself that seem to be represented by the changes in the reception of immigrants.

3. On the basis of the evidence offered in Howe's essay, write an essay in which you support the activities of humane, volunteer groups like HIAS and criticize those of the entrenched bureaucracy in any area of public concern.

4. Write an essay in which you analyze the stages by which the average bewildered and frightened immigrant became assimilated into American life.

5. Describe the immigrant experiences of your own family.

Facing Up to Death

ELISABETH KÜBLER-ROSS

Elisabeth Kübler-Ross, a physician, was born in Zurich, Switzerland, in 1926. Her youthful experiences during World War II impressed upon her indelibly the tragedy of the Nazi concentration camps and the agony of Europe's slaughtered millions, leading to a lifelong interest in the phenomenon of death. She is the author of a book-length study, *On Death and Dying,* and currently teaches psychiatry at the University of Chicago Medical School. One of the most important of her contributions to our understanding of the experience of death was a series of teaching seminars she conducted in 1965 at Billings Hospital in Chicago. Her purpose was to educate nursing and medical students, residents, and hospital staff in methods of dealing with the terminally ill. The essay that follows is in part a summary of the findings of those seminars.

1   People used to be born at home and die at home. In the old days, children were familiar with birth and death as part of life. This is perhaps the first generation of American youngsters who have never been close by during the birth of a baby and have never experienced the death of a beloved family member.

2   Nowadays when people grow old, we often send them to nursing homes. When they get sick, we transfer them to a hospital, where children are usually unwelcome and are forbidden to visit terminally ill patients—even when those patients are their parents. This deprives the dying patient of significant family members during the last few days of his life and it deprives the children of an experience of death, which is an important learning experience.

3   At the University of Chicago's Billings Hospital, some of my colleagues and I interviewed and followed approximately 500 terminally ill patients in order to find out what they could teach us and how we could be of more benefit, not just to them but to the members of their families as well. We were most impressed by the fact that even those patients who were not told of their serious illness were quite aware of its potential outcome. They were not only able to say that they were close to dying, but many were able to predict the approximate time of their death.

FACING UP TO DEATH   From *Today's Education,* January, 1972. Published by the National Education Association. Reprinted by permission of *Today's Education* and Elisabeth K. Ross.

4   It is important for next of kin and members of the helping professions to understand these patients' communications in order to truly understand their needs, fears, and fantasies. Most of our patients welcomed another human being with whom they could talk openly, honestly, and frankly about their predicament. Many of them shared with us their tremendous need to be informed, to be kept up-to-date on their medical condition, and to be told when the end was near. We found out that patients who had been dealt with openly and frankly were better able to cope with the imminence of death and finally to reach a true stage of acceptance prior to death.

5   Two things seem to determine the ultimate adjustment to a terminal illness. When patients were allowed hope at the beginning of a fatal illness and when they were informed that they would not be deserted "no matter what," they were able to drop their initial shock and denial rather quickly and could arrive at a peaceful acceptance of their finiteness.

6   Most patients respond to the awareness that they have a terminal illness with the statement, "Oh no, this can't happen to me." After the first shock, numbness, and need to deny the reality of the situation, the patient begins to send out cues that he is ready to "talk about it." If *we*, at that point, need to deny the reality of the situation, the patient will often feel deserted, isolated, and lonely and unable to communicate with another human being what he needs so desperately to share.

7   When, on the other hand, the patient has one person with whom he can talk freely, he will be able to talk (often for only a few minutes at a time) about his illness and about the consequences of his deteriorating health, and he will be able to ask for help. Sometimes, he'll need to talk about financial matters; and, toward the end of the life, he will frequently ask for some spiritual help.

8   Most patients who have passed the stage of denial will become angry as they ask the question, "Why me?" Many look at others in their environment and express envy, jealousy, anger, and rage toward those who are young, healthy, and full of life. These are the patients who make life difficult for nurses, physicians, social workers, clergymen, and members of their families. Without justification they criticize everyone.

9   What we have to learn is that the stage of anger in terminal illness is a blessing, not a curse. These patients are not angry at their families or at the members of the helping professions. Rather, they are angry at what these people represent: health, pep, energy.

10   Without being judgmental, we must allow these patients to express their anger and dismay. We must try to understand that the patients have to ask, "Why me?" and that there is no need on our part to answer this question concretely. Once a patient has ventilated his rage and his envy, then he can arrive at the bargaining stage. During this time, he's usually able to say, "Yes, it is happening to me—*but*." The *but* usually includes a prayer to God: "If you give me one more year to live, I will be a good Christian (or I'll go to the synagogue every day)."

11   Most patients promise something in exchange for prolongation of life.

Many a patient wants to live just long enough for the children to get out of school. The moment thay have completed high school, he may ask to live until the son gets married. And the moment the wedding is over, he hopes to live until the grandchild arrives. These kinds of bargains are compromises, the patient's beginning acknowledgement that his time is limited, and an expression of finiteness, all necessary in reaching a stage of acceptance. When a patient drops the *but,* then he is able to say, "Yes, me." At this point, he usually becomes very depressed. And here again we have to allow him to express his grief and his mourning.

12   If we stop and think how much we would grieve if we lost a beloved spouse, it will make us realize what courage it takes for a man to face his own impending death, which involves the loss of everyone and everything he has ever loved. This is a thousand times more crushing than to become a widow or a widower.

13   To such patients, we should never say, "Come on now, cheer up." We should allow them to grieve, to cry. And we should even convey to them that "it takes a brave person to cry," meaning that it takes courage to face death. If the patient expresses his grief, he will feel more comfortable, and he will usually go through the stage of depression much more rapidly than he will if he has to suppress it or hide his tears.

14   Only through this kind of behavior on our part are our patients able to reach the stage of acceptance. Here, they begin to separate themselves from the interpersonal relationships in their environment. Here, they begin to ask for fewer and fewer visitors. Finally, they will require only one beloved person who can sit quietly and comfortably near.

15   This is the time when a touch becomes more important than words, the time when a patient may simply say one day, "My time is very close now, and it's all right." It is not necessarily a happy stage, but the patient now shows no more fear, bitterness, anguish, or concern over unfinished business. People who have been able to sit through this stage with patients and who have experienced the beautiful feeling of inner and outer peace that they show will soon appreciate that working with terminally ill patients is not a morbid, depressing job but can be an inspiring experience.

16   The tragedy is that in our death-denying society, people grow up uncomfortable in the presence of a dying patient, unable to talk to the terminally ill and lost for words when they face a grieving person.

17   We tried to use dying patients as teachers. We talked with these patients so they could teach our young medical students, social work students, nurses, and members of the clergy about one part of life that all of us eventually have to face. When we interviewed them, we had a screened window setup in which we were able to talk with them in privacy while our students observed and listened. Needless to say this observation was done with the knowledge and agreement of our patients.

18   This teaching by dying patients who volunteered this service to us enabled

them to share some of their turmoil and some of their needs with us. But perhaps more important than that, they were able to help our own young students to face the reality of death, to identify at times with our dying patients, and to become aware of their own finiteness.

19   Many of our young students who originally were petrified at the thought of facing dying patients were eventually able to express to us their own concerns, their own fears, and their own fantasies about dying. Most of our students who have been able to attend one quarter or perhaps a semester of these weekly death-and-dying seminars have learned to come to grips with their own fears of death and have ultimately become good counselors to terminally ill patients.

20   One thing this teaches us is that it would be helpful if we could rear our children with the awareness of death and of their own finiteness. Even in a death-denying society, this can be and has been done.

21   In our hospital we saw a small child with acute leukemia. She made the rounds and asked the adults, "What is it going to be like when I die?" The grown-ups responded in a variety of ways, most of them unhelpful or even harmful for this little girl who was searching for an answer. The only message she really received through the grown-ups' response was that they had a lot of fear when it came to talking about dying.

22   When the child confronted the hospital chaplain with the same question, he turned to her and asked, "What do you think it's going to be like?" She looked at him and said, "One of these days I'm going to fall asleep and when I wake up I'm going to be with Jesus and my little sister." He then said something like "That should be very beautiful." The child nodded and happily returned to play. Perhaps this is an exaggerated example, but I think it conveys how children face the reality even of their own death if the adults in their environment don't make it a frightening, horrible experience to be avoided at all costs.

23   The most forgotten people in the environment of the dying patient are the brothers and sisters of dying children. We have seen rather tragic examples of siblings who were terribly neglected during the terminal illness of a brother or a sister. Very often those children are left alone with many unanswered questions while the mother attends the dying child in the hospital and the father doesn't come home from work because he wants to visit the hospital in the evening.

24   The tragedy is that these children at home not only are anxious, lonely, and frightened at the thought of their sibling's death, but they also feel that somehow their wish for a sibling to "drop dead" (which all children have at times) is being fulfilled. When such a sibling actually dies, they feel responsible for the death, just as they do when they lose a parent during the preschool years. If these children receive no help prior to, and especially immediately after, the death of a parent or a sibling, they are likely to grow up with abnormal fears of death and a lot of unresolved conflicts that often result in emotional illness later on in life.

25   We hope that teachers are aware of the needs of these children and can make themselves available to them in order to elicit expression of their fears, their fantasies, their needs. If they're allowed to express their anger for being neglected and their shame for having "committed a crime," then these children can be helped before they develop permanent emotional conflict.

26   A beautiful example of death education in an indirect way is expressed in a letter I received from a man who became aware of my work and felt the need to convey some of his life experiences to me. I will quote his letter verbatim because it shows what an early childhood memory can do for a man when he's faced with the imminent death of his own father.

27   Dear Dr. Ross: May I commend you and your colleagues who took part in the Conference on "death. . . ."

28   I am a production-line brewery worker here in Milwaukee who feels strongly on this subject. Because of your efforts, maybe one day we can all look death in the eye. . . . In reading and rereading the enclosed account of your meeting, I found myself with the urge to relate to you a personal experience of my own.

29   About six years ago, my dad was a victim of terminal cancer. He was a tough, life-loving 73-year-old father of 10 with 10 grandchildren who kept him aglow and always on the go. It just couldn't be that his time had come. The last time I saw him alive was the result of an urgent phone call from my sister. "You'd better come home as soon as possible; it's Pa."

30   The 500-mile drive to northern Minnesota wasn't the enjoyable trip that so many others had been. I learned after I arrived that he wasn't in the hospital, but at home. I also learned that "he didn't know." The doctor told the family that it was up to us to tell him or not tell him. My brother and sisters who live in the area thought it best "not to" and so advised me.

31   When I walked in on him, we embraced as we always did when we'd visit about twice or so each year. But this time it was different—sort of restrained and lacking the spirit of earlier get-togethers; and each of us, I know, sensed this difference.

32   Then, some hours later, after the usual kinds of questions and answers and talk, it was plain to me that he appeared so alone and withdrawn, almost moody or sulking. It was scary to see him just sitting there, head in hand, covering his eyes. I didn't know what to say or do. I asked if he'd care for a drink—no response. Something had to give. It all seemed so cruel. So I stepped into the kitchen and poured me a good one—and another. This was it, and if he didn't "know," he would now.

33   I went over and sat down beside and sort of facing him, and I was scared. I was always scared of my father, but it was a good kind of fear, the respectful kind. I put one hand on his shoulder and the other on his knee. I said, "Pa, you know why I came home, don't you? This is the last time we will be together." The dam burst. He threw his arms around me, and just hung on.

34   And here's the part I'll never forget and yet always cherish. I remember when our tears met, I recalled, in a sort of vivid flashback, a time 30 years before when I was five or six and he took me out into the woods to pick hazelnuts. My very first big adventure! I remembered being afraid of the woods. Afraid of bears or monsters or something that would eat me up. But even though I was

afraid, I at the same time was brave, because my big strong daddy was with me.

35   Needless to say, thanks to that hazelnut hunt, I knew how my dad was feeling at that moment. And I could only hope that I gave him some small measure of courage; the kind he had given me. I do know he was grateful and appreciated my understanding. As I remember, he regained his composure and authority enough to scold *me* for crying. It was at the kitchen table, after a couple or three fingers of brandy, that we talked and reminisced and planned. I would even guess he was eager to start a long search for his wife, who also had known how to die. . . .

36   What I am trying to convey is that everything depends on the way we rear our children. If we help them to face fear and show them that through strength and sharing we can overcome even the fear of dying, then they will be better prepared to face any kind of crisis that might confront them, including the ultimate reality of death.

Exercises

COMPREHENSION

Organization and Development

Complete the following outline. Find the statement of purpose, and then find the thesis statement, keeping in mind the difference between the two. Write them in the spaces provided. Then find the main divisions in the essay and the conclusion, and fill in the remaining spaces. Note the paragraphs for each section.

Statement of purpose: _____
Thesis statement: _____
I.   Introduction: _____ [   ]
II.   _____ [   ]
      A. _____ [   ]
      B. _____ [   ]
      C. _____ [   ]
      D. _____ [   ]
      E. _____ [   ]
III. _____ [   ]
IV.   _____ [   ]
V.   _____ [   ]
VI.   Conclusion: _____ [   ]

Content

Choose the answer that correctly completes each statement.

1. Kübler-Ross believes we need to be taught about death and dying because (a) it is *the* fundamental human experience (b) the circumstances of modern life prevent chil-

dren from gaining a familiarity with death or birth in the natural course of things (c) we might thus solve the riddle of the afterlife.

2. Kübler-Ross's research showed that (a) it is best not to tell the terminally ill patient of his impending death (b) it is impossible to tell someone gently of his coming death (c) a terminally ill patient is almost always quite aware of his impending death, even if he has not been "told."

3. The purpose of Kübler-Ross's research at Billings Hospital was to (a) determine in detail the stages through which the dying pass (b) find out what dying patients could teach about death and how medical personnel could be of more benefit to them and their families (c) analyze the differences between the ways in which the young and the old face impending death.

4. The first reaction of most patients when they become aware that they have a terminal illness is (a) anger (b) fear (c) denial.

5. Kübler-Ross refers to the depth of grief one would feel at the loss of a beloved spouse to show (a) that the feelings in such a circumstance are universal (b) how we should cheer the dying patient and keep his mind off the subject of death (c) how enormously greater is the grief one feels for one's own death, implying the loss of everyone and everything.

6. The letter from the Milwaukee brewery-worker exemplifies (a) how much nicer it is to die at home than in a hospital or nursing home (b) the way in which accepting and sharing in the dying person's experience can help to give him courage (c) the cruelty of telling the terminally ill person of his death before he is actually prepared to accept it.

7. Kübler-Ross's emphasis on "death-education" is, in this essay, directed principally toward improving (a) the way in which we prepare our children to face all crises, especially death (b) hospital care of the terminally ill (c) the chances for a terminally ill person to recover.

8. Which of the following best expresses the author's attitude toward death and dying? (a) No man is an island. (b) O Death, where is thy sting? (c) All that lives must die.

Paragraph Structure

Reorder the following sentences to form a unified, coherent paragraph. Identify one sentence as the topic sentence. Then check your version with the original.

1. Many a patient wants to live just long enough for the children to get out of school.

2. These kinds of bargains are compromises, the patient's beginning acknowledgement that his time is limited, and an expression of finiteness, all necessary in reaching a stage of acceptance.

3. And here again we have to allow him to express his grief and mourning.

4. Most patients promise something in exchange for prolongation of life.

5. And the moment the wedding is over, he hopes to live until the grandchild arrives.

6. When a patient drops the *but*, when he is able to say, "Yes, me."

7. The moment they have completed high school, he may ask to live until the son gets married.

8. At this point, he usually becomes very depressed.

VOCABULARY AND USAGE

Word Formation Table

Complete the following table by changing word endings or root forms to make new grammatical forms. Use your dictionary if necessary.

NOUN	VERB	ADJECTIVE	ADVERB
1. _____	die	_____	_____
2. justification	_____	_____	_____
3. _____	reminisce	_____	_____
4. courage	xxx	_____	_____
5. _____	_____	_____	terminally

Fill-Ins

Complete each of the sentences below using the words on the following list. You may need to use some words more than once. You may also find that some blanks can be completed correctly with more than one word. Add plural endings to nouns and change verb forms where necessary.

predicament	situation	hospital	imminent
finiteness	dying	experience	reality
depression	death	acknowledge	reminisce
anger	accept	support	morbid
courage	impending	convey	share

1. People used to be born at home and die at home, too; today they must _____ the _____ of _____ _____ in the frequently unpleasant or lonely circumstances of the large, modern _____.
2. The terminally ill patient usually knows he is _____, even if he has not been told; because he "knows," he needs to learn to _____ the fact of his own _____.
3. _____ patients, young or old, need emotional _____ from others who can _____ their feelings of _____ and _____.
4. It is difficult to _____ to someone who is _____ that others understand and _____ his _____ because in our culture so few people want to accept the ultimate _____ of _____.
5. _____ is the final _____ which each of us must _____; it is up to us whether we will face it with _____.
6. Kübler-Ross wants us to teach our children to understand and _____ the _____ of _____ as an everyday occurrence, instead of something _____, something which should be hidden from them.

DISCUSSION

1. What is the main *purpose* of this essay? How is it distinguished from the main *idea*?
2. What is the relationship between the statement that "people used to be born at home and die at home" and the repeated description of ours as a "death-denying society"? What, specifically, are the ways in which our society denies the reality of death? Does Kübler-Ross state the ways, or does she simply imply them?
3. This essay analyzes not the stages by which terminally ill patients die, but the stages by which they "arrive at a peaceful acceptance of their finiteness." What is the special significance of the term "finiteness," and how is it related—or distinguished from— the phrase "the ultimate reality of death"?
4. What are the stages through which the terminally ill person passes? In what specific way is each of these stages connected to the title "Facing Up to Death"?
5. What method or device does the author use to define and connect her discussion of each of the stages of dying? In what other way could she have organized these stages?

6. "No young man thinks that he will ever die; every old man knows he will." This quotation implies that advancing age is itself the means by which we become aware of the reality of death, but Kübler-Ross's essay indicates that even the dying may refuse to believe in their own deaths. Are these two views really at odds, or is there some way in which they complement each other? Discuss.

SUGGESTIONS FOR WRITING

1. Describe a personal experience in which you came to understand, for the first time, the concept of "finiteness." (This might be an experience in which your own life was endangered, the death of a family member, or even the loss of a beloved pet.) Or analyze the stages by which you came to such an understanding, perhaps through a number of different experiences.
2. Analyze the stages of some other fundamental human state or experience (for example, birth, childhood, education, crippling illness, marriage, divorce, falling in love, etc.)
3. Describe your own attitude toward death.
4. Write an essay about those aspects of our society that most particularly contribute to its ability to "deny the ultimate reality of death."
5. Compare the way in which death and dying are treated in another culture.

Moonshining as a Fine Art

THE FOXFIRE BOOK

The Foxfire Book was the inspiration of Eliot Wigginton, a graduate of Cornell University who began teaching English in 1966 at the 240-pupil Rabun Gap-Nacoochee School in the Appalachians of Georgia. Six weeks later, he "surveyed the wreckage"—bored, rebellious students and a frazzled, disenchanted teacher. He conceived of *Foxfire,* a magazine to be written, edited, and published by his students who were dispatched to interview old-time Georgia residents and to record their skills in crafts and arts, thereby preserving them for future generations. Four *Foxfire* books have since been published, each representing the writing efforts of Wigginton's ninth and tenth grade students. The following excerpt is from the section on moonshining, which explains how moonshiners hide stills and how revenuers find them.

1   The manufacture of illicit whiskey in the mountains is not dead. Far from it. As long as the operation of a still remains so financially rewarding, it will never die. There will always be men ready to take their chances against the law for such an attractive profit, and willing to take their punishment when they are caught.

2   Moonshining as a fine art, however, effectively disappeared some time ago. There were several reasons. One was the age of aspirin and modern medicine. As home doctoring lost its stature, the demand for pure corn whiskey as an essential ingredient of many home remedies vanished along with those remedies. Increasing affluence was another reason. Young people, rather than follow in their parents' footsteps, decided that there were easier ways to make money; and they were right.

3   Third, and perhaps most influential of all, was the arrival, even in moonshining, of that peculiarly human disease known to most of us as greed. One fateful night, some force whispered in an unsuspecting moonshiner's ear, "Look. Add this gadget to your still and you'll double your production. Double your production, and you can double your profits."

4   Soon the small operators were being forced out of business, and moonshining, like most other manufacturing enterprises, was quickly taken over by a breed of men bent on making money—and lots of it. Loss of pride in the product, and loss of time taken with the product increased in direct propor-

tion to the desire for production; and thus moonshining as a fine art was buried in a quiet little ceremony attended only by those mourners who had once been the proud artists, known far and wide across the hills for the excellence of their product. Too old to continue making it themselves, and with no one following behind them, they were reduced to reminiscing about "the good old days when the whiskey that was made was *really* whiskey, and no questions asked."

5   Suddenly moonshining fell into the same category as faith healing, planting by the signs, and all the other vanishing customs that were a part of a rugged, self-sufficient culture that is now disappearing.

Hiding The Still

6   Since the days of excise, moonshiners have been forced to hide their stills. Here are some of the ways they have used.

7   1. Since cold running water is an absolute necessity, stills are often high up on the side of a mountain near the source of a stream. Water on the north side of a hill flowing west was preferred by many. Some count on the inaccessibility of the spot they chose for protection. Others, however:

8   build a log shed over the still and cover this with evergreen branches;

9   bend living saplings over so they conceal the still. The branches continue growing and their leaves provide cover;

10   find a tree that has fallen over a ravine or gully and build the still under it, adding branches, if necessary, for additional coverage;

11   find a ravine, dig out its bottom, place the still in, and then set branches and saplings over the top like a roof. They should be arranged so that they blend in with the landscape;

12   find a cave and cover up the front of it;

13   find a large laurel thicket, crawl into the center of it, and cut out a room right in the middle of the thicket big enough for the still;

14   find a large spruce and put the still under its branches so it can't be seen from a plane.

15   2. The legend has grown that all one has to do to find a still is follow a likely looking branch up into a cove and then poke around until uncovering something suspicious. Moonshiners have countered by locating many stills in so-called "dry hollows." They find a cove that has no stream and pipe in the water they need from a higher, "wet" cove. Using all the hiding devices mentioned above, they:

16   buy two-inch piping, and run the pipe underground, around a ridge and into the dry hollow;

17   get plastic pipe and run it under leaves, or in a trench;

18   forget about the cove, and put the still right out on the top of a dry ridge, or in a laurel thicket, and pipe the water from a higher source.

19   3. Other moonshiners get far more elaborate and actually dig out an underground room big enough to stand in comfortably. Rows of beams are set in overhead, covered with dirt, and plant materials are actually planted

overhead. A small trapdoor in the center of the roof, also covered with a growth, lifts up, exposing a ladder which goes down into the room. A vent pipe, cleverly concealed, carries off fumes. Some rooms are even wired for electricity.

20   4. Another way to avoid detection is by moving constantly. Some men follow logging jobs, figuring that the loggers will destroy all signs of their moonshining activities. In fact, loggers themselves often run stills in conjunction with their logging job.

21   5. Some men set up in a site the revenuers have just cut down believing that they won't be back for at least two months unless they get another report of activity there.

22   6. Others place their stills right in existing buildings that are not often visited, or would not normally be suspected—barns, silos, smoke-houses, tool sheds, abandoned homes or buildings, even the basements of their own homes. Others run right in the center of town behind a false-fronted store or in a condemned building.

23   7. One man we know, believing that the revenuers will be looking for his still to be concealed, has it right out in the open, near the main highway, with only a few trees in front. He hasn't been caught yet.

24   8. Smoke, too, is a problem, but only at the beginning of the run. When the fire begins burning well, it gives off heat waves rather than smoke. Thus, often the fire is started just before dawn and is burning well enough by daylight to escape detection.

25   Others, however, worried about smoke, "burn their smoke." A worm or pipe which runs out the side of the furnace and back into the firebox recirculates the smoke and makes it invisible. We also have heard of a man who somehow piped his smoke so that it came up underwater—this supposedly dispersed it so effectively that it could not be seen. Others counted on the leaves and branches over their shelters to disperse the smoke.

26   Now any conceivable problem of smoke has been wiped out with the use of fuels such as butane or kerosene.

27   9. A dead giveaway as to the location of a still is a "sign" or trace of activity. Moonshiners constantly guard against this. An empty sugar bag, the lid from a fruit jar, a piece of copper—all can reveal their location.

28   An even bigger problem is that of trails. There are various ways they have dealt with it:

29   if the still is in the woods, always enter the woods from the road at a different point. Then, one hundred fifty yards up the hill, cross over to the main trail which begins as many yards or so off the road.

30   enter stills that are in a cove or hollow from the ridge above the still, instead of coming uphill from the front. One man who lives at the base of a high ridge said he could sit on his porch on a summer night and sometimes hear the voices of men, on the way to their still, shouting at the mules that were carrying in the supplies. If he looked carefully, he could see their lanterns winking high up on the ridge as they came in the back way to keep from being caught.

31   locate the still on a stream that runs into a lake, through brush, and far away from any road. Then always enter the still at night, by boat.

32   find a cut in the road the top of which is capped with a rock ledge, and is either level with or a little higher than a pickup truck bed. Load or unload from this rock to prevent leaving trails.

33   use fuel like butane gas to prevent leaving signs such as stumps or trees and wood chips and clipped off foliage.

Finding the Hidden Still

34   Law officers have used many methods for finding hidden stills. Each time one became popular, the blockaders countered by hiding it in a different way. Here, however, are some of the methods used.

35   1. They are always alert for signs. A brick dropped in the middle of the woods is an obvious one. Why would it be there except for a furnace? Spilled meal or sugar on the side of a road is suspicious. A ladder left at the top of a high cut in the road is an obvious signal; probably it is used to load and unload supplies from the back of a pickup. Other signs include an empty sugar bag, a broken jar, a place in the woods where trees have been cut, a pile of charcoal, an empty cement bag, a broken shovel handle, a barrel stave, a burlap sack.

36   2. With an officer on either side of a backwoods dirt road—each two hundred yards away from the road, walking parallel to it—they search for a place where a trail begins.

37   3. With a boat, they search the edges of a lake. They look for signs of activity near a place where a branch empties into the lake. Such signs might be places where a boat has been pulled up on shore or slick trails made by dragging heavy feed bags.

38   4. They stake out a road and watch for signs of unusual activity in the early morning hours. They follow any cars heading up little-used roads. Or an officer might stake out a section of woods and listen for sounds such as a hammer against metal, the sound of a thump barrel, etc.

39   5. Usually areas where moonshine is being made have a distinctive smell. Law officers may detect that while walking through forest.

40   Many stills are found by people like hunters who spend much time in the woods and merely stumble across one by accident. Others are found by searching small branches that flow from hillsides through heavy growth.

41   The most prevalent means of finding stills, however, remains the informer. Often, they are people with a grudge or an axe to grind. One moonshiner characterized them as people, "who don't have enough of their own business to mind, and so they feel obligated to mind th' business of other people. Th' lowest man I know," he continued, "is one who wins your confidence, buys your liquor, and then turns you in. I believe there's a special place for people like that after they die."

Analysis and Classification

Analysis is the examination and explanation of a subject or a thing through the study of its component parts (what it consists of) and their relationship to each other. Classification is a means of determining the relationships among things by assessing their similarities or likenesses and then placing them in classes or categories. An *analysis* of basic equipment for the kitchen, for instance, would probably begin by dividing the subject, "kitchen equipment," into categories: "major appliances, small appliances, equipment for food serving, furniture for storage, etc." *Classifying* the kitchen equipment would mean placing stove, refrigerator, and dishwasher together in the category of "major appliances." But classification is also the name for the commonplace task you perform whenever you straighten out the kitchen drawers and cupboards, putting the egg slicer, cheese grater, and corkscrew into the same drawer—a decision you make because, consciously or unconsciously, you have grouped these items together in the class of "small gadgets."

These two methods of organization, analysis and classification, are common in everyday thinking and activity, closely related, and frequently used in combination. Analysis may be carried out solely through the establishment of classes or categories (major appliances, small appliances; responsibility, optimism), as in the kitchen example and in Michener's essay on middle-class values. In turn, where classification rather than analysis is the primary aim, analysis still may be required: does the cheese grater have the properties of a small gadget, or is it a tool for slicing that belongs in the same category—and therefore in the same drawer—with the knives?

A crucial issue in both analysis and classification is keeping before you—as reader or writer—the subject or substance being studied, and the major divisions or classes that emerge from the analytic procedure. "Kitchen equipment" and "new appliances needed in my kitchen" are very different subjects for analysis. And even with a single subject, any change in purpose or point of view may alter the categories or divisions established by the analysis. ("Kitchen equipment" *could* be divided into "food preparation, serving, cleaning, storage." And "assumptions of the middle class" might break down into "security, safety, income level, etc.," instead of the categories chosen by Michener.)

Eric Sevareid's essay, "Velva, North Dakota," begins by establishing the subject for analysis—not the author's home town itself, but rather the *changes* that have occurred there in thirty years. The general subject, "changes," is then analyzed, broken down into elements, or classes: sights, sounds, the kinds of people in Velva, distance and time, consolidation. These categories are in turn developed by means of illustrations and examples, which in fact require the classification of specific aspects of the town's changed character. Ruth Benedict, too, carefully defines the scope of her analysis: it is *not* the rapidly changing character or the elements of decay in family life, but the family itself, in relation to the demands of the society in which it must survive. Her divisions then make sense *in relation to her subject*, a point that is true as well of the other essays in this section, and of all good analysis in general.

Apart from the scope of the analysis and its main divisions, it is also important to recognize the relationships among the elements or categories themselves. Are they logical? Are they equal? Do some deserve more emphasis than others? If one class or division can be included in another, then it is not really a separate class, but a subdivision. (In Sevareid's essay, is "consolidation" really a separate category, or is it a subdivision of "time and distance"? Does Benedict's discussion of the way the young American couple sets up housekeeping belong under the major category of "freedom" or "privacy"?)

Analysis is a vital and fundamental method of thinking as well as a means of organizing an essay. It is the function you must perform before you can outline your ideas in preparation for writing; it is the same manner of thinking you use when you try to outline an essay you have read. And, like almost every other means of expository development, it demands the exercise of your fundamental capacity to perceive relationships.

Velva, North Dakota

ERIC SEVAREID

Eric Sevareid began his career as a newspaperman, and during World War II he was a war correspondent in both Europe and China. After the war, he became a national correspondent for CBS in Washington; from 1964 until his retirement in 1977, he was a commentator on national and international affairs for the CBS Evening News. In this essay, he records the changes that time and progress have brought to his home town.

1   My home town has changed in these thirty years of the American story. It is changing now, will go on changing as America changes. Its biography, I suspect, would read much the same as that of all other home towns. Depression and war and prosperity have all left their marks; modern science, modern tastes, manners, philosophies, fears and ambitions have touched my town as indelibly as they have touched New York or Panama City.

2   Sights have changed: there is a new precision about street and home, a clearing away of chicken yards, cow barns, pigeon-crested cupolas, weed lots and coulees, the dim and secret adult-free rendezvous of boys. An intricate metal "jungle gym" is a common backyard sight, the sack swing uncommon. There are wide expanses of clear windows designed to let in the parlor light, fewer ornamental windows of colored glass designed to keep it out. Attic and screen porch are slowly vanishing and lovely shades of pastel are painted upon new houses, tints that once would have embarrassed farmer and merchant alike.

3   Sounds have changed; I heard not once the clopping of a horse's hoofs, nor the mourn of a coyote. I heard instead the shriek of brakes, the heavy throbbing of the once-a-day Braniff airliner into Minot, the shattering sirens born of war, the honk of a diesel locomotive which surely cannot call to faraway places the heart of a wakeful boy like the old steam whistle in the night. You can walk down the streets of my town now and hear from open windows the intimate voices of the Washington commentators in casual converse on the great affairs of state; but you cannot hear on Sunday morning the singing in Norwegian of the Lutheran hymns; the old country seems now part of a world left long behind and the old-country accents grow fainter in the speech of my Velva neighbors.

4   The people have not changed, but the *kinds* of people have changed: there

is no longer an official, certified town drunk, no longer a "Crazy John," spitting his worst epithet, "rotten chicken legs," as you hurriedly passed him by. People so sick are now sent to places of proper care. No longer is there an official town joker, like the druggist MacKnight, who would spot a customer in the front of the store, have him called to the phone, then slip to the phone behind the prescription case, and imitate the man's wife to perfection with orders to bring home more bread and sausage and Cream of Wheat. No longer anyone like the early attorney, J. L. Lee, who sent fabulous dispatches to that fabulous tabloid, the *Chicago Blade,* such as his story of the wild man captured on the prairie and chained to the wall in the drugstore basement. (This, surely, was Velva's first notoriety; inquiries came from anthropologists all over the world.)

5   No, the "characters" are vanishing in Velva, just as they are vanishing in our cities, in business, in politics. The "well-rounded, socially integrated" personality that the progressive schoolteachers are so obsessed with is increasing rapidly, and I am not at all sure that this is good. Maybe we need more personalities with knobs and handles and rugged lumps of individuality. They may not make life more smooth; more interesting they surely make it.

6   They eat differently in Velva now; there are frozen fruits and sea food and exotic delicacies we only read about in novels in those meat-and-potato days. They dress differently. The hard white collars of the businessmen are gone with the shiny alpaca coats. There are comfortable tweeds now, and casual blazers with a touch in their colors of California, which seems so close in time and distance.

7   It is distance and time that have changed the most and worked the deepest changes in Velva's life. The telephone, the car, the smooth highway, radio and television are consolidating the entities of our country. The county seat of Towner now seems no closer than the state capital of Bismarck; the voices and concerns of Presidents, French premiers and Moroccan pashas are no farther away than the portable radio on Aunt Jessey's kitchen table. The national news magazines are stacked each week in Harold Anderson's drugstore beside the new soda fountain, and the excellent *Minot Daily News* smells hot from the press each afternoon.

8   Consolidation. The nearby hamlets of Sawyer and Logan and Voltaire had their own separate banks and papers and schools in my days of dusty buggies and Model Ts marooned in the snowdrifts. Now these hamlets are dying. A bright yellow bus takes the Voltaire kids to Velva each day for high school. Velva has grown—from 800 to 1,300—because the miners from the Truax coal mine can commute to their labors each morning and the nearby farmers can live in town if they choose. Minot has tripled in size to 30,000. Once the "Magic City" was a distant and splendid Baghdad, visited on special occasions long prepared for. Now it is a twenty-five minute commuter's jump away. So P. W. Miller and Jay Louis Monicken run their businesses in Minot but live on in their old family homes in Velva. So Ray Michelson's two girls on his farm to the west drive up each morning to their jobs as maids in Minot

homes. Aunt Jessey said, "Why, Saturday night I counted sixty-five cars just between here and Sawyer, all going up to the show in Minot."

9   The hills are prison battlements no longer; the prairies no heart-sinking barrier, but a passageway free as the swelling ocean, inviting you to sail home and away at your whim and your leisure. (John and Helen made an easy little jaunt of 700 miles that weekend to see their eldest daughter in Wyoming.)

10   Consolidation. Art Kumm's bank serves a big region now; its assets are $2,000,000 to $3,000,000 instead of the $200,000 or $300,000 in my father's day. Eighteen farms near Velva are under three ownerships now. They calculate in sections; "acres," is an almost forgotten term. Aunt Jessey owns a couple of farms, and she knows they are much better run. "It's no longer all take out and no put in," she said. "Folks strip farm now; they know all about fertilizers. They care for it and they'll hand on the land in good shape." The farmers gripe about their cash income, and not without reason at the moment, but they will admit that life is good compared with those days of drought and foreclosure, manure banked against the house for warmth, the hand pump frozen at 30 below and the fitful kerosene lamp on the kitchen table. Electrification has done much of this, eased back-breaking chores that made their wives old as parchment at forty, brought life and music and the sound of human voices into their parlors at night.

11   And light upon the prairie. "From the hilltop," said Aunt Jessey, "the farms look like stars at night."

12   Many politicians deplore the passing of the old family-size farm, but I am not so sure. I saw around Velva a release from what was like slavery to the tyrannical soil, release from the ignorance that darkens the soul and from the loneliness that corrodes it. In this generation my Velva friends have rejoined the general American society that their pioneering fathers left behind when they first made the barren trek in the days of the wheat rush. As I sit here in Washington writing this, I can feel their nearness. I never felt it before save in my dreams.

13   But now I must ask myself: Are they nearer to one another? And the answer is no; yet I am certain that this is good. The shrinking of time and distance has made contrast and relief available to their daily lives. They do not know one another quite so well because they are not so much obliged to. I know that democracy rests upon social discipline, which in turn rests upon personal discipline; passions checked, hard words withheld, civic tasks accepted, work well done, accountings honestly rendered. The old-fashioned small town was this discipline in its starkest, most primitive form; without this discipline the small town would have blown itself apart.

14   For personal and social neuroses festered under this hard scab of conformity. There was no place to go, no place to let off steam; few dared to voice unorthodox ideas, read strange books, admire esoteric art or publicly write or speak of their dreams and their soul's longings. The world was not "too much with us," the world was too little with us and we were too much with one another.

15   The door to the world stands open now, inviting them to leave anytime they wish. It is the simple fact of the open door that makes all the difference; with its opening the stale air rushed out. So, of course, the people themselves do not have to leave, because, as the stale air went out, the fresh air came in.

16   Human nature is everywhere the same. He who is not forced to help his neighbor for his own existence will not only give him help, but his true good will as well. Minot and its hospital are now close at hand, but the people of Velva put their purses together, built their own clinic and homes for the two young doctors they persuaded to come and live among them. Velva has no organized charity, but when a farmer falls ill, his neighbors get in his crop; if a townsman has a financial catastrophe his personal friends raise a fund to help him out. When Bill's wife, Ethel, lay dying so long in the Minot hospital and nurses were not available, Helen and others took their turns driving up there just to sit with her so she would know in her gathering dark that friends were at hand.

17   It is personal freedom that makes us better persons, and they are freer in Velva now. There is no real freedom without privacy, and a resident of my home town can be a private person much more than he could before. People are able to draw at least a little apart from one another. In drawing apart, they gave their best human instincts room for expansion.

Exercises

COMPREHENSION

Organization and Development

Complete the following outline. Find the thesis statement and write it in the space provided. Then find the main divisions in the essay and fill in the remaining spaces. Note the paragraphs for each section.

Thesis statement: _____

_____

_____

I.   _____   [   ]
    A.   _____   [   ]
    B.   _____   [   ]
    C.   _____   [   ]
    D.   _____   [   ]
    E.   _____   [   ]
    F.   _____   [   ]
II.   _____   [   ]

Content

Choose the answer that correctly completes each statement.

1. The main idea of this essay is that (a) small rural towns like Velva are vanishing as technology and transportation improve (b) Velva has changed in the same ways the

country as a whole has changed in the past thirty years (c) on the surface Velva appears to have changed, but people's lives have actually changed very little.

2. Apparently, when the author was young (a) crazy people were put in mental hospitals (b) many of Velva's residents were European immigrants (c) a wild man was once captured and imprisoned in the drugstore basement.

3. The greatest changes in Velva have been brought about by time and (a) such inventions as the automobile, radio, and TV that have made the outside world closer (b) the depression and World War II (c) improved education and bussing of children to larger towns.

4. Small rural towns and family farms have become increasingly (a) democratic (b) isolated (c) consolidated.

5. Farm families now find their work easier principally because of (a) modern fertilizers (b) tractors and other machinery (c) electricity.

6. What has made all the difference between the old and the new in Velva is (a) a chance to escape and the influx of new ideas (b) postwar prosperity (c) more leisure time as technology improved people's lives.

7. According to the author, the passing of the small family farm has brought about (a) rivalry and hostility between former neighbors (b) a breakdown in social and personal discipline and the passing of a better way of life (c) freedom from slavery to the soil and a release from ignorance and loneliness.

8. People in Velva no longer need to (a) help their neighbors and friends (b) conform (c) compete.

Paragraph Structure

Reorder the following sentences to form a unified, coherent paragraph. Then check your version with the original.

1. It is the simple fact of the open door that makes all the difference; with its opening the stale air rushed out.

2. So, of course, the people themselves do not have to leave, because, as the stale air went out, the fresh air went in.

3. The door to the world stands open now, inviting them to leave anytime they wish.

VOCABULARY AND USAGE

Word Formation Table

Complete the following table by changing word endings or root forms to make new grammatical forms. Use your dictionary if necessary.

	NOUN	VERB	ADJECTIVE	ADVERB
1.	_____	_____	_____	individually
2.	_____	xxx	notorious	_____
3.	obsession	_____	_____	_____
4.	_____	compare	_____	_____
5.	_____	xxx	tyrannical	_____

Fill-Ins

Complete each of the sentences below using the words on the following list. You may need to use some words more than once. You may also find that some blanks can be completed correctly with more than one word. Add plural endings to nouns and change verb forms where necessary.

common	consolidation	unorthodox	compare
mourn	difficult	obsessed	lament
disappearance	vanish	restrain	desire
deplore	different	esoteric	uncommon
change	whim	unification	popular

1. Many politicians _____ the _____ of small family farms.
2. _____ to thirty years ago, the _____ that have occurred in Velva have made the farmers' lives less _____.
3. _____ of small family farms into larger units has been the major _____ in the rural areas.
4. If one _____ people's behavior in Velva with an earlier time, he will see that their good instincts have not _____.
5. Those who _____ to read _____ books or state _____ opinions are now freer to do so.
6. It is _____ for residents of Velva to feel _____ about what they believe; furthermore, they are no longer so _____ with conforming.

DISCUSSION

1. What is Sevareid's thesis? To what extent does he discuss the various influences he mentions in the last sentence of paragraph 1?
2. What can one infer from paragraph 2 about the kinds of changes Sevareid describes in the town's appearance? Beyond "precision," what is the motive behind the sprucing up? What lies behind the trend toward jungle gyms and away from front porches? What inference can we make about the town's inhabitants from these two illustrations of change?
3. Why does Sevareid mention the "wild man" dispatch that was sent to a Chicago newspaper? How does this incident relate to his thesis or to the changes he describes in the town? Does he make it clear how he knows that such "characters" as he describes no longer exist?
4. What are some ways in which technological inventions have changed the lives of rural residents? What inventions have caused the most far-reaching changes?
5. This essay *classifies* ideas, in this case, changes that Velva has undergone. What other method of development does the essay use?
6. Do you think Sevareid is right when he says that small towns now allow more freedom of expression and belief? What examples might you use to support an opposing view?

SUGGESTIONS FOR WRITING

1. Describe one or two "characters" whom you know or have observed—people who, according to Sevareid, have "knobs and handles and rugged lumps of individuality."
2. Trace the effects on your family of one major event (for example, World War II, social upheaval in the 1960s, or Vietnam).

3. Using Sevareid's method of contrast in distinguishing between the old and the new, describe changes that have occurred in your town, city, or region in your lifetime.
4. Review what Sevareid has to say in paragraph 14 about the "hard scab of conformity." Then write an essay in which you explain the degree to which your community or an institution you have been involved with expects its members to conform to an established standard.

The Family: *Genus Americanum*

RUTH BENEDICT

Ruth Benedict (1887–1948) was a distinguished anthropologist at Columbia University. Her best-known book, *Patterns of Culture,* was published in 1934. During her career, she made several field trips to study American Indian tribes, one of which is alluded to in this essay. Here, she examines the primary characteristics of the American family from an anthropological point of view; although published more than thirty years ago, her observations about the structure of the American family remain accurate and occasionally even prophetic.

1   A great many people today speak as if the family were in some special sort of danger in our times. We hear a great deal about "saving the family" and about "preserving the home." Authors and lecturers describe how the family is threatened by divorce, or by mothers who work outside of the home, or by unemployment, or by lack of religious training of children. Each of them, depending on his experience in his own home and on his observations in the families he knows, selects something which he thinks should be changed—or should be preserved—and says that, if this or that were done, the family would be "saved."

2   To an anthropologist such phrasings are dangerously misleading. He has studied the family among naked savages and in contemporary civilizations and he knows that it has survived in all human societies known in the record of mankind. Just as surely he knows that the family takes all kinds of different forms. It is not merely that unlettered primitive nomads have family arrangements different from Western industrial nations; even in Western nations around the Atlantic shores the family differs profoundly. The ethics of marriage, the specific close emotional ties which the family fosters, the disciplines and freedoms for the child, the nature of the dependency of the children upon the parents, even the personnel which makes up the family—all these differ in Western civilized nations. The anthropologist knows that the changes taking place in the home in any decade in any country do not mean that the family is now about to disintegrate under our eyes unless we do something about it. The problem as he states it is quite different: how do legal and customary arrangements in the family tally with the arrangements and premises of the whole way of life which is valued in

THE FAMILY: GENUS AMERICANUM   From *The Family: Its Function and Destiny* edited by Ruth Nanda Anshen. Copyright 1949 by Harper & Row, Publishers, Inc; Copyright © 1959 by Ruth Nanda Anshen. Reprinted by permission of Harper & Row, Publishers, Inc.

any tribe or nation? If, for instance, the father has a heavy, authoritarian hand upon his children, the anthropologist asks: Is this in keeping with authoritarianism in the state and in industry? Or is it at odds with a society which values non-authoritarianism and the pursuit of happiness? He asks the same kind of question about a nation's laws of inheritance from father to son, about the divorce laws, about the architectural layout of the house, about the reasons that are given to children when they are told to be good.

3   Customs enshrined in the family in any tribe or nation are likely to be sensitively adjusted to the values and customs of each particular people. This is no mystic correspondence; the persons who make up the family are the same people who are the citizens of that nation—the business men, the farmers, the churchgoers or non-churchgoers, the readers of newspapers, and the listeners to the radio. In all their roles they are molded more or less surely into a people with certain habits, certain hopes, and a certain *esprit de corps*. Americans come to share certain slogans, behavior, and judgments which differ from those of Frenchmen or Czechs. This is inevitable. And in the process the role of the family also becomes different. By the same token, just as economic and political changes occur over a period of time in the United States or in France or in Czechoslovakia, the family also changes.

4   An anthropologist, therefore, when he reads about the failure of the family, finds in such criticism a somewhat special meaning. He remembers how often the family is made a convenient whipping boy among many peoples who disapprove of the way their world is going. He has seen it in Amazon jungles and on the islands of the Pacific. The author remembers an American Indian tribe which used to talk about the family in a most uncomplimentary fashion. They were a people who, not long before, had roamed over the great plains hunting buffalo and proving their courage by war exploits. Now they lived on a reservation, and tending crops was no adequate substitute for their old way of life. Their old economic arrangements of boastful gift giving, their political life, and their religious practices had either been destroyed by circumstances or had lost their old meaningfulness. Life had become pointless to them. These men talked with gusto about the failure of the family. They said that in the family the children no longer learned manners, or religion, or generosity, or whatever it was the individual Indian favored as a cure-all. The family, too, weighed a man down, they said; it was a burden to him.

5   To the anthropologist studying this tribe, however, the family was precisely the best arranged, most trustworthy institution in their whole culture. It was hard beset and it had not escaped the tragic effects of the general disintegration of tribal life, but it was what provided the warm, human ties and the dependable security which were left in that Indian tribe. The children were loved and cared for, the husbands and wives often had comfortable relations with each other, and family hospitality had a graciousness that was absent in more public life. At birth and marriage and death the family still functioned as an effective institution. And there seemed to be no man or woman of childbearing age who was not married or would not have preferred to be.

6   The writer thinks of this Indian tribe when she hears Americans talk about the decay of the family. Instead of viewing the family with such alarm, suppose we look at it as it exists in this decade in this country and see how it is arranged to fulfill its functions in American schemes of life. Let us leave aside for the moment the questions of whether conditions are provided that would keep it from preventable overstrain and of whether as human beings we are able to get all the satisfaction we might out of this institution; let us consider only the arrangements of the family as we know it and how these fit in with our values and with the way we should like to plan our lives.

7   Suppose we take marriage first. Marriage sets up the new family, and it seems to make a great deal of difference whether a society dictates that the new home shall be begun in tears and heartache or with rejoicing. Many human societies would not recognize a marriage without a wailing bride and a sullen groom. Often the bride has to be surrounded by her mourning women, who lament her coming lifelong separation from her parents and her brothers and sisters, as well as her future misery as she goes to work for her mother-in-law. Often they cut her long hair and remove her jewelry as a sign that she is now a worker and no longer alluring. The groom's role, too, may be that of an unwilling victim. Often marriages are arranged by the parents without giving the two young people any chance to know each other.

8   All these circumstances are absent in marriage in the United States. The young people are hardly hampered in their choice of a mate; if occasionally parents deplore their choice, public opinion allows the young couple to outface them and expects the parents to accept the inevitable with as much decency as they can muster. We expect that the bride and groom will be in love or will have chosen each other for reasons known to themselves. Whether they marry for love or for money or to show they can win a sought-after mate from a rival, in any case they are making a personal choice and are not acting on command. Because in every field of life American culture puts such a high value on this kind of freedom and so bitterly resents its curtailment in peace time, the fact that young people do make their own choice of a mate is an important and auspicious arrangement. The arranged marriage which is traditional in France or the careful class restrictions which have been observed in Holland would be difficult to manage in the United States. The wide range of choice of a mate and the fact that the young people make their own selection are conditions which could hardly be made more satisfactory for Americans with their particular habits and demands.

9   After marriage, too, the new family has a wide range of choices about where to live, how the wife shall occupy herself, when to start a family, and a host of other important matters. Such freedom is extremely unusual in the world. Sometimes the couple must live with the husband's family, sometimes with the wife's. Often in other countries, until one or two children are born, the young man continues to work for his father and has no say about the farm or the flock and no money which he can control. But in the United States a young couple plans the family budget before the wedding and what they earn is theirs to spend.

10   The way the new family in this country sets up its own separate home makes possible a rare and delightful circumstance: the two of them can have an incomparable privacy. No matter how hard it has been to arrange for privacy before marriage, as soon as the wedding is over everybody expects them to have their own latch key and their own possessions around them. If they cannot manage this, they feel cheated and other people think something is wrong. It is the same if they have to give a home to a parent. In most civilized countries this is a duty to which as a good son and good daughter they are bound, but if it is necessary in the United States their friends and neighbors will regard them as exceptionally burdened. Even the scarcity and high wages of domestic servants give the young family a greater privacy. Considering that they have chosen each other to their own liking, this privacy in the home is made in order to gratify them; the only problem is whether they can use it to their own happiness.

11   When they cannot, and when they find that their choice of a mate was not fool-proof just because they made it on their own, there is in the United States great freedom to get a divorce. Our growing divorce rate is the subject of much viewing-with-alarm; yet in a culture built as ours is on ever expanding personal choice, an important goal of which is the pursuit of happiness, the right to terminate an unhappy marriage is the other side of the coin of which the fair side is the right to choose one's spouse. Weak and stunted individuals will of course abuse both privileges, yet it is difficult to see how divorce could consistently be denied in a culture like ours. Certainly if we accepted it more honestly as a necessary phase of our way of life, however sorrowful, and put honest effort and sympathy into not penalizing the divorced, we should be acting more appropriately and in our own best interests. At any rate, the high divorce rate in the United States is no attack on marriage, for it is precisely the divorced—those who have failed in one or two attempts—who have the highest rate of marriage. Between the ages of twenty-five and thirty-five not even the unmarried or the widowed marry at so great a rate as the divorced.

12   Besides free choice and privacy, the American family has unusual potential leisure because of the labor-saving devices, prepared foods, and ready-made clothes available under modern conditions. The basic labor-saver is running water in the sink, and Americans have little idea how many millions of homes in civilized countries do not have it. Thus we are saved an endless round of drudgery that ties down women—and men also—in countries where homes have no running water, no gas and electricity, no farm tools but those which are driven into the earth by human hands or are swung in human arms, and no use of ready-made soaps and foods and clothes. Americans put high value on lessened drudgery, but they deprecate having free spaces of truly leisure time; the more time they save the more they fill up their days and nights with a round of engagements and complications. They are unwilling to admit that they have leisure, but the schedules of their lives prove clearly how much they have.

13   Universal schooling in the United States also frees the family of many duties when children have come. It is hard for Americans to imagine the

difference which regular school hours makes in a mother's role. For a great part of the working day, American children are the responsibility of the teacher and not of the mother. As nursery schools spread over the country, younger and younger children get trained care outside the home and the mother's labors are correspondingly relieved. As the children grow older the mother's leisure increases, until finally she reaches that idle middle age with its round of card parties and clubs and window shopping and movies which engross and waste the energy of so many millions of American women. Her husband is earning more money now than when he was younger, and her children have flown; she has a plethora of privileges and freedom and leisure. In one sense she has everything.

14   It is obviously unfair to talk about the incomparable freedom from drudgery which the American home offers without emphasizing that interval of a few years when there is no leisure for the mother in the home—the years when the babies are little. In our great cities where each family is strange to all the others, a mother is likely to have to be baby tender every hour of the day, with no one to relieve her. Along with these duties she must do all her cooking and washing and cleaning. And, as all our magazines and women's pages reiterate, she must make efforts to keep her husband. She must keep herself looking attractive, must keep up social contacts, and be a companion to him. To European wives this program looks formidable. "I was always told that American women were so free," a Polish woman said to me, "but when I came here and saw how they had to manage with the babies and the house without any older women of the family to help, and then how they had to play around with their husbands in the evening to keep them happy, I decided I wouldn't change places with them for anything. In Poland a woman doesn't have to 'keep' her husband; it's all settled when they're married."

15   The striking fact about the nursery years in the United States is that in comparison with those in other countries they are so short and that nevertheless we do not really treat them as an interim. Mothers who are going through this period give remarkably little thought to the leisure that will come soon. They are often vocal enough about the turmoil of their present lives, and sometimes bitter, but the fact that the nursery years last so short a time in the United States and could be treated as an interim—like a professor's going into the government during war time—is all too seldom part of their thinking. No doubt this is due in part to a lag in our culture, since even with our grandparents conditions were different; but in part it is a result of the sentiment which selects this period, no matter how short, as the fulfillment of a woman's chief duty in life. A social engineer looking at the family, however, would certainly put his major effort into better arrangements for the overburdened mother during these years and into thinking about effecting some transition from this period into that next one during which, in the United States, millions of women become idle parasites upon society—and dull and unhappy into the bargain.

16   Another notable feature of the American family is its peculiarly non-authoritarian character. The old rules that a child should be seen and not heard and the adage, "Spare the rod and spoil the child," are anachronistic in the United States; they are dispensed with even in immigrant groups which honored them in their native country. The rule of the father over the family is still a reality in some European nations, but in the United States the mother is the chief responsible agent in bringing up her children; here the father's opinions are something the children are more likely to play off against the mother's, to their own advantage, rather than a court of last authority from which there is no appeal. Children take the noisy center of the stage at the breakfast table and in the living room in a way that is quite impossible in European countries. The fact that they are expected to know right from wrong in their tenderest years and to act upon it on their own is often commented on by European mothers who have lived here. A Dutch mother once spoke to the author about how hard we are on our children because we expect this of them; she said, "I don't expect it of my children before they are seven; until then, I am there to see that they act correctly." But an American mother expects a child of three or four to be a responsible moral agent, and she gives him great latitude in which to prove that he can manage his little affairs by himself.

17   All this lack of strong authoritarianism in American families accords well with the values that are chiefly sought after in this country. No strong father image is compatible with our politics or our economics. We seek the opportunity to prove that we are as good as the next person, and we do not find comfort in following an authoritarian voice—in the state or in the home, from the landowner or the priest—which will issue a command from on high. We learn as children to measure ourselves against Johnny next door, or against Mildred whose mother our mother knows in church, and this prepares us for living in a society with strongly egalitarian ideals. We do not learn the necessity of submitting to unquestioned commands as the children of many countries do. The family in the United States has become democratic.

18   These free-choice and non-authoritarian aspects of the family, along with its privacy and potential leisure, evidence only a few of the many ways in which it has become consistent with major emphases in our national life. They seem, when one compares them with arrangements in other civilized nations, to be quite well fitted to the role the family must play in a culture like the United States. This does not mean, however, that Americans capitalize to their own advantage upon all these consistently contrived arrangements which are institutionalized in the family as we know it. At the beginning of this essay two subjects were left for later discussion—how well our society protects the family from dangerous overstrain, and how well as human beings with special insights and blind spots we are able to get all the satisfactions we might out of our version of the home. These two subjects cannot be omitted.

19   In spite of all our American sentiment about the home and the family, we do not show great concern about buttressing it against catastrophe. Any well-considered national program must have regard for the children; if they are housed and fed below a certain minimum, if their health is not attended to, the nation suffers in the next generation. The lack of a tolerable economic floor under the family is especially crucial in a society like that of the United States, where competition is so thoroughly relied upon as an incentive and where so few families have anything but the weekly pay envelope to use for food and doctors' bills. When factories close, when inflation comes, the family gets little consideration in the United States. Especially in economic crises it gets the little end of the horn. Today the necessity of providing tens of thousands of new homes is of the greatest importance for healthy family life in the United States, but adequate housing programs are notoriously unsupported. Sickness insurance, too, which would provide preventive care as well as relieve the family budget of all expenses in a crisis, needs high priority in a national program. When one reads about families in trouble, it is clear that many of the reefs which are threatening shipwreck are avoidable by intelligent local, state, or national programs. Such programs have worked satisfactorily in non-communist countries—as, for instance, in the Scandinavian nations. But they cost money, and Americans have not been willing to be taxed for the sake of taking the excessive strain off the family and providing better circumstances for growing children. It could be done, and if it were done the incidental disadvantages of our highly competitive and unregulated economic system would be largely removed; it should be the surest way to ensure the successful continuance of what is known as the democratic way of life.

20   Besides this American political attitude toward the family, there is also a very different difficulty which threatens it. We have seen how as an institution it is particularly tailored to American ways of living. But the very best suit of clothes may be badly worn by a careless and irresponsible person. So, too, people may abuse a home well designed to suit them. It is no less true of marriage and the family. These exist as institutions remarkably well adjusted to American life. But many Americans are miserably unable to achieve happiness within them.

21   It is of course easy to say that a culture like that of the United States, which allows individuals so much free choice among alternatives, is asking a great deal of human beings. In social life, as in literature, some of the finest human achievements have been within restrictions as rigid as those of the sonnet form. Our American culture is more like a sprawling novel where every page may deal with a new encounter and with a special choice. We ask a great deal of individuals when we give them such wide latitude and so little respected authority. But the United States is built on the premise that this is possible, and if ever we as a people decide otherwise our nation will change beyond recognition. We shall have lost the very thing we have been trying to build in this country.

22   It must not be imagined that this craving for individual freedom is what prevents Americans from enjoying the family as much as it might be enjoyed. In so far as the family is an overheavy economic burden on some wage earners, a more careful welfare program could take care of this complaint. Certainly women and children have a freedom in the American family which is hard to match elsewhere in the world, and from all portents this will probably increase rather than diminish.

23   The crucial difficulty in American happiness in marriage, is, rather, a certain blind spot which is especially fostered in our privileged United States. An extreme instance of this was mentioned in connection with the millions of idle, middle-aged wives in this country. These are women who as a group are well set up and favored beyond any such great numbers of women in any other part of the world. But privilege to them is separate from responsibility. Comparatively few of them feel that it is compatible with their status to do responsible work in which they have had experience in their own households and which must now be done outside their homes, and few take the initiative in getting the training they would need in jobs which they can see need to be done—except in war time. In periods of peace they have a blind spot about what it takes to live happily. For that the motto is *noblesse oblige*, or, "Privilege obligates one to do something in return."

24   It is not only the middle-aged woman who accepts privilege without a sense of obligation. In marriage, the right of both men and women to choose their mates freely is a privilege which carries with it, if they are to live happily, an accompanying conviction that when things go wrong it is doubly their obligation—to themselves as well as to their spouses—to deal tolerantly. Perhaps a young man realizes that his wife is more petulant than he knew; exactly because he chose her, however, she is "a poor thing; but his own." Privileged as he was to choose her, he has a corresponding responsibility.

25   It is the same with children. In the United States the reason for having children is not, as it is in most of the world, the perpetuation of the family line down many generations. In most countries people have children because there must be someone to till the piece of land in the village where the family has lived for centuries, there must be an heir to inherit the *Hof*, or there must be a son to perform the ancestral rites. In our atomistic American families these motivations seldom arise. We have children, not because our parents are sitting in judgment, not because of the necessity of having an heir, but because we personally want them—whether as company in the home or to show our friends we can have them. It is a privileged phase of parenthood, and if it is to bring us happiness it implies an acceptance of responsibility. Nothing is all pleasure in this life, and bringing up two or three noisy children in our small urban apartments is no exception to the rule. But with us it is based on choice—far more than it is elsewhere in the world—and we can only make the most of a choice if we follow it through wholeheartedly in all its implications.

26   It is partly because of this blind spot in the American family, this walling off of privilege from responsibility and tolerance, that we so often ask of life an average happiness—as if it could be presented to us on a platter. Full normal happiness only comes to men and women who give as well as take—who, in this instance, give themselves warmly to their family life, and do not merely arrogate to themselves the rights they are so freely allowed in our society. In the United States, if happiness proves impossible they can get a divorce; but, until they have made this decision, they can capitalize on their privileges only if they bind around their arms the motto "Privilege has its obligations."

27   The family in the United States is an institution remarkably adapted to our treasured way of life. The changes that are occurring in it do not mean that it is decaying and needs to be saved. It offers a long array of privileges. It needs more consideration in political tax-supported programs, by means of which many difficulties that beset it could be eradicated. Finally, Americans, in order to get the maximum happiness out of such a free institution as the family in the United States, need to parallel their privileges with an awakening responsibility. It is hard to live up to being so privileged as we are in the United States, but it is not impossible.

Exercises

COMPREHENSION

Organization and Development

Complete the following outline. Find the sentence in the essay that best expresses the author's purpose and write it in the space provided. Then in your own words write a sentence summarizing the author's thesis. Finally, find the main divisions in the essay and fill in the remaining spaces. Note the paragraphs for each section.

Statement of purpose: _____

_____

_____

Thesis statement: _____

_____

_____

I.   _____   [   ]
II.   _____   [   ]
III. _____   [   ]

Content

Choose the answer that correctly completes each statement.

1. The author is concerned not about the family's possible disintegration, but about how (a) family members view their own roles and responsibilities (b) the family arrang-

ments agree with or reflect the values of the larger culture (c) the family will adjust to the demands of women for more freedom and self-fulfillment outside the home.

2. Many people use the family as a convenient whipping boy because (a) the forces threatening the family are more severe now than ever before (b) they disapprove of the way the world is going (c) it is the most visible symbol of the decline in American values.

3. The author emphasizes an Indian tribe she studied because (a) they rebelled against being forced to move to a reservation (b) they exhibited a breakdown in traditional values as well as in relationships between family members (c) all cultures—whether primitive or civilized—worry about the strength of the family structure.

4. A newly married American couple may feel cheated if they cannot (a) buy a house immediately (b) have an array of labor-saving devices to relieve them of drudgery (c) establish their own private household.

5. According to the author, the growing divorce rate in America is (a) merely an extension of the culture's emphasis on free, personal choice (b) truly a matter of concern and an argument for stricter divorce laws (c) not so alarming if one examines divorce statistics in other countries.

6. Women from other cultures feel that American women are (a) to be envied for their leisure time (b) too concerned with appearance and material goods (c) not as free as they appear at first glance.

7. Both the American family structure and child-raising techniques reflect a lack of (a) discipline (b) authoritarianism (c) equality between sexes.

8. The greatest difficulty facing the American family is (a) Americans' inability to accept responsibility with privilege (b) Americans' refusal to put the family above selfish interests (c) the anxiety and uncertainty that freedom brings with it.

Paragraph Structure

Reorder the following sentences to form a unified, coherent paragraph. Then check your version with the original.

1. Often in other countries, until one or two children are born, the young man continues to work for his father and has no say about the farm or the flock and no money which he can control.

2. After marriage, too, the new family has a wide range of choices about where to live, how the wife shall occupy herself, when to start a family, and a host of other important matters.

3. But in the United States a young couple plans the family budget before the wedding and what they earn is theirs to keep.

4. Sometimes the couple must live with the husband's family, sometimes with the wife's.

5. Such freedom is extremely unusual in the world.

VOCABULARY AND USAGE

Word Formation Table

Complete the following table by changing word endings or root forms to make new grammatical forms. Use your dictionary if necessary.

NOUN	VERB	ADJECTIVE	ADVERB
1. _____	_____	_____	sensitivity
2. lament	_____	_____	_____
3. _____	_____	bitter	_____
4. _____	_____	boastful	_____
5. _____	_____	dependable	_____

Fill-Ins

Complete each of the sentences below using the words on the following list. You may need to use some words more than once. You may also find that some blanks can be completed correctly with more than one word. Add plural endings to nouns and change verb forms where necessary.

lack	disapprove of	arrangement	survive
leisure	latitude	freedom	deplore
plethora	besides	premise	value
inevitably	disintegration	abundance	in addition to
terminate	failure	pattern	outcome

1. A great many people worry about the family's ability to _____, and they _____ the changes that they feel will _____ lead to the _____ of the family.
2. Anthropologists know that the family is not in danger of _____; rather, they ask how the family _____ agree with the customs and _____ of the whole culture.
3. American marriage _____ correspond to the general _____ of our society; that is, marriage is characterized by personal _____ and a _____ of authoritarianism.
4. American young people are given much _____ in their choice of a marriage partner; _____, even if the parents _____ the choice, they are expected to accept the _____ gracefully.
5. The divorce rate in this country simply proves that personal _____ of choice is highly _____ in our culture; if we have the right to choose our own spouse, it follows that we have the right to _____ a bad marriage.
6. _____ free choice and privacy, the American family has a(n) _____ of labor-saving devices and _____ time.

DISCUSSION

1. How does the title of this essay help reveal Benedict's point of view?
2. What is the reason for the author's discussion of marriage patterns among an American Indian tribe in paragraphs 4 and 5?
3. Which sentence (or sentences) best states the author's thesis? Be prepared to defend your choice.
4. What method of development does the author use in paragraph 4? In relation to paragraph 4, what is the method of development in paragraph 5?

5. Taken together, what method of exposition does the author use in paragraphs 7 and 8?
6. Underline the transitional devices in paragraphs 9 and 12.
7. What are the two stages in the American woman's life that Benedict feels are the most difficult? Why?
8. What does the phrase "noblesse oblige" (in paragraph 23) mean? Do you agree with her conclusion that the greatest defect in American marriages is our inability to accept responsibility commensurate with the privileges we enjoy?
9. According to the author, what are the primary characteristics of the American family? Do you agree with all her characterizations? Why or why not?
10. What are some examples that Benedict uses to support her thesis that the American family is "peculiarly non-authoritarian"?
11. What changes have been brought to the American family in the last 30 years since this essay was published? What characteristics have remained the same?

SUGGESTIONS FOR WRITING

1. Write a précis (a brief summary or condensed version) of the main ideas in Benedict's analysis.
2. Benedict's essay was published in 1949, and it is clear that in the intervening 30 years, the American family has undergone many changes, some of which may perhaps be more drastic threats to the family's stability than she could have foreseen. In an essay, analyze some of the social and economic changes that have taken place in your generation and assess their probable impact on the family.
3. Analyze several ways in which the American woman's role and status have changed or are different from those described in Benedict's essay.
4. Write an essay contrasting one culture's way of observing a custom or celebrating an event with that of another culture.
5. Contrast American methods of childrearing and discipline with those of another culture or subculture you may be familiar with.
6. Benedict, writing in the 1940s, could not have foreseen the phenomenon of increasing numbers of young people who live together without being married, or who are exploring nontraditional family patterns. Discuss the merits of this alternative (or alternatives) as it affects the American family unit, and come to a conclusion of your own about its long-range effects.

The Assumptions of the Middle Class

JAMES MICHENER

James Michener was born in 1907 in New York and was educated at Swarthmore College. He has received numerous degrees from other universities in this country and abroad, and has taught at Colorado State and Harvard University. It is not, however, as an academic but as a novelist that he is best known. His extensive experience and interest in the South Pacific are the basis of his Pulitzer Prize-winning *Tales of the South Pacific,* as well as other popular books, including *The Bridges at Toko-Ri, Sayonara,* and *Hawaii.* He has been active in political affairs as well, and is the author of *Report of the County Chairman* and *Kent State: What Happened and Why.*

The Assault Widens

1   From all sides the barrage continues. Thoughtful blacks in the cities do not want their children educated along the old middle-class lines which produced obedient stenographers and shipping clerks.

2   Young draftees simply cannot accept the simplistic postulates of World Wars I and II: "Congress has declared war. It's our duty to fight."

3   Young ministers, truly wrestling with the problems their congregations bring to them, cannot advise their younger members "to follow in the old paths and everything will work out all right."

4   Particularly, younger college professors gag at indoctrinating their students with a vision of happiness through working for I.B.M. or doing research for the Pentagon. Everywhere I look I find so much rebellion against the values that predominated when I was growing up that I have been forced to reevaluate them.

5   It seems to me that the assumptions upon which I operated as a young man can best be understood if they are summarized within certain categories. What follows is merely one man's recollection of the forces which formed him. Other men my age will recall other experiences and will identify other forces, but in general most lists would include roughly the same components.

The Puritan Noose

6   Within the Christian ethic American society has always inclined toward Puritanism. Any local businessman who wanted to get ahead, any political

leader who hoped for long life, has had to pay public homage to Puritan morality, and even the more liberal European Catholic Church, when implanted on our shores, found it expedient to advocate a censorship of, say, films, along ridiculously puritanical lines. I suppose that no single strand of middle-class values has been rejected more totally in recent years than this strangling rope of Puritanism which once bound us so strongly, and against which the young have rebelled with such contempt.

7   We have lived primarily within a Christian ethic, once largely Protestant, of late increasingly Catholic. Our father figures have been austere men like John Knox, John Calvin, Martin Luther, and Thomas Aquinas. To the perceptive young person today these moral leaders, who used to terrify me with their rectitude, seem slightly ridiculous. One evening, when I tried to introduce the matter of religious ethics to a young group, one girl said, "Please! Today the Pope is just as confused as we are."

The Three R's

8   A cornerstone of middle-class life has been reliance upon education. Through it, immigrants were salvaged and the children of the laboring class set free. A conspicuous feature of American life has been the fact that the upper classes have done precious little in this country for the education of anyone but themselves, whereas the middle and laboring classes have striven consistently for a free, widely dispersed education. I myself, a product of that middle-class faith in education, believe it has been the principal differentiator between America and the rest of the world.

9   Some years ago in Hawaii a barefooted Japanese cleaning woman demonstrated the middle-class attitude toward education. She told me one day as she was sweeping my apartment that she was worried about her two sons and asked if she might talk with me. I assumed that her boys had gotten themselves mixed up with girls or had stolen a car, but her problems were rather different. "First son, senior Harvard Law School. Top ten. When he graduate he can go into big law firm in New York. Or into government? Which one?" I said that since he was a Japanese boy trying to make his way in a Caucasian society it might be wise to establish himself first with his peers, then move into government. She agreed. "Second son, freshman M.I.T. Next year they starting accelerated course advanced calculus"—those were her exact words. "In regular calculus he get only B-minus. Should he try new course?" With wages earned by sweeping apartments, she had sent her sons to two of the best universities in America, five thousand miles from Hawaii.

Making It

10   A central belief of the middle class in which I grew up was that the son of a ditchdigger could become a college president, whereas the careless son of the top family in town could easily make mistakes from which he would not recover. These twin beliefs were not legendary; each year they were illustrated by specific lives in our community, and are still being illustrated. I

have lived in a good many countries in the world, and in no other is social mobility so easily attainable, or so dominant a factor in national life. I realize that I am begging the core question of "Mobility to what?" Young people ridicule the legendary middle-class struggle to achieve upward mobility because they see that a man is often no better off "ahead" than he was when he started. For the moment I shall avoid that challenge.

Competence

11   At home, in school, and in church I was reared on the stern belief that in the long run competence sets the limits as to what a man could become, and this was drummed into my generation wherever we turned. If you wanted to play third base in the big leagues you had to learn how to handle ground balls smashed toward the bag. If you shied away from stabbing your hand out at the speeding white bullet, you were not going to be a third baseman. You could be something else, but not that. This was true, we were taught, of all professions. If you wanted to be a lawyer, you went to law school. If you wanted to go into business, you mastered arithmetic and the art of quick decision. The penalty for sliding through life without having mastered any competence was a sentence to mediocrity.

12   By no means did we equate competence with formal education. Horse traders, garage mechanics, and trainmen stood high in our value judgments; and I can still remember the approval with which one of my teachers read that admirable passage from Emerson in which he described how much he admired the farm girl who knew how to subdue a fractious calf by letting the animal suck on her finger as if it were a teat. "I admire people who know how to do things," said Emerson, the high priest of middle-class values, and we shared his enthusiasm. To this day I retain a sense of awe in the presence of anyone who knows how to do something.

Hierarchy

13   I have always felt that in America our middle-class values were strongly rooted in a sense of hierarchy, and the fact that we have eschewed the trappings of royalty has blinded us, I think, to the other fact that we are the most royalist of all peoples. I remember when Arnold Bennett unleashed one of his periodic attacks on the British royal family to the great distress of some Englishmen who were at that moment visiting America. They were outraged that Bennett had dared to speak ill of royalty but were consoled by their New Jersey host, who explained, "Never worry about what your English fools like Arnold Bennett say of your royal family. England may go off the gold standard. She may have a Socialist government. But she will never discard or in any way abuse the royal family, because the people of Iowa would not permit it."

14   I find this principle of hierarchy, or class consciousness if you prefer, strongly ingrained in American life, and much of the protest of the young today has been a legitimate rejection of our country-club pretensions. On the

other hand, I do feel that our responsible affection for position and order has been a strong factor in accounting for our stability.

Responsibility

15   At the core of the middle-class life has stood the doctrine of responsibility. Not only was a man largely responsible for himself and his family, but groups of families were responsible for their community. If I were asked to specify a major difference between life as it is actually lived in the United States and in Japan or Spain, for example, I would stress the fact that in those other countries there is no public tradition of support for art museums, hospital complexes, universities, and a multitude of other public charities, whereas this sense of responsibility has been strong in America. For tragic and historic reasons, we have not up to now been willing to allow this responsibility to operate in certain areas like race relations or the preservation of our cities, but the tradition for the exercise of such responsibility exists and is available for new creative uses. I would judge this commitment to responsibility to be a major characteristic of American middle-class life.

Accumulation

16   No one should underestimate the powerful urge felt by the middle class toward accumulation, either of money, or property, or the sillier accouterments of success. I judge this to be one of our strongest motivating factors and one most subject to abuse. The tradition began, I suppose, on the frontier, when it was patently better to have 640 acres of cleared land than a quarter of an acre.

17   I spoke recently with a man who had just bought a comfortably sized insurance business, and even before he had moved into his new office he was planning for a second, a third, and a fourth office in nearby towns. He explained, "Of course I could make a comfortable living from my new office, but only for a few years. In this business you build volume or the major insurance companies take away your franchise. It's impossible to stay little. You grow big or you perish."

18   If our middle-class mania for accumulation is subject to abuse, it is also subject to ridicule, and many a father who has spent the years from 22 to 52 in a mad race to accumulate now finds himself powerless to answer his children who ask, "Why did you do it, Pop? What good did you get out of it? What have you to show for the rat race except two cars and three picture windows?" These are terrifying questions to throw at a man in his fifties, for they undermine his hitherto unquestioned faith in accumulating.

Optimism

19   One of the most appealing of the middle-class virtues has been the tendency toward optimism. There has been reason for this, for in spite of wars, depressions, and other setbacks of considerable dimension, the American middle class has been living in an expanding economy, in which social justice has made conspicuous gains. The middle-class response has been a general euphoria. After all, Kaiser Wilhelm and Adolf Hitler were defeated. Communism was more or less contained, and although a stubborn Democratic party did make frequent incursions to power, the Republican party did return at comforting intervals to run things pretty much as we had grown accustomed to seeing them run. It did not seem preposterous for the middle class to cling to its optimism.

20   Of course, at its most blatant our optimism took the pathetic form demonstrated by George Babbitt of Zenith City and was properly ridiculed. One of the most disastrous cultural influences ever to hit America was Walt Disney's Mickey Mouse, that idiot optimist who each week marched forth in Technicolor against a battalion of cats, invariably humiliating them with one clever trick after another. I suppose the damage done to the American psyche by this foolish mouse will not be specified for another fifty years, but even now I place much of the blame for Vietnam on the bland attitudes sponsored by our cartoons.

21   When the original version of this essay was published, I received much criticism for this passage on Mickey Mouse. Some vilified me for having spoken ill of one of our nation's folk heroes. Others rebuked me for having taken seriously what was intended merely as a fairy tale, and one that they revered. And a great many asked, "You didn't mean what you said seriously, did you? Wasn't it all a put-on?" I supose nothing proves more clearly that I did mean what I said than the seriousness of the criticism that overtook me.

22   I do indeed believe that the narcotic nonsense of these cartoons—and similar daydreams of American life—dull our sensitiveness to real problems. . . .

Comparison and Contrast

Like other methods of exposition, comparison and contrast reflects a basic arrangement of ideas, a pattern of thinking translated into writing. While for convenience the term "comparison" may be used in reference to contrast as well, and while an essay developed in this way generally will employ both methods, there *is* a difference. Comparison points specifically to likenesses—mainly between things we usually think of as different (television viewing and air travel). Contrast focuses on differences—principally between things usually seen as similar (the motives that brought European colonists to the New World from Spain and England). Recognizing likenesses and differences is one of the most common and natural of human thought processes—it is, in fact, something *only* human beings can do, and we all do it constantly. It is useful in everyday activities like decision making (shall I buy this car or that?), evaluation (which of these movies is better?), and classification (even though it flies, the bat must be a mammal because it nurses its young, a characteristic of mammals *only*).

Like most expository writing, the comparison and contrast essay ordinarily has a point to make, a conclusion to draw, and is never merely an exercise in highlighting either the obvious or the obscure. Thus, Campa underscores the cultural differences between Anglo and Hispanic colonists in order to show the reader the reasons for contemporary conflict between their descendants, as well as the possibility of their resolution. Arlen not only makes a neat comparison between the passivity of the air traveler and the television viewer, he suggests a much larger inquiry into the quality of modern life. And Twain not only differentiates between his view of the river before and after his training as a pilot, he unexpectedly draws one aspect of the contrast into the heart of his discussion: instead of the expanded pleasure and status we tend to associate with increased knowledge, Twain stresses the loss of innocence that comes with experience.

The fundamental requirement for a good comparison—as for all good exposition—is clarity. First, the writer must make clear what it is he is comparing (the air traveler and the television viewer, *not* the air traveler and a character in a poem by T. S. Eliot). Second, he must make clear the basis on which the comparison is made, the points being compared (not simply Anglo-Hispanic cultural differences, but Anglo-Hispanic cultural differences that cause conflict). Third, he must reveal the purpose for making the comparison. (Compare, for example, Campa's opening paragraph, his declaration of intention, with Arlen's more implicit and delayed revelation of the underlying purpose for presenting his lengthy comparison.)

Fortunately, there are only two basic methods for arranging such an essay. The first is the subject-by-subject method—here exemplified in "Prufrock Before the Television Set"—where one of two or more subjects of comparison or contrast is dealt with fully, point by point, and then the other is presented. This method works best where the comparison is brief or the items are not so complex that the reader has trouble, in the second half, remembering what he read in the first. The items being compared must always be discussed in the same terms; that is, the same points of comparison must be used for both. Having chosen to speak first of airline travel in terms of the kind of behavior it encourages or requires in the passenger, Arlen can later compare it to television viewing only by using the *same* basis of comparison: the kind of behavior the activity requires or encourages. (While in another context one might legitimately discuss television viewing in terms of its expense or intellectual appeal, here it would be illogical—in fact, it would not be a comparison at all.)

The second method, used by Campa in "Anglo vs. Chicano: Why?" is the point-by-point method. Here the bases for comparison (the geography of England and Spain; the moral values of England and Spain; the English and Spanish motives for colonization, etc.) are discussed, one by one, in paragraphs or sections of the essay that present each of these issues side by side with *both* Anglo and Hispanic relationships to them. This method offers the reader a kind of "running tally" of the comparison or contrast, which gradually adds up to a total picture of the subjects under discussion.

Of course, a skillful writer can combine both the subject-by-subject and the point-by-point methods, which is what Twain does in "Life on the Mississippi: Reading the River."

To help you in your own efforts at comparison/contrast writing, here are examples of the two basic plans by which one might organize, through comparison and contrast, an evaluation of the advantages of living at home and living on campus while attending college. (You should be aware that this abbreviated format omits two essentials—the statement of purpose and the conclusion to be drawn from the comparison.)

METHOD A (SUBJECT BY SUBJECT)

I. Living at Home
   A. Expense
   B. Convenience
   C. Freedom

II. Living on Campus
   A. Expense
   B. Convenience
   C. Freedom

METHOD B (POINT BY POINT)

I. Expense
   A. At home
   B. On campus

II. Convenience
   A. At home
   B. On campus

III. Freedom
   A. At home
   B. On campus

Prufrock Before the Television Set

MICHAEL ARLEN

Michael Arlen now lives in Chicago. Formerly a staff writer for *The New Yorker,* he currently writes a regular column as its television critic. Two collections of his writings on TV have been published: *Living Room War,* about TV and the Vietnam War, and *The View from Highway One.* The "Prufrock" of the title is an allusion to the hero of T. S. Eliot's poem, "The Love Song of J. Alfred Prufrock" (1915). Prufrock, a failure and a mediocrity, is torn between a desire to live life to the fullest or to remain unassertive and timid. This selection, from Arlen's *New Yorker* television column, compares airplane travel and television viewing and concludes that both encourage unassertive, Prufrock-like behavior in the passenger/viewer.

1   A few days ago, while seated snugly in an airplane seat on my way back to New York from Chicago, with a drink in front of me, and last week's copy of *Sports Illustrated* on my lap, and the soothing hum of the engines washing over my ears (and with the memory of the taxi ride and traffic jam and ticket-counter chaos already receding), it occurred to me that there was a rather striking similarity between what I was experiencing then, flying in a modern airliner, and what I've felt often happens as I watch television. To begin with, both are largely passive experiences; or, rather, they have been made into passive experiences. But this passivity is, itself, interesting and complicated, for not only does it involve obvious conditions of quietude and inaction, as well as the illusion of privacy; it also implies, and sometimes makes explicit, a quite formal undertaking of non-aggressive behavior on the part of the passenger or viewer. In fact, there is something to be said for the notion that much of the "pleasure" involved with riding in a commercial airliner, or in watching an evening's television schedule, has to do as much with this subjective state of non-aggression (in contrast with the aggressions of the "outside world") as it has with the supposedly greater and more evident pleasure of the trip or the actual programs.

2   Consider, for example, the airplane journey. In many ways, levels of ordinary comfort for passengers have been, if anything, decreasing since the days of the old Pan American "Yankee Clipper." Even so, there is undoubted pleasure to be had in a routine jetliner trip of reasonable length (and admittedly one without crying babies or furious grandparents on one's lap). As an extreme example of this, I mention the experience of a friend who,

PRUFROCK BEFORE THE TELEVISION SET   From an article in *The New Yorker* of Nov. 8, 1976. Reprinted by permission; © 1976 The New Yorker Magazine, Inc.

being harried to exhaustion by a project in New York, determined suddenly to fly to California for a few days by the sea. As soon as he was airborne on the way out, he began to relax. Five hours later in California, however, as soon as he was on the ground, dealing with baggage and car rentals and freeways and finally his motel-by-the-sea, he began again to unravel. The same evening, he drove back to the airport, took a return flight to New York, and, after five more hours of airplane massage, was in a suitable condition for resuming work.

3   People still talk of the romance of travel, and perhaps it is still romance for fashionable visitors to Ethiopian ruins, or even for cruise-ship passengers. Indeed, travel was once an active and difficult undertaking, with the pleasure therein consisting in actively engaging in the difficulties and surmounting them—though even surmounting them wasn't always all that important. The important thing was to participate, to experience. But in much travel nowadays, it seems to me, the key element is non-participation. Not only is aggressive behavior discouraged or proscribed but non-aggressive behavior is formally encouraged as the norm. Thus, the pleasure of much of modern travel lies in the restful illusion that non-aggressive behavior is "being oneself."

4   On an airplane, for instance, the passenger lumpishly settles into his narrow seat, usually dishevelled in mind or spirit from the hurly-burly of the outside world, sometimes still quivering from the hazards of actually getting to the airplane. The stewardess has already relieved him of his coat and briefcase, his downtown symbols. Sometimes, wifelike, she will have given him an initial, token reward for having reached her: a cup of coffee, a ginger ale, a Bloody Mary. Prufrock has arrived home. Prufrock need do nothing more, except buckle himself to his seat, and follow modest instructions "for his own safety," and act unaggressively. In fact, for doing so, he will be rewarded: by great speed and forward motion (i.e., by progress), by the benign smiles of the stewardess, by the loan of a magazine, by the outright gift of an airline magazine ("Yours to keep"), by drinks, by the hospitality of a meal, even by the appurtenances of an overnight guest—a pillow and blanket. A shower of benefits is rained upon the passenger by the authorities of the airplane (including periodic descriptions of the unseen ground being traversed, delivered over loudspeaker by the unseen captain), who ask in return only that the passenger do nothing, stay quiet, keep still. Bathroom privileges are given, but can easily be revoked. Primary addictive substances, such as cigarettes, are permitted the passengers more rapidly and easily than secondary substances, such as alcohol, which might cause disquiet or might "spill." When all the right conditions are met, modest walking about is allowed, but since there is usually no place to walk to, it is a privilege rarely accepted. Even when the seat-belt sign has been turned off, so the captain has announced, one would do well to keep buckled.

5   In short, passivity reigns in the modern airliner. And when aggression reappears, it is sternly chastised. For example, after the plane has landed but

before it has arrived at the gate, several passengers—doubtless summoned again to aggressive behavior by the imminence of the outside world—will leap to their feet and begin reaching for coats and bags like children who have been held too long in school. At this point, the formerly benign stewardess becomes severe and quickly reprimands the aggressive passengers. If these passengers do not abandon their aggressive behavior and return to the passivity of their seats, she says, they will be deprived of the one thing they still lack: further forward motion. Thereupon, the misbehaving passengers feign non-aggressive behavior until the second the plane has docked at the gate and they have been released from passivity. Immediately, aggression returns and now all the passengers push past each other down the airport corridors and once again start fighting over baggage, taxis, buses, or parking space.

6   The experience of watching most commercial television seems to involve a similar voyage and a similar stylized passivity. Here, of course, the seat belts are figurative rather than actual, though I notice that there are a variety of "TV lounge chairs" now on the market, whose chief function seems to be safely to enclose the viewer during his nightly journey. Also, it is an interesting (if taste-numbing) coincidence that the TV dinner and the standard airline meal are made the same way, with the same technology and the same results. With television, the forward motion is through time, not space; but the effect is somewhat the same, since in the modern world final destinations rarely exist. The end of each day's program schedule, as with O'Hare Airport, is as much a beginning as a terminus.

7   Rewards for good behavior flow ceaselessly throughout the evening, according to a set routine. In return for sitting still in front of his television set, the viewer is rewarded not only by the vague, general, forward-seeming flow of the entertainment but, more specifically, by periodic "messages" from the authority of the television station which promise him two levels of benefits. On the higher, symbolic level, there is the romantic promise of an upward alteration or enhancement of his life, by the acquisition of a new car, or a new deodorant, or a new kind of floor tile. This is deeply moving but it is remote, as is the promise of romance in travel. On a more immediate level, then, the viewer is rewarded by a trip to the bathroom or another bottle of beer from the refrigerator: these are stand-ins for the larger, dreamlike rewards.

8   Aggressive behavior is not actively prohibited, but it is discouraged. There are almost no viewer phone-in programs, as on radio. Live audiences are few. Real audience participation is almost nonexistent, save for the inflated hysteria of a few game shows. Indeed, even some of the new game shows have become quite stylized and remote, with earnest, sedate couples trying to guess the authorship of "Hamlet" in the company of a lonely host and much electronic paraphernalia. On what are described as comedy or drama or adventure programs, there remains scarcely any nourishment of the viewer's active participation, in the form of emotionally involving stories. Thus, a

middling detective series such as "Baretta" becomes oddly noticeable, as if it contained a certain gritty substance that somehow spoke to the still-awake part of the viewer's mind—that part persistently untouched by the noisiest bang-bang of cop-show revolvers or even by the sight of artillery explosions in foreign lands. In recent years, many news programs have taken steps toward greater informality and a semblance of involvement on the part of the newscasters. But the involvement of these newsmen has been mostly with each other. The audience continues voyaging, buckled into its Barcaloungers, attending no longer to the voice of a single, solemn captain but to the equally distant, cheery chitchat of two or three of them.

9   What is strange about this new passivity, regarding both travel and broadcasting, is that not so long ago the reverse was considered normal. That is, flying was once a highly participatory activity—as was automobile driving, as was broadcasting. Thirty-five years ago, the driver of an ordinary car was intimately involved with the event of driving, by means of direct access to his steering wheel, brakes, transmission, and the outside environment. In the same period, a listener to Edward R. Murrow's broadcasts from London was directly involved with the event of broadcasting as well as the events of the Second World War that Murrow was describing. Since then, however, the automobile driver has given up his direct involvement in favor of power controls, automatic transmission, and sealed-in passenger interiors, while the television audience has largely given up its involvement with drama and news in favor of undemanding, mechanical entertainment and uninvolving news. Nowadays, only aggressive people insist on direct, or participatory, driving, by means of sports cars; at least, they are owned by people who are willing to appear aggressive. And only an aggressive minority, perhaps of a different, cultural, nature, appears to prefer participatory television, such as the music and serious drama programs that now and then are shown on public television.

10   The question remains: Have we somehow demanded this period of passivity for ourselves (one in which we may, so to speak, draw a breath in order to reach the summit of this peculiar century), or has it been foisted upon us by the onrush of technical systems? Certainly it's true that technical systems assert a logic of their own, as well as clearly seeming to "prefer" a passivity on the part of their components, whether semiconductors or passengers or viewers. At the same time, if fear of flying evoked the seat belt and the stewardess, then fear of another kind has surely evoked our present uninvolving programs, news and entertainment both. Is it fear of communication, of "too much"? Or fear of ourselves? Are we the people meekly buckled in by seat belts or the people rushing pell-mell down the airport corridors and fighting over taxis? Or is there any difference?

11   At least, nowadays when one has something to think about one can usually find the time and space for it, either by flying to Chicago or by turning on the television set.

Exercises

COMPREHENSION

Organization and Development

Complete the following outline. In your own words write a sentence stating the author's thesis in the space provided. Then find the main divisions in the essay and fill in the remaining spaces. Note the paragraphs for each section.

Thesis statement: _____

_____

_____

I.   Introduction: _____   [   ]
II. _____   [   ]
III. _____   [   ]
IV. _____   [   ]

Content

Choose the answer that correctly completes each statement.

1. In his discussion of air travel and television watching, Arlen primarily (a) compares—shows the similarities (b) contrasts—shows the differences (c) both compares and contrasts.

2. According to Arlen, not only are airplane travel and TV watching passive experiences, but in fact the passenger or viewer must (a) not complain if he is dissatisfied (b) formally accept a condition of non-aggressive behavior (c) let his mind go completely blank and think of nothing.

3. Arlen makes a distinction between the supposedly pleasurable state of non-aggression and the (a) active participation required by most TV programs (b) romance of travel to exotic places (c) aggressions of the outside world.

4. Arlen supports his contention about the kind of behavior expected from airline passengers with a series of (a) examples and illustrations (b) analogies (c) forceful arguments.

5. We can infer that Arlen's comments about the behavior of airline passengers refer mostly to (a) families on vacation (b) businessmen who travel regularly (c) people unaccustomed to flying.

6. Arlen says that the TV viewer is rewarded not only by entertainment, but also by "messages," by which he means (a) editorials and public service messages (b) commericals that promise him the things of the good life (c) moral lessons implied in the dramatic or detective programs he watches.

7. Arlen's chief complaint about TV is that it provides few opportunities for (a) the viewer's active participation (b) intellectual or emotional stimulation (c) in-depth analyses of important social issues.

8. Arlen concludes his essay by (a) presenting a series of recommendations for improving both the airline and television industries (b) contrasting the television and movie industries (c) asking a series of rhetorical questions about the origins of our new penchant for passivity.

Paragraph Structure

Reorder the following sentences to form a unified, coherent paragraph. Identify one sentence as the topic sentence. Then check your version with the original.

1. Indeed, travel was once an active and difficult undertaking, with the pleasure therein consisting in actively engaging in the difficulties and surmounting them—though even surmounting them wasn't always all that important.
2. But in much travel nowadays, it seems to me, the key element is non-participation.
3. People still talk of the romance of travel, and perhaps it is still romance for fashionable visitors to Ethiopian ruins, or even for cruise-ship passengers.
4. The important thing was to participate, to experience.
5. Thus, the pleasure of much of modern travel lies in the restful illusion that non-aggressive behavior is "being oneself."
6. Not only is aggressive behavior discouraged or proscribed but non-aggressive behavior is formally encouraged as the norm.

VOCABULARY AND USAGE

Word Formation Table

Complete the following table by changing word endings or root forms to make new grammatical forms. Use your dictionary if necessary.

	NOUN	VERB	ADJECTIVE	ADVERB
1.	chaos	xxx	_____	_____
2.	_____	xxx	passive	_____
3.	_____	prohibit	_____	_____
4.	acquisition	_____	_____	_____
5.	_____	xxx	aggressive	_____

Fill-Ins

Complete each of the sentences below using the words on the following list. You may need to use some words more than once. You may also find that some blanks can be completed correctly with more than one word. Add plural endings to nouns and change verb forms where necessary.

passive	illusion	figurative	metaphorical
condition	discourage	experience	for example
thus	but	kind	aggressive
reprimand	benign	state	similarity
technological	proscribe	prohibit	active

1. Arlen says that there was a striking _____ between what he has _____ while flying in an airplane and watching television.
2. Not only are both _____ largely _____, _____ also the two activities require non-_____ behavior.
3. Both television viewing and airplane travel inhibit one's _____ participation;

_____, _____ behavior on an airplane is not only _____, it is _____ as well.

4. The stewardess's _____ manner may change abruptly if a passenger breaks the rules, and he may quickly be _____.

5. _____, television and air travel show certain _____, partly because both are the products of a _____ society; _____, TV dinners and airline food are nearly identical, _____ Arlen admits that the seat belts on TV lounge chairs are _____ rather than actual.

6. Arlen apparently dislikes the _____ of television programs available because the viewer is _____ into accepting passive behavior as normal.

DISCUSSION

1. What is Arlen's thesis, and how does he qualify it later in paragraph 1?

2. What method of development does Arlen use in paragraph 4? Write a topic sentence for it.

3. With respect to what precedes it, what is the function of the first sentence of paragraph 5? Underline the transitional expressions in the same paragraph and explain how each functions.

4. Which paragraph in the essay is pivotal; that is, which connects the two main parts of the body?

5. In paragraph 6, Arlen refers to TV as involving a "similar stylized passivity." What does he mean by "stylized," and how can his description of airplane travel be considered in this way? Refer to a dictionary if you are unsure.

6. "Baretta," to which Arlen refers in paragraph 8, was canceled by ABC in 1978. What did "Baretta" represent to Arlen? Can you think of other programs on the three commercial networks that somehow stand out as "oddly noticeable"? What makes them so?

7. What is the function of paragraph 9, and how does it relate to the body of the essay?

8. In paragraph 9, Arlen says that the TV audience has given up its involvement with drama and news in favor of undemanding entertainment and uninvolving news. How can news by "uninvolving"? If he is right, what are some reasons for this reversal in our preferences?

9. What is the effect of paragraph 11, and is its tone consistent with the tone he has established elsewhere? Explain.

SUGGESTIONS FOR WRITING

1. Following Arlen's organization, discuss the similarities (or perhaps some differences as well) between two activities—for example, building a house and writing a paper; taking an exam and getting a job; changing a diaper and wrapping a gift.

2. In an essay, contrast two ways of doing something—for example, dieting, stopping smoking, learning to ski, or breaking up with a girlfriend or boyfriend. Your conclusion should indicate which is the better method.

3. Examine some ways in which your beliefs or attitudes are different from those of your parents. If it is appropriate, you may also want to include a discussion of similarities in your thinking.

Anglo vs. Chicano: Why?

ARTHUR L. CAMPA

Arthur L. Campa (1905–1978) was born in Guaymas, Mexico, the son of American citizens who were missionaries there. He held degrees from the University of New Mexico and Columbia University, and from 1946 on he was chairman of the Department of Modern Languages at the University of Denver as well as Director of the Center of Latin American Studies in Denver. He also served in the United States Air Force, filled the post of cultural attaché in several foreign embassies, and wrote extensively on varied subjects—all in addition to his distinguished career as an educator.

1   The cultural differences between Hispanic and Anglo-American people have been dwelt upon by so many writers that we should all be well informed about the values of both. But audiences are usually of the same persuasion as the speakers, and those who consult published works are for the most part specialists looking for affirmation of what they believe. So, let us consider the same subject, exploring briefly some of the basic cultural differences that cause conflict in the Southwest, where Hispanic and Anglo-American cultures meet.

2   Cultural differences are implicit in the conceptual content of the languages of these two civilizations, and their value systems stem from a long series of historical circumstances. Therefore, it may be well to consider some of the English and Spanish cultural configurations before these Europeans set foot on American soil. English culture was basically insular, geographically and ideologically; was more integrated on the whole, except for some strong theological differences; and was particularly zealous of its racial purity. Spanish culture was peninsular, a geographical circumstance that made it a catchall of Mediterranean, central European and north African peoples. The composite nature of the population produced a market regionalism that prevented close integration, except for religion, and led to a strong sense of individualism. These differences were reflected in the colonizing enterprise of the two cultures. The English isolated themselves from the Indians physically and culturally; the Spanish, who had strong notions about *pureza de sangre* [purity of blood] among the nobility, were not collectively averse to adding one more strain to their racial cocktail. Cortés led the way by siring the first *mestizo* in North America, and the rest of the conquistadores

ANGLO VS. CHICANO: WHY?   Originally published in *Western Review,* 1972. Reprinted by permission of Mrs. Arthur L. Campa.

followed suit. The ultimate products of these two orientations meet today in the Southwest.

3   Anglo-American culture was absolutist at the onset; that is, all the dominant values were considered identical for all, regardless of time and place. Such values as justice, charity, honesty were considered the superior social order for all men and were later embodied in the American Constitution. The Spaniard brought with him a relativistic viewpoint and saw fewer moral implications in man's actions. Values were looked upon as the result of social and economic conditions.

4   The motives that brought Spaniards and Englishmen to America also differed. The former came on an enterprise of discovery, searching for a new route to India initially, and later for new lands to conquer, the fountain of youth, minerals, the Seven Cities of Cíbola and, in the case of the missionaries, new souls to win for the Kingdom of Heaven. The English came to escape religious persecution, and once having found a haven, they settled down to cultivate the soil and establish their homes. Since the Spaniards were not seeking a refuge or running away from anything, they continued their explorations and circled the globe 25 years after the discovery of the New World.

5   This peripatetic tendency of the Spaniard may be accounted for in part by the fact that he was the product of an equestrian culture. Men on foot do not venture far into the unknown. It was almost a century after the landing on Plymouth Rock that Governor Alexander Spotswood of Virginia crossed the Blue Ridge Mountains, and it was not until the nineteenth century that the Anglo-Americans began to move west of the Mississippi.

6   The Spaniard's equestrian role meant that he was not close to the soil, as was the Anglo-American pioneer, who tilled the land and built the greatest agricultural industry in history. The Spaniard cultivated the land only when he had Indians available to do it for him. The uses to which the horse was put also varied. The Spanish horse was essentially a mount, while the more robust English horse was used in cultivating the soil. It is therefore not surprising that the viewpoints of these two cultures should differ when we consider that the pioneer is looking at the world at the level of his eyes while the *caballero* [horseman] is looking beyond and down at the rest of the world.

7   One of the most commonly quoted, and often misinterpreted, characteristics of Hispanic peoples is the deeply ingrained individualism in all walks of life. Hispanic individualism is a revolt against the incursion of collectivity, strongly asserted when it is felt that the ego is being fenced in. This attitude leads to a deficiency in those social qualities based on collective standards, an attitude that Hispanos do not consider negative because it manifests a measure of resistance to standardization in order to achieve a measure of individual freedom. Naturally, such an attitude has no *reglas fijas* [fixed rules].

8   Anglo-Americans who achieve a measure of success and security through institutional guidance not only do not mind a few fixed rules but demand them. The lack of a concerted plan of action, whether in business or in

politics, appears unreasonable to Anglo-Americans. They have a sense of individualism, but they achieve it through action and self-determination. Spanish individualism is based on feeling, on something that is the result not of rules and collective standards but of a person's momentary, emotional reaction. And it is subject to change when the mood changes. In contrast to Spanish emotional individualism, the Anglo-American strives for objectivity when choosing a course of action or making a decision.

9   The Southwestern Hispanos voiced strong objections to the lack of courtesy of the Anglo-Americans when they first met them in the early days of the Santa Fe trade. The same accusation is leveled at the *Americanos* today in many quarters of the Hispanic world. Some of this results from their different conceptions of polite behavior. Here too one can say that the Spanish have no *reglas fijas* because for them courtesy is simply an expression of the way one person feels toward another. To some they extend the hand, to some they bow and for the more *íntimos* there is the well-known *abrazo*. The concepts of "good or bad" or "right and wrong" in polite behavior are moral considerations of an absolutist culture.

10   Another cultural contrast appears in the way both cultures share part of their material substance with others. The pragmatic Anglo-American contributes regularly to such institutions as the Red Cross, the United Fund and a myriad of associations. He also establishes foundations and quite often leaves millions to such institutions. The Hispano prefers to give his contribution directly to the recipient so he can see the person he is helping.

11   A century of association has inevitably acculturated both Hispanos and Anglo-Americans to some extent, but there still persist a number of culture traits that neither group has relinquished altogether. Nothing is more disquieting to an Anglo-American who believes that time is money than the time perspective of Hispanos. They usually refer to this attitude as the "*mañana* psychology." Actually, it is more of a "today psychology," because Hispanos cultivate the present to the exclusion of the future; because the latter has not arrived yet, it is not a reality. They are reluctant to relinquish the present, so they hold on to it until it becomes the past. To an Hispano, nine is nine until it is ten, so when he arrives at nine-thirty, he jubilantly exclaims: "*¡Justo!*" [right on time]. This may be why the clock is slowed down to a walk in Spanish while in English it runs. In the United States, our future-oriented civilization plans our lives so far in advance that the present loses its meaning. January magazine issues [including ID's] are out in December; 1973 cars have been out since October; cemetery plots and even funeral arrangements are bought on the installment plan. To a person engrossed in living today the very idea of planning his funeral sounds like the tolling of the bells.

12   It is a natural corollary that a person who is present oriented should be compensated by being good at improvising. An Anglo-American is told in advance to prepare for an "impromptu speech," but an Hispano usually can improvise a speech because "*Nosotros lo improvisamos todo*" [we improvise everything].

13   Another source of cultural conflict arises from the difference between

being and *doing.* Even when trying to be individualistic, the Anglo-American achieves it by what he does. Today's young generation decided to be themselves, to get away from standardization, so they let their hair grow, wore ragged clothes and even went barefoot in order to be different from the Establishment. As a result they all ended up doing the same things and created another stereotype. The freedom enjoyed by the individuality of *being* makes it unnecessary for Hispanos to strive to be different.

14 In 1963 a team of psychologists from the University of Guadalajara in Mexico and the University of Michigan compared 74 upper-middle-class students from each university. Individualism and personalism were found to be central values for the Mexican students. This was explained by saying that a Mexican's value as a person lies in his *being* rather than, as is the case of the Anglo-Americans, in concrete accomplishments. Efficiency and accomplishments are derived characteristics that do not affect worthiness in the Mexican, whereas in the American it is equated with success, a value of highest priority in the American culture. Hispanic people disassociate themselves from material things or from actions that may impugn a person's sense of being, but the Anglo-American shows great concern for material things and assumes responsibility for his actions. This is expressed in the language of each culture. In Spanish one says, *"Se me cayó la taza"* [the cup fell away from me] instead of "I dropped the cup."

15 In English, one speaks of money, cash and all related transactions with frankness because material things of this high order do not trouble Anglo-Americans. In Spanish such materialistic concepts are circumvented by referring to cash as *efectivo* [effective] and when buying or selling as something *al contado* [counted out], and when without it by saying *No tengo fondos* [I have no funds]. This disassociation from material things is what produces *sobriedad* [sobriety] in the Spaniard according to Miguel de Unamuno, but in the Southwest the disassociation from materialism leads to *dejadez* [lassitude] and *desprendimiento* [disinterestedness]. A man may lose his life defending his honor but is unconcerned about the lack of material things. *Desprendimiento* causes a man to spend his last cent on a friend, which when added to lack of concern for the future may mean that tomorrow he will eat beans as a result of today's binge.

16 The implicit differences in words that appear to be identical in meaning are astonishing. Versatile is a compliment in English and an insult in Spanish. An Hispano student who is told to apologize cannot do it, because the word doesn't exist in Spanish. *Apología* means words in praise of a person. The Anglo-American either apologizes, which is a form of retraction abhorrent in Spanish, or compromises, another concept foreign to Hispanic culture. *Compromiso* means a date, not a compromise. In colonial Mexico City, two hidalgos once entered a narrow street from opposite sides, and when they could not go around, they sat in their coaches for three days until the viceroy ordered them to back out. All this because they could not work out a compromise.

17 It was that way then and to some extent now. Many of today's conflicts in the Southwest have their roots in polarized cultural differences, which need not be irreconcilable when approached with mutual respect and understanding.

Exercises

COMPREHENSION

Organization and Development

Complete the following outline. Find the author's statement of purpose and thesis statement and write them in the spaces provided. Then find the main divisions and the conclusion of the essay and fill in the remaining spaces. Note the paragraphs for each section.

Statement of purpose: _____

_____

_____

Thesis statement: _____

_____

_____

I.   _____ [   ]
   A._____ [   ]
   B._____ [   ]
   C._____ [   ]
   D._____ [   ]
II. _____ [   ]
   A._____ [   ]
   B._____ [   ]
   C._____ [   ]
III. _____ [   ]
   A._____ [   ]
   B._____ [   ]
   C._____ [   ]
   D._____ [   ]
Conclusion: _____ [   ]

Content

Choose the answer that correctly completes each statement.

1. The purpose of Campa's essay is to (a) compare Anglo and Hispanic motives for colonization of the New World (b) compare and contrast the cultural values that are covertly expressed in the English and Spanish languages (c) explore some of the basic cultural differences that cause conflict in the Southwest, where Hispanic and Anglo-American cultures meet.

2. In Campa's discussion of the two original cultures, the English and Spanish, one of the most fundamental distinctions is that between a(n) (a) Protestant and a Catholic religious hierarchy (b) constitutional government and a monarchy (c) insular and a peninsular situation.

3. The fact that the English colonists isolated themselves from the Indians while the Spanish mingled and intermarried freely is (a) seen as a reflection of basic distinctions that existed between the two cultures before these Europeans came to America (b) cited as one of the first major differences to develop between the two European groups once they came to America (c) mentioned as the root cause of the racial antagonism that exists today between Anglo- and Hispanic-Americans.
4. The Spaniards came to America on an enterprise of discovery, and the English came to (a) seek refuge from religious persecution (b) save souls for the Kingdom of Heaven (c) find the fountain of youth.
5. While both the Anglo-Americans and the Spanish are characterized by a sense of individualism, (a) Anglo individualism is not often a result of adherence to rules or collective standards (b) Hispanic individualism rises out of a need for careful plans of action in all situations (c) Anglo individualism is objective and follows fixed rules; Hispanic individualism is emotional and changeable.
6. The anecdote about the hidalgos who sat in their coaches for three days until the viceroy ordered them to move is used to exemplify the (a) extreme pride and stubbornness of the Spaniard (b) fact that neither the Spanish language nor the Spanish culture includes the concept of compromise (c) rigid hierarchical order on which Hispanic society is based.
7. One of the most familiar aspects of the Hispanic culture, one that we usually refer to as the "*mañana* psychology," really describes the Spanish tendency to (a) live for the future (b) cultivate the present to the exclusion of the future (c) live in the past to the exclusion of the present or the future.
8. Campa's conclusion is that (a) the two cultures are so dissimilar in language and values that conflict is inevitable (b) another century of association will erase all cultural differences between these two groups (c) conflicts that have their roots in polarized cultural differences need not be irreconcilable.

Paragraph Structure

Reorder the following sentences to form a unified, coherent paragraph. Write a sentence that can serve as a topic sentence for the reorganized paragraph. Then check your version with the original.

1. The Spaniard cultivated the land only when he had Indians available to do it for him.
2. The Spanish horse was essentially a mount, while the more robust English horse was used in cultivating the soil.
3. The Spaniard's equestrian role meant that he was not close to the soil, as was the Anglo-American pioneer, who tilled the land and built the greatest agricultural industry in history.
4. It is therefore not surprising that the viewpoints of these two cultures should differ when we consider that the pioneer is looking at the world at the level of his eyes while the *caballero* [horseman] is looking beyond and down at the rest of the world.
5. The uses to which the horse was put also varied.

VOCABULARY AND USAGE

Word Formation Table

Complete the following table by changing word endings or root forms to make new grammatical forms. Use your dictionary if necessary.

NOUN	VERB	ADJECTIVE	ADVERB
1. _____	_____	conceptual	_____
2. _____	_____	averse	_____
3. _____	_____	_____	implicitly
4. _____	_____	abhorrent	_____
5. condition	_____	_____	_____

Fill-Ins

Complete each of the sentences below using the words on the following list. You may need to use some words more than once. You may also find that some blanks can be completed correctly with more than one word. Add plural endings to nouns and change verb forms where necessary.

Hispanic	culture	society	value
Anglo	difference	conflict	belief
insular	colonize	individualism	moral
explorer	peninsular	money	understand
discovery	differ	distinction	contrast

1. Campa tries to make the reader _____ that _____ and _____ _____ have very great _____ in _____.
2. In _____ to the English, who came to _____ America because they were persecuted in England for their religious _____, the Spanish came to the New World on voyages of _____.
3. One major _____ between the _____-American and the _____-American is that the former can talk easily about _____, and the latter cannot, but must employ euphemism.
4. Campa cites the _____ in the ways in which the two _____ relate to the horse as an illustration of the great _____ between their _____ and _____.
5. While the _____ colonists came from a(n) _____ _____, the _____ _____ were rooted in a _____ place, and even the two languages reflect the _____.

DISCUSSION

1. Why does Campa depend almost exclusively on contrast in this essay? Is there any point at which he uses comparison? Which are the most important issues or points of contrast between the Anglo and Hispanic cultures?
2. Which of the two methods of arranging a comparison-contrast essay does Campa employ? Do you think the other method would be as effective? Why or why not?
3. In paragraphs 5 and 6, Campa focuses on the role of the horse in the English and Spanish cultures. What specific distinctions does he make, and what are the effects that stem from the different uses of the horse? How reliable is the cause-effect relationship Campa tries to establish here? Are there other cause-effect relationships established elsewhere in the essay? If so, what are they, and how convincingly are they established?
4. Paragraphs 7 and 8 stand in contrast to most of the rest of the essay because the author does not supply specific, concrete examples of the generalization he is making

about Hispanic individualism. Supply a concrete example of a "revolt against the incursion of collectivity, strongly asserted when it is felt the ego is being fenced in." What are "those social qualities based on collective standards" in which Hispanos are deficient? Why do you think the author has not supplied concrete illustrations?

5. Think of situations that would illustrate concretely the idea of individualism achieved "through action and self-determination" versus that which is "based on feeling, on something that is the result not of rules and collective standards but of a person's momentary, emotional reaction . . . subject to change when the mood changes" [paragraph 8]. When these abstractions are defined concretely, do they appear to be truly different manifestations of the same idea, or do they seem simply different?

6. Is Campa completely objective, or do you find that he values some traits (of either culture) more highly than their opposite numbers? How, if at all, is his preference expressed?

7. What aspects of Anglo culture seem to be direct or indirect results of its emphasis on *doing*? What aspects of Hispanic culture seem to be the results of the emphasis on *being*?

SUGGESTIONS FOR WRITING

1. Using Campa's method, examine the unique traits and values of some other subculture within the American society (or any other society you are familiar with). Use your analysis to elicit greater respect and understanding for that group.

2. Write a précis of Campa's discussion of the values fostered by Anglo and Hispanic cultures.

3. Write an essay in which you compare and/or contrast the specific effects on individual behavior of the two time perspectives—the Hispanic idea of *mañana* (orientation to the present) and the Anglo idea that time is money (orientation to the future).

4. Compare or contrast the attitudes toward material possessions in our culture and another culture (or subculture). You may wish to reread the essays by Coles and Toffler before you begin.

5. Describe in detail an individual who typifies the values and standards of Anglo-American culture (or of Hispanic-American, or any other culture you are familiar with).

6. Analyze the experience and cultural changes of some more recent group of immigrants. Include as well some reference to the changes, if any, brought about in the larger culture by the advent of the newcomers.

Life on the Mississippi: Reading the River

SAMUEL CLEMENS (MARK TWAIN)

Samuel Langhorne Clemens (1835–1910), better known as Mark Twain, is one of America's most celebrated writers. He spent his boyhood in the Mississippi River town of Hannibal, Missouri, later immortalized in *The Adventures of Tom Sawyer* and *The Adventures of Huckleberry Finn*. His formal education ended with elementary school, after which he worked at a variety of jobs, including a stint as a printer and, some years later, a newspaper editor in Virginia City, Nevada, and San Francisco.

But his greatest love remained the early years he spent as a Mississippi River pilot. Clemens's pseudonym itself, Mark Twain, is a term used by riverboat men in sounding the depth of a passage. Young Clemens signed on as an apprentice in 1857 and stayed on the river as pilot until the outbreak of the Civil War halted all travel. In those prewar days, the Mississippi was America's principal North-South artery for both commercial and passenger traffic, and the riverboat pilot was a highly skilled, respected, and well-paid man—much like the airline pilot of today.

Clemens's record of the river experience, *Life on the Mississippi,* includes an account of his reactions when, toward the end of his intricate training, he made a serious error of judgment (confusing a wind reef and a bluff reef) from which his mentor, Captain Bixby, had to rescue both him and the boat. To the cub pilot's frustrated query, "But it is exactly like a bluff reef. How am I ever going to tell them apart?" the captain responded, "I can't tell you. It is an instinct. By and by you will just naturally *know* one from the other, but you never will be able to explain why or how you know them apart." The following passage records the cub pilot's thoughtful musings on Bixby's advice and his own newly acquired knowledge of the river.

1   It turned out to be true. The face of the water, in time, became a wonderful book—a book that was a dead language to the uneducated passenger, but which told its mind to me without reserve, delivering its most cherished secrets as if it uttered them with a voice. And it was not a book to be read once and thrown aside, for it had a new story to tell every day. Throughout the long twelve hundred miles there was never a page that was void of interest, never one that you could leave unread without loss, never one that you would want to skip, thinking you could find higher enjoyment in some other thing. There never was so wonderful a book written by man; never one whose interest was so absorbing, so unflagging, so sparklingly renewed with every reperusal. The passenger who could not read it was

LIFE ON THE MISSISSIPPI: READING THE RIVER   From *Life on the Mississippi* by Samuel Clemens (1883).

charmed with a peculiar sort of faint dimple on its surface (on the rare occasions when he did not overlook it altogether); but to the pilot that was an *italicized* passage; indeed, it was more than that, it was a legend of the largest capitals, with a string of shouting exclamation points at the end of it, for it meant that a wreck or a rock was buried there that could tear the life out of the strongest vessel that ever floated. It is the faintest and simplest expression the water ever makes, and the most hideous to a pilot's eye. In truth, the passenger who could not read this book saw nothing but all manner of pretty pictures in it, painted by the sun and shaded by the clouds, whereas to the trained eye these were not pictures at all, but the grimmest and most dead-earnest of reading-matter.

2   Now when I had mastered the language of this water, and had come to know every trifling feature that bordered the great river as familiarly as I knew the letters of the alphabet, I had made a valuable acquisition. But I had lost something, too. I had lost something which could never be restored to me while I lived. All the grace, the beauty, the poetry, had gone out of the majestic river! I still kept in mind a certain wonderful sunset which I witnessed when steamboating was new to me. A broad expanse of the river was turned to blood; in the middle distance the red hue brightened into gold, through which a solitary log came floating, black and conspicuous; in one place a long, slanting mark lay sparkling upon the water; in another the surface was broken by boiling, tumbling rings, that were as many-tinted as an opal; where the ruddy flush was faintest, was a smooth spot that was covered with graceful circles and radiating lines, ever so delicately traced; the shore on our left was densely wooded, and the somber shadow that fell from this forest was broken in one place by a long, ruffled trail that shone like silver; and high above the forest wall a clean-stemmed dead tree waved a single leafy bough that glowed like a flame in the unobstructed splendor that was flowing from the sun. There were graceful curves, reflected images, woody heights, soft distances; and over the whole scene, far and near, the dissolving lights drifted steadily, enriching it every passing moment with new marvels of coloring.

3   I stood like one bewitched. I drank it in, in a speechless rapture. The world was new to me, and I had never seen anything like this at home. But as I have said, a day came when I began to cease from noting the glories and the charms which the moon and the sun and the twilight wrought upon the river's face; another day came when I ceased altogether to note them. Then, if that sunset scene had been repeated, I should have looked upon it without rapture, and should have commented upon it, inwardly, after this fashion: "This sun means that we are going to have wind to-morrow; that floating log means that the river is rising, small thanks to it; that slanting mark on the water refers to a bluff reef which is going to kill somebody's steamboat one of these nights, if it keeps on stretching out like that; those tumbling 'boils' show a dissolving bar and a changing channel there; the lines and circles in the slick water over yonder are a warning that that troublesome place is shoaling up dangerously; that silver streak in the shadow of the forest is the

'break' from a new snag, and he has located himself in the very best place he could have found to fish for steamboats; that tall dead tree, with a single living branch, is not going to last long, and then how is a body ever going to get through this blind place at night without the friendly old landmark?"

4   No, the romance and beauty were all gone from the river. All the value any feature of it had for me now was the amount of usefulness it could furnish toward compassing the safe piloting of a steamboat. Since those days, I have pitied doctors from my heart. What does the lovely flush in a beauty's cheek mean to a doctor but a "break" that ripples above some deadly disease? Are not all her visible charms sown thick with what are to him the signs and symbols of hidden decay? Does he ever see her beauty at all, or doesn't he simply view her professionally, and comment upon her unwholesome condition all to himself? And doesn't he sometimes wonder whether he has gained most or lost most by learning his trade?

Analogy

Comparison shows similarities between like things, things in the same general class: lions and tigers (both "big cats"), lions and bears (both "wild animals"), or even lions and elephants (both "wild animals that can be trained for circus acts"). An analogy is a special kind of comparison in which two essentially unlike things, members of totally different classes (girls and flowers, street life and theatrical productions, cities and living organisms) are brought together in order to call attention to, to emphasize, or to explain the qualities in the one that are already obvious in the other. Often one of the subjects in an analogy is familiar and the other unfamiliar; when *both* subjects seem familiar, it is their characteristics that are joined in the pattern of familiar and unfamiliar.

When the poet, for instance, says, "My love is like a red, red rose," he underscores the qualities *he* finds in the girl that we *all* find in the rose: beauty, fragility, a delicate air of transience—and the challenging danger of the surrounding thorns. The poet is making a metaphor, and metaphor is the ultimate analogy, the most extreme coupling of essentially unlike objects: only by an intellectual effort can we see the likeness between the girl and the rose. At the other extreme of relationship-making is the simple comparison: a red rose is like a geranium. Here we can see quite easily the real, concrete likeness in color, form, etc. Between these extremes is the analogy, where the objects compared possess certain concrete similarities (sloburbs and slime molds are both apparently formless; the movements of both dancers and city dwellers reveal a pattern). But basically, the total relationship presented in an analogy is one of great difference rather than of similarity in concrete or tangible terms.

Jane Jacobs's essay proposes an analogy between the daily activities of her city neighborhood and the intricately ordered and disciplined movements of a ballet. The familiar ritualized order of the ballet highlights her vision of life on Hudson Street as calm, predictable, safe—ritualized and orderly. (Someone else's portrait of city life, of another neighborhood, might make a very different analogy—between the city and the jungle, for example, as Willwerth does.) Krutch uses a double analogy—first generally comparing the organization of a metropolis to that of a living organism, and then ultimately pairing the sloburb and the slime mold. This is Krutch's way of insisting that the American suburb is one of the lowest forms of life.

While the essays in this section use analogy as a dominant mode of organization, it is a vivid and imaginative method of illustrating or emphasizing a point that can be used in support of other methods of development (see the essays by Maynard and Mitford).

The Hudson Street Ballet

JANE JACOBS

Jane Jacobs is a writer on urban affairs. In *The Death and Life of Great American Cities* from which this excerpt comes, she attacks city planning and urban renewal, the ill effects of which she had observed when she covered New York's rebuilding projects as editor of *Architectural Forum*. The essay below is a description of the daily sidewalk activities of the street she lived on in Greenwich Village in New York City.

1   Under the seeming disorder of the old city, wherever the old city is working successfully, is a marvelous order for maintaining the safety of the streets and the freedom of the city. It is a complex order. Its essence is intricacy of sidewalk use, bringing with it a constant succession of eyes. This order is all composed of movement and change, and although it is life, not art, we may fancifully call it the art form of the city and liken it to the dance—not to a simple-minded precision dance with everyone kicking up at the same time, twirling in unison and bowing off en masse, but to an intricate ballet in which the individual dancers and ensembles all have distinctive parts which miraculously reinforce each other and compose an orderly whole. The ballet of the good city sidewalk never repeats itself from place to place, and in any one place is always replete with new improvisations.

2   The stretch of Hudson Street where I live is each day the scene of an intricate sidewalk ballet. I make my own first entrance into it a little after eight when I put out the garbage can, surely a prosaic occupation, but I enjoy my part, my little clang, as the droves of junior high school students walk by the center of the stage dropping candy wrappers. (How do they eat so much candy so early in the morning?)

3   While I sweep up the wrappers I watch the other rituals of morning: Mr. Halpert unlocking the laundry's handcart from its mooring to a cellar door, Joe Cornacchia's son-in-law stacking out the empty crates from the delicatessen, the barber bringing out his sidewalk folding chair, Mr. Goldstein arranging the coils of wire which proclaim the hardware store is open, the wife of the tenement's superintendent depositing her chunky three-year-old with a toy mandolin on the stoop, the vantage point from which he is learning the English his mother cannot speak. Now the primary children, heading for St. Luke's, dribble through to the south; the children for St. Veronica's cross, heading to the west, and the children for P.S. 41, heading toward the east.

Two new entrances are being made from the wings: well-dressed and even elegant women and men with brief cases emerge from doorways and side streets. Most of these are heading for the bus and subways, but some hover on the curbs, stopping taxis which have miraculously appeared at the right moment, for the taxis are part of a wider morning ritual: having dropped passengers from midtown in the downtown financial district, they are now bringing downtowners up to midtown. Simultaneously, numbers of women in housedresses have emerged and as they crisscross with one another they pause for quick conversations that sound with either laughter or joint indignation, never, it seems, anything between. It is time for me to hurry to work too, and I exchange my ritual farewell with Mr. Lofaro, the short, thick-bodied, white-aproned fruit man who stands outside his doorway a little up the street, his arms folded, his feet planted, looking solid as earth itself. We nod; we each glance quickly up and down the street, then look back to each other and smile. We have done this many a morning for more than ten years, and we both know what it means: All is well.

4   The heart-of-the-day ballet I seldom see, because part of the nature of it is that working people who live there, like me, are mostly gone, filling the roles of strangers on other sidewalks. But from days off, I know enough of it to know that it becomes more and more intricate. Longshoremen who are not working that day gather at the White Horse or the Ideal or the International for beer and conversation. The executives and business lunchers from the industries just to the west throng the Dorgene restaurant and the Lion's Head coffee house; meat-market workers and communications scientists fill the bakery lunchroom. Character dancers come on, a strange old man with strings of old shoes over his shoulders, motor-scooter riders with big beards and girl friends who bounce on the back of the scooters and wear their hair long in front of their faces as well as behind, drunks who follow the advice of the Hat Council and are always turned out in hats, but not hats the Council would approve. Mr. Lacey, the locksmith, shuts up his shop for a while and goes to exchange the time of day with Mr. Slube at the cigar store. Mr. Koochagian, the tailor, waters the luxuriant jungle of plants in his window, gives them a critical look from the outside, accepts a compliment on them from two passersby, fingers the leaves on the plane tree in front of our house with a thoughtful gardener's appraisal, and crosses the street for a bite at the Ideal where he can keep an eye on customers and wigwag across the message that he is coming. The baby carriages come out, and clusters of everyone from toddlers with dolls to teen-agers with homework gather at the stoops.

5   When I get home after work, the ballet is reaching its crescendo. This is the time of roller skates and stilts and tricycles, and games in the lee of the stoop with bottletops and plastic cowboys; this is the time of bundles and packages, zigzagging from the drug store to the fruit stand and back over to the butcher's; this is the time when teen-agers, all dressed up, are pausing to ask if their slips show or their collars look right; this is the time when beautiful girls get out of MG's; this is the time when the fire engines go through; this is the time when anybody you know around Hudson Street will go by.

6   As darkness thickens and Mr. Halpert moors the laundry cart to the cellar door again, the ballet goes on under lights, eddying back and forth but intensifying at the bright spotlight pools of Joe's sidewalk pizza dispensary, the bars, the delicatessen, the restaurant and the drug store. The night workers stop now at the delicatessen, to pick up salami and a container of milk. Things have settled down for the evening but the street and its ballet have not come to a stop.

7   I know the deep night ballet and its seasons best from waking long after midnight to tend a baby and, sitting in the dark, seeing the shadows and hearing the sounds of the sidewalk. Mostly it is a sound like infinitely pattering snatches of party conversation and, about three in the morning, singing, very good singing. Sometimes there is sharpness and anger or sad, sad weeping, or a flurry of search for a string of beads broken. One night a young man came roaring along, bellowing terrible language at two girls whom he had apparently picked up and who were disappointing him. Doors opened, a wary semicircle formed around him, not too close, until the police came. Out came the heads, too, along Hudson Street, offering opinion, "Drunk . . . Crazy . . . A wild kid from the suburbs."[1]

8   Deep in the night, I am almost unaware how many people are on the street unless something calls them together, like the bagpipe. Who the piper was and why he favored our street I have no idea. The bagpipe just skirled out in the February night, and as if it were a signal the random, dwindled movements of the sidewalk took on direction. Swiftly, quietly, almost magically a little crowd was there, a crowd that evolved into a circle with a Highland fling inside it. The crowd could be seen on the shadowy sidewalk, the dancers could be seen, but the bagpiper himself was almost invisible because his bravura was all in his music. He was a very little man in a plain brown overcoat. When he finished and vanished, the dancers and watchers applauded, and applause came from the galleries too, half a dozen of the hundred windows on Hudson Street. Then the windows closed, and the little crowd dissolved into the random movements of the night street.

9   The strangers on Hudson Street, the allies whose eyes help us natives keep the peace of the street, are so many that they always seem to be different people from one day to the next. That does not matter. Whether they are so many always-different people as they seem to be, I do not know. Likely they are. When Jimmy Rogan fell through a plate-glass window (he was separating some scuffling friends) and almost lost his arm, a stranger in an old T-shirt emerged from the Ideal bar, swiftly applied an expert tourniquet and, according to the hospital's emergency staff, saved Jimmy's life. Nobody remembered seeing the man before and no one has seen him since. The hospital was called in this way: a woman sitting on the steps next to the accident ran over to the bus stop, wordlessly snatched the dime from the hand of a stranger who was waiting with his fifteen-cent fare ready, and raced into the Ideal's phone booth. The stranger raced after her to offer the nickel too.

---

[1]He turned out to be a wild kid from the suburbs. Sometimes, on Hudson Street, we are tempted to believe the suburbs must be a difficult place to bring up children.

Nobody remembered seeing him before, and no one has seen him since. When you see the same stranger three or four times on Hudson Street, you begin to nod. This is almost getting to be an acquaintance, a public acquaintance, of course.

10   I have made the daily ballet of Hudson Street sound more frenetic than it is, because writing it telescopes it. In real life, it is not that way. In real life, to be sure, something is always going on, the ballet is never at a halt, but the general effect is peaceful and the general tenor even leisurely. People who know well such animated city streets will know how it is. I am afraid people who do not will always have it a little wrong in their heads—like the old prints of rhinoceroses made from travelers' descriptions of rhinoceroses.

11   On Hudson Street, the same as in the North End of Boston or in any other animated neighborhoods of great cities, we are not innately more competent at keeping the sidewalks safe than are the people who try to live off the hostile truce of Turf in a blind-eyed city. We are the lucky possessors of a city order that makes it relatively simple to keep the peace because there are plenty of eyes on the street. But there is nothing simple about that order itself, or the bewildering number of components that go into it. Most of those components are specialized in one way or another. They unite in their joint effect upon the sidewalk, which is not specialized in the least. That is its strength.

Exercises

COMPREHENSION

Organization and Development

Complete the following outline. Find the thesis statement and write it in the space provided. Then find the main divisions in the essay and fill in the remaining spaces. Note the paragraphs for each section.

Thesis statement: _____

_____

_____

I.   _____   [   ]
II.   _____   [   ]
III. _____   [   ]
IV.   _____   [   ]
V.   _____   [   ]

Content

Choose the answer that correctly completes each statement.

1. Apparently, the neighborhood the author lives in is composed mainly of (a) skyscrapers and office buildings (b) residences as well as shops and restaurants (c) theaters, nightclubs, and other places of entertainment.

2. The author particularly emphasizes the street's daily (a) conversations (b) bizarre events (c) rituals.
3. The character dancers described in the essay are actually (a) longshoremen and truck drivers (b) teenagers showing off (c) strange people who don't fit into the neighborhood.
4. When a little old man came to play his bagpipes late at night (a) many people in the neighborhood gathered to listen and applaud (b) the police took him away (c) people yelled from their windows for him to go away.
5. In reality, the general tenor of Hudson Street is (a) frantic and fast-paced (b) calm and leisurely (c) hostile and tense.
6. At night the street (a) continues its intricate motions, though they are different from the daytime activities (b) becomes so unsafe for the unwary resident that few people venture outdoors (c) becomes the site for teenagers cruising in sports cars.
7. According to the author, what keeps Hudson Street safe is the (a) gangs of juveniles who patrol the street and keep troublemakers away (b) watchful eyes of all who live there (c) kind actions of strangers who help out in emergencies.
8. When the author describes the "hostile truce of Turf in a blind-eyed city," she means (a) ghettoes where arson and vandalism are common (b) areas victimized by gangs of juveniles whose residents don't want to get involved (c) areas whose residents form patrol groups who watch the neighborhood for suspicious activities.

Paragraph Structure

Reorder the following sentences to form a unified, coherent paragraph. Identify one sentence as the topic sentence. Then check your version with the original.

1. One night a young man came roaring along, bellowing terrible language at two girls whom he had apparently picked up and who were disappointing him.
2. Mostly it is a sound like infinitely pattering snatches of party conversation and, about three in the morning, singing, very good singing.
3. Doors opened, a wary semicircle formed around him, not too close, until the police came.
4. I know the deep night ballet and its seasons best from waking long after midnight to tend a baby and, sitting in the dark, seeing the shadows and hearing the sounds of the sidewalk.
5. Sometimes there is a sharpness and anger or sad, sad weeping, or a flurry of search for a string of beads broken.
6. Out came the heads, too, along Hudson Street, offering opinion, "Drunk . . . Crazy . . . A wild kid from the suburbs."

VOCABULARY AND USAGE

Word Formation Table

Complete the following table by changing word endings or root forms to make new grammatical forms. Use your dictionary if necessary.

	NOUN	VERB	ADJECTIVE	ADVERB
1.	_____	apply	_____	xxx
2.	_____	_____	wary	_____
3.	_____	xxx	_____	infinitely
4.	_____	intensify	_____	_____
5.	_____	xxx	intricate	_____

Fill-Ins

Complete each of the sentences below using the words on the following list. You may need to use some words more than once. You may also find that some blanks can be completed correctly with more than one word. Add plural endings to nouns and change verb forms where necessary.

complex	praise	ritual	distinctive
build	watch	lively	animated
unaware	compliment	bewildering	intricate
observe	cautious	specialized	emerge
unless	intensify	wary	and

1. On Hudson Street each person plays his own _____ role to produce a(n) _____ dance that the author finds fascinating to _____.
2. Every morning the author _____ the same _____ take place: People _____ from their houses to leave for work _____ shopkeepers open their stores.
3. Some passerby _____ Mr. Koochagian's plants, _____ Mr. Lacey, the locksmith, carries on a(n) _____ conversation with Mr. Slube at the cigar store.
4. The author is _____ of how many people are actually on the street _____ something occurs to bring them together; a fight, for example, draws a _____ crowd of observers as if by magic.
5. After working hours, the movement of the street becomes more _____, with children and teenagers everywhere, _____ the tempo _____ until it reaches its peak.
6. The street's movements are not at all simple; in fact, they are quite _____ because of the _____ number of components, each of which has a _____ part to play.

DISCUSSION

1. What is the function of paragraph 1? How does it relate to the rest of the essay? Would the essay be as effective (or as clear) if it began with paragraph 2 and the thesis statement?
2. In what ways are the activities on Hudson Steet analogous to a ballet? Go through the essay and pick out references to the dance that serve to unify the theme.
3. How does the analogy strengthen the point Jacobs wants to make about her neighborhood? What would the description lose if she had written about the street prosaically?
4. Why is the midday ballet more intricate than the morning rituals? [See paragraph 4.] What makes it so?
5. Aside from the ballet analogy, what other analogy or thematic device does Jacobs use throughout the essay to unify her description? Why is this device appropriate?
6. How would you characterize the relations between neighbors and storekeepers on Hudson Street? Find some illustrations from the essay to support your answer.
7. What is the source of the "strength" that Jacobs refers to in paragraph 11?
8. What order of development does the essay follow?

SUGGESTIONS FOR WRITING

1. Describe your street's daily rituals. Use chronological order and be sure to describe your neighbors and their activities both specifically and concretely.

2. Jacobs mentions in paragraph 9 the kindness shown by strangers who saved a boy's life. Relate an incident you have observed or experienced in which a stranger came to the rescue, from altruism, not from the expectation of a reward.
3. Following Jacobs's model of establishing an analogy between two dissimilar things, write an essay in which you describe a scene in terms of something else. Some examples might be a bus station waiting room, a registration line, a rock concert, a McDonald's, or a city street. Keep in mind that an analogy is an *extended* comparison, not simply a metaphor stated once.

The Sloburbs

JOSEPH WOOD KRUTCH

Joseph Wood Krutch (1893–1970) was a well-known American journalist, naturalist, and drama critic. He taught at Columbia University and at the New School for Social Research. After a period as drama critic for *The Nation,* he became its editor. When he retired, he moved to Tucson, Arizona, one place that in particular has witnessed the relentless spread of the suburban sprawl called "sloburbs" described in this essay.

1   At Los Angeles we were told that the San Francisco Airport was fogged in, and we were given a choice. We could go to a hotel for the night and hope that the weather would clear or we could resign ourselves to a nine-hour bus ride. I chose the bus while reflecting sourly on the paradoxes of today's travel. A few months before I had come to San Francisco from Tokyo in exactly the same time it would take me to get there from Los Angeles. But one compensation—if you can call it that—did develop. I got the most extensive view I have ever had of what is now commonly called the sloburbs. Also, the fullest realization of their horror.

2   Nowhere are they worse than in the Los Angeles area and nowhere are they more extensive. For several hours the same dismal scenes changed so little that it was hard to believe one was moving at all. Gas station, motel, car lot, bar, hamburger stand; then gas station, motel, car lot, bar and hamburger stand again—all bathed in the hellish glow of neon. Daylight would have made everything look shabbier but not more attractive.

3   Los Angeles can, of course, be accused of no more than a bad eminence. Nearly all American towns, even quite small ones, present a more or less extensive version of the same picture. The newer and the faster growing the community the more it tends to be a sloburb and nothing else, and sloburbs are so much alike that if you were carried into one blindfolded you would often find it impossible to say not only where you were, but even whether you were north or south or east or west.

4   Tucson, where I now live, is no exception. In fact, it is rather worse than many because so much of its explosive growth is recent and takes the form of rapidly spreading sloburbs. They have not yet reached the area where I live but they are creeping towards it, and as I drove home the other day through spreading ugliness I was again amazed that this sort of anti-city could be so

characterless. Everything looks improvised, random, unrelated to everything else, as though it had no memory of yesterday and no expectation of tomorrow.

5   Nor is this true only of the motel, bar, hamburger-stand complex. It is almost equally so of a new kind of "business district," which is less a district than a ribbon of commercial establishments growing longer and longer as "downtown" shrinks or stagnates. Here the repetitive succession is not unlike that of the only slightly frowzier parade of eateries, drinkeries and sleeperies. The supermarkets (one every few hundred yards) are the most imposing of the commercial establishments. Between them come drugstores (which sell more toys, sporting equipment and sandwiches than they do drugs), dime stores, TV repair shops and auto supply emporia in a sort of procession which is repeated as soon as the repertory has completed itself.

6   Yet this is far from being a depressed area. It is actually a very prosperous one and real-estate prices skyrocket in what is only a little better than a sort of shantytown. Poverty, I reminded myself, creates slums and slums can be even uglier. But I wondered if ever before in history a prosperous people had consented to live in communities so devoid of every grace and dignity, so slum-like in everything except the money they represent. They are something new and almost uniquely unattractive—neither country nor village nor town nor city—just an agglomeration without plan, without any sense of unity or direction, as though even offices and shops were thought of as disposable, like nearly everything else in our civilization, and therefore not worth considering from any standpoint except the make-do of the moment.

7   A real metropolis has a quasi-organic unity. There is a nerve center more or less elaborate which includes whatever public buildings, theaters, auditoriums and major commerical emporia the community can support. From the impressiveness of this nerve center one can judge pretty accurately just to what degree it is a metropolis rather than a town or a village. Its suburbs and even its slums are related to the whole. But a large sloburb like that which surrounds and all but engulfs Los Angeles differs from that of the village on the highway in nothing except area. You could cut a piece of it and set the piece down anywhere and you could not tell that it had grown up around Los Angeles, rather than where you found it. A suburb implies a city to which it is attached but what we are increasingly developing are huge agglomerations which cannot be called suburbs beause there is no urbs to own them.

8   Why, then, have the sloburbs become the most characteristic aspect of modern America? Why are they the only real urban development new to our time, as much our special contribution to the look and feel of our environment as the skyscraper was that of the first half of the century?

9   If you accept the now usual assumption that whatever we do or are is the necessary result of "evolving technology," then the answer is easy. Technological progress has made the population explosion supportable and necessitated rapid growth. The automobile has made us mobile, and prosperity has not only created the demand for the superfluities to which two-thirds of the

enterprises in the sloburbs cater but also encouraged the tendency to regard everything, including architecture, as disposable. Stores, office buildings and even churches will be "turned in" for new ones in a year or two. That is progress.

10   If on the other hand you believe that evolving technology is only half the story, that human beings are capable of resisting as well as of yielding to pressures, then the question why we have consented to the sloburbs remains; why we are to all appearances so contented with them. Remember that sloburbs are the product of wealth and abundance. The motel-café regions cater to those who have much leisure; the merchandising sloburbs depend at least as much upon what might be called luxury goods as they do upon necessities. Why is there so little luxurious, or even decently dignified, about the buildings which house them, the merchandising methods they employ? Why should an abundant society be content to accept communities so obviously the antithesis of that "graceful living" which the service magazines talk about and declare to be nowadays open to all?

11   Some of the frequent answers to that question also are easy: Americans have no taste, no sense of dignity, no ability to discriminate between the informality to which they are committed and the slovenliness of the sloburbs. Their civic pride does not extend beyond pride in increasing size and that prosperity which means that most of its citizens are making money building sloburbs or operating them. Given the primary fact of profit, nothing else is very important. Certainly aesthetic considerations are not. Arizona, for instance, tempts the tourist with the pretense that its proudest boast is its natural beauty. But it really prefers billboards, as is evidenced by the fact that it recently again rejected the offer of the national government to grant a bonus if it would keep the main highways clear of them.

12   These also are, of course, familiar charges and not without an element of truth. But they are not quite the whole story, not quite fair. The typical American is not indifferent to everything except profit. He is merely indifferent to some of the things which others consider important. He has, for example, an enormous faith in schooling—which he assumes to be the same thing as education. In Tucson, for example, by far the most imposing buildings are the absurdly elaborate schools, which the same citizens who prefer billboards to scenic grandeur, seem willing to support through very high taxes. The consensus seems to be essentially this: It is just that citizens should be taxed heavily and also expected to contribute generously. But they should never, under any circumstances, be prevented from making a profit. Hospitals also seem to be among the non-profit institutions to which citizens point with pride. But they are unwilling to do anything to slow the spread of sloburbs. The zoning regulations are a farce. If an area is zoned for residents only, that usually means that no business can be established there until somebody wants to establish one—at which time the zoning is promptly changed. Order, dignity, grace and beauty are things that are simply not worth paying even a small price for. Schooling, recreation and health should

be supported. But the other parts of, and provisions for, the good life are not the community's business. Perhaps this tolerance is part of the kindly sloven-liness in manners and morals to which we seem more and more inclined. But it is enough to permit the development of communities which it is impossible to imagine an earlier generation submitting to without protest.

13   Some years ago I decided that for me the city was paying diminishing returns and I moved away from it. This was a choice I have never regretted but it was related to my time of life as well as to certain aspects of my temperament. It did not mean that I had no regard for cities and what they have contributed to civilization. But the sloburbs have none of the advantages of country, village or genuine city life. They do not, like real cities, provide a sufficiently large minority of citizens of intellectual and artistic taste to support cultural institutions proportionate to the size of their populations. Neither do they provide that "life of the streets" which is another of the chief attractions offered by a real city. Anywhere in a sloburb one may buy gasoline, cocktails, beer and hamburgers. But one cannot go window-shopping or indulge in any of the other activities which in New York or San Francisco draw strollers down the streets of the urban core. Neither, of course, can one breathe fresh air or enjoy the beauties of nature. One can only breathe gas fumes and revel in the glow of neon. Of all the places into which one's lot may be cast, few—not even those minimum-security prisons called garden apartments of the sort I pass on my way once or twice a year from Manhattan to Kennedy—strike me as more dismal.

14   Thinking of a real city as something analogous to a living creature where highly differentiated organs are all related to, and coordinated by, a central nervous system, I found myself wondering to just what sort of creature an individual sloburb might be compared. Most of even the so-called primitive organisms are wholes in the sense that the parts are related to one another and cannot exist except in connection with some center. You can't, in most cases, just break off a section and expect it to survive. Neither can most of such simple organisms grow indefinitely without any natural boundaries or shape. Hence, if a sloburb is analogous to any living thing it must be, I think, to one of the myxomycetes or slime molds. These remarkable blobs found especially in damp, rotting logs have no shape, no characteristic size and no community center. They consist of an agglomeration of one-celled individu-als without a trace of the differentiation characteristic of even the more primitive multi-cellular organisms. You may break one blob into a hundred pieces and each will prosper as satisfactorily as it did when it was part of a larger blob. Put the pieces into contact again and they will merge much as the sloburbs spreading out from two communities merge when they meet. And given favorable conditions, the size of the blob grows and grows without there being any theoretical reason why it should not ultimately cover the earth. Such an eventuality might make a good horror movie. But no better than one that showed the whole face of America covered ultimately by one vast sloburb.

Cause and Effect

Expository writing that seeks to establish a relationship between a cause (something in the past) and its effect (a future consequence) is sometimes called "causal analysis." It tries to show that the first thing made or makes the second thing happen, or it explains *why* something happened or will happen. (The coming of telephone service to Squaw Gap, a *cause*—"has revolutionized life here"—its *effect*.)

One way to make a causal analysis is first to consider a cause and then to demonstrate, or at least try to determine or explain, its effect. Any effort to look into the future, to predict the results of actions not yet taken, requires the formation of this type of cause-effect relationship. (What would happen if . . .? What kind of job will I get if I major in . . .?) "The Telephone Comes to Squaw Gap" is a particularly clear-cut example of reasoning from cause to effect, because the installation of phone service in this prairie community is so easily isolated as a cause, and because it had such instantaneous and easily-identifiable results. The historian's effort to determine the far-reaching effects of historical events (What were the results of granting the vote to women?) is another illustration of this pattern of causal analysis. Of course, with any complex cause—whether the constant exposure of children to television or a major event—it is far more difficult to identify and trace a direct line of connection to specific effects.

Another way to organize this type of essay is to start with a known effect and trace it back to a known or probable cause. (How did *this* happen? Who made *this* mess?) This is the pattern of analysis your doctor follows when, after looking at your stuffy nose and itchy eyes (*effects*), he tries to identify the unknown substance (or *cause*) provoking your allergic reaction. The essays by Winn and Crew also follow the doctor's basic plan in seeking to assign causes (television viewing, the misplaced values of physical education teachers) to known or visible effects (the breakdown of American family life, the author's physical ineptitude).

If you had only to decide whether to trace from cause to effect, or from effect back to cause, this method of exposition would be simple. But, as these examples show, causal analysis is based on a highly abstract thought process, and so it is one of the most difficult forms of organization, one with a number of built-in problems. These can, however, be avoided for the most part by the careful thinker and writer.

First, it is crucial to remember that in logic and in fact, causes precede effects. You must avoid the common fallacy of assuming that because event B (you break out in hives) happens immediately after or simultaneously with event A (you eat a slice of wheat bread), A must necessarily have caused B. In fact, your rash *may* have been caused by the patch of poison ivy you sat in while eating your sandwich.

Then again, the rash may have resulted from something else in the sandwich, like the mayonnaise, illustrating the principle that an effect may be produced by more than one cause. And a single cause may result in multiple effects, or multiple causes may be necessary to produce a single effect. Thus, all relevant conditions must be considered in establishing a causal relationship, not just some. Winn, for example, may be at fault in lightly dismissing many factors in American society which contribute along with television to the deterioration of family life.

Next, you need to distinguish between immediate causes (those nearest to the effect—the bread you ate just before you became ill), and ultimate or remote causes (those most distant from the effect—the metabolic deficiency that prevents you from digesting wheat products). In the allergy example, *both* immediate and remote causes may be relevant and important. But in other cases, such as why you lost the tennis championship, the causal connections may be insufficiently clear, so it is better to concentrate on the immediate causes—your weak serve or a headache on the day of the competition—rather than retreat to remote causes, like the influence of your lunar sign or the neurotic anxiety produced by your early toilet training. Also, ultimate causes may themselves bring about effects that in turn become causes, making a chain of causes and effects, as in the old nursery rhyme, "For want of a nail the shoe was lost, for want of a shoe the horse was lost, for want of a horse the rider was lost . . . and all for want of a nail."

Another problem concerns the difference between what logicians call necessary and sufficient causes. A necessary cause must be present for an effect to occur, but it cannot *by itself* cause that effect. Telephone service may be *necessary* to the 50 percent increase in Goldsberry's Squaw Gap quarterhorse business, but other factors (advertising? fine horses?) may also be required. A sufficient cause, on the other hand, is one that can produce an effect by itself: in the case of Mrs. Whited's ability to make medical appointments in advance, the phone is a sufficient cause.

Finally, remember that even some philosophers question the possibility of ever asssigning a direct relationship between some causes and some effects, and as a student reader and writer, you should be wary of trying to prove the unprovable or connect the unconnectable.

The Telephone Comes to Squaw Gap

ANDREW MALCOLM

Andrew Malcolm has been a reporter and correspondent for the *New York Times* since 1967. One of his assignments was to travel around the country in search of "unknown America." The result was a series of short vignettes of Americana published daily in the *Times;* they have since been collected in a book, *Unknown America.* In the following selection, Malcolm explains what happened when a small North Dakota town finally got telephone service.

1   There's a strange clicking sound in Squaw Gap these days, coming from within the new, pink cement-block building over by the crumbling community hall. Every so often a workman visits the windowless structure, but the clicking continues. And that's just fine with everyone here. For that sound, about the only unnatural one heard for scores of miles in this rugged, rolling corner of North Dakota, symbolizes the end of isolation for the few people of Squaw Gap and the beginning of a new way of life.

2   It is the sound of an automatic telephone switching center. Six months ago, it brought to 93 families here their first telephone service.

3   Spread over 1000 square miles of northwest North Dakota, these people lived in the largest inhabited area of the United States without phones. For years they have had electricity, dishwashers, television sets, washing machines, and air-conditioners. But until Dec. 15, 1971, a day etched in local memory on a par with Pearl Harbor, they had no phone service. Then, at 1:30 P.M., Mountain Standard Time, with more than 200 excited people in attendance at the community hall, Squaw Gap—after 23 years of trying—was connected with the rest of the nation.

4   The telephone has already revolutionized life here, saving countless hours, many dollars, much wasted effort, and probably a few lives. It has made better friends of some and caused friction with others. It has boosted business for many, saved at least one rancher from costly disaster, and probably spurred a couple of teen-age romances. "The phone," said Sharon Whited, "is simply wonderful." All this with no thanks to the Bell System, which, despite dozens of meetings, petitions, and pleas since 1948, maintained that it could not economically serve Squaw Gap's cattle ranchers and wheat farmers.

5   Squaw Gap, an area and a town named for a now-fallen rock formation

THE TELEPHONE COMES TO SQUAW GAP   Originally titled "Squaw Gap, North Dakota." From *Unknown America* by Andrew H. Malcolm. Copyright © 1975 by Andrew H. Malcolm. Reprinted by permission of Quadrangle/The New York Times Book Co.

resembling a squaw, is indeed isolated. It appears on no road maps. The "town" consists of a T-shaped, dirt-road intersection with eight buildings—four of them outhouses. The town's population on a winter weekday evening is one. On the weekend, it's none, because Mrs. Ethel Franz, the schoolteacher for four students, goes back to Sidney, Montana. Even Sidney is more than 40 dusty miles away across the stark buttes and rolling grassland, where cattle, deer, and antelope graze and the only sound is the swishing of the grasses in the 30-mile-an-hour prairie wind.

6   It is an area that is 45 times bigger than Manhattan. But it has about 1/26,000 the number of phones. It wasn't long ago that the residents were doubtful about ever getting any. "Here I could watch astronauts go to the moon on color TV," said Ray Macik, "but I couldn't phone my next-door neighbor." Then someone wrote the Reservation Telephone Cooperative, a small, independent system in Parshall, North Dakota. With a hefty loan from the federal government, its officers said they could bury about 200 miles of cable and give everyone a private dial line for a $50 membership fee and $12 a month.

7   Last September, the digging began, skepticism waned, and excitement rose. One night in early December, Mr. Macik's wife recalled, their newly installed but dormant phone suddenly rang. Instant bedlam engulfed the house—children shouted, parents cheered, dogs barked, papers flew. It was only a workman testing the line, but it signaled progress.

8   On December 15, Mrs. Franz canceled classes and Squaw Gap staged the biggest do here since 1916, when Buffalo Bill Cody is said to have passed through. The historic first call, to Secretary of Agriculture Earl L. Butz, was disconnected by a Washington secretary. But after that afternoon, life here will never be the same.

9   When Mr. Macik's order of 100 baby chickens arrived in Sidney, the agent could call him instead of mailing a postcard. That saved several days and probably several chickens. Mrs. Whited can now make advance appointments by phone at her beautician and her children's doctor instead of taking a chance. Vernon Goldsberry's quarter-horse business is up 50 percent now that he can advertise with a phone number. "People don't like to write any more," he said.

10   Melvin Leland now knows exactly when a truck is due to pick up his cattle so he won't waste time hanging around the house with the animals penned up and losing weight. And his wife, Luella, shares a telephone coffee break twice daily with her sister, Betty Wersland. Mr. Goldsberry's wife talked with her brother in Portland, Oregon, the other day for the first time in 15 years. Mrs. Loretta Tescher's morale had sagged every winter when she was snowbound for days and the mail came once a week or so. "Now it's just wonderful," she said, "I can chat with a neighbor and it lets me put off my housework." More important, it saved her family several thousand dollars. About three months ago, 2 of their 500 cattle died unexpectedly. Although snowed in, the family could telephone the veterinarian with the symptoms.

He diagnosed it as a form of food poisoning and saved dozens of other cattle, many of them pregnant, from the same feed.

11   Around midnight just a couple of weeks ago, lightning cracked into Milton Brunsvold's field. Soon the horizon was lit by the ominous glow that can mean only one thing out here—prairie fire. Within minutes, 100 men, summoned by an impromptu telephone relay, were dashing the flames with wet gunnysacks. The fire burned 160 acres. Four years ago, a similar blaze roared across 3000 acres before couriers in cars could round up enough help. In other times, people perished, unwarned of such fires or of flash floods.

12   There are, however, some problems with the telephone. Almost every call is long distance, so monthly bills hover around $50. Some children away at college have discovered, to their parents' dismay, the collect phone call. And some farmhands, juiced up after a Friday night at a Sidney bar, still think it is hilarious to telephone their boss at 3 A.M. to discuss the marvels of modern communication.

13   "Sometimes," said Mr. Macik, "I'd like to know how to turn this fool thing off."

Exercises

COMPREHENSION

Organization and Development

Complete the following outline. Find the thesis statement and write it in the space provided. Then find the main divisions in the essay and fill in the remaining spaces. Note the paragraphs for each section.

Thesis statement: _____

_____

_____

    I.   _____   [   ]
    II. _____   [   ]
    III. _____   [   ]

Content

Choose the answer that correctly completes each statement.

1. The primary purpose of this selection is to describe the (a) efforts of Squaw Gap's residents to get telephone service (b) effects of telephone service on Squaw Gap's residents (c) importance of the telephone as a means of communication.

2. Apparently, the residents of Squaw Gap (a) also lacked electricity (b) had been trying to get telephone service for 23 years (c) resisted the idea of having telephones installed.

3. Squaw Gap is (a) only an intersection, a crossroads with a population of 100 (b) a

busy farm town in a remote farming area (c) both a town and an area comprising about 1000 square miles.

4. One resident of Squaw Gap found it ironic that he could not get phone service although he could (a) have a washer and dryer (b) watch astronauts go to the moon on TV (c) fight prairie fires with teams of volunteers working in relays.

5. To receive telephone service, each family had to (a) sign a petition (b) take out a loan (c) pay a membership fee to a cooperative.

6. The Bell System did not want to install a phone system in the area because it was (a) difficult technologically (b) uneconomical (c) unnecessary.

7. The only real disadvantage for families with telephones is the (a) bills (b) loss of privacy (c) lost custom of letter writing.

8. It is clear that the telephone has not only improved business and saved lives in Squaw, Gap, but, more important, it has (a) allowed teenagers to have a better social life (b) provided housewives with an opportunity to chat with friends (c) ended the isolation that residents used to experience.

Paragraph Structure

Reorder the following sentences to form a unified, coherent paragraph. Write a sentence that can serve as a topic sentence for the reorganized paragraph. Then check your version with the original.

1. Soon the horizon was lit by the ominous glow that can mean only one thing out here—prairie fire.

2. Four years ago, a similar blaze roared across 3000 acres before couriers in cars could round up enough help.

3. Around midnight just a couple of weeks ago, lightning cracked into Milton Brunsvold's field.

4. In other times, people perished, unwarned of such fires or of flash floods.

5. Within minutes, 100 men, summoned by an impromptu telephone relay, were dashing the flames with wet gunnysacks.

6. The fire burned 160 acres.

VOCABULARY AND USAGE

Word Formation Table

Complete the following table by changing word endings or root forms to make new grammatical forms. Use your dictionary if necessary.

	NOUN	VERB	ADJECTIVE	ADVERB
1.	_____	diagnose	_____	_____
2.	_____	revolutionize	_____	xxx
3.	_____	xxx	hilarious	_____
4.	_____	perish	_____	_____
5.	_____	symbolize	_____	_____

Fill-Ins

Complete each of the sentences below using the words on the following list. You may need to use some words more than once. You may also find that some blanks can be completed correctly with more than one word. Add plural endings to nouns and change verb forms where necessary.

isolation	before	when	signal
revolutionize	symbolize	diagnose	die
perish	doubtful	decrease	probably
wane	until	inhabitant	surround
skeptical	ominous	similar	represent

1. _____ the telephone switching center was installed, it _____ the end of Squaw Gap's _____.
2. Not only has the telephone _____ people's lives, but it has _____ saved a few lives, too.
3. _____ the phones were actually working, the _____ of Squaw Gap were _____ they would ever have telephone service.
4. _____ telephone service arrived, neighbors lived in _____ and often they _____ in unreported fires or floods.
5. The Maciks' skepticism _____ and their excitement rose _____ they heard the first _____ from their phone.
6. With the phone, a veterinarian was able to _____ the symptoms of some sick cattle who would _____ have _____ otherwise.

DISCUSSION

1. What is the dominant impression of Squaw Gap before telephone service began?
2. By what rhetorical means does the author show the effects of phone service on the residents of the area?
3. This essay uses a cause and effect method of organization. Which paragraph (or paragraphs) states the *cause*, and which the *effects*?
4. Write a topic sentence to incorporate the details of paragraph 9.
5. What were some of the difficulties the residents of Squaw Gap had to put up with before the telephone came?
6. How do you feel about the telephone? What would you do without it? Would you like to get rid of it? (Note: According to the *Wall Street Journal*, there are 160 million telephones in the United States, which has a population of 220 million.)

SUGGESTIONS FOR WRITING

1. Using a cause and effect method of organization, describe the changes in your family (or perhaps in your town or city) resulting from some innovation or new technological device. If it is pertinent, you might include an explanation of how the device was acquired.
2. Malcolm's essay is intended to inform the reader that ordinary technological devices like the telephone should not be taken for granted, and his description implies what life without the telephone must be like. Explain, in a similar fashion, the changes— positive or negative—in your daily life that would result if you did not have one of the following: a car, a television, a stove, a refrigerator, electricity, running water.

The Plug-In Drug: TV and the American Family

MARIE WINN

Marie Winn was born in Czechoslovakia and educated at Radcliffe and Columbia. She is the author of ten books for parents and children, among them *The Playgroup Book, The Sick Book,* and *The Baby Reader.* She is also a frequent contributor to *The New York Times Magazine, The Village Voice,* and other publications. She lives in New York City with her husband, two children, and one small black and white television set, which is used only on special occasions.

1   A quarter of a century after the introduction of television into American society, a period that has seen the medium become so deeply ingrained in American life that in at least one state the television set has attained the rank of a legal necessity, safe from repossession in case of debt along with clothes, cooking utensils, and the like, television viewing has become an inevitable and ordinary part of daily life. Only in the early years of television did writers and commentators have sufficient perspective to separate the activity of watching television from the actual content it offers the viewer. In those early days writers frequently discussed the effects of television on family life. However, a curious myopia afflicted those early observers: almost without exception they regarded television as a favorable, beneficial, indeed, wondrous influence upon the family.

2   "Television is going to be a real asset in every home where there are children," predicts a writer in 1949.

3   "Television will take over your way of living and change your children's habits, but this change can be a wonderful improvement," claims another commentator.

4   "No survey's needed, of course, to establish that television has brought the family together in one room," writes *The New York Times* television critic in 1949.

5   Each of the early articles about television is invariably accompanied by a photograph or illustration showing a family cozily sitting together before the television set, Sis on Mom's lap, Buddy perched on the arm of Dad's chair, Dad with his arm around Mom's shoulder. Who could have guessed that twenty or

so years later Mom would be watching a drama in the kitchen, the kids would be looking at cartoons in their room, while Dad would be taking in the ball game in the living room?

6   Of course television sets were enormously expensive in those early days. The idea that by 1975 more than 60 percent of American families would own two or more sets was preposterous. The splintering of the multiple-set family was something the early writers could not foresee. Nor did anyone imagine the number of hours children would eventually devote to television, the common use of television by parents as a child pacifier, the changes television would effect upon child-rearing methods, the increasing domination of family schedules by children's viewing requirements—in short, the *power* of the new medium to dominate family life.

7   After the first years, as children's consumption of the new medium increased, together with parental concern about the possible effects of so much television viewing, a steady refrain helped to soothe and reassure anxious parents. "Television always enters a pattern of influences that already exist: the home, the peer group, the school, the church and culture generally," write the authors of an early and influential study of television's effects on children. In other words, if the child's home life is all right, parents need not worry about the effects of all that television watching.

8   But television does not merely influence the child; it deeply influences that "pattern of influences" that is meant to ameliorate its effects. Home and family life has changed in important ways since the advent of television. The peer group has become television-oriented, and much of the time children spend together is occupied by television viewing. Culture generally has been transformed by television. Therefore it is improper to assign to television the subsidiary role its many apologists (too often members of the television industry) insist it plays. Television is not merely one of a number of important influences upon today's child. Through the changes it has made in family life, television emerges as *the* important influence in children's lives today.

9   Television's contribution to family life has been an equivocal one. For while it has, indeed, kept the members of the family from dispersing, it has not served to bring them *together*. By its domination of the time families spend together, it destroys the special quality that distinguishes one family from another, a quality that depends to a great extent on what a family *does*, what special rituals, games, recurrent jokes, familiar songs, and shared activities it accumulates.

10   "Like the sorcerer of old," writs Urie Bronfenbrenner, "the television set casts its magic spell, freezing speech and action, turning the living into silent statues so long as the enchantment lasts. The primary danger of the television screen lies not so much in the behavior it produces—although there is danger there—as in the behavior it prevents: the talks, the games, the family festivities and arguments through which much of the child's learning takes place and through which his character is formed. Turning on the television set can turn off the process that transforms children into people."

11   Yet parents have accepted a television-dominated family life so completely that they cannot see how the medium is involved in whatever problems they might be having. A first-grade teacher reports:

12   "I have one child in the group who's an only child. I wanted to find out more about her family life because this little girl was quite isolated from the group, didn't make friends, so I talked to her mother. Well, they don't have time to do anything in the evening, the mother said. The parents come home after picking up the child at the baby-sitter's. Then the mother fixes dinner while the child watches TV. Then they have dinner and the child goes to bed. I said to this mother, 'Well, couldn't she help you fix dinner? That would be a nice time for the two of you to talk,' and the mother said, 'Oh, but I'd hate to have her miss "Zoom." It's such a good program!' "

13   Even when families make efforts to control television, too often its very presence counterbalances the positive features of family life. A writer and mother of two boys aged 3 and 7 described her family's television schedule in an article in *The New York Times:*

> We were in the midst of a full-scale War. Every day was a new battle and every program was a major skirmish. We agreed it was a bad scene all around and were ready to enter diplomatic negotiations. . . . In principle we have agreed on 2 ½ hours of TV a day, "Sesame Street," "Electric Company" (with dinner gobbled up in between) and two half-hour shows between 7 and 8:30 which enables the grown-ups to eat in peace and prevents the two boys from destroying one another. Their pre-bedtime choice is dreadful, because, as Josh recently admitted, "There's nothing much on I really like." So . . . it's "What's My Line" or "To Tell the Truth." . . . Clearly there is a need for first-rate children's shows at this time. . . .

14   Consider the "family life" described here: Presumably the father comes home from work during the "Sesame Street"—"Electric Company" stint. The children are either watching television, gobbling their dinner, or both. While the parents eat their dinner in peaceful privacy, the children watch another hour of television. Then there is only a half-hour left before bedtime, just enough time for baths, getting pajamas on, brushing teeth, and so on. The children's evening is regimented with an almost military precision. They watch their favorite programs, and when there is "nothing much on I really like," they watch whatever else is on—because *watching* is the important thing. Their mother does not see anything amiss with watching programs just for the sake of watching; she only wishes there were some first-rate children's shows on at those times.

15   Without conjuring up memories of the Victorian era with family games and long, leisurely meals, and large families, the question arises: isn't there a better family life available than this dismal, mechanized arrangement of children watching television for however long is allowed them, evening after evening?

16   Of course, families today still do *special* things together at times: go camping in the summer, go to the zoo on a nice Sunday, take various trips

and expeditions. But their *ordinary* daily life together is diminished—that sitting around at the dinner table, that spontaneous taking up of an activity, those little games invented by children on the spur of the moment when there is nothing else to do, the scribbling, the chatting, and even the quarreling, all the things that form the fabric of a family, that define a childhood. Instead, the children have their regular schedule of television programs and bedtime, and the parents have their peaceful dinner together.

17   The author of the article in the *Times* notes that "keeping a family sane means mediating between the needs of both children and adults." But surely the needs of adults are being better met than the needs of the children, who are effectively shunted away and rendered untroublesome, while their parents enjoy a life as undemanding as that of any childless couple. In reality, it is those very demands that young children make upon a family that lead to growth, and it is the way parents accede to those demands that builds the relationships upon which the future of the family depends. If the family does not accumulate its backlog of shared experiences, shared *everyday* experiences that occur and recur and change and develop, then it is not likely to survive as anything other than a caretaking institution.

Family Rituals

18   Ritual is defined by sociologists as "that part of family life that the family likes about itself, is proud of and wants formally to continue." Another text notes that "the development of a ritual by a family is an index of the common interest of its members in the family as a group."

19   What has happened to family rituals, those regular, dependable, recurrent happenings that gave members of a family a feeling of *belonging* to a home rather than living in it merely for the sake of convenience, those experiences that act as the adhesive of family unity far more than any material advantages?

20   Mealtime rituals, going-to-bed rituals, illness rituals, holiday rituals, how many of these have survived the inroads of the television set?

21   A young woman who grew up near Chicago reminisces about her childhood and gives an idea of the effects of television upon family rituals:

22   "As a child I had millions of relatives around—my parents both come from relatively large families. My father had nine brothers and sisters. And so every holiday there was this great swoop-down of aunts, uncles, and millions of cousins. I just remember how wonderful it used to be. These thousands of cousins would come and everyone would play and ultimately, after dinner, all the women would be in the front of the house, drinking coffee and talking, all the men would be in the back of the house, drinking and smoking, and all the kids would be all over the place, playing hide and seek. Christmas time was particularly nice because everyone always brought all their toys and games. Our house had a couple of rooms with go-through closets, so there were always kids running in a great circle route. I remember it was just wonderful.

23   "And then all of a sudden one year I remember becoming suddenly aware of how different everything had become. The kids were no longer playing Monopoly or Clue or the other games we used to play together. It was because we had a television set which had been turned on for a football game. All of that socializing that had gone on previously had ended. Now everyone was sitting in front of the television set, on a holiday, at a family party! I remember being stunned by how awful that was. Somehow the television had become more attractive."

24   As families have come to spend more and more of their time together engaged in the single activity of television watching, those rituals and pastimes that once gave family life its special quality have become more and more uncommon. Not since prehistoric times when cave families hunted, gathered, ate, and slept, with little time remaining to accumulate a culture of any significance, have families been reduced to such a sameness.

Real People

25   It is not only the activities that a family might engage in together that are diminished by the powerful presence of television in the home. The relationships of the family members to each other are also affected, in both obvious and subtle ways. The hours that the young child spends in a one-way relationship with television people, an involvement that allows for no communication or interaction, surely affect his relationships with real-life people.

26   Studies show the importance of eye-to-eye contact, for instance, in real-life relationships, and indicate that the nature of a person's eye-contact patterns, whether he looks another squarely in the eye or looks to the side or shifts his gaze from side to side, may play a significant role in his success or failure in human relationships. But no eye contact is possible in the child-television relationship, although in certain children's programs people purport to speak directly to the child and the camera fosters this illusion by focusing directly upon the person being filmed. (Mr. Rogers is an example, telling the child "I like you, you're special," etc.) How might such a distortion of real-life relationships affect a child's development of trust, of openness, of an ability to relate well to other *real* people?

27   Bruno Bettelheim writes:

> Children who have been taught, or conditioned, to listen passively most of the day to the warm verbal communications coming from the TV screen, to the deep emotional appeal of the so-called TV personality, are often unable to respond to real persons because they arouse so much less feeling than the skilled actor. Worse, they lose the ability to learn from reality because life experiences are much more complicated than the ones they see on the screen. . . .

28   A teacher makes a similar observation about her personal viewing experiences:

29   "I have trouble mobilizing myself and dealing with real people after watching a few hours of television. It's just hard to make that transition from watching television to a real relationship. I suppose it's because there was no effort necessary while I was watching, and dealing with real people always requires a bit of effort. Imagine, then, how much harder it might be to do the same thing for a small child, particularly one who watches a lot of television every day."

30   But more obviously damaging to family relationships is the elimination of opportunities to talk, and perhaps more important, to argue, to air grievances, between parents and children and brothers and sisters. Families frequently use television to avoid confronting their problems, problems that will not go away if they are ignored but will only fester and become less easily resolvable as time goes on.

31   A mother reports:

32   "I find myself, with three children, wanting to turn on the TV set when they're fighting. I really have to struggle not to do it because I feel that's telling them this is the solution to the quarrel—but it's so tempting that I often do it."

33   A family therapist discusses the use of television as an avoidance mechanism:

34   "In a family I know the father comes home from work and turns on the television set. The children come and watch with him and the wife serves them their meal in front of the set. He then goes and takes a shower, or works on the car or something. She then goes and has her own dinner in front of the television set. It's a symptom of a deeper-rooted problem, sure. But it would help them all to get rid of the set. It would be far easier to work on what the symptom really means without the television. The television simply encourages a double avoidance of each other. They'd find out more quickly what was going on if they weren't able to hide behind the TV. Things wouldn't necessarily be better, of course, but they wouldn't be anesthetized."

35   The decreased opportunities for simple conversation between parents and children in the television-centered home may help explain an observation made by an emergency room nurse at a Boston hospital. She reports that parents just seem to sit there these days when they come in with a sick or seriously injured child, although talking to the child would distract and comfort him. "They don't seem to know *how* to talk to their own children at any length," the nurse observes. Similarly, a television critic writes in *The New York Times*: "I had just a day ago taken my son to the emergency ward of a hospital for stitches above his left eye, and the occasion seemed no more real to me than Maalot or 54th Street, south-central Los Angeles. There was distance and numbness and an inability to turn off the total institution. I didn't behave at all; I just watched. . . ."

36   A number of research studies substantiate the assumption that television interferes with family activities and the formation of family relationships. One survey shows that 78 percent of the respondents indicated no conversa-

tion taking place during viewing except at specified times such as commercials. The study notes: "The television atmosphere in most households is one of quiet absorption on the part of family members who are present. The nature of the family social life during a program could be described as 'parallel' rather than interactive, and the set does seem to dominate family life when it is on." Thirty-six percent of the respondents in another study indicated that television viewing was the only family activity participated in during the week.

37   In a summary of research findings on television's effect on family interactions James Gabardino states: "The early findings suggest that television had a disruptive effect upon interaction and thus presumably human development. . . . It is not unreasonable to ask: 'Is the fact that the average American family during the 1950's came to include two parents, two children and a television set somehow related to the psychosocial characteristics of the young adults of the 1970's?' "

Undermining the Family

38   In its effect on family relationships, in its facilitation of parental withdrawal from an active role in the socialization of their children, and in its replacement of family rituals and special events, television has played an important role in the disintegration of the American family. But of course it has not been the only contributing factor, perhaps not even the most important one. The steadily rising divorce rate, the increase in the number of working mothers, the decline of the extended family, the breakdown of neighborhoods and communities, the growing isolation of the nuclear family—all have seriously affected the family.

39   As Urie Bronfenbrenner suggests, the sources of family breakdown do not come from the family itself, but from the circumstances in which the family finds itself and the way of life imposed upon it by those circumstances. "When those circumstances and the way of life they generate undermine relationships of trust and emotional security between family members, when they make it difficult for parents to care for, educate and enjoy their children, when there is no support or recognition from the outside world for one's role as a parent and when time spent with one's family means frustration of career, personal fulfillment and peace of mind, then the development of the child is adversely affected," he writes.

40   But while the roots of alienation go deep into the fabric of American social history, television's presence in the home fertilizes them, encourages their wild and unchecked growth. Perhaps it is true that America's commitment to the television experience masks a spiritual vacuum, an empty and barren way of life, a desert of materialism. But it is television's dominant role in the family that anesthetizes the family into accepting its unhappy state and prevents it from struggling to better its condition, to improve its relationships, and to regain some of the richness it once possessed.

41   Others have noted the role of mass media in perpetuating an unsatisfactory *status quo*. Leisure-time activity, writes Irving Howe, "must provide relief from work monotony without making the return to work too unbearable; it must provide amusement without insight and pleasure without disturbance—as distinct from art which gives pleasure through disturbance. Mass culture is thus oriented towards a central aspect of industrial society: the depersonalization of the individual." Similarly, Jacques Ellul rejects the idea that television is a legitimate means of educating the citizen: "Education . . . takes place only incidentally. The clouding of his consciousness is paramount. . . ."

42   And so the American family muddles on, dimly aware that something is amiss but distracted from an understanding of its plight by an endless stream of television images. As family ties grow weaker and vaguer, as children's lives become more separate from their parents', as parents' educational role in their children's lives is taken over by television and schools, family life becomes increasingly more unsatisfying for both parents and children. All that seems to be left is Love, an abstraction that family members *know* is necessary but find great difficulty giving each other because the traditional opportunities for expressing love within the family have been reduced or destroyed.

43   For contemporary parents, love toward each other has increasingly come to mean successful sexual relations, as witnessed by the proliferation of sex manuals and sex therapists. The opportunities for manifesting other forms of love through mutual support, understanding, nurturing, even, to use an unpopular word, *serving* each other, are less and less available as mothers and fathers seek their independent destinies outside the family.

44   As for love of children, this love is increasingly expressed through supplying material comforts, amusements, and educational opportunities. Parents show their love for their children by sending them to good schools and camps, by providing them with good food and good doctors, by buying them toys, books, games, and a television set of their very own. Parents will even go further and express their love by attending PTA meetings to improve their children's schools, or by joining groups that are acting to improve the quality of their children's television programs.

45   But this is love at a remove, and is rarely understood by children. The more direct forms of parental love require time and patience, steady, dependable, ungrudgingly given time actually spent *with* a child, reading to him, comforting him, playing, joking, and working with him. But even if a parent were eager and willing to demonstrate that sort of direct love to his children today, the opportunities are diminished. What with school and Little League and piano lessons and, of course, the inevitable television programs, a day seems to offer just enough time for a good-night kiss.

Exercises

COMPREHENSION

Organization and Development

Complete the following outline. In your own words, write a sentence stating the author's thesis in the space provided. Then find the main divisions in the essay and fill in the remaining spaces. Note the paragraphs for each section.

Thesis statement: _____

_____

_____

    I. _____ [   ]

   II. _____ [   ]

  III. _____ [   ]

  IV. _____ [   ]

   V. _____ [   ]

  VI. _____ [   ]

Content

Choose the answer that correctly completes each statement.

1. Almost without exception, early observers of television predicted that its effect on the American family would be (a) disastrous (b) favorable, beneficial, indeed wondrous (c) insignificant and short-lived.
2. By 1975, the number of American families owning two or more television sets had risen to over (a) 94% (b) 60% (c) 27%.
3. According to this essay, television is (a) only one of a number of important influences on today's children (b) the least important influence on children's lives (c) the most important influence on children's lives today.
4. The author believes that television destroys (a) the family's control of the child's moral development (b) parental authority in matters of discipline (c) the special quality that distinguishes one family from another.
5. Family rituals, those special patterns of behavior at meals, bedtime, holidays, are (a) less important than the intellectual stimulation of television (b) becoming more and more uncommon in America because of television (c) relatively unimportant features of any culture.
6. Some critics believe that television viewing distorts the child's relationships with real-life people because (a) real people arouse less feeling and are more complicated than people on television (b) the average child spends more time watching television than being with real people (c) all Americans have begun to behave like television actors.
7. Television helps to damage family relationships because (a) constant viewing cuts down on the opportunity for families to talk, even to argue, together (b) television shows family situations that may be happier than those attainable by real families (c) commercials make children ask for things their parents cannot afford.
8. The essay concludes by arguing that television is just one of many factors that interfere with (a) the parents' obligation to be involved in their children's education (b) important after-school activities, such as piano lessons and Little League (c) real, direct forms of parental love, which demand actual time spent with children.

Paragraph Structure

Reorder the following sentences to form a unified, coherent paragraph. Identify one sentence as the topic sentence. Then check your version with the original.

1. Television is not merely one of a number of important influences on today's child.
2. The peer group has become television-oriented, and much of the time children spend together is occupied by television viewing.
3. But television does not merely influence the child; it deeply influences that "pattern of influences" that is meant to ameliorate its effects.
4. Therefore it is improper to assign to television the subsidiary role its many apologists (too often members of the television industry) insist it plays.
5. Through the changes it has made in family life, television emerges as *the* important influence in children's lives today.
6. Home and family life have changed in important ways since the advent of television.
7. Culture generally has been transformed by television.

VOCABULARY AND USAGE

Word Formation Table

Complete the following table by changing word endings or root forms to make new grammatical forms. Use your dictionary if necessary.

	NOUN	VERB	ADJECTIVE	ADVERB
1.	apologists	_____	_____	_____
2.	_____	_____	recurrent	_____
3.	alienation	_____	_____	XXX
4.	_____	anesthetize	_____	_____
5.	culture	_____	_____	_____

Fill-Ins

Complete each of the sentences below using the words on the following list. You may need to use some words more than once. You may also find that some blanks can be completed correctly with more than one word. Add plural endings to nouns and change verb forms where necessary.

beneficial	plight	perpetuate	disintegration
culture	decrease	substantiate	grievance
isolated	recurrent	complaint	although
diminish	alienated	dismal	nevertheless
sufficient	depressing	demonstrate	anger

1. _____ in the early days critics believed that television would have a _____ effect on family life, the _____ state of the family today does not _____ their predictions.
2. In the television-centered home, there are _____ opportunities for conversation between family members, who often cannot even express _____ to each other.
3. Ironically, television viewing may keep the family "together"; _____ the members are still _____ from each other.

4. Family rituals are _____ activities that _____ a family's sense of its own unity.

5. One of this essay's major _____ is that American _____ in general has been transformed by television; _____, the essay does not offer _____ evidence to _____ this claim.

6. Is television really the cause of the American family's _____, or is it another effect of the increasing _____ of our _____?

DISCUSSION

1. Which of the following introductory tags gives you the most confidence in the reliability of any evidence that might follow? Which the least? Rank all the others in between and explain your decisions.

   (a) a young woman who grew up near Chicago . . .

   (b) a mother reports . . .

   (c) the New York *Times* television critic . . .

   (d) Bruno Bettelheim writes . . .

   (e) one survey shows . . .

   (f) a teacher makes a similar observation . . .

   (g) a family therapist says . . .

   (h) a writer and a mother of two boys . . .

2. With what specific evidence does Winn answer these questions (paragraphs 19–20): "What has happened to family rituals . . . ?" ". . . how many of these have survived the inroads of the television set?" Does the evidence seem adequate to support her conclusion (paragraph 24)? If not, what kind of support do you think should have been furnished?

3. Winn tries to establish that it is the act of viewing itself, rather than program content, which ought to concern parents. What are the major negative effects of simply watching television, according to Winn?

4. What kinds of television programs are usually criticized by concerned parents, psychologists, or teachers? After reading this essay, how do you feel about this conventional criticism (of violence on television, for example)?

5. Discuss family rituals as you understand them. Winn never suggests that television viewing itself might be a kind of family ritual. Is it? If so, how does it differ from those you know of, or those rituals that the author sees in a positive light?

SUGGESTIONS FOR WRITING

1. Describe your family's patterns of television viewing.

2. Describe a particular family ritual, showing its relationship to your family's special character or sense of itself.

3. Winn says that "culture generally has been transformed by television." Using this as a thesis statement, discuss several aspects of our culture beyond the family circle and show how they have been "transformed" by television.

4. Using Winn's method of establishing a cause-effect relationship, *refute* her arguments, establishing some favorable, beneficial, positive effects of television on the family.

5. Winn does not discuss the actual content of television programming, but only the effects of watching on the viewer. Discuss the effects of certain *kinds* of television shows on children. Be sure that you establish a logical cause-effect relationship insofar as it is possible.

The Physical Miseducation of a Former Fat Boy

LOUIE CREW

Louie Crew was born in Anniston, Alabama, in 1936, and holds degrees in English and Rhetoric from Baylor University, Auburn University, and the University of Alabama. He has also been a Wurlitzer Foundation fellow. His career as an educator has included teaching positions at the University of Alabama and private schools in Georgia, Delaware, and London, England. He has also served as director of the academic program of the Experiment in International Living in England, and has written on subjects ranging from Black English to the novels of Charles Dickens. He is currently associate professor of English at Ft. Valley State College, Ft. Valley, Georgia and is, as far as we know, still formerly fat.

1   When I was six, a next-door neighbor gave me my first candy bar, and I fattened immediately in a home where food was love. It is hardly surprising that when I first entered physical education courses in the eighth grade my coaches were markedly unimpressed or that thereafter I compensated by working harder at books, where I was more successful. Although I did learn to take jokes about my size and experienced the "bigness" of being able to laugh at myself (the standard fat man's reward), at thirty-five I am furious to recall how readily and completely my instructors defaulted in their responsibilities to me. Some remedies I have learned in my thirties persuade me that it is not inevitable that the system will continue to fail other fat boys.

2   My personal remedies for physical ineptitude have a firm base in ideas. Four years ago I weighed 265 pounds. Only my analyst needs to know how much I consequently hated myself. In six months I took off 105 pounds and initiated a regular jogging and exercising schedule that has gradually, very gradually, led to increased self-confidence. Yet my physical education teachers in secondary school and college never showed the least interest in my physical problems, never sat down and initiated the simplest diagnosis of my physical needs, never tempted me into the personal discoveries that I had to wait more than a decade to make for myself.

3   Instead, my physical educators offered two alternatives. Either I could enter the fierce competitive sports that predominate in our culture and therein make and accept the highest mark I could achieve; or I could opt for the less-competitive intramurals, modeled after the big boys' games, and

accept my role as a physically incompetent human being, sitting on the sidelines to cheer for a chosen team of professionals. These limited alternatives were repeatedly justified as teaching me how it is out in the "real world," in "the game of life," allegedly divided between the participators and the watchers.

4   Now, as I jog in midwinter dawn, all muffled with socks over my hands, making tracks with the rabbits in Carolina dew, I am not competing with anyone, unless I whimsically imagine Father Time having to add another leaf to my book. I am celebrating me, *this* morning, *this* pair of worn-out tennis shoes, the tingle in my cheeks, the space being cleared in my stomach for my simple breakfast when I get back. . . . I was very articulate at fourteen—fat but articulate—and I believe that a sympathetic, interested coach could have shared this type of insight, this type of reality, with me, and perhaps thereby he could have teased me into the discoveries I had to make many years later. But the coach would have had to love kids like me more than he loved winning if he had hoped to participate in my physical education. I had no such coach.

5   Perhaps an athletic friend could have shared insights into my physical needs and suggested alternative fulfillments. I certainly had many athletic friends, because I sought avidly to compensate for my physical failures by liking and being liked by athletes. Unfortunately, these friends were all schooled in the competitive rules of keeping trade secrets and of enjoying and hoarding compliments. Human sharing had not been a part of their education.

6   I recall how at thirty-two I tentatively jogged around a block for the first time, how the fierce hurt in my gut was less bothersome than the fear that I would not make it. I had to learn to love myself for making it, and for making it again the next day, rather than to participate in my hecklers' mockery of the sweating fat man. I remember jogging no faster at sixteen and being laughed at by the coach, who kept me that much longer a prisoner in my role as the jovial class clown.

7   I became a water boy and trainer, winning the school's award for "most unselfish service." Is not the role familiar? I even served two summers as a camp counselor. I could not walk to first base without puffing, but I could call a kid "out" with a tongue of forked lightning. I had been taught well.

8   My physical educators were signally unimaginative. We played only the few sports that had always been played in our area. Further, they maintained a rigid separation between "sports" and "play." Football, baseball, basketball, and track were "sports." Fishing, hiking, boating, and jogging were "play." Golf was "play" until you had a team that won five trophies; then you developed the cool rhetoric of "sport."

9   I remember going on a boy-scout trip in the Talledega National Forest in Alabama for a week. My anticipation was immense. I liked the woods. I liked walking. I liked the sky, trees, rocks, ferns. . . . We were to walk only about five or ten miles a day through a wilderness, camping out around an authentic chuck wagon that would move in advance during the day. The trip

itself, however, was a nightmare for me. The coach/scoutmaster led at a frantic pace, because he wanted to get each lap done with and, as he said, he wanted "to make men" out of us. The major activity was to race ahead so as to enjoy "breathers" while waiting to heckle us slower folk when we caught up. When we came to a clearing overlooking the vast chasms of blue-green shimmer, the biggest breach of the unwritten code would have been to stop to look for ten minutes. The trip was to get somewhere (nobody quite knew why or where), not to be somewhere.

10   For a long time I treasured illusions that my experiences with physical miseducation resulted merely from my provincial isolation, that real professionals elsewhere had surely identified and rectified these ills. But as I have moved from south to west to east, even to England, I have found very few real physical educators. Almost no one is interested in educating individuals to discover their own physical resources and to integrate them with all the other personal experiences. Almost everyone is interested in developing ever-better professionals to provide vicarious entertainment for a physically inept society.

11   Most of the professional literature describes the training of professional sportsmen and evaluates the machinery developed to serve this training. My favorite example of this perverse pedantry is my friend's M.A. thesis studying the effects of various calisthenics on sweat samples. One is scared to imagine what secretions he will measure for his doctoral dissertation. Yet it is fashionable to mock medieval scholars for disputing how many angels could stand on the head of a pin!

12   Once while working out in a gymnasium at the University of Alabama, I jestingly asked some professionals how many pounds I would have to be able to lift to be a man. To my surprise, I received specific answers: one said 280 pounds (he could lift 285); another said "one's own weight"; another. . . . But I was born a man! It is surely perverse for a man to trap himself by confusing *being* with *becoming*.

Definition

Definition—telling what a word, phrase, or term means—also implies limitation, the setting of boundaries, and the explanation of the essential nature of a thing. All these senses converge in the problem of definition that faces the writer. A writer must define or limit adequately words that may have several meanings, especially key terms in an essay, if he is to communicate clearly. In fact, defining controversial or abstract language may itself be the subject of an expository piece.

There are three main methods of definition. The first is by synonym, presenting another word that means the same as the one in question ("a marguerite is a daisy"). The second is the formal definition, which requires that the word being defined be placed in a class ("a marguerite is a common flowering plant"), and then carefully distinguished from all other members of that class ("a marguerite is a common flowering plant, *Chrysanthemum frutescens*, whose blossoms have white or pale yellow petals around a yellow center"). The addition of distinguishing characteristics is vital to the formal definition: there are thousands of "common flowering plants"; only one, the marguerite, is distinguished by these particular details.

The third method, the one we are mainly concerned with here, is the extended definition, which is normally used for clarification—to ensure that reader and writer are on the same track. This may involve the careful limiting, in a paragraph or two within an essay, of an abstraction or a key term—as we see in Ciardi's definition of Thoreau's idea of a "high" or Davis's definition of an "Indian equivalent." Further, an entire essay—for example, "Is Everybody Happy?"—may address itself to the definition of a single important, controversial, or abstract term. Abstractions in particular—words like "truth" or "injustice" or "happiness"—need to be defined because they allow for so many possible interpretations that ultimate confusion results if reader and writer do not share the same idea. And, as Davis's essay shows, even a familiar word like "overpopulation" may be reinterpreted by a writer without baffling the reader—but only if the term has been carefully redefined before it is used in an unconventional manner.

Several methods are especially helpful in developing an extended definition. First, the writer may supply a historical background or other factual information about the term he is defining, as Ciardi does in his opening paragraphs, and as Davis does in a more limited way with his descriptions of the daily activities of Indian villagers and American suburbanites. A second method, used extensively in "Is Everybody Happy?" is negation—telling what a word does *not* mean, what a thing is *not*. Finally, the specific qualities or characteristics of the subject may be enumerated, almost in the fashion of description or illustration, as Ciardi does in paragraph 7, and as Davis does in paragraphs 4 and 5.

But any or all of the basic methods of expository development may be brought to bear in an extended definition, particularly when that definition constitutes the whole, or nearly the whole, of the essay. Thus, Ciardi depends heavily on illustration and example, but he also employs analysis, formal definition, and description in support of his major purpose. Davis uses contrast, example, factual detail, process, and analysis, among other techniques—all within the scope of an essay that, with its extended definition, is designed to persuade the reader to adopt a new point of view.

Is Everybody Happy?

JOHN CIARDI

John Ciardi was born in Boston in 1916, and was educated at Bates, Tufts, and the University of Michigan. He taught English at Harvard and Rutgers, and was for many years the poetry editor of *The Saturday Review*. He has received numerous awards and prizes for his own volumes of poetry, which include *Homeward to America, Other Skies,* and *I Met a Man* (a book of nonsense verses for children). He has also translated *The Inferno of Dante* and written many essays, some of which are collected in *Manner of Speaking,* from which the following essay was selected.

While Ciardi is popularly known as a master of the short essay and the well-turned phrase, his best-known work is probably *How Does a Poem Mean?*—a classic text on appreciating poetry—and Ciardi sees himself as principally a poet and serious critic of poetry whose avowed aim is to raise the taste of his audience to the heights of good poetry. This penchant for elevating the public taste and sensitivity can be seen in the criticism of certain American values that forms an essential part of the following essay's definition.

1   The right to pursue happiness is issued to Americans with their birth certificates, but no one seems quite sure which way it ran. It may be we are issued a hunting license but offered no game. Jonathan Swift seemed to think so when he attacked the idea of happiness as "the possession of being well-deceived," the felicity of being "a fool among knaves." For Swift saw society as Vanity Fair, the land of false goals.

2   It is, of course, un-American to think in terms of fools and knaves. We do, however, seem to be dedicated to the idea of buying our way to happiness. We shall all have made it to Heaven when we possess enough.

3   And at the same time the forces of American commercialism are hugely dedicated to making us deliberately unhappy. Advertising is one of our major industries, and advertising exists not to satisfy desires but to create them— and to create them faster than any man's budget can satisfy them. For that matter, our whole economy is based on a dedicated insatiability. We are taught that to possess is to be happy, and then we are made to want. We are even told it is our duty to want. It was only a few years ago, to cite a single example, that car dealers across the country were flying banners that read "You Auto Buy Now." They were calling upon Americans, as an act approaching patriotism, to buy at once, with money they did not have, au-

tomobiles they did not really need, and which they would be required to grow tired of by the time the next year's models were released.

4   Or look at any of the women's magazines. There, as Bernard DeVoto once pointed out, advertising begins as poetry in the front pages and ends as pharmacopoeia and therapy in the back pages. The poetry of the front matter is the dream of perfect beauty. This is the baby skin that must be hers. These, the flawless teeth. This, the perfumed breath she must exhale. This, the sixteen-year-old figure she must display at forty, at fifty, at sixty, and forever.

5   Once past the vaguely uplifting fiction and feature articles, the reader finds the other face of the dream in the back matter. This is the harness into which Mother must strap herself in order to display that perfect figure. These, the chin straps she must sleep in. This is the salve that restores all, this is her laxative, these are the tablets that melt away fat, these are the hormones of perpetual youth, these are the stockings that hide varicose veins.

6   Obviously no half-sane person can be completely persuaded either by such poetry or by such pharmacopoeia and orthopedics. Yet someone is obviously trying to buy the dream as offered and spending billions every year in the attempt. Clearly the happiness market is not running out of customers, but what are we trying to buy?

7   The idea "happiness," to be sure, will not sit still for easy definition: the best one can do is to try to set some extremes to the idea and then work in toward the middle. To think of happiness as acquisitive and competitive will do to set the materialistic extreme. To think of it as the idea one senses in, say, a holy man of India will do to set the spiritual extreme. That holy man's ideal of happiness is in needing nothing from outside himself. In wanting nothing, he lacks nothing. He sits immobile, rapt in contemplation, free even of his own body. Or nearly free of it. If devout admirers bring him food he eats it; if not, he starves indifferently. Why be concerned? What is physical is an illusion to him. Contemplation is his joy and he achieves it through a fantastically demanding discipline, the accomplishment of which is itself a joy within him.

8   Is he a happy man? Perhaps his happiness is only another sort of illusion. But who can take it from him? And who will dare say it is more illusory than happiness on the installment plan?

9   But, perhaps because I am Western, I doubt such catatonic happiness, as I doubt the dreams of the happiness market. What is certain is that his way of happiness would be torture to almost any Western man. Yet these extremes will still serve to frame the area within which all of us must find some sort of balance. Thoreau—a creature of both Eastern and Western thought—had his own firm sense of that balance. His aim was to save on the low levels in order to spend on the high.

10   Possession for its own sake or in competition with the rest of the neighborhood would have been Thoreau's idea of the low levels. The active discipline of heightening one's perception of what is enduring in nature would have been his idea of the high. What he saved from the low was time and effort he could spend on the high. Thoreau certainly disapproved of starvation, but he

would put into feeding himself only as much effort as would keep him functioning for more important efforts.

11   Effort is the gist of it. There is no happiness except as we take on life-engaging difficulties. Short of the impossible, as Yeats put it, the satisfactions we get from a lifetime depend on how high we choose our difficulties. Robert Frost was thinking in something like the same terms when he spoke of "the pleasure of taking pains." The mortal flaw in the advertised version of happiness is in the fact that it purports to be effortless.

12   We demand difficulty even in our games. We demand it because without difficulty there can be no game. A game is a way of making something hard for the fun of it. The rules of the game are an arbitrary imposition of difficulty. When the spoilsport ruins the fun, he always does so by refusing to play by the rules. It is easier to win at chess if you are free, at your pleasure, to change the wholly arbitrary rules, but the fun is in winning within the rules. No difficulty, no fun.

13   The buyers and sellers at the happiness market seem too often to have lost their sense of the pleasure of difficulty. Heaven knows what they are playing, but it seems a dull game. The Indian holy man seems dull to us, I suppose, because he seems to be refusing to play anything at all. The Western weakness may be in the illusion that happiness can be bought. Perhaps the Eastern weakness is in the idea that there is such a thing as perfect (and therefore static) happiness.

14   Happiness is never more than partial. There are no pure states of mankind. Whatever else happiness may be, it is neither in having nor in being, but in becoming. What the Founding Fathers declared for us as an inherent right, we should do well to remember, was not happiness but the *pursuit* of happiness. What they might have underlined, could they have foreseen the happiness market, is the cardinal fact that happiness is in the pursuit itself, in the meaningful pursuit of what is life-engaging and life-revealing, which is to say, in the idea of *becoming*. A nation is not measured by what it possesses or wants to possess, but by what it wants to become.

15   By all means let the happiness market sell us minor satisfactions and even minor follies so long as we keep them in scale and buy them out of spiritual change. I am no customer for either puritanism or asceticism. But drop any real spiritual capital at those bazaars, and what you come home to will be your own poorhouse.

Exercises

COMPREHENSION

Organization and Development

Complete the following outline. Find the author's statement of purpose and thesis statement and write them in the spaces provided. Then find the main divisions in the essay and fill in the remaining spaces. Note the paragraphs for each section.

Statement of purpose: _____
_____
_____

Thesis statement: _____
_____
_____

    I.   _____ [   ]
    II. _____ [   ]
        A. _____ [   ]
        B. _____ [   ]
    III. _____ [   ]
    Conclusion: _____ [   ]

Content

Choose the answer that correctly completes each statement.

1. According to Ciardi, advertising exists to (a) spur the economy (b) inform people of useful new products (c) create desires that can never be satisfied fully.
2. The main purpose of this essay is to (a) define happiness (b) criticize American materialism and commercialism (c) show admiration for the seductive appeal of the Indian holy man.
3. Ciardi's method of defining happiness is to (a) state specifically what makes him happy (b) show what happiness is not (c) examine the extremes of the concept in order to reach some middle ground of definition.
4. For Ciardi, the ideal lies in a balance between the Eastern and Western versions of happiness and is best illustrated by the life of (a) Swift (b) Thoreau (c) Gandhi.
5. The references to the images of flawless beauty offered in women's magazines and the image of the Indian holy man, immobile, rapt in contemplation, are both designed to illustrate (a) the impossibility of achieving either the Western or the Eastern extreme of happiness (b) Ciardi's sensitivity to the fundamental cultural differences that determine happiness (c) the flesh and the devil as symbols of opposing objects of bliss.
6. Ciardi says that one of the weaknesses in the Western version of happiness is in the (a) failure to work hard enough in the pursuit of happiness (b) illusion that happiness can be bought (c) sense that we have a legal right to happiness.
7. The major weakness in the Eastern vision of happiness lies in the idea that (a) happiness is a game (b) there is such a thing as perfect happiness (c) happiness cannot exist in the material world.
8. The main point to be made about happiness is that (a) there is no happiness without effort (b) happiness can be achieved only in dreams (c) there is no way to achieve happiness except by buying it.

Paragraph Structure

Reorder the following sentences to form a unified, coherent paragraph. Identify one sentence as the topic sentence. Then check your version with the original.

1. To think of happiness as acquisitive and competitive will do to set the materialistic extreme.
2. That holy man's ideal of happiness is in needing nothing from outside himself.
3. Why be concerned?
4. Or nearly free of it.

5. The idea "happiness," to be sure, will not sit still for easy definition: the best one can do is to try to set some extremes to the idea and then work in toward the middle.
6. What is physical is an illusion to him.
7. To think of it as the idea one senses in, say, a holy man of India will do to set the spiritual extreme.
8. Contemplation is his joy and he achieves it through a fantastically demanding discipline, the accomplishment of which is itself a joy within him.
9. In wanting nothing, he lacks nothing.
10. He sits immobile, rapt in contemplation, free even of his own body.
11. If devout admirers bring him food he eats it; if not, he starves indifferently.

VOCABULARY AND USAGE

Word Formation Table

Complete the following table by changing word endings or root forms to make new grammatical forms. Use your dictionary if necessary.

	NOUN	VERB	ADJECTIVE	ADVERB
1.	illusion	xxx	_____	_____
2.	_____	xxx	mortal	_____
3.	_____	perceive	_____	_____
4.	_____	_____	arbitrary	_____
5.	_____	define	_____	_____

Fill-Ins

Complete each of the sentences below using the words on the following list. You may need to use some words more than once. You may also find that some blanks can be completed correctly with more than one word. Add plural endings to nouns and change verb forms where necessary.

concept	difficulty	effort	happiness
idea	material	lack	create
definition	pursue	achieve	seek
advertising	dream	attain	desire
extreme	balance	illusion	spiritual

1. Ciardi seeks to define _____ by pointing out the _____ versions of the _____.
2. The Eastern _____ of _____ is _____, one in which the individual abandons all _____ for _____ objects.
3. Since the Eastern holy man _____ nothing, he _____ nothing.
4. Ciardi says it is a(n) _____ to think that _____ can be _____ in either the Eastern or the Western sense alone.
5. Thoreau exemplifies a _____ between the Eastern and Western _____, between the _____ and _____ _____ of happiness.
6. The most important thing to remember is that human beings _____ _____ and find more of pleasure if they _____ happiness than if they _____ it.

DISCUSSION

1. Where else in the essay does the author use images or references that are related to the reference to Vanity Fair in paragraph 1? What is the function of these repeated references?
2. What purpose is served by the references in paragraphs 4 and 5 to beauty aids and women's magazines? What is the relationship between these specific examples and the discussion of automobile advertising in paragraph 3?
3. Trace Ciardi's use of words or other references that relate to the general idea of *illusion*. Where do these references occur and what effect do they have on the argument? Do the same thing for words, phrases, or references having to do with the marketplace.
4. In paragraph 7, Ciardi presents a striking visual image of his impression of the spiritual conception of happiness. Does the essay provide a similarly striking image of the material version of happiness? If so, what is it?
5. What does Ciardi mean by the term "life-engaging difficulties" in paragraph 11? Can you provide some concrete examples from your own experience?
6. Ciardi's accusation that Americans are dedicated to the idea of buying happiness is a common one. Give reasons why you think the criticism is or is not fair. Cite if you can specific illustrations that support another vision of the American philosophy of happiness.

SUGGESTIONS FOR WRITING

1. Write your own personal, extended definition of happiness.
2. Following Ciardi's example, write an extended definition of some abstract term (discipline, success, or devotion, for example) by first looking at and defining its extremes and then seeking a middle ground of definition.
3. Discuss those aspects of our culture that seem most to exemplify the Western extreme of happiness; compare them with those aspects of the society that seem most to approximate Thoreau's sense of balance.
4. Describe as specifically as you can the life of someone who has struck the balance of which Ciardi speaks.
5. Analyze the means by which advertising works to keep us perpetually dissatisfied.

Overpopulated America

WAYNE DAVIS

Wayne Davis, a professor of biology at the University of Kentucky, is a specialist in mammalian ecology. He has also written a column called "Man and Environment" for the Louisville *Courier-Journal*. This article, which forces the reader to reconsider the "foreign" problem of overpopulation as a pressing domestic issue, aroused great controversy when it first appeared in *The New Republic*. In the essay, Davis proposes a radical redefinition of the term "overpopulation," designed to alter the reader's understanding of the economic, environmental, and human aspects of this world problem. Although some of the figures—on population and gross national product, for example—have altered since this essay was written, the central issues of population growth and the relationship of the affluent nations to the world's natural resources are, if anything, even more pressing today.

1   I define as most seriously overpopulated that nation whose people by virtue of their numbers and activities are most rapidly decreasing the ability of the land to support human life. With our large population, our affluence and our technological monstrosities the United States wins first place by a substantial margin.

2   Let's compare the US to India, for example. We have 203 million people, whereas she has 540 million on much less land. But look at the impact of people on the land.

3   The average Indian eats his daily few cups of rice (or perhaps wheat, whose production on American farms contributed to our one percent per year drain in quality of our active farmland), draws his bucket of water from the communal well and sleeps in a mud hut. In his daily rounds to gather cow dung to burn to cook his rice and warm his feet, his footsteps, along with those of millions of his countrymen, help bring about a slow deterioration of the ability of the land to support people. His contribution to the destruction of the land is minimal.

4   An American, on the other hand, can be expected to destroy a piece of land on which he builds a home, garage and driveway. He will contribute his share to the 142 million tons of smoke and fumes, seven million junked cars, 20 million tons of paper, 48 billion cans, and 26 billion bottles the overburdened

environment must absorb each year. To run his air conditioner we will strip-mine a Kentucky hillside, push the dirt and slate down into the stream, and burn coal in a power generator, whose smokestack contributes to a plume of smoke massive enough to cause cloud seeding and premature precipitation from Gulf winds which should be irrigating the wheat farms of Minnesota.

5   In his lifetime he will personally pollute three million gallons of water, and industry and agriculture will use ten times this much water in his behalf. To provide these needs the U.S. Army Corps of Engineers will build dams and flood farmland. He will also use 21,000 gallons of leaded gasoline containing boron, drink 28,000 pounds of milk and eat 10,000 pounds of meat. The latter is produced and squandered in a life pattern unknown to Asians. A steer on a Western range eats plants containing minerals necessary for plant life. Some of these are incorporated into the body of the steer which is later shipped for slaughter. After being eaten by man these nutrients are flushed down the toilet into the ocean or buried in the cemetery, the surface of which is cluttered with boulders called tombstones and has been removed from productivity. The result is a continual drain on the productivity of range land. Add to this the erosion of overgrazed lands, and the effects of the falling water table as we mine Pleistocene deposits of groundwater to irrigate to produce food for more people, and we can see why our land is dying far more rapidly than did the great civilizations of the Middle East, which experienced the same cycle. The average Indian citizen, whose fecal material goes back to the land, has but a minute fraction of the destructive effect on the land that the affluent American does.

6   Thus I want to introduce a new term, which I suggest be used in future discussions of human population and ecology. We should speak of our numbers in "Indian equivalents." An Indian equivalent I define as the average number of Indian citizens required to have the same detrimental effect on the land's ability to support human life as would the average American. This value is difficult to determine, but let's take an extremely conservative working figure of 25. To see how conservative this is, imagine the addition of 1000 citizens to your town and 25,000 to an Indian village. Not only would the Americans destroy much more land for homes, highways and a shopping center, but they would contribute far more to environmental deterioration in hundreds of other ways as well. For example, their demand for steel for new autos might increase the daily pollution equivalent of 130,000 junk autos which *Life* tells us that U.S. Steel Corp. dumps into Lake Michigan. Their demand for textiles would help the cotton industry destroy the life in the Black Warrior River in Alabama with endrin. And they would contribute to the massive industrial pollution of our oceans (we provide one third to one half the world's share) which has caused the precipitous downward trend in our commercial fisheries landings during the past seven years.

7   The per capita gross national product of the United States is 38 times that of India. Most of our goods and services contribute to the decline in the ability of the environment to support life. Thus it is clear that a figure of 25 for an

Indian equivalent is conservative. It has been suggested to me that a more realistic figure would be 500.

8   In Indian equivalents, therefore, the population of the United States is at least four billion. And the rate of growth is even more alarming. We are growing at one percent per year, a rate which would double our numbers in 70 years. India is growing at 2.5 percent. Using the Indian equivalent of 25, our population growth becomes 10 times as serious as that of India. According to the Reinows in their recent book *Moment in the Sun,* just one year's crop of American babies can be expected to use up 25 billion pounds of beef, 200 million pounds of steel and 9.1 billion gallons of gasoline during their collective lifetime. And the demands on water and land for our growing population are expected to be far greater than the supply available in the year 2000. We are destroying our land at a rate of over a million acres a year. We now have only 2.6 agricultural acres per person. By 1975 this will be cut to 2.2, the critical point for the maintenance of what we consider a decent diet, and by the year 2000 we might expect to have 1.2.

9   You might object that I am playing with statistics in using the Indian equivalent on the rate of growth. I am making the assumption that today's Indian child will live 35 years (the average Indian life span) at today's level of affluence. If he lives an American 70 years, our rate of population growth would be 20 times as serious as India's.

10   But the assumption of continued affluence at today's level is unfounded. If our numbers continue to rise, our standard of living will fall so sharply that by the year 2000 any surviving Americans might consider today's average Asian to be well off. Our children's destructive effects on their environment will decline as they sink ever lower into poverty.

11   The United States is in serious economic trouble now. Nothing could be more misleading than today's affluence, which rests precariously on a crumbling foundation. Our productivity, which had been increasing steadily at about 3.2 percent a year since World War II, has been falling during 1969. Our export over import balance has been shrinking steadily from $7.1 billion in 1964 to $0.15 billion in the first half of 1969. Our balance of payments deficit for the second quarter was $3.7 billion, the largest in history. We are now importing iron ore, steel, oil, beef, textiles, cameras, radios and hundreds of other things.

12   Our economy is based upon the Keynesian concept of a continued growth in population and productivity. It worked in an under-populated nation with excess resources. It could continue to work only if the earth and its resources were expanding at an annual rate of 4 to 5 percent. Yet neither the number of cars, the economy, the human population, nor anything else can expand indefinitely at an exponential rate in a finite world. We must face this fact *now*. The crisis is here. When Walter Heller says that our economy will expand by 4 percent annually through the latter 1970s he is dreaming. He is in a theoretical world totally unaware of the realities of human ecology. If the economists do not wake up and devise a new system for us now somebody else will have to do it for them.

13   A civilization is comparable to a living organism. Its longevity is a function of its metabolism. The higher the metabolism (affluence), the shorter the life. Keynesian economics has allowed us an affluent but shortened life span. We have now run our course.

14   The tragedy facing the United States is even greater and more imminent than that descending upon the hungry nations. The Paddock brothers in their book, *Famine 1975!*, say that India "cannot be saved" no matter how much food we ship her. But India will be here after the United States is gone. Many millions will die in the most colossal famines India has ever known, but the land will survive and she will come back as she always has before. The United States, on the other hand, will be a desolate tangle of concrete and ticky-tacky, of strip-mined moonscape and silt-choked reservoirs. The land and water will be so contaminated with pesticides, herbicides, mercury fungicides, lead, boron, nickel, arsenic and hundreds of other toxic substances, which have been approaching critical levels of concentration in our environment as a result of our numbers and affluence, that it may be unable to sustain human life.

15   Thus as the curtain gets ready to fall on man's civilization let it come as no surprise that it shall first fall on the United States. And let no one make the mistake of thinking we can save ourselves by "cleaning up the environment." Banning DDT is the equivalent of the physician's treating syphilis by putting a bandaid over the first chancre to appear. In either case you can be sure that more serious and widespread trouble will soon appear unless the disease itself is treated. We cannot survive by planning to treat the symptoms such as air pollution, water pollution, soil erosion, etc.

16   What can we do to slow the rate of destruction of the United States as a land capable of supporting human life? There are two approaches. First, we must reverse the population growth. We have far more people now than we can continue to support at anything near today's level of affluence. American women average slightly over three children each. According to the *Population Bulletin* if we reduced this number to 2.5 there would still be 300 million people in the nation at the end of the century. And even if we reduced this to 1.5 we would have 57 million more people in the year 2000 than we have now. With our present longevity patterns it would take more than 30 years for the population to peak even when reproducing at this rate, which would eventually give us a net decrease in numbers.

17   Do not make the mistake of thinking that technology will solve our population problem by producing a better contraceptive. Our problem now is that people want too many children. Surveys show the average number of children wanted by the American family is 3.3. There is little difference between the poor and the wealthy, black and white, Catholic and Protestant. Production of children at this rate during the next 30 years would be so catastrophic in effect on our resources and the viability of the nation as to be beyond my ability to contemplate. To prevent this trend we must not only make contraceptives and abortion readily available to everyone, but we must establish a system to put severe economic pressure on those who produce children and

reward those who do not. This can be done within our system of taxes and welfare.

18   The other thing we must do is to pare down our Indian equivalents. Individuals in American society vary tremendously in Indian equivalents. If we plot Indian equivalents versus their reciprocal, the percentage of land surviving a generation, we obtain a linear regression. We can then place individuals and occupation types on this graph. At one end would be the starving blacks of Mississippi; they would approach unity in Indian equivalents, and would have the least destructive effect on the land. At the other end of the graph would be the politicians slicing pork for the barrel, the highway contractors, strip-mine operators, real estate developers, and public enemy number one—the U.S. Army Corps of Engineers.

19   We must halt land destruction. We must abandon the view of land and minerals as private property to be exploited in any way economically feasible for private financial gain. Land and minerals are resources upon which the very survival of the nation depends, and their use must be planned in the best interests of the people.

20   Rising expectations for the poor is a cruel joke foisted upon them by the Establishment. As our new economy of use-it-once-and-throw-it-away produces more and more products for the affluent, the share of our resources available for the poor declines. Blessed be the starving blacks of Mississippi with their outdoor privies, for they are ecologically sound, and they shall inherit a nation. Although I hope that we will help these unfortunate people attain a decent standard of living by diverting war efforts to fertility control and job training, our most urgent task to assure this nation's survival during the next decade is to stop the affluent destroyers.

Argument and Persuasion

The fourth of the major modes of discourse, argument and persuasion, has been placed near the end of the text because the making of an effective and successful argument demands the ability to call upon the techniques of the other three modes—narration, description, and exposition in all its forms. Both argument and persuasion are written forms of debate originating in the oral presentations of the public forums and law courts of ancient Greece and Rome. In ancient times, argument meant a fixed form of public speech designed to present a rational, logical appeal to the intellect on some matter of public policy. Persuasion was a variation of this form, used by Athenian lawyers trying to gain acquittal for their clients in the courts of law. To argue in this sense does not mean to quarrel, but to convince, and to convince solely through the presentation of facts, reasoned logic, appeals to the intellect. Persuasion, too, seeks to convince the listener or reader to adopt another position, another manner of thinking, another solution to a problem; but it differs from argument in its legitimate and expected use of techniques that appeal to the emotions. At its best, the emotional appeal of persuasion rests on the same fundamentally rational approach that defines argument. It is the difference in motivation between argument and persuasion, between achieving some public good and saving a client's life, which accounts for the addition of emotional appeals to persuasive prose.

Today, most of what we call "argument" or "persuasion" is really a combination of the two methods of approaching a problem, and examples of this form of discourse range from a sample ballot's carefully reasoned arguments for and against new zoning regulations or school bonds to the completely emotional and irrational appeal of the television commercial urging you to buy a product because "it's better." Nevertheless, all good argument and most persuasion still rests on the basic forms of ancient times, requiring the inclusion of four essential elements. First, the problem must be analyzed or at least clearly presented. Next, the proposed solution must be offered and developed or supported by factual and logical details and evidence. Then, if there is an opposing position, it should be answered or refuted when this seems possible or necessary. Finally, the writer should conclude with a restatement of his own position.

Persuasion follows essentially the same formula, except for its additional appeals to the emotions, accomplished mainly through diction and tone and the careful selection of examples. (Compare Baruch's definition of the problem as "a choice between the quick and the dead" and Einstein's reference to "this most important political question." Or examine carefully the details selected by the pro and con writers to illustrate the actual slaughter of the animals or the economic impact of sealing on the economy of Newfoundland.)

The essays in this section offer two approaches to the study of argument and persuasion. The pieces on "Hunting the Harp Seal" present opposing views of a single controversial issue. Both should be carefully analyzed. Do they reveal the basic outlines of argument as indicated above? How convincing are they? What methods and facts do they employ to motivate a change of mind in the reader? How much reasoned argument, how much purely emotional assertion is used to build either side of the case?

The extra readings again address themselves to a single issue—control of atomic weapons. But this time, both writers argue the same side; only their methods differ: one arguing dispassionately, the other persuading with great feeling. Studied with careful attention to diction, imagery, and arrangement of ideas, this pair of essays should provide an unusually controlled opportunity for distinguishing between argument and persuasion and for evaluating the effects of emotional, persuasive rhetoric in contrast to logical appeals to the intellect.

Hunting the Harp Seal

The two essays that follow present opposing views of the dispute over Canada's annual baby harp seal hunt. The controversy touches on many issues—economic, environmental, and moral—as protest groups such as the Greenpeace Foundation's battle with government officials over whether or not the hunt is "humane" or "brutal." The central question seems to be whether or not affluent, technological nations have the right to hunt animals on the endangered species list.

The best-known endangered animal is the humpback whale, still hunted by the Soviet Union and Japan despite heavy opposition from other nations and environmental and animal welfare organizations. The most provocative of these organizations is Greenpeace, whose members put their own lives on the line by going out in small boats and interposing themselves between the harpoons and the threatened whale.

The hunting nations assert that these animals are essential as a source of food; the protesters charge that the carcasses are also used for nonessential items like cosmetics and fur coats. And so the hunt—and the controversy surrounding it—goes on.

The Seal's in No Danger of Extinction

PARKER BARSS DONHAM

Parker Barss Donham was formerly associate editor of the *Cape Breton Post* in Sydney, Nova Scotia. He is now a journalist with the Canadian Broadcast Company.

1   The 1978 Canadian seal hunt came to an end early this month, and with it the protest that annually vilifies Newfoundlanders as a special breed of barbarians who get their jollies by clubbing and skinning live baby harp seals, a species said to be hovering perilously close to extinction.

2   The protesters make such sophisticated use of the news media that few Americans even question their view of the hunt as a cruel and greedy business. It is a view that infuriates residents of Canada's Atlantic provinces, who know that it bears not the faintest resemblance to the truth.

3   The key to understanding the seal hunt controversy is the fact that harp seal pups are cute. Their pictures carry instant appeal for animal lovers throughout the world. If seal pups looked like lobsters or codfish or even chickens, their harvest would inspire no protest.

4   The anti-sealing campaign is a consequence, not of any objective complaint about sealing, but of the seal pups' ability to raise the funds that pay the salaries of professional protesters.

5   The campaigns are astonishingly successful. Brian Davies, head of the International Fund for Animal Welfare, an organization which exists solely to protest the annual seal hunt, flies around in the organization's very own helicopter and pays himself a salary of $40,000. This summer Mr. Davies will move his headquarters from Fredericton, New Brunswick, to Cape Cod, Massachusetts, a move which will bring him closer to the computer firm which handles the organization's fund-raising mailing list.

6   Last month, a former director of the Greenpeace Foundation, the other group that annually protests the seal hunt, wrote an open letter to Canadian newspapers denouncing the 1978 Greenpeace leaders as "professional opportunists (who) are as dependent upon the continuation of the seal hunt as the sealers themselves."

7   "When the seal hunt ends," wrote Paul F. Watson, "so also will end the fat checks which pay Greenpeace salaries, rent for their Vancouver office, jet fare for their globe-trotting escapades and of course the charter fee for the annual Greenpeace summer ocean cruise to 'save' the whales."

8   Stripped of its rhetoric and emotionalism, the case against the seal hunt rests on two contentions: That the seal pups suffer a prolonged, painful death, and that the harp seal's future is endangered by the hunt. Fortunately, both of these issues have been subjected to careful research, and it's possible to draw firm conclusions about them.

9   Veterinarians working for the Canadian government and for a variety of humane organizations have studied the best means of killing seals, looking at such alternatives as guns, drugs, carbon monoxide, and concussion bolts. They have concluded that the best method is clubbing with a hardwood bat or with a Norwegian instrument known as a hakapik. Because seal pups have a paper-thin skull, clubbing results in instant death or in a state of deep, irreversible unconsciousness.

10   Contrary to the anti-sealing propaganda, seal pups are not skinned alive. The muscular motion sometimes observed during slaughter is a reflex contraction similar to that found in many animals shortly after death. Nor do mother seals ordinarily show signs of bereavement common to dogs and other animals. Among the organizations which have sent observers to the seal hunt are the Canadian Federation of Humane Societies, the Society for the Prevention of Cruelty to Animals, the Ontario Humane Society,

11   The slaughter of animals on a mass scale is not a pretty sight. When the abattoir happens to be an open ice field, and the animals destined for slaughter have large, childlike eyes, the scene is hard to stomach, especially for people unfamiliar with animal slaughter. But ours is not a vegetarian culture. We have shown no aversion to using animal products in shoes and clothing. In terms of humaneness with which it is conducted, the Canadian seal hunt compares favorably with the slaughter of domesticated animals, and represents a vast improvement over the way most wild animals are captured and killed.

12   The question of assuring the continued survival of the harp seal is complicated by the difficulty of counting the seal population accurately. Nevertheless, no biologist who has studied the question believes the harp seal is in danger of extinction. Far from it. The harp seal is the second most abundant species of seal in the world, outnumbered only by Antarctic's crabeater seal. There is now widespread agreement that the herd is growing.

13   A few years ago, there was a disagreement among the scientific community, if not about the possible extinction of the harp seal, then about the appropriate quotas for harvesting. It's worth noting, however, that some of the biologists who originally questioned the quotas have moved closer to the government's view. One of these, David M. Lavigne of the University of Guelph in Guelph, Ontario, is quoted extensively in the anti-sealing literature of protest groups. At the outset of this year's hunt, Lavigne held a news conference in St. John's, Newfoundland, to complain that the protest groups were quoting him out of context, and that he does not oppose the hunt.

14   Driving the herd to extinction would serve no one's interests. On the other hand, an unlimited herd would not be desirable either. Elimination of the seal pup hunt would greatly increase the pressure on the already depleted

Atlantic fishery. Even at their present levels, harp seals annually consume an estimated 300,000 to 500,000 metric tons of capelin, which are in turn a vital link in the food chain for a vast number of cod, sea birds, seals and great whales.

15   Perhaps the aspect of the hunt which Americans understand least is the role it plays in the economy and history of Newfoundland. Protest groups dismiss the economic impact of the hunt—a few million dollars per year—as making an insignificant contribution to the economy of Newfoundland. Their argument betrays a profound ignorance of life in the outports and villages of the Atlantic Provinces, where families piece together a meager subsistence from half a dozen sources. Unemployment in Newfoundland hovers around 25 percent.

16   A 1976 survey indicated that the average seal hunter earned an annual income of $7500 to support 3.5 dependents. For those working off large vessels, $2400 of this income was earned during the month spent sealing. About half of this money came from the sale of meat and blubber, contrary to the protesters' claim that seals are used only for fur coats and trinkets. This income might seem small by U.S. standards, but its elimination would hurt some of the poorest families in North America.

17   The Newfoundland seal hunt has been an annual event ever since white people settled the island 350 years ago, and for unknown eons before that by Indians.

18   As recently as a few decades ago, sealers worked under appalling conditions, and the hunt today remains a grueling way to make part of a living. The men who head for the ice floes each spring are regarded by Newfoundlanders as folk heroes. When they are confronted by a collection of aspiring movie starlets, airline stewardesses, and well-heeled protest executives, the people at this end of Canada have little trouble deciding which side they're on.

The Brutal Slaughter Must Be Stopped

ROBERT O. TAUNT III

Robert O. Taunt III is a spokesman and an organizer of both the antiwhaling and antisealing campaigns for the Greenpeace Foundation of America in San Francisco.

1   "The mother seals would screech and put up a helpless fight while their babies were skinned in front of them—mostly alive. It was the cruelest, most bloodthirsty thing I've ever seen and I've traveled the world," stated Fred Joyce, a sealer aboard the Martin Karlsen last month in Newfoundland. Joyce said the crew got so angry at the bad conditions (aboard the sealing ships) that they took out their frustrations on the baby harp seals and many of the seals were skinned alive.

2   In an interview with Moira Farrow of the Vancouver Sun, he stated further, ". . . when the sealers saw a fisheries officer approaching they would go back to the carcasses and bash in the skulls so the officer would believe the seal pup had been dead before it was skinned."

3   This is not Greenpeace emotionalism or rhetoric; it is a statement of a 43-year-old seaman who had to eat beef that had been frozen for five years and hamburger that was black. He is not a "well-heeled protest executive," as we have been charged, but a seaman that dared to come forward and tell his story to the world. It went mostly unnoticed by the Canadian press due to a tendency on the part of much of the press in Canada to ignore the more negative aspects of the Canadian seal slaughter.

4   Our helicopter put down on the ice around 8:30 a.m. on March 18, 1978, off the coast of Labrador. As I stepped from the chopper I found myself surrounded with the carcasses of baby seals taken hours before—frozen in the snow with their eyes fixed toward the sky and nothing but dried blood, bone and entrails strewn everywhere. We had arrived at the annual seal slaughter in Canada.

5   Our Flight to Save the Seals had been a long, tedious battle of lawyers, Canadian federal officials, and bureaucratic lies upon lies. But we made it to the ice floes where the mother seals were nursing their young.

6   The seal slaughter is not humane. It is one of the most brutal and mismanaged operations I have ever personally witnessed. There is no control on the ice, and sealers move with complete freedom anywhere and without

THE BRUTAL SLAUGHTER MUST BE STOPPED   From *This World, San Francisco Sunday Chronicle,* May 7, 1978. Copyright Chronicle Publishing Co., 1978. Reprinted by permission of the author and the publisher.

direct supervision. Their primary task is to kill as many baby seals as possible. Period.

7   One should be very careful about comparing the killing of harp seals with the killing of cattle in the United States. Cattle here are used for human consumption and are not an endangered species. Baby harp seals are killed for fashion and there is an extreme difference between the end result of the two examples given.

8   The Canadian government is very expert at stretching statistics as one would stretch a rubber band. But even taking official Canadian government statistics (a highly risky matter) we find that of the $5.5 million gained from sealing, less than .2 percent (two-tenths of one percent) of the annual Newfoundland Gross Provincial Income is derived from sealing.

9   To put this in partial perspective, the introduction of the 200-mile limit has increased the income of the Newfoundland fishing industry by $70 million over the past two years, with even greater increases possible as fish stocks recover from the ocean-stripping effects of foreign draggers.

10   Of that $5.5 million gained through sealing, only $702,000, or 12 percent went to 3045 landsmen involved in the "hunt" in 1976. The remaining $4,795,078 (88 percent) went to only 29 percent of those involved. The real profits derived from sealing never reached the people who risk their lives in the "hunt." The real profits are funneled into the pockets of the large ship owners and the European, mainly Norwegian, companies who turn pelts into finished products.

11   In 1976, the last year statistics were available for any of this data, 7819 sealing licenses were issued in Newfoundland. However, less than 4000 Newfoundland sealers earned any money from the hunt that year. Taking the Canadian government's gross annual income range to $1000, only 2.4 percent of those participating received over $1000 while 30.4 percent made $0.

12   The blood on the ice was everywhere. It was like an Easter egg hunt, one could easily walk up to any baby seal basking in the sun and it would move ever so slightly. The baby seals are totally defenseless. Greenpeace asserts it has as much right to protect the life of a seal as the sealers contend they have the right to kill a seal. Under the "Seal Protection Act" of Canada, it is illegal to move a seal from point "A" to point "B" to save its life but perfectly legal to kill it.

13   Congressman Leo Ryan of California and Congressman Jim Jeffords of Vermont accompanied Greenpeace to the ice as factfinders from the U.S. Congress. They were treated with every possible rudeness by federal officials in St. Anthony, Newfoundland, who were in daily contact with Ottawa. Congressman Ryan was later to call the "hunt" a "slaughterhouse on ice."

14   The truth is beginning to spread all over the world: the slaughter must be stopped. We must co-exist with nature and simply because Russia and Japan have the technology to kill whales doesn't give them the right to do so. The same applies to Canada and Norway which annually slaughter seals.

15   The world is opposing the seal slaughter and Canadian officials are sweat-ing. So much so that they have arrested two persons connected with Green-

peace: Dr. Patrick Moore for "knowingly interfering with the seal hunt" and, amazingly, our legal advisor, Peter Ballem. Moore tried to save the life of one seal. You are not allowed to save the life of a seal in Canada. It is against the law.

Exercises

COMPREHENSION

Organization and Development

On a separate piece of paper, state each author's major premise in your own words. Then list the major pieces of evidence each writer uses to support his argument.

Content

Choose the answer that correctly completes each statement.
Essay by Parker Barss Donham

1. Donham asserts that most residents of Canada's Atlantic provinces regard the American news coverage of the annual seal hunt as distorted because (a) the Canadian government makes it difficult for observers to be present at the hunt (b) it portrays the seal hunt unfairly and gives a false picture (c) the media sympathizes with Greenpeace's campaign and thus does not give an objective portrayal.
2. Donham says that the controversy over the seal hunt exists primarily because (a) Greenpeace and other animal welfare groups rely on the hunt to raise funds (b) the seal hunt is not really crucial to Newfoundland's economy (c) the harp seals are cuter than other animals hunted routinely.
3. The author sets forth two basic contentions in his argument for the seal hunt: that the seals do not suffer a prolonged, painful death, and that the (a) goods made from the harp seals are essential items (b) harp seal is not in danger of extinction (c) harp seal herds deplete the fish supply off the Atlantic coast.
4. To support his opinion, Donham relies mostly on (a) economic statistics and the opinion of experts in the field (b) emotional statements and challenges to the opposition (c) statements from government officials and the testimony of a few sealers.
5. Aside from his comments about the harp seal herds' potential survival, Donham emphasizes the (a) importance of the harp seal as a source of food (b) economic necessity of the hunt for Newfoundlanders (c) tradition of the hunt in Newfoundland culture not only for whites but also for the Indians before them.

Essay by Robert O. Taunt III

1. The sealer's statements that open this essay reveal one cause of the sealers' brutal treatment of the pups; it is (a) the absence of supervision by government wildlife officials (b) indifference to public sentiment against the sealers' methods (c) the bad conditions aboard the sealing ships, which make the crew take out their frustrations on the baby seals.

2. This seaman's story went largely unnoticed by the Canadian press because (a) he was widely regarded as a bad sport (b) the press usually ignores negative statements about the seal hunt (c) the press refuses to print information publicized by Greenpeace.
3. The annual harp seal hunt occurs (a) right after breeding season ends (b) when the baby seals are nursing (c) just after the baby seals have been weaned.
4. Taunt says that less than .2 percent of the annual Newfoundland Gross Provincial Income derives from sealing, but more important, that (a) the government takes a large percentage of the sealers' income (b) only half the people engaged in sealing make a decent living from it since the demand for seal coats has diminished (c) the majority of the profits goes not to the sealers, but to the ship owners and European companies who buy the pelts.
5. Underlying Taunt's argument is a fundamental belief that (a) other governments should pressure Canada to outlaw the annual hunt (b) the Canadian government must exercise more control and supervision over the hunt (c) nations with advanced technology to kill animals do not have the right to do so.

Paragraph Structure

Reorder the following sentences to form a unified, coherent paragraph. Identify one sentence as the topic sentence. Then check your version with the original.

1. We have shown no aversion to using animal products in shoes and clothing.
2. The slaughter of animals on a mass scale is not a pretty sight.
3. But ours is not a vegetarian culture.
4. In terms of humaneness with which it is conducted, the Canadian seal hunt compares favorably with the slaughter of domesticated animals, and represents a vast improvement over the way most wild animals are captured and killed.
5. When the abattoir happens to be an open ice field, and the animals destined for slaughter have large, childlike eyes, the scene is hard to stomach, especially for people unfamiliar with animal slaughter.

VOCABULARY AND USAGE

Word Formation Table

Complete the following table by changing word endings or root forms to make new grammatical forms. Use your dictionary if necessary.

	NOUN	VERB	ADJECTIVE	ADVERB
1.	barbarian	xxx	_____	_____
2.	_____	_____	_____	perilously
3.	_____	_____	humane	_____
4.	_____	destine	_____	xxx
5.	_____	_____	brutal	_____

Fill-Ins

Complete each of the sentences below using the words on the following list. You may need to use some words more than once. You may also find that some blanks can be completed correctly with more than one word. Add plural endings to nouns and change verb forms where necessary.

emotionalism	meager	rhetoric	brutal
annual	dangerously	controversy	extinction
contrary	compare	defend	dispute
slaughter	content	in contrast	argue
humane	economy	perilously	hunt

1. Donham _____ that the antisealers' charge of the harp seal's being _____ close to _____ is nothing but _____.

2. _____ to the anti-sealing propaganda, Donham says that the methods used in the _____ harp seal _____ are not _____.

3. Donham _____ the _____ by _____ that it is necessary for Newfoundland's _____, even though the wages the sealers earn are _____.

4. Greenpeace got involved in the _____ because its members were concerned that what the sealers call a _____ was actually a _____.

5. Taunt _____ that the seal _____ is not _____; in fact, he calls it one of the most _____ operations he has ever witnessed.

6. Donham says that the sealing operation _____ favorably with the _____ of domesticated animals; _____, Taunt _____ that we should be careful about _____ the killing of cattle and the killing of seals since cattle are not in danger of _____.

DISCUSSION

Examine both essays closely before you attempt to answer these questions. You might also refer to the list of supporting statements you wrote for the organization and development exercise.

1. What major evidence does each author cite? What kind of evidence does each author rely on most? Is the evidence in each essay verifiable and well documented?

2. Are there any unsubstantiated assertions?

3. What authorities are cited?

4. Are there any instances where the authors' feelings take the place of logical argument? Are there any examples of unfair statements or prejudiced arguments?

5. Is there any evidence that either author has anticipated the arguments of the opposing side?

6. Do the writers contradict each other in any way?

7. Does either author omit evidence that you think would be crucial to the argument? Does either essay leave unanswered questions?

8. What was your opinion of the harp seal controversy before you read these articles? What evidence was your previous conviction based on? Did either essay persuade you to change or at least to reexamine your previous conviction?

9. Which essay presents the more logical evidence? Which did you find more convincing?

SUGGESTIONS FOR WRITING

1. Analyze the strengths and weaknesses of each writer's position and come to a conclusion of your own about the harp seal controversy.

2. At the end of his essay, Taunt raises a peripheral issue when he says, "We must

co-exist with nature and simply because Russia and Japan have the technology to kill whales doesn't give them the right to do so. The same applies to Canada and Norway which annually slaughter seals." Use this statement as an introduction to an essay in which you examine the conflicting values of ecology, which is international, and economic self-interest, which is national. [See also Wayne Davis, "Overpopulated America."]

3. At the library gather statistics and other kinds of factual evidence on a controversial subject you feel strongly about. Then write a persuasive essay that uses the evidence to bolster your conviction.

4. Do some research in the library and investigate the process by which some other once-endangered species became extinct (or nearly extinct). Draw some conclusions about the forces that led to this destruction. Some examples are the Great American bison, the snowy egret, and the bald eagle.

Control of Atomic Weapons

BERNARD BARUCH

Bernard Baruch (1870–1965) was a brilliant economist and financier who made and lost a million dollars on Wall Street before he was thirty. He later made millions more, which he gave away to many philanthropic causes. In addition to his charitable interests, he was an author, statesman, and economic adviser to every president from Wilson to Eisenhower. The role for which the public probably remembers him best is that of park-bench philosopher, a gentle elder statesman who issued almost daily bulletins from his bench in Central Park in New York.

He was United States representative to the United Nations Atomic Energy Commission and the author of the American plan for international control of atomic weapons. His passionate interest in this issue is made clear in the following speech, delivered at the opening session of the Atomic Energy Commission of the United Nations, in New York City, on June 14, 1946.

1   We are here to make a choice between the quick and the dead.

2   That is our business.

3   Behind the black portent of the new atomic age lies a hope which, seized upon with faith, can work our salvation. If we fail, then we have damned every man to be the slave of fear. Let us not deceive ourselves: We must elect world peace or world destruction.

4   Science has torn from nature a secret so vast in its potentialities that our minds cower from the terror it creates. Yet terror is not enough to inhibit the use of the atomic bomb. The terror created by weapons has never stopped man from employing them. For each new weapon a defense has been produced, in time. But now we face a condition in which adequate defense does not exist.

5   Science, which gave us this dread power, shows that it can be made a giant help to humanity, but science does not show us how to prevent its baleful use. So we have been appointed to obviate that peril by finding a meeting of the minds and the hearts of our peoples. Only in the will of mankind lies the answer.

6   In this crisis we represent not only our governments but, in a larger way, we represent the peoples of the world. We must remember that the peoples do not belong to the governments, but that the governments belong to the

CONTROL OF ATOMIC WEAPONS   From *The World's Great Speeches*, edited by Lewis Copeland and Lawrence W. Lamm (Dover Publications, 1973). Reprinted by permission of the publisher.

peoples. We must answer their demands; we must answer the world's longing for peace and security.

7   In that desire the United States shares ardently and hopefully. The search of science for the absolute weapon has reached fruition in this country. But she stands ready to proscribe and destroy this instrument—to lift its use from death to life—if the world will join in a pact to that end.

8   In our success lies the promise of a new life, freed from the heart-stopping fears that now beset the world. The beginning of victory for the great ideals for which millions have bled and died lies in building a workable plan. Now we approach the fulfillment of the aspirations of mankind. At the end of the road lies the fairer, better, surer life we crave and mean to have.

9   Only by a lasting peace are liberties and democracies strengthened and deepened. War is their enemy. And it will not do to believe that any of us can escape war's devastation. Victor, vanquished and neutrals alike are affected physically, economically and morally.

10   Against the degradation of war we can erect a safeguard. That is the guerdon for which we reach. Within the scope of the formula we outline here, there will be found, to those who seek it, the essential elements of our purpose. Others will see only emptiness. Each of us carries his own mirror in which is reflected hope—or determined desperation—courage or cowardice.

11   There is famine throughout the world today. It starves men's bodies. But there is a greater famine—the hunger of men's spirit. That starvation can be cured by the conquest of fear, and the substitution of hope, from which springs faith—faith in each other; faith that we want to work together toward salvation; and determination that those who threaten the peace and safety shall be punished.

12   The peoples of these democracies gathered here have a particular concern with our answer, for their peoples hate war. They will have a heavy exaction to make of those who fail to provide an escape. They are not afraid of an internationalism that protects; they are unwilling to be fobbed off by mouthings about narrow sovereignty, which is today's phrase for yesterday's isolationism.

13   The basis of a sound foreign policy, in this new age, for all the nations here gathered, is that: anything that happens, no matter where or how, which menaces the peace of the world, or the economic stability, concerns each and all of us.

14   That, roughly, may be said to be the central theme of the United Nations. It is with that thought we gain consideration of the most important subject than can engage mankind—life itself.

15   Now, if ever, is the time to act for the common good. Public opinion supports a world movement toward security. If I read the signs aright, the peoples want a program, not composed merely of pious thoughts, but of enforceable sanctions—an international law with teeth in it.

16   We of this nation, desirous of helping to bring peace to the world and realizing the heavy obligations upon us, arising from our possession of the means for producing the bomb and from the fact that it is part of our

armament, are prepared to make our full contribution toward effective control of atomic energy.

17   But before a country is ready to relinquish any winning weapons, it must have more than words to reassure it. It must have a guarantee of safety, not only against the offenders in the atomic area, but against the illegal users of other weapons—bacteriological, biological, gas—perhaps—why not?—against war itself.

18   In the elimination of war lies our solution, for only then will nations cease to compete with one another in the production and use of dread "secret" weapons which are evaluated solely by their capacity to kill. This devilish program takes us back not merely to the Dark Ages, but from cosmos to chaos. If we succeed in finding a suitable way to control atomic weapons, it is reasonable to hope that we may also preclude the use of other weapons adaptable to mass destruction. When a man learns to say "A" he can, if he chooses, learn the rest of the alphabet, too.

19   Let this be anchored in our minds:

20   Peace is never long preserved by weight of metal or by an armament race. Peace can be made tranquil and secure only by understanding and agreement fortified by sanctions. We must embrace international co-operation or international disintegration.

21   Science has taught us how to put the atom to work. But to make it work for good instead of for evil lies in the domain dealing with the principles of human duty. We are now facing a problem more of ethics than of physics.

22   The solution will require apparent sacrifice in pride and in position, but better pain as the price of peace than death as the price of war.

Peace in the Atomic Age

ALBERT EINSTEIN

Albert Einstein (1879–1955), the greatest theoretical physicist since Newton, was born in Germany and died in Princeton, New Jersey. His theory of relativity, formulated during the early years of the twentieth century, changed the course of modern physics and of civilization itself, making his name a household word. A Jew, he renounced his German citizenship in 1933 when Hitler came to power, and emigrated to the United States, where he was appointed a life member of the Institute for Advanced Studies at Princeton University.

Einstein was also a man deeply committed to the ideal of the morally responsible scientist as well as to every humanitarian cause. After the bombing of Hiroshima in 1945 and the terrible destruction that resulted, Einstein became a powerful advocate of world government. Among the many causes to which he lent both the prestige of his name and his own energies were the vigorous postwar efforts to ensure a lasting peace and a halt to the further development of the nuclear weapons that his own theory had made possible. This is the subject of the speech that follows, delivered on February 12, 1950.

1   I am grateful to you for the opportunity to express my conviction in this most important political question.

2   The idea of achieving security through national armament is, at the present state of military technique, a disastrous illusion. On the part of the United States this illusion has been particularly fostered by the fact that this country succeeded first in producing an atomic bomb. The belief seemed to prevail that in the end it were possible to achieve decisive military superiority.

3   In this way, any potential opponent would be intimidated, and security, so ardently desired by all of us, brought to us and all of humanity. The maxim which we have been following during these last five years has been, in short: security through superior military power, whatever the cost.

4   The armament race between the U.S.A. and the U.S.S.R., originally supposed to be a preventive measure, assumes hysterical character. On both sides, the means to mass destruction are perfected with feverish haste—behind the respective walls of secrecy. The H-bomb appears on the public horizon as a probably attainable goal.

5   If successful, radioactive poisoning of the atmosphere and hence annihila-

PEACE IN THE ATOMIC AGE   From *The World's Great Speeches,* edited by Lewis Copeland and Lawrence W. Lamm (Dover Publications, 1973). Reprinted by permission of the publisher.

tion of any life on earth has been brought within the range of technical possibilities. The ghostlike character of this development lies in its apparently compulsory trend. Every step appears as the unavoidable consequence of the preceding one. In the end, there beckons more and more clearly general annihilation.

6   Is there any way out of this impasse created by man himself? All of us, and particularly those who are responsible for the attitude of the U.S. and the U.S.S.R., should realize that we may have vanquished an external enemy, but have been incapable of getting rid of the mentality created by the war.

7   It is impossible to achieve peace as long as every single action is taken with a possible future conflict in view. The leading point of view of all political action should therefore be: What can we do to bring about a peaceful co-existence and even loyal cooperation of the nations?

8   The first problem is to do away with mutual fear and distrust. Solemn renunciation of violence (not only with respect to means of mass destruction) is undoubtedly necessary.

9   Such renunciation, however, can only be effective if at the same time a supra-national judicial and executive body is set up empowered to decide questions of immediate concern to the security of the nations. Even a declaration of the nations to collaborate loyally in the realization of such a "restricted world government" would considerably reduce the imminent danger of war.

10   In the last analysis, every kind of peaceful cooperation among men is primarily based on mutual trust and only secondly on institutions such as courts of justice and police. This holds for nations as well as for individuals. And the basis of trust is loyal give and take.

Style

Style is an elusive quality. We can all usually recognize it, but few of us can analyze or define it. Two girls are wearing apparently identical outfits—but one has "style" and the other does not. This year's Chevrolet leaves you cold—the 1956 Bel Air is your dream car. The forward on the local basketball team is a crowd pleaser, a star; the center, also a fine athlete, hasn't a fan in the stands. We all know that such mysterious distinctions exist, and we freely label them "style"—but what exactly does that mean?

A closer look tells you that one girl has a special way of turning up her collar, rolling her jeans, tying her sash. The style—and appeal—of the twenty-year-old car is defined by the bumpers, the hood ornament, the headlights, or the armrests. Similarly, the way one athlete bends his knees, shakes his hips, or waves to the crowd spells out his personal "style."

It is the same with prose. It is easy to see, for example, that the essays by Woiwode and Cousins are quite different. And without much probing, we can also see that this difference, this variation in style, is located in, and the result of, differences in a number of details. But how to describe this? With writers, as with girls, cars, and athletes, "style" is a simple and conventional label for something very complex: the combination of several elements, with many highly individual and distinctive differences, often so small that alone they are undetectable but that, added together, form an unmistakable, identifying pattern.

In prose, style means specifically an author's individual pattern of writing and the overall impression the written work makes on the reader. The details that distinguish prose style rest largely in the patterns created by the writer's unique combination of the elements of point of view (perspective), tone (manner of expression), diction (choice of words), and sentence structure (syntax). And just as it is a good idea to take a second look at girls, cars, and ball players, looking more closely at the details of the works you read can add much to your understanding and appreciation of them. This kind of analysis can also help you to understand *why* you respond as you do to a particular writer (or girl or car). Even more to the point, the closer look that constitutes analysis of prose style can help you to locate the strengths, weaknesses, and most of all, the distinctive traits of your own writing style.

But while practical aims (like the improvement of your own writing) may demand that from time to time you try to isolate the elements of style, remember that, ultimately, the genius of any piece of prose writing is in the aggregate, the harmonious union of these elements.

Point of View and Tone

Point of view is one of the most basic determinants of style. It affects profoundly the other elements—tone, diction, and sentence structure. In some senses, especially where tone is concerned, it might even be said to create or control the other elements of style. In any case, virtually everything the writer does is in some way marked by the angle of vision, the position from which he views his subject and, implicitly, his audience. If you think for a moment of the writer as a photographer, the point becomes quite clear: the position from which a subject is photographed, the angle of the lens, the lighting—all add up to the photographer's "point of view," and all function to determine almost every aspect of the photograph he produces. It is the same with prose, only for the writer it is more often the intellectual and emotional rather than the physical attitude that determines the "camera angle" or point of view. And, of course, the available information (comparable to the photographer's available light) and the writer's own capacity for processing the information (comparable to the quality of the camera) also shape the perspective, which in turn determines the actual treatment of the subject and, finally, contributes to the reader's own point of view.

Because the two short pieces in this section both concern a single topic, the death of the boxer Benny Paret, they offer an excellent opportunity to examine the way in which point of view alone affects prose style. Mailer, writing ostensibly as an observer and reporter, is nevertheless not completely objective, for he not only describes the event, he interprets it for us as well. The heart of the essay (paragraph 5) does indeed seem to offer a sports reporter's ringside, blow-by-blow account of the fight. But a closer look reveals that Mailer—from a perspective more subjective, personal, and evaluative than that of the ordinary reporter—has employed techniques of selection, description, and diction that inevitably shape the reader's own point of view. What does he choose to include—or not include? If Griffith is a cat, then what role is implied for Paret? And what words does he select to convey these impressions? Mailer wants the reader to see this fight not necessarily as it actually was, but as he, Mailer, saw it. While the description springs as much from his own feelings about the killing as from the event, these impressions are appropriately revealed in metaphor ("a baseball bat demolishing a pumpkin"), rather than concealed by direct but judgmental commentary. Mailer surrenders the reporter's camera and the black and white news photo in order to produce an impressionistic painting of the fight.

Cousins, unlike Mailer, did not witness Paret's death. But his lack of personal involvement does not matter; it is in fact an asset, for his chosen angle of vision is that of judge, not eyewitness observer. His camera is focused somewhere offstage, behind the scenes, on causes rather than effects; and his language is cool and concrete, bare of the emotional and psychological interest or impact of Mailer's diction. This is because his interest, his point of view—his purpose, in fact—is to explore broad, underlying causes, while Mailer is interested in reporting what happened, what he, a sensitive man, personally witnessed. Cousins constructs a persuasive argument, in climactic order, and the account of the fight itself (paragraphs 6–8) is at once so bare and so excessively elaborate in its recording of objective detail that the reader is forced, step by step, to reconsider the real implications of this event—forced finally to adopt Cousins's point of view.

While these examples demonstrate that a writer's perspective in prose may be determined by either his actual or intellectual perspective on the subject, as well as by his purpose, there are other possible relationships between writer and topic that also shape point of view and that you will want to consider when reading other selections in the text. Is the writer himself personally involved in the action, an "insider" (like Adam Smith in "You Deserve a Break Today"), or is he merely an outside observer (like Roy Harris in "The Dinosaur Man")? In addition to actual physical participation, there is, of course, the possibility of the writer's psychological involvement—sympathetic or hostile. And the writer's personal attitudes may not be immediately clear to the reader. Nora Ephron is a supposedly neutral observer in "Baking Off," but her language betrays strongly subjective feelings. And how does a writer like James Willwerth really stand in relation to his subject, Jones the mugger? In such cases, the reader must determine the writer's point of view and any influence it has on the objectivity of the material presented. Where the writer's personal involvement is so intense that it amounts to open advocacy or opposition (as in the selections on hunting the harp seal), the reader's position is somewhat easier. If the writer's bias is clear from the outset, the reader is at least forewarned to exercise reasonable caution in evaluating the honesty and objectivity of what he reads.

Another important factor in determining perspective is distance: could Willie Morris or Robert Coles have produced the same sense of Yazoo or of the Allen family if they had gained their information at second hand? And time as well can be used and manipulated in many ways: the essays by White, Kingston, and Anderson all offer memoirs of past events seen now from a distance in time, which inevitably colors them. Further, a writer may consciously and deliberately wrench the reader's point of view away from a habitual perspective to a fresh one—as Brown does in his retelling of the familiar history of America's colonization, and as Davis does in his redefinition of the concept of overpopulation.

These examples show that the writer can shape his own and the reader's perspective by his handling of virtually any aspect of his subject. As a reader you must be on the alert for any special manipulation of perspective and conscious of your own responsibility for evaluating the writer's motivation to persuade you to adopt or change a particular point of view.

Finally, a word about tone—the writer's manner of expression—an important yet elusive and amorphous quality. It is both an element of style and a function of point of view, rising from and at the same time creating or emphasizing the writer's perspective and language. Tone designates the overall impression, the almost indefinable aura generated by the writer's feelings and expressed through a particular combination of diction and sentence structure. Actually, the writer's tone or manner of expression is essentially the same as the "tone of voice" we use and respond to in spoken communications. And in written prose as in oral language, tone conveys the entire range of human feeling, from joy to sorrow, anger to sympathy, mockery to praise. Again, as in spoken language, tone is the product of a writer's purpose and of his feeling, his attitude, his point of view or relationship to both subject and audience.

Tone is the voice you hear as you read. But unlike the speaker, the writer does not have at his disposal the facial expression, the body language, or the actual rise and fall of the human voice to expand upon or even to temper the actual meaning of the individual word or phrase. For example, a mother may say to her child "Beat it" in a soft and gentle tone of voice, with a smile on her face, and a warm and loving touch on the shoulder as she propels the interrupting tot from the room. The harsh command implied by the words is transformed into a pleasant request by these nonverbal additions—this *tone*. A writer, however, has only the mark of punctuation ("Beat it!"), the capital letter ("BEAT IT!"), or the additional word or phrase ("Please beat it") to temper the inherently peremptory or even angry sense of the actual words. And so for the writer, the *choice* of words—diction—becomes more crucial, more imperative than for the speaker. But diction is itself an important and separate element of style that will be discussed in the next section.

The Death of Benny Paret

NORMAN MAILER

Norman Mailer was born in New Jersey in 1923, and was raised in Brooklyn, New York. He began writing fiction even before his graduation from Harvard in 1943; and after serving with the U.S. Army in the Pacific, he wrote what continues to be his most popular novel, the powerful war story *The Naked and the Dead*. His later novels include *The Deer Park* and *An American Dream*. He has not confined himself to fiction, but has written widely on important contemporary issues, including the Vietnam war, the radical movement of the 1960s, and women's liberation. Among his more controversial and best-known writings are *Marilyn* (a biography of Marilyn Monroe), *Armies of the Night* (a chronicle of the great antiwar march on Washington), and *The Prisoner of Sex* (Mailer's personal manifesto of male chauvinism). Many of his miscellaneous writings have been collected in *The Presidential Papers*, from which this piece was selected.

1   On the afternoon of the night Emile Griffith and Benny Paret were to fight a third time for the welterweight championship, there was murder in both camps. "I hate that kind of guy," Paret had said earlier to Pete Hamill about Griffith. "A fighter's got to look and talk and act like a man." One of the Broadway gossip columnists had run an item about Griffith a few days before. His girl friend saw it and said to Griffith, "Emile, I didn't know about you being that way." So Griffith hit her. So he said. Now at the weigh-in that morning, Paret had insulted Griffith irrevocably, touching him on the buttocks, while making a few more remarks about his manhood. They almost had their fight on the scales.

2   The accusation of homosexuality arouses a major passion in many men; they spend their lives resisting it with a biological force. There is a kind of man who spends every night of his life getting drunk in a bar, he rants, he brawls, he ends in a small rumble on the street; women say, "For God's sakes, he's homosexual. Why doesn't he just turn queer and get his suffering over with." Yet men protect him. It is because he is choosing not to become homosexual. It was put best by Sartre who said that a homosexual is a man who practices homosexuality. A man who does not, is not homosexual—he is entitled to the dignity of his choice. He is entitled to the fact that he chose not to become homosexual, and is paying presumably his price.

3   The rage in Emile Griffith was extreme. I was at the fight that night, I had

never seen a fight like it. It was scheduled for fifteen rounds, but they fought without stopping from the bell which began the round to the bell which ended it, and then they fought after the bell, sometimes for as much as fifteen seconds before the referee could force them apart.

4   Paret was a Cuban, a proud club fighter who had become welterweight champion because of his unusual ability to take a punch. His style of fighting was to take three punches to the head in order to give back two. At the end of ten rounds, he would still be bouncing, his opponent would have a headache. But in the last two years, over fifteen-round fights, he had started to take some bad maulings.

5   This fight had its turns, Griffith won most of the early rounds, but Paret knocked Griffith down in the sixth. Griffith had trouble getting up, but made it, came alive and was dominating Paret again before the round was over. Then Paret began to wilt. In the middle of the eighth round, after a clubbing punch had turned his back to Griffith, Paret walked three disgusted steps away, showing his hindquarters. For a champion, he took much too long to turn back around. It was the first hint of weakness Paret had ever shown, and it must have inspired a particular shame, because he fought the rest of the fight as if he were seeking to demonstrate that he could take more punishment than any man alive. In the twelfth, Griffith caught him. Paret got trapped in a corner. Trying to duck away, his left arm and his head became tangled on the wrong side of the top rope. Griffith was in like a cat ready to rip the life out of a huge boxed rat. He hit him eighteen right hands in a row, an act which took perhaps three or four seconds. Griffith making a pent-up whimpering sound all the while he attacked, the right hand whipping like a piston rod which has broken through the crankcase, or like a baseball bat demolishing a pumpkin. I was sitting in the second row of that corner—they were not ten feet away from me, and like everybody else, I was hypnotized. I had never seen one man hit another so hard and so many times. Over the referee's face came a look of woe as if some spasm had passed its way through him, and then he leaped on Griffith to pull him away. It was the act of a brave man. Griffith was uncontrollable. His trainer leaped into the ring, his manager, his cut man, there were four people holding Griffith, but he was off on an orgy, he had left the Garden, he was back on a hoodlum's street. If he had been able to break loose from his handlers and the referee, he would have jumped Paret to the floor and whaled on him there.

6   And Paret? Paret died on his feet. As he took those eighteen punches something happened to everyone who was in psychic range of the event. Some part of his death reached out to us. One felt it hover in the air. He was still standing in the ropes, trapped as he had been before, he gave some little half-smile of regret, as if he were saying, "I didn't know I was going to die just yet," and then, his head leaning back but still erect, his death came to breathe about him. He began to pass away. As he passed, so his limbs descended beneath him, and he sank slowly to the floor. He went down more slowly than any fighter had ever gone down, he went down like a large ship which turns on end and slides second by second into its grave. As he went

down, the sound of Griffith's punches echoed in the mind like a heavy ax in the distance chopping into a wet log.

Exercises

COMPREHENSION

Organization and Development

Complete the following outline. In your own words, write the thesis, which is implied rather than openly stated in this primarily descriptive essay. Then find the main divisions in the essay and fill in the remaining spaces. Note the paragraphs for each section.

Thesis statement: _____

_____

_____

I.   _____ [   ]
    A. _____ [   ]
    B. _____ [   ]
II.   _____ [   ]
    A. _____ [   ]
    B. _____ [   ]
III. _____ [   ]
    A. _____ [   ]
    B. _____ [   ]

Content

Choose the answer that correctly completes each statement.

1. Mailer begins by establishing the fact that on the eve of the fight (a) both Paret and Griffith expected to win easily (b) Paret was getting ready to spend his winnings on his girlfriend (c) there was murder in both camps.
2. Before the fight, Paret had insulted Griffith by implying that Griffith was a (a) coward (b) wife-beater (c) homosexual.
3. Mailer emphasizes the fact that Griffith and Paret continued to fight for as long as 15 seconds after the bell in every round because this shows that (a) they really wanted to please the crowd (b) they were enraged, and fighting on a personal level, not just as professionals (c) each wanted to wear out the other boxer early in the fight.
4. Paret's basic strength as a boxer came from his unusual ability to (a) come back from behind and win at the end of a match (b) avoid being caught in the ropes (c) take an unusual amount of punishment.
5. Mailer especially notes an incident in the eighth round when Paret's back was momentarily turned on his opponent because it shows (a) the hint of weakness in Paret that inspired him to show he could take a lot of punishment (b) the real reason for Paret's desire to kill Griffith (c) in Paret's lack of caution, his apparent contempt for Griffith's ability as a fighter.

6. Mailer's description of the last round of the fight compares Griffith and Paret to a (a) cat and a trapped rat (b) snake and a caged rabbit (c) lion and a frightened deer.
7. Mailer says he himself had never before seen a man (a) hit another man so many times (b) killed in the ring (c) whose right fist could demolish a human skull.
8. While he was beating Paret to death, Griffith was (a) remorseful (b) happy (c) uncontrollable.

Paragraph Structure

Reorder the following sentences to form a unified, coherent paragraph. Identify one sentence as the topic sentence. Then check your version with the original.

1. His style of fighting was to take three punches to the head in order to give back two.
2. But in the last two years, over the fifteen-round fights, he had started to take some bad maulings.
3. Paret was a Cuban, a proud club fighter who had become welterweight champion because of his unusual ability to take a punch.
4. At the end of ten rounds, he would still be bouncing, his opponent would have a headache.

VOCABULARY AND USAGE

Word Formation Table

Complete the following table by changing word endings or root forms to make new grammatical forms. Use your dictionary if necessary.

	NOUN	VERB	ADJECTIVE	ADVERB
1.	_____	_____	_____	presumably
2.	dignity	_____	_____	_____
3.	_____	hate	_____	_____
4.	_____	breathe	_____	_____
5.	protection	_____	_____	_____

Fill-Ins

Complete each of the sentences below using the words on the following list. You may need to use some words more than once. You may also find that some blanks can be completed correctly with more than one word. Add plural endings to nouns and change verb forms where necessary.

murder	fight	death	orgy
boxer	bout	shame	crowd
gossip	round	punch	referee
champion	punishment	ring	uncontrollable
challenge	rage	insult	irrevocably

1. The _____ between Paret and Griffith was one in which Griffith _____ Paret, who was the welterweight _____.
2. Mailer says that Paret _____ Griffith, _____, on the eve of the _____.

3. Mailer thinks that when Paret turned his back on Griffith in the eighth _____, Griffith saw it as a(n) _____, a(n) _____.
4. Paret seems to have felt some _____ after this incident in the eighth _____, and was determined to show he could still take a _____.
5. Mailer says Griffith was _____, like someone who, in his imagination, had left the _____ and was off at a street brawl, a(n) _____.
6. Griffith's _____ was so extreme that it took four men, including the _____, to pull him off Paret.

DISCUSSION

1. From what point of view does Mailer write about the fight?
2. Mailer's language is simple, direct, and concrete. How is his choice of words connected with his point of view? Can you single out other devices that he uses to establish his perspective?
3. Which details does Mailer use to characterize each of the boxers? What qualities does he seem to think most important?
4. The main description of the fight (paragraph 3) contains three vivid similes. The last paragraph includes two more striking images. What are they? What attitude or feeling does each one seem designed to produce in the reader?
5. What is the relationship between Mailer's use of these images and his point of view? Is there a relationship between these figures of speech, Mailer's perspective, and the reader's own point of view?
6. Which parts of Mailer's description seem to you to be most objective? Which seem most heavily to rely on impression and inference, rather than accurate reporting of what has been observed? Do you think Mailer manipulates our view of the fight? If so, how?
7. Do you think Mailer is a good sports reporter? Why or why not?

SUGGESTIONS FOR WRITING

1. Write a description of an event (it need not be an athletic contest) in which something surprising, totally unexpected, or shocking occurs.
2. Describe an event first as a reporter, that is, from a presumably objective point of view. Then rewrite your description from another perspective, one in which you deliberately slant your discussion to provide praise or criticism of the scene or situation in question.
3. Write a "ringside" account of a situation, person, or event that we are unaccustomed to seeing at close range. (For example, you might write an "eyewitness" account of a historical event in the distant past, or you might position yourself within intimate range of a person we are accustomed to "seeing" only at a distance.)

Who Killed Benny Paret?

NORMAN COUSINS

Norman Cousins was born in 1913. He is best known for his long and distinguished career as editor of *The Saturday Review,* which he used as a forum for expression of his humanitarian concern for the ideals of democracy, international understanding, and world unity. He is the author of many books, including *The Democratic Chance, Who Speaks for Man?, The Last Defense in a Nuclear Age,* and *Present Tense,* from which this selection is taken.

1   Sometime about 1935 or 1936 I had an interview with Mike Jacobs, the prize-fight promoter. I was a fledgling newspaper reporter at that time; my beat was education, but during the vacation season I found myself on varied assignments, all the way from ship news to sports reporting. In this way I found myself sitting opposite the most powerful figure in the boxing world.

2   There was nothing spectacular in Mr. Jacobs's manner or appearance; but when he spoke about prize fights, he was no longer a bland little man but a colossus who sounded the way Napoleon must have sounded when he reviewed a battle. You knew you were listening to Number One. His saying something made it true.

3   We discussed what to him was the only important element in successful promoting—how to please the crowd. So far as he was concerned, there was no mystery to it. You put killers in the ring and the people filled your arena. You hire boxing artists—men who are adroit at feinting, parrying, weaving, jabbing, and dancing, but who don't pack dynamite in their fists—and you wind up counting your empty seats. So you searched for the killers and sluggers and maulers—fellows who could hit with the force of a baseball bat.

4   I asked Mr. Jacobs if he was speaking literally when he said people came out to see the killer.

5   "They don't come out to see a tea party," he said evenly. "They come out to see the knockout. They come out to see a man hurt. If they think anything else, they're kidding themselves."

6   Recently a young man by the name of Benny Paret was killed in the ring. The killing was seen by millions; it was on television. In the twelfth round he was hit hard in the head several times, went down, was counted out, and never came out of the coma.

WHO KILLED BENNY PARET?   From *Saturday Review,* May 5, 1962. Reprinted by permission of the author.

7   The Paret fight produced a flurry of investigations. Governor Rockefeller was shocked by what happened and appointed a committee to assess the responsibility. The New York State Boxing Commission decided to find out what was wrong. The District Attorney's office expressed its concern. One question that was solemnly studied in all three probes concerned the action of the referee. Did he act in time to stop the fight? Another question had to do with the role of the examining doctors who certified the physical fitness of the fighters before the bout. Still another question involved Mr. Paret's manager; did he rush his boy into the fight without adequate time to recuperate from the previous one?

8   In short, the investigators looked into every possible cause except the real one. Benny Paret was killed because the human fist delivers enough impact, when directed against the head, to produce a massive hemorrhage in the brain. The human brain is the most delicate and complex mechanism in all creation. It has a lacework of millions of highly fragile nerve connections. Nature attempts to protect this exquisitely intricate machinery by encasing it in a hard shell. Fortunately, the shell is thick enough to withstand a great deal of pounding. Nature, however, can protect man against everything except man himself. Not every blow to the head will kill a man—but there is always the risk of concussion and damage to the brain. A prize fighter may be able to survive even repeated brain concussions and go on fighting, but the damage to his brain may be permanent.

9   In any event, it is futile to investigate the referee's role and seek to determine whether he should have intervened to stop the fight earlier. This is not where the primary responsibility lies. The primary responsibility lies with the people who pay to see a man hurt. The referee who stops a fight too soon from the crowd's viewpoint can expect to be booed. The crowd wants the knockout; it wants to see a man stretched out on the canvas. This is the supreme moment in boxing. It is nonsense to talk about prize fighting as a test of boxing skills. No crowd was ever brought to its feet screaming and cheering at the sight of two men beautifully dodging and weaving out of each other's jabs. The time the crowd comes alive is when a man is hit hard over the heart or the head, when his mouthpiece flies out, when blood squirts out of his nose or eyes, when he wobbles under the attack and his pursuer continues to smash at him with poleax impact.

10   Don't blame it on the referee. Don't even blame it on the fight managers. Put the blame where it belongs—on the prevailing mores that regard prize fighting as a perfectly proper enterprise and vehicle of entertainment. No one doubts that many people enjoy prize fighting and will miss it if it should be thrown out. And that is precisely the point.

Exercises

COMPREHENSION

Organization and Development

Complete the following outline. Find the thesis and restate it in your own words. Then find the main divisions in the essay and fill in the remaining spaces. Note the paragraphs for each section.

Thesis statement: _____

_____

   I.   _____ [   ]

  II.   _____ [   ]

 III.   _____ [   ]

Content

Choose the answer that correctly completes each statement.

1. Cousins begins the essay with an anecdote about his interview with Mike Jacobs, the promoter, in order to establish the point that (a) the author has had a long career as a sports reporter and is thoroughly familiar with boxing (b) the death of Benny Paret was actually planned by his promoters (c) prize fighting exists not to show the skill of the boxers but to satisfy the crowd's desire to see a man getting hurt.

2. Cousins says that when you talked with Mike Jacobs "you knew you were listening to Number One" because he wants to establish that (a) Jacobs's intervention might have saved Paret's life (b) Jacobs should have been in charge of the Griffith-Paret match (c) Jacobs's opinions about what pleases a crowd must be considered as true, the voice of authority.

3. According to Jacobs, a promoter who hires boxing artists instead of killers will wind up with (a) empty seats (b) Olympic champions (c) a small but loyal group of fans.

4. The Paret fight was followed by a (a) temporary ban on boxing in New York state (b) plea by Governor Rockefeller for the permanent suspension of Griffith (c) flurry of investigations.

5. All three groups that probed Paret's death solemnly studied (a) the referee's action (b) Griffith's psychiatric record (c) Paret's previous physical condition.

6. Cousins says Paret's death was really caused by the (a) failure of the referee to stop the fight in time (b) capacity of the human fist to deliver enough impact against the head to produce a massive hemorrhage in the brain (c) inadequacy of the doctors who examined Paret before the fight.

7. Cousins says the primary responsibility for Paret's death lies with (a) the referee (b) Paret's trainers (c) the people who pay to see a man hurt.

8. Cousins's conclusion is that (a) boxing should be restricted to amateurs (b) boxing should be thrown out (c) the boxing commission should make better provisions for the safety of the fighters.

Paragraph Structure

Reorder the following sentences to form a unified, coherent paragraph. Identify one sentence as the topic sentence. Then check your version with the original.

1. The New York State Boxing Commission decided to find out what was wrong.
2. Did he act in time to stop the fight?
3. The Paret fight produced a flurry of investigations.
4. Still another question involved Mr. Paret's manager; did he rush his boy into the fight without adequate time to recuperate from the previous one?
5. Governor Rockefeller was shocked by what happened and appointed a committee to assess the responsibility.
6. Another question had to do with the role of the examining doctors who certified the physical fitness of the fighters before the bout.
7. One question that was solemnly studied in all three probes concerned the action of the referee.
8. The District Attorney's office expressed its concern.

VOCABULARY AND USAGE

Word Formation Table

Complete the following table by changing word endings or root forms to make new grammatical forms. Use your dictionary if necessary.

	NOUN	VERB	ADJECTIVE	ADVERB
1.	_____	_____	powerful	_____
2.	season	xxx	_____	_____
3.	_____	xxx	true	_____
4.	_____	expect	_____	_____
5.	probe	_____	_____	_____

Fill-Ins

Complete each of the sentences below using the words on the following list. You may need to use some words more than once. You may also find that some blanks can be completed correctly with more than one word. Add plural endings to nouns and change verb forms where necessary.

knockout	impact	mores	ban
successful	crowd	brain	killer
fledgling	fist	cheering	boxing
mauler	people	skill	adroit
bout	intervene	investigate	referee

1. Jacobs told Cousins that the way to be a _____ promoter of _____ matches was to put _____ or _____ in the ring.
2. The _____ does not care about seeing _____ athletes dancing around the ring; _____ want to see a _____.
3. There was no point in criticizing the _____ at the Griffith-Paret _____; the human _____ was responsible for Paret's death.
4. You will not find a crowd jumping to its feet and _____ unless someone has been hurt, unless, possibly, there has been a _____.
5. Cousins blames Paret's death on the _____ and the prevailing _____ that regard _____ as a perfectly proper enterprise and vehicle of entertainment.

6. The essay says it is useless to blame the _____, to question whether he _____ in time.

DISCUSSION

1. The essay begins with an anecdote that is apparently unrelated to the death of Benny Paret. How, in fact, does the story of Cousins's meeting with Mike Jacobs relate to the point of this essay?
2. Why does Cousins restrict his description of Paret's death to two sentences (paragraph 6)? How does this contrast with Mailer's description of the same event? What conclusions can you draw regarding Cousins's point of view in relationship to Mailer's perspective?
3. Why does Cousins provide the detailed description (paragraph 8) of the capacity of the human fist to produce hemorrhage, and of the structure of the human brain and nature's provisions for its protection?
4. Why is it "nonsense" to talk about prize fighting as "a test of boxing skills"? What is the relationship of this remark to the earlier comments about "boxing artists" (paragraph 3)? What is the implied evaluation of prize fighting in relation to other sports?
5. What basic attitude about human nature is implied by Cousins's remark (paragraph 9) about "the time the crowd comes alive . . ."? Is this how you see human beings?
6. "One picture is worth a thousand words." Which of the two essays about the death of Benny Paret do you think is more likely to persuade or move a reader to seek the elimination of prize fighting? Carefully consider purpose and point of view in formulating an answer.

SUGGESTIONS FOR WRITING

1. Argue, as Cousins does, for the elimination or banning of something that pleases the public and that the public wants, but that is nevertheless harmful to at least some members of the society and, in a larger sense, subversive of the most basic values or ideals of our culture.
2. Answer Cousins's argument by presenting an argument in favor of prize fighting.
3. Compare Cousins's statement with Mailer's as an effective means of arousing the public against the violence of prize fighting.
4. Describe in detail the "prevailing mores" of our society, specifically pointing out those that regard prize fighting as a proper vehicle of entertainment. Are these values in conflict with any others? If so, develop your essay, at least in part, by comparison and contrast.

Diction and Sentence Structure

Diction is the writer's language, his choice of words—a highly subjective, individualized aspect of prose style, and one that is particularly interesting in a language as rich in synonyms as English. Diction is generally described or measured with respect to three main qualities: formality, concreteness, and literal or emotional meaning.

Diction may be studied and formal, or it may be casual, informal, and colloquial. Words like *languished, seared, hew*, and *degenerate* mark Martin Luther King's prose as formal because, like formal evening clothes, these words are not ordinarily seen in everyday usage. In casual conversation, or informal prose, most of us would express King's ideas through their less formal synonyms: *weakened, burned, carve, decay.* Diction is conventionally measured along a scale of usage marked at one end by the extreme formality of words that are almost never used in ordinary conversation, but only in writing (*redemptive, synchrony*), and at the other end by colloquial and slang expressions reserved for and appropriate only to casual speech (*gimmicks, conned*). Within a particular essay, an author usually assumes and maintains unmixed a certain level of discourse, whether it is relatively formal or informal— just as you would probably not mix sneakers with your tuxedo. But a good writer may consciously violate this rule for his own purposes, as King himself does in using the colloquial expression "to blow off steam" in the midst of his generally far more formal diction. (When in doubt about the level of usage of any word, consult your dictionary, where labels will indicate any deviation from the range of standard, acceptable usage.)

In addition to the relative formality or informality of the level of discourse, a writer's language may be marked by the degree to which he uses words that are concrete and vivid in their close, visible association to the physical, tangible world —as in Woiwode's powerful image of "a shattered shin and hoof . . . steaming in the red-beaded snow." Or language may be abstract, avoiding the clear, material image, as in Lewis Thomas's reference to the regulation of "human behavior according to today's view of nature." (Along with the concrete and the abstract qualities of diction are their companions, the specific and the general—all four constituting an important feature of language that is more fully discussed and illustrated in the discussion of description, page 37.)

A third important aspect of diction is the relation between word or symbol and meaning. Denotation is the term for the objective, generally agreed upon meaning of a word, the literal or dictionary definition that clearly links symbol (word) and referent (the object symbolized by the word). The denotation is the meaning everyone shares when, for example, the word *chair* is used and we all think of some version of "a piece of furniture consisting of a seat, legs, a back, and often arms, designed to accommodate one person." The connotation is the feeling or emotional response that certain words tend to evoke. Some words obviously carry very little of this emotionally weighted meaning, while others bear a great deal. The word *chair*, for example, is unlikely to arouse any particular feeling in the reader—unless, of course, his associations are to the electric chair or to some other powerfully positive or negative object. In that case, the connotative meaning would be strictly personal and subjective. In contrast, words like *mother* and *home* bear more universal emotional "charges," connotations tending to elicit a feeling response from almost everyone. Some words, like *democracy, communism, liberal,* or *conservative,* are frequently used with reference only to their positive or negative connotations, leaving concrete, denotative meaning behind altogether.

Finally, any study of diction must include some mention of jargon, the term for language or terminology peculiar to a particular field of interest or activity. Jargon may itself become the foundation of a writer's diction. This phenomenon is seen at its best in Lewis Thomas's use of the scientific jargon without which he would be unable to express his ideas or their basis in the facts of biology. At its worst, jargon is represented by the kind of vague, needlessly abstract, reality-obscuring language we have come to associate with bureaucracy, and which Maynard mocks in her ironic repetition of the jargon of educators ("poor motivating factor," "adapting to the group").

But words alone do not make up prose or prose style. Like musical notes, which achieve their full significance only when arranged in rhythmic order, words too must be joined together in orderly patterns, in sentences. And the English sentence is especially flexible in its structure, rich in its susceptibility to a wide variety of patterns and rhythms. The main elements of sentence structure that concern us here are length, pattern, and grammatical structure. Additionally, the patterns created within sentences may be altered or reinforced by the larger patterns resulting from the arrangment of sentences of varying shape and size within a paragraph.

To begin with, there is length. Even the most casual reader will be struck by an unusually long or short sentence. And in English, the sentence may be very short indeed ("Stop!"), or extraordinarily long (see Woiwode's paragraph 5, composed of a single sentence). English syntax also allows for enormous variation in the positioning or patterning of the basic elements of the sentence. What we think of as the "normal" pattern is a basically forceful, essentially progressive movement from subject to verb to object or complement: "We cannot walk alone"; "I once choked a chicken to death"; "I have an earnest proposal to make." Modifying phrases and clauses may be added, almost endlessly, to this basic pattern. If they occur mainly *after* the basic subject-verb-complement pattern, the heart of every English sentence, grammarians call the sentence "loose." These modifications may be brief and simple or long and elaborate (as they are in the very first sentence of Maynard's essay). If the core sentence is saved for the end, preceded and built up to by other elements, then the sentence is called "periodic." A periodic sentence, too, may be brief ("And if America is to be a great nation this must become true"), or it may be lengthy and involved (as in the second sentence in Maynard's opening paragraph).

But whether long or short, loose or periodic, English sentences are all built up from this essential core of subject-verb-complement. And the third feature of sentence structure—grammatical variation from the simple to the compound, the complex, or the compound-complex sentence—is more or less subject to the other, larger variations of length and looseness or periodicity of pattern. It is important to remember that the predictable emphasis in English is on subject and verb, and the basic, expected arrangement is that of the loose sentence. In music, when a theme or motif has been established, the counterpointing of another motif derives its force and importance from its departure from the expected. It is the same with these variations on the basic pattern and rhythm of the subject-verb-complement pattern of "John hit the ball" or "I have a dream today": powerful prose takes much of its strength from the writer's ability to ring the changes on the basic and expected sentence patterns, to enforce the significance of his ideas in effective sentences that both echo and depart from the expected patterns.

Beyond the variation possible in the shape of the individual sentence is the potential for creating pattern by the arrangement of sentences within a paragraph. A writer may monotonously keep his sentences equal or nearly so in length, or he may vary their weight, achieving emphasis and impact merely by the juxtaposition of the unusually long and the unusually short—as Woiwode does to great effect in the first three sentences of paragraph 8.

Two other devices—repetition and parallelism—are also widely employed, often together, to reinforce the writer's ideas. Parallelism is the expression of similar ideas in similar grammatical forms; repetition is the technique of deliberately repeating a word or phrase for emphasis and feeling. Nowhere in this book are these devices more powerfully and effectively employed than in Martin Luther King's moving speech, where they become, in fact, the dominant stylistic feature. Notice, for example, the four emphatic "now's" that arrest the reader's attention at the end of paragraph 4. At the same time, parallelism emphasizes the four related yet separate goals. Later, in paragraph 9, King makes yet another effective use of repetition ("Go back to Mississippi, go back to Alabama, go back to South Carolina . . ."). And at the conclusion, in the most famous and best remembered passage, "I have a dream," he again uses repetition and parallelism to drive home the message that no one who has heard or read this speech can ever forget.

Guns

LARRY WOIWODE

Larry Woiwode, a writer of fiction and essays, was born in Carrington, North Dakota, in 1941. He is a graduate of the University of Illinois, and has been a writer-in-residence at the University of Wisconsin, as well as a Guggenheim fellow. His first novel, *What I'm Going to Do, I Think*, won the William Faulkner Award for Best First Novel. He is also the author of a second novel, *Beyond the Bedroom Wall*, and a frequent contributor to the *New Yorker*, the *Atlantic Monthly*, *Esquire*, *McCall's*, *Mademoiselle*, *Partisan Review*, and other national magazines.

1   Once in the middle of a Wisconsin winter I shot a deer, my only one, while my wife and daughter watched. It had been hit by a delivery truck along a country road a few miles from where we lived and one of its rear legs was torn off at the hock; a shattered shin and hoof lay steaming in the red-beaded snow. The driver of the truck and I stood and watched as it tried to leap a fence, kicked a while at the top wire it was entangled in, flailing the area with fresh ropes of blood, and then went hobbling across a pasture toward a wooded hill. Placid cows followed it with a curious awe. "Do you have a rifle with you?" the driver asked. "No, not with me. At home." He looked once more at the deer, then got in his truck and drove off.

2   I went back to our Jeep where my wife and daughter were waiting, pale and withdrawn, and told them what I was about to do, and suggested that they'd better stay at home. No, they wanted to be with me, they said; they wanted to watch. My daughter was three and a half at the time. I got my rifle, a .22, a foolishly puny weapon to use on a deer but the only one I had, and we came back and saw that the deer was lying in some low brush near the base of the hill; no need to trail its blatant spoor. When I got about a hundred yards off, marveling at how it could have made it so far in its condition through snow that came over my boot tops, the deer tried to push itself up with its front legs, then collapsed. I aimed at the center of its skull, thinking, *This will be the quickest*, and heard the bullet ricochet off and go singing through the woods.

3   The deer was on its feet, shaking its head as though stung, and I fired again at the same spot, quickly, and apparently missed. It was now moving at its fastest hobble up the hill, broadside to me, and I took my time to sight a heart shot. Before the report even registered in my mind, the deer went down

GUNS   First published in *Esquire Magazine*, December 1975. Copyright © 1975 by Larry Woiwode. Reprinted by permission of Candida Donadio & Associates, Inc.

in an explosion of snow and lay struggling there, spouting blood from its stump and a chest wound. I was shaking by now. Deer are color-blind as far as science can say, and as I went toward its quieting body to deliver the coup de grace, I realized I was being seen in black and white, and then the deer's eye seemed to home in on me, and I was struck with the understanding that I was its vision of approaching death. And then I seemed to enter its realm through its eye and saw the countryside and myself in shades of white and gray. *But I see the deer in color*, I thought.

4   A few yards away, I aimed at its head once more, and there was the crack of a shot, the next-to-last round left in the magazine. The deer's head came up, and I could see its eye clearly now, dark, placid, filled with an appeal, it seemed, and then felt the surge of black and white surround and subsume me again. The second shot, or one of them, had pierced its neck; a gray-blue tongue hung out over its jaw; urine was trickling from below its tail; a doe. I held the rifle barrel inches from its forehead, conscious of my wife's and daughter's eyes on me from behind, and as I fired off the final and fatal shot, felt myself drawn by them back into my multicolored, many-faceted world again.

5   I don't remember my first gun, the heritage is so ingrained in me, but know I've used a variety of them to kill birds, reptiles, mammals, amphibians, plant life, insects (bees and butterflies with a shotgun), fish that came too close to shore—never a human being, I'm quick to interject, although the accumulated carnage I've put away with bullets since boyhood is probably enough to add up to a couple of cows, not counting the deer; and have fired, at other targets living and fairly inert, an old ten gauge with double hammers that left a welt on my shoulder that lasted a week, a Mauser, a twelve-gauge sawed-off shotgun, an M-16, at least a dozen variations on the .22—pump, bolt action, level action, target pistols, special scopes and sights and stocks—a .410 over-and-under, a zip gun that blew up and scattered shrapnel that's still imbedded in my arm, an Italian carbine, a Luger, and, among others, a fancily engraved, single-trigger, double-barreled twenty gauge at snowballs thrown from behind my shoulder out over a bluff; and on that same bluff on the first day of this year, after some wine and prodding, I found myself at the jittering rim of stutters from a paratrooper's lightweight machine gun with a collapsible, geometrically reinforced metal stock, watched the spout of its trajectory of tangible tracers go off across the night toward the already-set sun, and realized that this was perhaps the hundredth weapon I'd had performing in my hands.

6   I was raised in North Dakota, near the edge of the West, during the turbulence and then the aftermath of the Second World War, which our country ended in such an unequivocal way there was a sense of vindication about our long-standing fetish for guns, not to say pride in it, too. "Bang! Bang! You're dead," returns to me from that time without the least speck of friction or reflection. When we weren't playing War, or Cowboys and Indians, or Cops and Robbers, we were reading War Comics (from which you could order for less than a dollar little cardboard chests of plastic weaponry and

soldiers to stage your own debacles), or Westerns, or listening to *The Lone Ranger* and *Richard Diamond, Private Detective*, and other radio shows—all of which openly glorified guns, and the more powerful the better.

7   My fantasies, when I was frustrated, angry, or depressed, were rife with firearms of the most lethal sort, flying shot, endless rounds of shattering ammunition; the enemy bodies blown away and left in bloody tableaux. And any gun was an engineered instrument—much more far-ranging and accurate than bows and arrows or slingshots—that detached you from your destructiveness or crime or sometimes even from being a source of death.

8   I've only owned three firearms in my life as an adult. Two I brought back to the shops within a week after I'd bought them, realizing I was trying to reach out in some archaic way, and the limits to my maturity and imagination that that implied, plus the bother to my daughter of their powing sounds; and the third, the .22, after trembling over it a few years and using it to shoot holes in the floor to enact a between-the-legs suicide, I gave away. To my younger brother. Who was initiated into the buck-fever fraternity in the forests of northern Wisconsin when he was an adolescent by a seasoned local who said to him, "If you see anything moving out there tomorrow, boy, *shoot it*. You can check out later what it is. Nobody gives a shit up here." And on a hunting trip years later, an acquaintance from the village my brother lived in then, a lawyer, was shot in the head with a deer rifle, but somehow survived. And even went back to practicing law. It was thought to be an accident at first, what with all the bullets embroidering the air that day, and then rumor had it that another member of the party hunting on adjoining land, an old friend of the lawyer's, had found out a week before the season that the lawyer had been having his wife for a while. The two men were polite enough to one another in the village after that, my brother said, but not such good friends, of course. Just balanced, justice-balanced males.

9   For months and seasons after I'd shot the crippled doe, every time we passed the field in our Jeep, my daughter would say, "Here's where Daddy shooted the deer." In exactly that manner, using the tone and detachment of a storyteller or tourist guide. And I'd glance into the rearview mirror and see her in her car seat, studying the hill with troubled and sympathetic eyes. One day I stopped. "Does it bother you so much that I shot it?" I asked. There was no answer, and then I saw that she was nodding her head, her gaze still fixed on the hill.

10   "Well, if I wouldn't have, it could have suffered a long time. You saw how badly hurt it was. It couldn't have lived that way. I didn't like doing it, either, but it was best for the deer. When I told the game warden about it, he even thanked me and said, 'leave it for the foxes and crows.' They have to eat, too, you know, and maybe the deer made the winter easier for them." And I thought, Oh, what a self-justifying fool and ass and pig you are. Why didn't you leave her at home? Why didn't you go to the farmer whose land the deer was on, which would have been as quick or quicker than going back for the .22—a man who would have had a deer rifle, or at least a shotgun with rifled slugs, and would have put the deer away with dispatch in one shot and might

have even salvaged the hide and venison? And who could say it wouldn't have lived, the way some animals do after tearing or chewing off a limb caught in a trap? Who was to presume it wouldn't have preferred to die a slow death in the brush, looking out over the pasture, as the crimson stain widening in the snow drew away and dimmed its colorless world until all went black? Why not admit that I was a common back-country American and, like most men of my mold, had used an arsenal of firearms to kill and was as excited about putting away a deer as moved by compassion for its suffering? Then again, given my daughter's understanding and the person I am, perhaps she sensed this, and more.

11   I once choked a chicken to death. It was my only barefaced, not to say barehanded, confrontation with death and the killer in me and happened on my grandparents' farm. I couldn't have been more than nine or ten and no firearms were included or necessary. I was on my knees and the chicken fluttered its outstretched wings with the last of the outraged protest. I gripped, beyond release, above its swollen crop, its beak gaping, translucent eyelids sliding up and down. An old molting specimen. A hen, most likely; a worse loss, because of eggs, than a capon or cock. My grandfather, who was widely traveled and world-wise, in his eighties then, and had just started using a cane from earlier times, came tapping at that moment around the corner of the chicken coop and saw what I was doing and started gagging at the hideousness of it, did a quick assisted spin away and never again, hours later nor for the rest of his life, for that matter, ever mentioned the homicidal incident to me. Keeping his silence, he seemed to understand; and yet whenever I'm invaded by the incident, the point of it seems to be his turning away from me.

12   My wife once said she felt I wanted to kill her. A common enough feeling among long-married couples, I'm sure, and not restricted to either sex (I know, for instance, that there were times when she wanted to kill me), but perhaps with firsthand experience infusing the feeling, it became too much to endure. I now live in New York City, where the clock keeps moving toward my suitcase, alone, and she and my daughter in the Midwest. The city has changed in the seven years since the three of us lived here together. There are more frivolous and not-so-frivolous wares—silk kerchiefs, necklaces and rings, roach clips, rolling papers, socks, a display of Florida coral across a convertible top, books of every kind—being sold in the streets than anybody can remember seeing in recent years. People openly saying that soon it will be like the thirties once were, with us *all* in the streets selling our apples, or whatever, or engaged in a tacit and friendly sort of gangsterism to survive. Outside my window, a spindly deciduous species has a sign strung on supporting posts on either side of it, in careful handlettering, that reads, THIS TREE GIVES OXYGEN. GIVE IT LOVE. More dogs in the streets and parks than they'd remembered, and more canine offal sending up its open-ended odor; at least half the population giving up cigarette smoking, at last, for good, they say, and many actually are. The mazed feeling of most everywhere now of being in the midst of a slowly forging and forgiving reciprocity. An air of bravura

about most everybody in maintaining one's best face, with a few changes of costumish clothing to reflect it, perhaps, no matter what might yet evolve. A unisex barbershop or boutique on nearly every other block, it seems.

13   Sometimes I think this is where I really belong. Then a man is gunned down in a neighborhood bar I used to drop into and the next day a mob leader assassinated, supposedly by members of his own mob. *Perhaps this is where I'm most at home,* I equivocate again and have an image of myself in a Stetson traveling down a crosstown street at a fast-paced and pigeon-toed shamble toward the setting sun (setting this far east, but not over my wife and daughter yet), my eyes cast down and shoulders forward, hands deep in my empty Levi's pockets, a suspect closet-faggot-cowboy occasionally whistled at by queens.

14   I won't (and can't) refute my heritage, but I doubt that I'll use a firearm again, or, if I do, only in the direst sort of emergency. Which I say to protect my flanks. The bloody, gunfilled fantasies seldom return now, and when they do they're reversed: I'm the one being shot, or shot at, or think I am.

Exercises

COMPREHENSION

Organization and Development

Complete the following outline. Find the thesis statement (partly implicit) and write it in the space provided. Then find the main divisions in the essay and fill in the remaining spaces. Note the paragraphs for each section.

Thesis statement: _____

_____

_____

I.   _____   [   ]

II.   _____   [   ]

III. _____   [   ]

IV.   _____   [   ]

V.   _____   [   ]

VI. Conclusion: _____   [   ]

Content

Choose the answer that correctly completes each statement.

1. The narrative of the killing of the deer is (a) the central point of the essay (b) intended to illustrate and exemplify the main point (c) not really directly relevant to the main point.

2. Woiwode presents the catalogue of guns to demonstrate (a) his complete, ingrained, lifelong familiarity with guns and slaughter (b) the variety of weapons available to any American boy (c) the improvements in weaponry since his youth.

3. Woiwode describes himself in his relationship to guns as (a) more sensitive and gentle than most American men (b) a common, back-country American who, like most men of his type, had used an arsenal of firearms to kill (c) someone whose nature has been brutalized by his lifelong intimacy with guns and killing.
4. Woiwode's daughter constantly reminds him of the shooting of the deer, causing him to (a) move back to New York without her (b) resolve to give up hunting forever (c) reexamine his real motives for shooting the deer as he had.
5. Long after the actual incident, the author admits to himself that he shot the deer with a .22, even though it was an unsuitable weapon and caused the animal unnecessary suffering, because (a) it was really the quickest way to end the situation (b) he didn't have a deer rifle and couldn't bear to see the animal die a slow, painful death (c) he was really as excited at the prospect of killing a deer as he was moved by compassion for it.
6. The significance of the chicken-killing story is that it (a) revealed Woiwode's boyish willingness to destroy a useful animal (b) was the only time he ever killed anything barehanded (c) revealed to the grandfather something in the boy—a love of killing, perhaps—from which he had to retreat.
7. When Woiwode tells us, following his catalogue of youthful experience with guns, that he has only owned three firearms as an adult and that he kept none for very long, he implies that (a) for him, guns represent a childish, immature response to life (b) guns do not belong in New York City (c) he cannot afford to own a weapon now that he has a family.
8. Woiwode concludes that he will probably (a) never use a firearm again (b) never kill another animal (c) leave New York City to return to country life.

Paragraph Structure

Reorder the following sentences to form a unified, coherent paragraph. Write a sentence that can serve as a topic sentence for the reorganized paragraph. Then check your version with the original.

1. In exactly that manner, using the tone and detachment of a storyteller or tourist guide.
2. There was no answer, and then I saw that she was nodding her head, her gaze still fixed on the hill.
3. One day I stopped.
4. For months and seasons after I'd shot the crippled doe, every time we passed the field in our Jeep, my daughter would say, "Here's where Daddy shooted the deer."
5. And I'd glance into the rearview mirror and see her in her car seat, studying the hill with troubled and sympathetic eyes.
6. "Does it bother you so much that I shot it?" I asked.

VOCABULARY AND USAGE

Word Formation Table

Complete the following table by changing word endings or root forms to make new grammatical forms. Use your dictionary if necessary.

NOUN	VERB	ADJECTIVE	ADVERB
1. reciprocity	_____	_____	_____
2. _____	refute	_____	xxx
3. _____	presume	_____	_____
4. image	_____	_____	_____
5. _____	xxx	frivolous	_____

Fill-Ins

Complete each of the sentences below using the words on the following list. You may need to use some words more than once. You may also find that some blanks can be completed correctly with more than one word. Add plural endings to nouns and change verb forms where necessary.

unequivocal	firearm	kill	weapon
glorify	deer	gun	experience
clear	destroy	shoot	carnage
fantasy	animal	color	blood
image	incident	immature	killer

1. The author makes it _____ that he has had a lifetime of _____ with _____.
2. This essay argues that popular culture in America _____ the use of _____; the author refers to his childhood _____ of Cops and Robbers, filled with _____, to emphasize this belief.
3. The _____ of the strangled chicken, as well as the author's youthful _____ of _____, _____, and _____, imply that there lurks a _____ in each of us.
4. The opening paragraphs concentrate on the _____ of the dying _____ which the author later decides he _____ because he wanted to _____ it, more than because he felt compassion.
5. The _____ of the gun-slinging cowboy is an essential part of our national _____.
6. Woiwode connects his personal enthusiasm for _____ and the _____ that _____ their use with a(n) _____ state of mind.

DISCUSSION

1. List the descriptive words or details in paragraphs 3 and 4. How many are adjectives? How many are verbs? Adverbs? Adverbial phrases? In what sense are the nouns descriptive? Most readers would call this a vivid description. Can you explain what makes it so vivid?
2. Analyze the first four sentences of paragraph 8. Diagram each one, study its punctuation, and then think about the interrelationship of the four. What is the effect of the varying lengths? Why does Woiwode employ fragments? Try rewriting these sentences in shorter, clearer, more "correct" forms. What happens?
3. This essay does not have an obvious structure or pattern, which does not mean it is not carefully organized. Examine the main incidents of the narrative(s), the relationships between the parts of the essay, and the transitions between paragraphs. What

techniques does the author employ to weave together into a coherent whole such apparently unrelated incidents as the death of the deer, the strangled chicken, and the assassination of a New York gangster?

4. In paragraph 5, Woiwode says, "I don't remember my first gun, the heritage is so ingrained in me. . . ." What does he mean by "the heritage," a term he uses again in the final paragraph? In what way is this word related to his underlying conviction about guns?

5. Why does Woiwode introduce the apparently irrelevant detail about the color-blindness of the deer? What effect is achieved by the imagined contrast between the deer's black and white vision and the author's "multi-colored, many-faceted world"? In what other ways is color used to influence our attitude toward the deer's death and Woiwode's role in it?

6. Paragraphs 10, 11, and 12 each contain an admission or confession. How are these revelations related to each other and to the implied thesis of the essay?

7. Woiwode's essay suggests in various ways that ours is a violent society that glorifies guns and killing. Exactly how does the author gradually develop this view?

SUGGESTIONS FOR WRITING

1. Discuss your own experience with and attitude toward firearms.

2. Argue for or against the banning of privately owned firearms as a means of controlling the violence in our society.

3. Write an essay in which you use factual detail to make a statement about firearms and the American character similar to the one Woiwode makes by citing personal experience. (Figures on your community's crime rate, national homicide statistics, etc., should provide some help.)

4. Using your own personal knowledge and experience, as well as films, television programs, and other references, analyze the national fascination with the romanticized image of the gun-slinging cowboy that Woiwode alludes to in paragraph 13.

5. Analyze the American obsession with automobiles (or some other fetish) as an emblem of manhood.

The Lion Tamers

JOYCE MAYNARD

Joyce Maynard, a graduate of Yale University, grew up in Durham, New Hampshire, the location of Oyster River School. *Looking Back: A Chronicle of Growing Up Old in the 60's*, written when Maynard was a sophomore at Yale, examines the forces that have shaped her generation. "The Lion Tamers" describes her memories of elementary and junior high school.

1   I watch them every year, the six-year-olds, buying lunch boxes and snap-on bow ties and jeweled barrettes, swinging on their mothers' arms as they approach the school on registration day or walking ahead a little, stiff in new clothes. Putting their feet on the shoe salesman's metal foot measurer, eying the patent leather and ending up with sturdy brown tie oxfords, sitting rigid in the barber's chair, heads balanced on white-sheeted bodies like cherries on cupcakes, as the barber snips away the kindergarten hair for the new grown-up cut, striding past the five-year-olds with looks of knowing pity (ah, youth) they enter elementary school, feigning reluctance—with scuffing heels and dying TV cowboy groans shared in the cloakroom, but filled with hope and anticipation of all the mysteries waiting in the cafeteria and the water fountain and the paper closet, and in the pages of the textbooks on the teachers' desks. With pink erasers and a sheath of sharpened pencils, they file in so really bravely, as if to tame lions, or at least subdue the alphabet. And instead, I long to warn them, watching this green young crop pass by each year, seeing them enter a red-brick, smelly-staircase world of bathroom passes and penmanship drills, gongs and red x's, and an unexpected snap to the teacher's slingshot voice (so slack and giving, when she met the mothers). I want to tell them about the back pages in the teacher's record book, of going to the principal's office or staying behind an extra year. Quickly they learn how little use they'll have for lion-taming apparatus. They are, themselves, about to meet the tamer.

2   I can barely remember it now, but I know that I once felt that first-day eagerness too. Something happened, though, between that one pony-tail-tossing, skirt-flouncing, hand-waving ("*I* know the answer—call on *me*") day and the first day of all the other years I spent in public school. It wasn't just homework and the struggle to get up at seven every morning, it was the *kind*

of homework assignments we were given and the prospect of just what it was that we were rousing ourselves for—the systematic breaking down, workbook page by workbook page, drill after drill, of all the joy we started out with. I don't think I'm exaggerating when I say that, with very few exceptions, what they did to (not *for*) us in elementary school was not unlike what I would sometimes do to my cats: dress them up in doll clothes because they looked cute that way.

3   We were forever being organized into activities that, I suspect, looked good on paper and in school board reports. New programs took over and disappeared as approaches to child education changed. One year we would go without marks, on the theory that marks were a "poor motivating factor," "an unnatural pressure," and my laboriously researched science and social studies reports would come back with a check mark or a check plus inside the margin. Another year every activity became a competition, with posters tacked up on the walls showing who was ahead that week, our failures and our glories bared to all the class. Our days were filled with electrical gimmicks, film strips and movies and overhead projectors and tapes and supplementary TV shows, and in junior high, when we went audio-visual, a power failure would have been reason enough to close down the school.

4   But though the educational jargon changed, the school's basic attitude remained constant. Anything too different (too bad or too exceptional), anything that meant making another column in the record book, was frowned upon. A lone recorder, in a field of squeaking flutophones, a reader of Dickens, while the class was laboring page by page (out loud, pace set by the slowest oral readers) with the adventures of the Marshall family and their dog Ranger, a ten-page story when the teacher had asked for a two-pager—they all met with suspicion. Getting straight A's was fine with the school as long as one pursued the steady, earnest, unspectacular course. But to complete a piece of work well, without having followed the prescribed steps—that seemed a threat to the school, proof that we could progress without it. Vanity rears its head everywhere, even in the classroom, but surely extra guards against it should be put up there. I remember an English teacher who wouldn't grant me an A until second term, an indication, for whoever cared about that sort of thing, that under her tutelage I had *improved*. Every composition was supposed to have evolved from three progressively refined rough drafts. I moved in just the opposite direction for the school's benefit: I wrote my "final drafts" the first time around, then deliberately aged them a bit with earnest-looking smudges and erasures.

5   Kids who have gone through elementary school at the bottom of their class might argue here that it *was* the smart ones who got special attention—independent study groups, free time to spend acting in plays and writing novels (we were always starting autobiographies) and researching "Special Reports"—all the things that kept our groups self-perpetuating, with the children lucky enough to start out on top forever in the teachers' good graces, and those who didn't start there always drilling on decimals and workbook extra-work pages. But Oyster River was an exemplary democratic school and

showed exemplary concern for slow students—the underachievers—and vir-
tuously left the quick and bright to swim for themselves, or tread water
endlessly.

6   It always seemed to me as a Group One member, that there was little
individual chance to shine. It was as if the school had just discovered the
division of labor concept, and oh, how we divided it. Book reports, math
problems, maps for history and even art projects—we did them all in
committee. Once we were supposed to write a short story that way, pooling
our resources of Descriptive Adjectives and Figures of Speech to come up with
an adventure that read like one of those typing-book sentences ("A quick
brown fox . . ."), where every letter of the alphabet is represented. Our
group drawings had the look of movie magazine composites that show the
ideal star, with Paul Newman's eyes, Brando's lips, Steve McQueen's hair.
Most people loved group work—the kids because working together meant not
working very hard, tossing your penny in the till and leaving it for someone
else to count, the teachers because committee projects prepared us for
community work, (getting along with the group, leadership abilities . . .)
and, more important, I think, to some of them, they required a lot less
marking time than individual projects did. The finished product didn't
matter so much—in fact, anything too unusual seemed only to rock our
jointly rowed canoe.

7   The school day was for me, and for most of us, I think, a mixture of
humiliation and boredom. Teachers would use their students for the entertainment of the class. Within the first few days of the new term, someone
quickly becomes the class jester, someone is the class genius, the "brain"
who, the teacher, with doubtful modesty, reminds us often, probably has a
much higher IQ than she. Some student is the trouble-maker black sheep (the
one who always makes her sigh), the one who will be singled out as the
culprit when the whole class seems like a stock exchange of note passing,
while all the others stare at him, looking shocked.

8   Although their existence is denied now, in this modern, psychologically
enlightened age, teachers' pets are still very much around, sometimes in the
form of the girl with superneat penmanship and Breck-clean hair, sometimes
in the person of the dependable Brain, who always gets called on when the
superintendent is visiting the class. Teachers, I came to see, could be intimidated by a class, coerced or conned into liking the students who were popular
among the kids, and it was hard not to miss, too, that many teachers were
not above using unpopular students to gain acceptance with the majority.
They had an instinct, teachers did, for who was well-liked and who wasn't;
they learned all the right nicknames and turned away, when they could, if
one of their favorites was doing the kind of thing that brought a 3 in conduct.
We saw it all, like underlings watching the graft operations of ambitious
politicians, powerless to do anything about it.

9   That was what made us most vulnerable: our powerlessness. Kids don't
generally speak up or argue their case. No one is a child long enough, I
suppose, or articulate enough, while he is one, to become a spokesman for his

very real, and often oppressed, minority group. And then when we outgrow childhood, we no longer care, and feel, in fact, that if *we* went through it all, so should the next generation. Children are *expected* to be adversaries of school and teachers, so often, in the choosing up of sides, parents will side with the school. Nobody expects children to like school; therefore it's no surprise when they don't. What should be a surprise is that they dislike it for many good reasons.

10   It would be inaccurate to say I hated school. I had a good time sometimes, usually when I was liked, and therefore on top. And with all the other clean-haired girls who had neat penmanship and did their homework, I took advantage of my situation. When I was on the other side of the teacher's favor though, I realized that my sun-basking days had always depended on there being someone in the shade. That was the system—climbing up on one another's heads, putting someone down so one's own stature could be elevated. Elementary school was a club that not only reinforced the class system but created it—a system in which the stutterer and the boy who can't hit a baseball start out, and remain, right at the bottom, a system where being in the middle—not too high or low—is best of all.

11   I had imagined, innocently, on my first day of school, that once the kids saw how smart I was, they'd all be my friends. I see similar hopes on the faces I watch heading to the front every September—all the loved children, tops in their parents' eyes, off to be "re-evaluated" in a world where only one of thirty can be favorite, each child unaware, still, that he is not the only person in the universe, and about to discover that the best means of survival is to blend in (adapting to the group, it's called), to go from being one to being one in a crowd of many, many others.

Exercises

COMPREHENSION

Organization and Development

Complete the following outline. Write a sentence stating the author's purpose in the space provided. Then find the thesis statement. Finally, find the main divisions in the essay and fill in the remaining spaces. Note the paragraphs for each section.

Statement of Purpose: _____

_____

Thesis statement: _____

_____

I.   _____   [   ]
II.   _____   [   ]
III. Conclusion: _____   [   ]

Content

Choose the answer that correctly completes each statement.

1. The theme of this essay is (a) bitterness (b) disillusionment (c) cynicism.
2. In reality, the "lion tamers" are the (a) school system (b) teachers (c) children.
3. Maynard recalls that homework assignments (a) broke down the children's joy of learning (b) were unimportant since the teachers seemed not to care if they were completed (c) only helped the good students.
4. Apparently, the educational programs changed according to (a) fashion (b) the principal's wishes (c) the parents' demands.
5. Maynard says that at Oyster River School, bright students were (a) ignored or left on their own in favor of the slower ones (b) pushed and encouraged to excel (c) asked to tutor the poor students in special reading groups.
6. Maynard recalls that teachers (a) attempted to treat all students equally (b) singled out the smart ones and ignored the rest (c) labeled students and used the unpopular ones to entertain or to gain favor.
7. With respect to the school system and the maneuverings of teachers, Maynard says the children were (a) innocent and unaware (b) powerless and vulnerable (c) intimidated and oppressed.
8. The lesson Maynard came away with from elementary school is (a) obedience: always doing what one is asked, no matter how trivial the task (b) mediocrity: blending in with the group so that one does not stand out too much (c) slyness: learning how to manipulate the system to one's own purposes.

Paragraph Structure

Reorder the following sentences to form a unified, coherent paragraph. Identify one sentence as the topic sentence. Then check your version with the original.

1. Our days were filled with electrical gimmicks, film strips and movies and overhead projectors and tapes and supplementary TV shows, and in junior high, when we went audio-visual, a power failure would have been reason enough to close down the school.
2. One year we would go without marks, on the theory that marks were a "poor motivating factor," "an unnatural pressure," and my laboriously researched science and social studies reports would come back with a check mark or a check plus inside the margin.
3. We were forever being organized into activities that, I suspect, looked good on paper and in school board reports.
4. Another year every activity became a competition, with posters tacked up on the walls showing who was ahead that week, our failures and our glories bared to all the class.
5. New programs took over and disappeared as approaches to child education changed.

VOCABULARY AND USAGE

Word Formation Table

Complete the following table by changing word endings or root forms to make new grammatical forms. Use your dictionary if necessary.

NOUN	VERB	ADJECTIVE	ADVERB
1. _____	xxx	vulnerable	_____
2. _____	_____	_____	progressively
3. _____	coerce	_____	_____
4. _____	_____	intimidated	xxx
5. exception	_____	_____	_____

Fill-Ins

Complete each of the sentences below using the words on the following list. You may need to use some words more than once. You may also find that some blanks can be completed correctly with more than one word. Add plural endings to nouns and change verb forms where necessary.

feign	learn	appear	adversary
weak	enemy	discover	in fact
deliberately	vulnerable	threat	conquer
or	when	subdue	prescribed
force	coerce	intimidate	powerless

1. Maynard describes the excitement of first graders who, though _____ reluctance, are really eager to _____ the lions _____ at least the alphabet.
2. _____ Maynard sees a new crop of students she knows they will, _____, be _____ themselves by a system that _____ destroys eagerness and creativity.
3. Maynard _____ that teachers and students were _____, and that school was a struggle between the strong and the _____.
4. Teachers were also _____ by bright students, who were _____ to conform to a particular standard; _____, any success achieved in a different way from the _____ one was considered a _____ to the entire system.
5. _____ Maynard wrote essays and failed to follow the _____ format, she _____ smudged the copies so that they _____ to have been revised.
6. Maynard notes that one reason children are _____ is that they can't speak up for themselves, and _____, _____ they're older, they think other children should be _____ to go through the same experience.

DISCUSSION

1. Paragraph 1 contains many concrete details about the typical six-year-old's preparation for first grade. What emotional attitude do these details convey? Which suggest innocence? Which suggest eagerness? Are any of them irrelevant, or do they all serve a function?
2. Why is the metaphor "lion tamers" appropriate to Maynard's thesis? The metaphor has a dual function in paragraph 1. What is it? After paragraph 1, the author does not mention the lion tamers again. What details nevertheless reinforce and continue the metaphor introduced at the beginning?
3. Tone refers to the emotional attitude of the writer toward the subject and also the mood or feeling the work arouses in the reader. What are some examples of

Maynard's word choice that help reveal her tone? In addition, you should explain how each example affects your own perception of her ideas.

4. Where does Maynard state her thesis? What would be the effect if the thesis were presented at or near the beginning of the essay? Do the illustrations of Maynard's grammar school experience lead conclusively and convincingly to the thesis, or does the thesis seem unwarranted?

5. What are the topic sentences in paragraphs 6 and 7, and what methods of development do they represent?

6. What does Maynard mean in paragraph 10 when she says, "I realized that my sun-basking days had always depended on there being someone in the shade"? What do "sun" and "shade" denote? What do they connote?

7. What effect does the last paragraph have on the reader? What contributes to that effect? Why is "re-evaluated" in quotation marks?

8. What is Maynard's real complaint about her elementary school? To what extent do her illustrations support her contention that the school system fostered mediocrity? In light of your own experience, do you think that she is right? To what extent are high school or college different from the system she describes?

SUGGESTIONS FOR WRITING

1. Write a sketch of the best teacher you have ever had. Include a description of the teacher's physical appearance as well as a discussion, supported by examples or illustrations, of the qualities that impressed you most.

2. Write an essay describing your own elementary school experience, using illustrations and concrete details. Your essay might be organized inductively, so that your illustrations lead to or anticipate your thesis.

3. Define what to you would be an ideal school (at any level).

4. Using specific details, write a narrative essay about an incident in your past that taught you a lesson about life or that forced you to redefine earlier, or perhaps naive ideas.

5. Maynard restricts her criticism of the educational system to elementary and junior high schools. Write an essay in which you analyze how college courses dampen the student's enthusiasm for learning. Use specific examples to give credibility to your analysis.

I Have A Dream . . .

MARTIN LUTHER KING, JR.

Until his assassination in 1968, Martin Luther King, Jr., president of the Southern Christian Leadership Conference, was the foremost leader of the civil rights movement. During the late 1950s and early 1960s, he led many of the early sit-ins and demonstrations in the South. A proponent of nonviolence, he applied the principles of Gandhi and Thoreau to the fight for racial equality.

During the centennial year of the Emancipation Proclamation, many demonstrations and marches were staged in an effort to impress upon the nation's conscience the urgency of granting first-class status to blacks. The largest and most impressive of these rallies was the March on Washington for Jobs and Freedom by over 200,000 people on August 28, 1963. Of all the speeches delivered that day before the Lincoln Memorial, King's speech, "I Have a Dream . . .," has been called "the emotional crescendo of an emotional day." According to an associate, King wrote his speech in longhand the night before the march, and finished it at four in the morning. The peroration, or conclusion, is one of the most stirring pieces of rhetoric ever delivered.

1   Five score years ago, a great American, in whose symbolic shadow we stand, signed the Emancipation Proclamation. This momentous decree came as a great beacon light of hope to millions of Negro slaves who had been seared in the flames of withering injustice. It came as a joyous daybreak to end the long night of captivity.

2   But one hundred years later, we must face the tragic fact that the Negro is still not free. One hundred years later, the life of the Negro is still sadly crippled by the manacles of segregation and the chains of discrimination. One hundred years later, the Negro lives on a lonely island of poverty in the midst of a vast ocean of material prosperity. One hundred years later, the Negro is still languished in the corners of American society and finds himself an exile in his own land. So we have come here today to dramatize an appalling condition.

3   In a sense we have come to our nation's Capital to cash a check. When the architects of our republic wrote the magnificent words of the Constitution and the Declaration of Independence, they were signing a promissory note to which every American was to fall heir. This note was a promise that all men would be guaranteed the unalienable rights of life, liberty, and the pursuit of happiness.

4   It is obvious today that America has defaulted on this promissory note insofar as her citizens of color are concerned. Instead of honoring this sacred obligation, America has given the Negro people a bad check; a check which has come back marked "insufficient funds." But we refuse to believe that the bank of justice is bankrupt. We refuse to believe that there are insufficient funds in the great vaults of opportunity of this nation. So we have come to cash this check—a check that will give us upon demand the riches of freedom and the security of justice. We have also come to this hallowed spot to remind America of the fierce urgency of *now*. This is no time to engage in the luxury of cooling off or to take the tranquilizing drug of gradualism. *Now* is the time to make real the promises of Democracy. *Now* is the time to rise from the dark and desolate valley of segregation to the sunlit path of racial justice. *Now* is the time to open the doors of opportunity to all of God's children. *Now* is the time to lift our nation from the quicksands of racial injustice to the solid rock of brotherhood.

5   It would be fatal for the nation to overlook the urgency of the moment and to underestimate the determination of the Negro. This sweltering summer of the Negro's legitimate discontent will not pass until there is an invigorating autumn of freedom and equality. 1963 is not an end, but a beginning. Those who hope that the Negro needed to blow off steam and will now be content will have a rude awakening if the nation returns to business as usual. There will be neither rest nor tranquillity in America until the Negro is granted his citizenship rights. The whirlwinds of revolt will continue to shake the foundations of our nation until the bright day of justice emerges.

6   But there is something that I must say to my people who stand on the warm threshold which leads into the palace of justice. In the process of gaining our rightful place we must not be guilty of wrongful deeds. Let us not seek to satisfy our thirst for freedom by drinking from the cup of bitterness and hatred. We must forever conduct our struggle on the high plane of dignity and discipline. We must not allow our creative protest to degenerate into physical violence. Again and again we must rise to the majestic heights of meeting physical force with soul force. The marvelous new militancy which has engulfed the Negro community must not lead us to a distrust of all white people, for many of our white brothers, as evidenced by their presence here today, have come to realize that their destiny is tied up with our destiny and their freedom is inextricably bound to our freedom. We cannot walk alone.

7   And as we walk, we must make the pledge that we shall march ahead. We cannot turn back. There are those who are asking the devotees of civil rights, "When will you be satisfied?" We can never be satisfied as long as the Negro is the victim of the unspeakable horrors of police brutality. We can never be satisfied as long as our bodies, heavy with the fatigue of travel, cannot gain lodging in the motels of the highways and the hotels of the cities. We cannot be satisfied as long as the Negro's basic mobility is from a smaller ghetto to a larger one. We can never be satisfied as long as a Negro in Mississippi cannot vote and a Negro in New York believes he has nothing for which to vote. No,

no, we are not satisfied, and we will not be satisfied until justice rolls down like waters and righteousness like a mighty stream.

8   I am not unmindful that some of you have come here out of great trials and tribulations. Some of you have come fresh from narrow jail cells. Some of you have come from areas where your quest for freedom left you battered by the storms of persecution and staggered by the winds of police brutality. You have been the veterans of creative suffering. Continue to work with the faith that unearned suffering is redemptive.

9   Go back to Mississippi, go back to Alabama, go back to South Carolina, go back to Georgia, go back to Louisiana, go back to the slums and ghettos of our northern cities, knowing that somehow this situation can and will be changed. Let us not wallow in the valley of despair.

10   I say to you today, my friends, that in spite of the difficulties and frustrations of the moment I still have a dream. It is a dream deeply rooted in the American dream.

11   I have a dream that one day this nation will rise up and live out the true meaning of its creed: "We hold these truths to be self-evident; that all men are created equal."

12   I have a dream that one day on the red hills of Georgia the sons of former slaves and the sons of former slaveowners will be able to sit down together at the table of brotherhood.

13   I have a dream that one day even the state of Mississippi, a desert state sweltering with the heat of injustice and oppression, will be transformed into an oasis of freedom and justice.

14   I have a dream that my four little children will one day live in a nation where they will not be judged by the color of their skin but by the content of their character.

15   I have a dream today.

16   I have a dream that one day the state of Alabama, whose governor's lips are presently dripping with the words of interposition and nullification, will be transformed into a situation where little black boys and black girls will be able to join hands with little white boys and white girls and walk together as sisters and brothers.

17   I have a dream today.

18   I have a dream that one day every valley shall be exalted, every hill and mountain shall be made low, the rough places will be made plains, and the crooked places will be made straight, and the glory of the Lord shall be revealed, and all flesh shall see it together.

19   This is our hope. This is the faith with which I return to the South. With this faith we will be able to hew out of the mountain of despair a stone of hope. With this faith we will be able to transform the jangling discords of our nation into a beautiful symphony of brotherhood. With this faith we will be able to work together, to pray together, to struggle together, to go to jail together, to stand up for freedom together, knowing that we will be free one day.

20   This will be the day when all of God's children will be able to sing with new meaning

> My country, 'tis of thee,
> Sweet land of liberty,
>   Of thee I sing:
> Land where my fathers died,
> Land of the pilgrims' pride,
> From every mountain-side
>   Let freedom ring.

21   And if America is to be a great nation this must become true. So let freedom ring from the prodigious hilltops of New Hampshire. Let freedom ring from the mighty mountains of New York. Let freedom ring from the heightening Alleghenies of Pennsylvania!

22   Let freedom ring from the snowcapped Rockies of Colorado!

23   Let freedom ring from the curvacious peaks of California!

24   But not only that; let freedom ring from Stone Mountain of Georgia!

25   Let freedom ring from Lookout Mountain of Tennessee!

26   Let freedom ring from every hill and molehill of Mississippi. From every mountainside, let freedom ring.

27   When we let freedom ring, when we let it ring from every village and every hamlet, from every state and every city, we will be able to speed up that day when all of God's children, black men and white men, Jews and Gentiles, Protestants and Catholics, will be able to join hands and sing in the words of the old Negro spiritual, "Free at last! free at last! thank God almighty, we are free at last!"

An Earnest Proposal

LEWIS THOMAS

Lewis Thomas is a physician and teacher; he is currently president and chief executive officer of Memorial–Sloan Kettering Cancer Center in New York. Since 1971 he has written a series of essays for the *New England Journal of Medicine,* ranging in subject from primitive one-celled organisms to the complex social systems of human beings. Many of these essays have been collected in *The Lives of a Cell: Notes of a Biology Watcher.* In "An Earnest Proposal," Thomas suggests that before we allow computers to program our own destruction, we should first compile a complete set of information on one living organism. His suggestion: the protozoan *Myxotricha paradoxa,* a parasite that lives in the digestive tract of Australian termites, where it joins with its host to form a fascinating ecosystem.

1   There was a quarter-page advertisement in the London *Observer* for a computer service that will enmesh your name in an electronic network of fifty thousand other names, sort out your tastes, preferences, habits, and deepest desires and match them up with opposite numbers, and retrieve for you, within a matter of seconds, and for a very small fee, friends. "Already," it says, "it [the computer] has given very real happiness and lasting relationships to thousands of people, and it can do the same for you!"

2   Without paying a fee, or filling out a questionnaire, all of us are being linked in similar circuits, for other reasons, by credit bureaus, the census, the tax people, the local police station, or the Army. Sooner or later, if it keeps on, the various networks will begin to touch, fuse, and then, in their coalescence, they will start sorting and retrieving each other, and we will all become bits of information on an enormous grid.

3   I do not worry much about the computers that are wired to help me find a friend among fifty thousand. If errors are made, I can always beg off with a headache. But what of the vaster machines that will be giving instructions to cities, to nations? If they are programmed to regulate human behavior according to today's view of nature, we are surely in for apocalypse.

4   The men who run the affairs of nations today are, by and large, our practical men. They have been taught that the world is an arrangement of adversary systems, that force is what counts, aggression is what drives us at the core, only the fittest can survive, and only might can make more might.

Thus, it is in observance of nature's law that we have planted, like perennial tubers, the numberless nameless missiles in the soil of Russia and China and our Midwestern farmlands, with more to come, poised to fly out at a nanosecond's notice, and meticulously engineered to ignite, in the centers of all our cities, artificial suns. If we let fly enough of them at once, we can even burn out the one-celled green creatures in the sea, and thus turn off the oxygen.

5   Before such things are done, one hopes that the computers will contain every least bit of relevant information about the way of the world. I should think we might assume this, in fairness to all. Even the nuclear realists, busy as their minds must be with calculations of acceptable levels of megadeath, would not want to overlook anything. They should be willing to wait, for a while anyway.

6   I have an earnest proposal to make. I suggest that we defer further action until we have acquired a really complete set of information concerning at least one living thing. Then, at least, we shall be able to claim that we know what we are doing. The delay might take a decade; let us say a decade. We and the other nations might set it as an objective of international, collaborative science to achieve a complete understanding of a single form of life. When this is done, and the information programmed into all our computers, I for one would be willing to take my chances.

7   As to the subject, I propose a simple one, easily solved within ten years. It is the protozoan *Myxotricha paradoxa*, which inhabits the inner reaches of the digestive tract of Australian termites.

8   It is not as though we would be starting from scratch. We have a fair amount of information about this creature already—not enough to understand him, of course, but enough to inform us that he means something, perhaps a great deal. At first glance, he appears to be an ordinary, motile protozoan, remarkable chiefly for the speed and directness with which he swims from place to place, engulfing fragments of wood finely chewed by his termite host. In the termite ecosystem, an arrangement of Byzantine complexity, he stands at the epicenter. Without him, the wood, however finely chewed, would never get digested; he supplies the enzymes that break down cellulose to edible carbohydrate, leaving only the nondegradable lignin, which the termite then excretes in geometrically tidy pellets and uses as building blocks for the erection of arches and vaults in the termite nest. Without him there would be no termites, no farms of the fungi that are cultivated by termites and will grow nowhere else, and no conversion of dead trees to loam.

9   The flagellae that beat in synchrony to propel myxotricha with such directness turn out, on closer scrutiny with the electron microscope, not to be flagellae at all. They are outsiders, in to help with the business: fully formed, perfect spirochetes that have attached themselves at regularly spaced intervals all over the surface of the protozoan.

10   Then, there are oval organelles, embedded in the surface close to the point of attachment of the spirochetes, and other similar bodies drifting through

the cytoplasm with the particles of still undigested wood. These, under high magnification, turn out to be bacteria, living in symbiosis with the spirochetes and protozoan, probably contributing enzymes that break down the cellulose.

11   The whole animal, or ecosystem, stuck for the time being halfway along in evolution, appears to be a model for the development of cells like our own. Margulis has summarized the now considerable body of data indicating that the modern nucleated cell was made up, part by part, by the coming together of just such prokaryotic animals. The blue-green algae, the original inventors of photosynthesis, entered partnership with primitive bacterial cells, and became the chloroplasts of plants; their descendants remain as discrete separate animals inside plant cells, with their own DNA and RNA, replicating on their own. Other bacteria with oxidative enzymes in their membranes, makers of ATP, joined up with fermenting bacteria and became the mitochondria of the future; they have since deleted some of their genes but retain personal genomes and can only be regarded as symbionts. Spirochetes, like the ones attached to *M. paradoxa*, joined up and became the cilia of eukaryotic cells. The centrioles, which hoist the microtubules on which chromosomes are strung for mitosis, are similar separate creatures; when not busy with mitosis, they become the basal bodies to which cilia are attached. And there are others, not yet clearly delineated, whose existence in the cell is indicated by the presence of cytoplasmic genes.

12   There is an underlying force that drives together the several creatures comprising myxotricha, and, then drives the assemblage into union with the termite. If we could understand this tendency, we would catch a glimpse of the process that brought single separate cells together for the construction of metazoans, culminating in the intervention of roses, dolphins, and, of course, ourselves. It might turn out that the same tendency underlies the joining of organisms into communities, communities into ecosystems, and ecosystems into the biosphere. If this is, in fact, the drift of things, the way of the world, we may come to view immune reactions, genes for the chemical marking of self, and perhaps all reflexive responses of aggression and defense as secondary developments in evolution, necessary for the regulation and modulation of symbiosis, not designed to break into the process, only to keep it from getting out of hand.

13   If it is in the nature of living things to pool resources, to fuse when possible, we would have a new way of accounting for the progressive enrichment and complexity of form in living things.

14   I take it on faith that computers, although lacking souls, are possessed of a kind of intelligence. At the end of the decade, therefore, I am willing to predict that the feeding in of all the information then available will result, after a few seconds of whirring, in something like the following message, neatly and speedily printed out: "Request more data. How are spirochetes attached? Do not fire."

Index of Authors and Titles

A 9
B 0
C 1
D 2
E 3
F 4
G 5
H 6
I 7
J 8